Feminist
Rhetorical
Theories

Feminist Rhetorical Theories

Karen A. Foss • Sonja K. Foss • Cindy L. Griffin

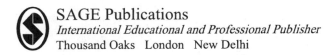

SAGE Publications
International Educational and Professional Publisher
Thousand Oaks   London   New Delhi

For information:

SAGE Publications, Inc.
2455 Teller Road
Thousand Oaks, California 91320
E-mail: order@sagepub.com

SAGE Publications Ltd.
6 Bonhill Street
London EC2A 4PU
United Kingdom

SAGE Publications India Pvt. Ltd.
M-32 Market
Greater Kailash I
New Delhi 110 048 India

Printed in the United States of America

Library of Congress Cataloging-in-Publication Data

Foss, Karen A.
 Feminist rhetorical theories / Karen A. Foss, Sonja K. Foss, and Cindy L. Griffin.
  p. cm.
 Includes bibliographical references and index.
 ISBN 0-7619-0346-1
 ISBN 0-7619-0347-X (pbk.)
 1. Rhetoric. 2. Feminist theory. I. Foss, Sonja K. II. Griffin,
Cindy L. III. Title.
 P301.F67 1998
 808′.0082—ddc21   98-25536

This book is printed on acid-free paper.

99 00 01 02 03 04 05 7 6 5 4 3 2 1

Acquiring Editor:	Margaret H. Seawell
Editorial Assistant:	Renée Piernot
Production Editor:	Astrid Virding
Designer/Typesetter:	Janelle LeMaster
Cover Designer:	Candice Harman
Indexer:	Molly Hall

Contents

Acknowledgments

Like most scholarship, this book is a collaborative effort that incorporates and relies on the ideas and support of numerous individuals. We would like to thank the many people who provided their assistance and support to this project in so many ways.

We are particularly grateful to the nine feminist theorists whose ideas are featured here: Cheris Kramarae, bell hooks, Gloria Anzaldúa, Mary Daly, Starhawk, Paula Gunn Allen, Trinh T. Minh-ha, Sally Miller Gearhart, and Sonia Johnson. Their ideas and work constitute the heart of this book and suggest the myriad transformations of rhetorical theory that we hope will have exciting impacts on the discipline of rhetorical studies. Our appreciation extends beyond their work as theorists; many of them assisted us in numerous ways as the book progressed—providing *curricula vitae*, bibliographic materials, and photographs; offering information in interviews, conversations, e-mail exchanges, and other correspondence; and reviewing drafts of our chapters. To these women, we offer a heartfelt thank you for your ideas, generosity, time, and enthusiasm.

Many individuals helped us gather materials and verify information for this book. Marian Chavez, Barbara Korbal, Kelci Lowe, Chris Rodgers, and Emily Plec at the University of New Mexico; Erin Reser, Kate Savage, Linda Scholz, and Derek Sweet at Colorado State University; and Ming-chu Chen, Gail J. Chryslee, Laura K. Hahn, and Sharon M. Varallo at Ohio State University provided research assistance. Thank you for your time, patience, perseverance, and competence. A Coca-Cola Grant for Research on Women from the Department of Women's Studies at Ohio State University helped to provide funding for some of these researchers.

We also wish to thank Sophy Craze, the Sage Publications editor who first proposed publication of this book and whose enthusiasm encouraged us to begin writing what had been a tangle of ideas in our minds for several years. Margaret H. Seawell, an acquisitions editor at Sage, assumed the oversight function of the book from Sophy and supported us with patience, gentle humor, and trust in the final product.

We used various chapters from this book in manuscript form in our classes, and the insights of our students were invaluable in clarifying and refining our ideas. The classes in which we tried out our ideas were Contemporary Rhetorical Theory at the Women's College, University of Denver, spring 1997; Culture and Discourse at the University of New Mexico, spring 1997; Feminist Rhetorical Theories at the University of Colorado at Denver, fall 1997; Feminist Theories of Discourse at Colorado State University, fall 1997; and Contemporary Feminist Theory at the University of New Mexico, fall 1997.

As we worked on this project, several women helped us refine our ideas and created environments of support and safety in the process. These women include Bessie Gallegos, Kathy Domenici, Leslie Fagre, Jennifer Gruenewald, Ann Skinner-Jones, Deborah Fort, Barb Willard, Ann Gill, Kimberly Barnett Gibson, Cin Chubb, Mary Jane Collier, Lenore Langsdorf, and Melissa McCalla. To all of these women, we express our deepest appreciation. We hope that you recognize the a-mazing women's world that you represent and invaluable friendship and support you offered us as this book progressed.

Finally, we thank our families—Anthony J. Radich, Stephen W. Littlejohn, and Michael J. Harte and Joseph S. Griffin-Harte—for providing us with the space in which to work, nourishment of all kinds, a good dose of perspective, much patience, and lots of laughter and love.

Photo Credits

Photograph of Cheris Kramarae provided by Jack Liu, Eugene, OR.

Photograph of bell hooks provided by John Pinderhughes.

Photograph of Gloria Anzaldúa provided by Jean Weisinger.

Photograph of Mary Daly provided by Gail Bryan, copyright © 1991. All rights reserved.

Photograph of Starhawk provided by Deborah Jones.

Photograph of Paula Gunn Allen provided by Tama Rothschild Photography, Beverly Hills, CA.

Photograph of Trinh T. Minh-ha provided by Jean-Paul Bourdier, Berkeley, CA.

Photograph of Sally Gearhart provided by Betsy Swart.

Photograph of Sonia Johnson provided by Pat Stroud.

Permission Credits

In Chapter 3, excerpts from "Shaking the Conventions of Higher Education or Appropriate and Appropriated Technology," presented by Cheris Kramarae at the Women, Information and Technology in Industry and Education Conference, Queensland University of Technology, Brisbane, Australia (December 5, 1997); and from *A Feminist Dictionary,* edited by Cheris Kramarae and Paula A. Treichler, with Ann Russo (Boston: Pandora, 1985), are reprinted by permission of Cheris Kramarae.

In Chapter 4, excerpts from *Feminist Theory: From Margin to Center,* by bell hooks, and from *Talking Back: Thinking Feminist, Thinking Black,* by bell hooks, are reprinted with permission from the publisher, South End Press, 116 Saint Botolph Street, Boston, MA 02115.

In Chapter 5, excerpts from *Borderlands/La Frontera: The New Mestiza,* © 1990 by Gloria Anzaldúa, and from *Making Face, Making Soul/Haciendo Caras: Creative and Critical Perspectives by Feminists of Color,* © 1990 by Gloria Anzaldúa, are reprinted by permission of Aunt Lute Books.

In Chapter 7, excerpts from *Truth or Dare: Encounters with Power, Authority, and Mystery,* by Starhawk, copyright © 1987 by Miriam Simos, are reprinted by permission of HarperCollins Publishers, Inc.

In Chapter 8, excerpts from *The Secret Hoop: Recovering the Feminine in American Indian Traditions,* by Paula Gunn Allen © 1986, 1992 by Paula Gunn Allen, are reprinted by permission of Beacon Press, Boston. Excerpts from "Sipapu: A Cultural Perspective" (unpublished doctoral dissertation, University of New Mexico), by Paula Gunn Allen, are reprinted by permission of the author. Excerpts from "The Horse That I Ride: The Life Story of Paula Gunn Allen" (unpublished manuscript), by Jacqueline L. Collins, are reprinted by permission of the author.

In Chapter 9, excerpts from *When the Moon Waxes Red: Representtion, Gender and Cultural Politics,* by Trinh T. Minh-ha, copyright © 1991, and from *Framer Framed,* by Trinh T. Minh-ha, copyright © 1992, are reproduced by permission of Routledge, Inc.

In Chapter 10, excerpts from "Notes from a Recovering Activist," by Sally Miller Gearhart, are reprinted from *Sojourner: The Women's Forum,* vol. 21, no. 1, September 1995, with permission from the Sojourner Feminist Institute. Excerpts from "The Womanization of Rhetoric," by Sally Miller Gearhart, are reprinted from *Women's Studies International Quartery,* vol. 2, pp. 195-201, 1979, with permission from Elsevier Science.

In Chapter 11, excerpts from *From Housewife to Heretic, Going Out of Our Minds: The Metaphysics of Liberation, Wildfire: Igniting the She/Volution,* and *The Ship That Sailed into the Living Room: Sex and Intimacy Reconsidered,* by Sonia Johnson, and from *Out of This World: A Fictionalized True-Life Adventure,* by Sonia Johnson and Jade DeForest, are reprinted by permission of the authors.

CHAPTER 1

Introduction

"Re-vision—the act of looking back, of seeing with fresh eyes, of entering an old text from a new critical direction—is for women more than a chapter in cultural history: it is an act of survival."[1] Adrienne Rich's notion of re-visioning is the inspiration for this book, which is about seeing rhetoric in new ways and, in particular, through the lens of feminist perspectives. The nine feminists included here—Cheris Kramarae, bell hooks, Gloria Anzaldúa, Mary Daly, Starhawk, Paula Gunn Allen, Trinh T. Minh-ha, Sally Miller Gearhart, and Sonia Johnson—offer theories of rhetoric that are substantially different from traditional rhetorical theory. They re-vision rhetoric and encourage scholars to rethink traditional constructs from new critical perspectives.

As its title implies, this book features the three themes of *feminism, rhetoric,* and *theory,* and we begin with a discussion of what these key terms mean to us. In the process of defining these terms, we will share experiences from our lives to provide sufficient context for readers to understand the perspectives on feminism, rhetoric, and theory that we hold. We also hope that our experiences reinforce the importance of re-visioning rhetoric from feminist perspectives because these experiences served, in many instances, as the impetus for our thinking that new approaches to rhetoric are needed.

Feminism

For us, feminism is a vital, engaging, and exciting perspective from which to view virtually every facet of life. Feminism is so integral to our lives that we cannot imagine not being feminists. This perspective may seem surprising,

1

given that feminism has such negative connotations in popular culture. When many people think of feminism and feminists, they envision angry women— perhaps in combat boots, flannel shirts, and no makeup—who spout harsh, anti-male slogans or otherwise assert power over men. Although some feminists may engage in some of these activities, not all feminists do. What is important to note is that there are many kinds of feminisms and feminists, and feminism is a much more complex mode of being in the world than any of these images suggest.

Most definitions of feminism are ones that we believe many individuals would support if they understood feminism apart from its stereotypically negative associations. Rebecca West, writing in the *Clarion* on November 14, 1913, suggests that self-definition is central to her understanding of the term: "I myself have never been able to find out precisely what feminism is: I only know that people call me a feminist whenever I express sentiments that differentiate me from a doormat."[2] Women's articulations of their own experiences and ideas and their claims to the right to determine how their lives will proceed, then, are key aspects of feminism.

Other definitions of feminism focus on the concept of equity, with a goal of reorganizing society on the basis of equality for the sexes in all areas of social relations. Definitions rooted in equity focus on the achievement of equality for women with men and the development of opportunities for women's expression and self-fulfillment in all realms of life, without the constraints of gender expectations. Feminists who embrace this definition of feminism seek an equal share of the opportunities to which men have access.

Other feminists are concerned with the development of alternative social systems and ways of being in the world—ways that are grounded in woman-centered principles and values. Some of these feminists separate from men in order to discover the kinds of lives that are possible for women outside of patriarchy. Still others believe that separation from men is infeasible or unrealistic and that a woman-centered perspective can be enacted in the current world despite the ongoing persistence of patriarchy.

Many feminists now expand the use of the term *feminism* to include eliminating the oppression of all people who are marginalized by the dominant culture, including but not limited to people of color, people with disabilities, people of different ages and socioeconomic classes, and lesbians and gay men. Such definitions of feminism suggest the treatment of all humans in accordance with such feminist values as respect, caring, reciprocity, self-determination, and interconnection. Some feminists extend these values to all creatures on the planet as well as the planet itself. In other words, they see all living beings as entitled to live life fully and to be affirmed and valued as unique and significant contributors to the universe.

These myriad definitions of and perspectives on feminism suggest that there are a variety of kinds of feminists and feminisms. Rather than confuse, we suggest that this variety opens up choices and possibilities and speaks to the very nature of feminism. It is rooted in choice and self-determination and does not prescribe one "official" position that feminists must hold. Feminism also is an evolving process that necessarily changes as conditions in the world change and as feminists develop new understandings. Our own definitions of and perspectives on feminism have followed this same pattern and have changed dramatically over the years. This evolution has resulted in our current focus, in which we have chosen to apply our energies toward reconceptualization and re-visioning in our professional and personal lives.

Because of generational differences (Sonja and Karen are eight years older than Cindy), our experiences with gender issues and the feminist movement have occurred in different ways. For Karen and Sonja, their father's death in an automobile accident when they were high school seniors instantly pointed out the difficulties with traditional gender roles for white, middle-class women. Not only was their mother forced to assume the financial support of the family (at her husband's insistence, she had not worked at jobs that earned any significant income), but she had to take on a number of masculine gender-role tasks she had not had to do before, such as mowing the lawn and having the car serviced.

Sonja and Karen also worked in a cannery one summer, sorting the bad vegetables from the good as they came by on a conveyor belt. While the women had to wear dresses and hair nets and stood throughout their shifts in a couple of inches of cold water, at the end of the conveyor belt stood a man, with long hair, dressed comfortably in jeans, boots, and no hair net. His job was simply to empty the box of vegetables when it filled up—about every 15 minutes—a job for which he was paid 50 cents more per hour than the women. Defining the term *feminism* to mean a commitment to equitable treatment for women seemed very relevant at the end of that summer. This experience and others like it prompted Karen and Sonja to work for the ratification of the Equal Rights Amendment and to enact feminism as equality in their personal lives. Both kept their family name when they married, and both figured out how to share equally in the domestic and financial responsibilities of marriage with their husbands.

Cindy does not recall a specific moment when the inequity of the world in terms of the treatment of women and men dawned on her. Rather, she remembers always moving through the world with the feeling that she did not have access to certain benefits as a female, although she did not have the words to articulate what was wrong. She remembers riding her bike when she was in about the sixth grade, thinking about the different treatment accorded her and her brother, and wondering why she did not have the options available to her that her brother did.

Although we began our feminist evolutions in different ways, our experiences very quickly led us in similar directions—toward an understanding of the need for a different kind of world. Cindy remembers longing for a different world, one not based on arbitrary hierarchical standards that encourage the judgment and rank ordering of masculine and feminine skills, tasks, and characteristics. She also remembers looking at how the world was organized in high school and thinking, "If this is all there is, I'm in big trouble!" The only option she saw was to try to create a different world, a world she later would label as *feminist.*

Cindy's experiences as both graduate student and mother probably most explicitly led her to understand that a world with feminist values is possible. The birth of her son during her first year of graduate school caused her to develop ways of being and living that managed the contradictory identities of student and mother, two roles usually not seen as appropriate in the same world. Because her child is a boy, she faced additional contradictions. Certain that she would have a girl (so she could raise another feminist), she realized with the birth of a boy that she would have to create a world that was different from the one she saw around her. She knew that she needed to and could create a world in which a boy could embrace the values she saw as important—sensitivity, respect, care for others, interconnection, collaboration, and nurturance.

Sonja's and Karen's understandings of the possibilities of a different world, a world in which different values from the current world were celebrated, emerged most clearly from their experiences as counselors at a Camp Fire Girls camp. In this all-female environment, in which girls and women were valued and allowed to express themselves as they chose, apart from male prescriptions and expectations, they immediately felt at home. Their camp experience literally gave them a glimpse of the possibilities of a women's world and enabled them to begin to articulate the components and importance of a woman-centered reality.

The three of us, then, eventually came to see feminism as more than the effort to achieve equality for women with men and as the means to create a different kind of world characterized by different practices and values. Once we saw feminism as a way of being, we began to create more consciously the worlds in which we wanted to live. We are all university professors and have come to realize, for example, that we do not approach our classrooms, advisees, colleagues, or institutions in the ways that many of our colleagues do. In this context, we often engage in practices that we see as feminist and are committed to creating what we believe are more humane environments. For both Cindy and Sonja, a particular graduate class at the University of Oregon composed largely of feminist women in which they both participated—Sonja as professor and Cindy as student—showed them clearly the possibilities of a feminist world in the academy. Karen realizes that she has chosen to direct women's studies programs—seven years in all—not so much because she enjoys administration but because of the largely all-female space created in such programs, a space that often is quite different from the rest of the university.

Our journeys, then, ultimately have led us to articulate feminism as a commitment to a set of principles or values. In our initial involvements with feminism, these commitments dealt solely with women and gender, but they now are more inclusive and recognize the oppressions that individuals other than women experience. We are committed to enacting in the world the values of self-determination, immanent value, affirmation, mutuality, and care, and we want to eliminate oppression, domination, and hierarchy in all of their manifestations. Feminism for us is not an abstract philosophy but a way of living our lives by acting in ways that allow others to make choices, that affirm them and their perspectives, and that do not oppress and exploit.

For us, feminism is an important perspective for at least three reasons. It validates values and experiences often associated with women. Some of our most meaningful experiences have involved women, and feminism celebrates and honors such experiences. This validation does not mean that we wish to maintain current gender divisions, believe that women have certain inherent characteristics that are better than those of men, or see feminism as applicable only to women. Rather, we simply have found that ways of communicating, approaches to the world, and experiences traditionally associated with the feminine gender are important to us, and feminism allows them to be validated.

Feminism also is important because it gives voice to individuals marginalized and devalued by the dominant culture and thus provides a more holistic understanding of the world. Feminism takes seriously not only the experiences associated with women but those of all marginalized groups, whether people of color, people with disabilities, lesbians and gay men, or any other group that is not featured in the dominant culture. Feminism takes seriously their perspectives and suggests that these perspectives are as valuable as those that characterize the dominant culture. The result is a greater repertoire of options for living and communicating for all individuals.

Finally, we believe feminism is important because it establishes and legitimates a value system that privileges mutuality, respect, caring, power-with, interconnection, and immanent value. These values stand in direct contrast to those that characterize the dominant culture—hierarchy, competition, domination, alienation, and power-over, for example. We believe that although feminist values are devalued in Western culture, they are far more sustainable and life affirming than the ones currently in place. Feminism, we suggest, offers a model for different ways of living in the world.

Rhetoric

Definitions of rhetoric are as abundant and varied as are definitions of feminism, and, like feminism, rhetoric has its share of negative connotations. When not conceptualized as ornamental, flowery speech devoid of any real content, rhetoric commonly is associated with the empty words used by politicians to win votes. Action is seen as antithetical to rhetoric in this negative view. In contrast to these images of emptiness, deceit, and passivity, we see rhetoric as something quite positive and useful in our lives.

The earliest definitions associated the term *rhetoric* with persuasion and with the production and study of formal, intentional, spoken discourse. More recent definitions have broadened the scope of rhetoric to include any kind of symbol use—verbal, visual, formal, informal, completed, or emergent—and even the intentional and persuasive aspects of early conceptualizations of rhetoric have come to be questioned. Although still viewed traditionally by some rhetorical theorists, rhetoric usually is seen now as incorporating virtually any humanly created symbols from which audiences derive meanings. Architecture, paintings, performances, films, advertisements, conversations, debates, speeches, books, and the like are considered legitimate artifacts for rhetorical study.

Traditionally, rhetoric also was associated strictly with human symbolic efforts to discern truth. Some classical perspectives suggest that individuals use rhetoric to discover the truth, which exists in the world in some kind of knowable and verifiable fashion. More recent perspectives, however, assume that rhetoric constructs, through interaction, a shared understanding of the world, which is the closest individuals can come to truth. Such views of the function of rhetoric raise questions about whose construction of reality is privileged in a culture and whether reality exists in an external form and fashion or whether it is constructed through symbolic interaction.

The site of or location for rhetoric also has been defined variously throughout the rhetorical tradition. Classical definitions suggest that rhetoric occurs in a narrowly defined public sphere—the sphere of political debate, law, religion, or public ceremony—a view that affects the way in which the rhetor is conceptualized. Appropriate occupants of this public sphere, until recently, tended to be famous, male, and white. Other possibilities for the site of rhetoric are beginning to emerge, however. In these conceptions, the proper sphere for rhetoric has been expanded so that the private realm can be a viable location for rhetoric. The result of this expansion is that individuals who do not necessarily have easy access to the political arena—women and other marginalized groups, for instance—are being seen as viable subjects for study.

For us, the study of rhetoric and the various debates around it are fascinating. We are intrigued by the ways symbols affect us and others and how they create particular realities. Like many rhetorical scholars, however, we came to the formal study of rhetoric through the back door—in this case, through the study of other languages. Cindy studied American Sign Language and Karen and Sonja studied Spanish and French as undergraduates in college. Intrigued by symbol use and how it works for different individuals in different cultures, we realized not only that we could not be full members of the cultures whose languages we studied but that our interests really were in larger questions about the nature and functions of symbolicity. We turned to the study of rhetoric and to the various ways that symbols are used to construct particular realities.

As we began to study rhetoric, however, we realized that traditional rhetorical theory did not represent or include our experiences as women. The focus of our early study was on Aristotelian and other classical rhetorical theories, and we struggled to find the connection between this material and women's rhetorical activities. We came to realize that a bias existed in our chosen field—one that did not value or make easy the inclusion in rhetorical theory of practices associated with women.

Ultimately, by bringing our feminism to the study of rhetoric, we developed what we see as a more comprehensive understanding of rhetoric. We define rhetoric as any kind of human symbol use that functions in any realm—public, private, and anything in between. The rhetors we study can be anyone—they need not hold certain positions or speak in particular fields in order to be worthy of our investigation. Our goal for studying rhetoric also has changed from our initial understanding of the notion. It no longer is to learn how to persuade others; rather, it is to understand how people construct the worlds in which they live and how those worlds make sense to them.

The study of rhetoric is important to us for two reasons. Rhetoric is integral to our lives. Individuals are surrounded by symbols continually, and we want to be conscious of the ways in which these symbols function in our lives and influence us as well as those around us. We also value rhetoric because it can and does create reality. We believe that rhetoric is an important way in which individuals create worlds, perspectives, and identities. In almost any situation, innumerable options exist for how to act and respond. Understanding how rhetoric functions allows us to make conscious choices about the kinds of worlds we want to create, who and how we want to be in those worlds, and the values we want those worlds to embody. The study of rhetoric, then, enables us to understand and articulate the various ways individuals create and enact the worlds in which they choose to live.

Theory

The third term that is important to this book is *theory,* and we realize that this is yet another word that often fails to excite people. The word *theory* regularly conjures up images of an abstract, mystifying, inaccessible treatise or formula that has no clear relationship to everyday life. These esoteric images, however, have little to do with our view of theory and how we conceptualize it in this book.

Traditional conceptualizations of theory suggest that only the expert, trained individual—the individual who has researched and read extensively about a subject—can produce theory. This conceptualization has tended to foster arbitrary divisions between those who can produce knowledge and those who cannot. Cheris Kramarae, the subject of Chapter 3, suggests that traditional conceptualizations of theory foster the belief that only a few can know or explain, and those few usually are male. Women often have not been acknowledged as capable of producing theory, Kramarae explains; to do so would "acknowledge that these women are experts and have created serious, impressive, contending" bodies of knowledge. We believe, with Kramarae, that theory is "not the activity of a few, but the articulation, open to all, of our practical, knowing activities."[3]

The re-visioning of who can theorize led to a transformation of the ways in which theories are produced and validated. In traditional definitions, theory production was limited to formal arenas—science and politics, for example— and theories were verified only after extensive formal research and testing of hypotheses. Some contemporary scholars, however, have begun to suggest that theories can be produced in less formal settings—the home or the workplace, for example—and validated through the daily experiences of individuals. Although some scholars continue to place tight boundaries around the production and verification of theory, many others now suggest that theory can be produced from the most simple and basic of human experiences and can be tested and verified through everyday practices and observations.

By *theory,* then, we mean a way of framing an experience or event—an effort to understand and account for something and the way it functions in the world. We see theory and theorizing as a natural part of life; theorizing is a process in which most people engage on a daily basis. Individuals theorize when they try to figure out answers for, develop explanations about, and organize what is happening in their worlds. Because we see theory as a way to organize, describe, name, or explain phenomena and recognize that all individuals can theorize, we do not believe that there is only one theory that correctly describes or captures any particular situation or activity. Consistent with our definitions of feminism and rhetoric, we suggest that multiple—and sometimes even contradictory— theories are possible and viable for a given event or situation.

Our entry into the world of theorizing follows similar paths as did our development of a feminist consciousness and our conceptualization of rhetoric. Looking back, we realize that the three of us felt that we never quite fit into the worlds in which we lived, and we recognize now that we used theorizing to make sense of these experiences. For Cindy, years of competitive swimming gave her the time and place to reflect on the nature of a world in which she did not belong. Her family virtually required that she swim competitively, but she always came in last in the meets in which she participated. Although she worked out as vigorously as the rest of her family and the swim team, her small physical build prevented her from excelling at this sport. Over the years, Cindy had to organize and interpret this experience so that she could make sense of her place on the swim team as well as within her family.

Sonja's and Karen's experiences with theorizing came because, as adolescents, they were too shy to engage comfortably in public situations and felt as though they did not have a place in the public world. They remember hiding out in the language lab in high school to avoid things like pep rallies—activities that seemed silly and made little sense to them because of their emphasis on winning and competition. They tried to make sense of their feelings about high school through theorizing—framing and reframing their experiences to be able to articulate the nature of the constraints they felt and the alternative world in which they wished to live. Because they are twins, they were able to theorize and develop coping strategies together for responding to their world.

Our experiences with theorizing have led us to value theory for one fundamental reason. At its most basic level, theorizing helps clarify thinking. Gloria Anzaldúa, the subject of Chapter 5, defines theory as "a mental viewing, an idea or mental plan of the way to do something."[4] In the process of theorizing, individuals are encouraged to move from the particulars of their own experiences to larger patterns or frames and to decide what those patterns mean. Theorizing assists individuals in organizing what might at first seem to be chaotic or unrelated information in order to make sense of those experiences and, ultimately, their lives.

Organizing ideas and experiences into theories can promote action. When individuals make sense of their worlds through theory, they are better equipped to understand situations and to see the possibilities for responding and taking action in those situations. Rather than remain confused or immobilized by seemingly chaotic experiences or information, individuals can use the theorizing process to order and then respond to events in a more systematic and coherent way. Organizing painful events into larger patterns of experiences has the potential to politicize those events, connecting them to the larger systemic forces and structures that negatively affect their lives. Theory's very basic function of organizing information, in sum, facilitates the process of articulating experiences about, acting in, and making sense of life. Anzaldúa's perspective on theory provides an apt summary of theory's emancipatory function: "If we have been gagged and disempowered by theories, we can also be loosened and empowered by theories."[5]

In labeling the work of the women in this book *theories,* we are saying that we believe they have important contributions to make in the area of rhetoric—ways of organizing communication that are distinct, insightful, and important to rhetorical studies. We also suggest that their theories are very much out-growths of their daily lives, not distant, abstract, or removed explanations about rhetoric. We believe that even though these theorists might not agree on various points—indeed, might even seem to be in deep disagreement with one an-other—all of their theories are plausible, valid, and important explanations of how rhetoric works in the world.

Preview

The nine theorists included here—Cheris Kramarae, bell hooks, Gloria Anzaldúa, Mary Daly, Starhawk, Paula Gunn Allen, Trinh T. Minh-ha, Sally Miller Gearhart, and Sonia Johnson—are contemporary feminists who offer important insights into rhetoric. Although we could have included many other feminist theorists in this book, we chose to feature the ideas and works of these nine theorists for several reasons. A primary reason we included these women is their diversity. They represent different perspectives and positions on feminism that derive from standpoints that vary across race, ethnicity, and class, as well as sexual, spiritual, and political orientations. The result of these differences is a multiplicity and expansion of perspectives on rhetoric.

We also selected these nine theorists for inclusion because all of them have substantial bodies of written work in which they have articulated feminist theories relevant to rhetoric. All of these theorists have made issues of symbol use central to their views of the world, and the resulting theories have transfor-mative potential for rhetorical theory. We do not mean to suggest, however, that all of these women have developed rhetorical theories deliberately or explicitly; in fact, most of them would not consider themselves to be rhetorical theorists. Only two—Kramarae and Gearhart—formally associate with the communica-tion discipline and see their work in specifically rhetorical terms. Nevertheless, a rhetorical perspective and theory clearly are evident in the works of all nine theorists.

Accessibility also was a criterion in our selection of these women. In keeping with our commitment to theory that is grounded in experience and our commit-ment to the disruption of practices of domination and elitism, we chose to feature theorists who not only provide insightful ideas but also present them in ways that are accessible, even to those without much background in feminism or rhetoric. With bell hooks, the subject of Chapter 4, we ask, "[O]f what use is feminist theory . . . that leaves [women] stumbling bleary-eyed from class-room settings," trapped in jargon and technical detail such that the major ideas and their potential applications are lost?[6] Rather than select theorists who have the potential to keep individuals distanced from and struggling with feminist theory, we have included scholars who enact accessibility in their work.

Finally, we chose to feature these nine individuals because of their strong influences on our own work. Their varied definitions of feminism, their descriptions of the world, and their particular approaches to social change resonate with us and have refined our thinking about rhetoric. These are women we admire, and our inclusion of them constitutes a celebration of their work as well as an invitation to others to consider and make use of their ideas.

Our goal in the chapters about the theorists is to present and explicate their feminist rhetorical theories as they articulate them. We envision each chapter functioning as a starting point—a point of entry into the theorist's original work—and we hope to lay the groundwork from which readers can theorize, debate, critique, and extend the ideas presented as they see fit.

Each chapter or theory is organized around six components. For each theorist, we offer a brief biography to provide a context for understanding her orientation to the world and some of the particular experiences that have influenced the development of her ideas. We then discuss the nature of the world as explicated by the theorist. This discussion provides the theorist's view of the realm for rhetoric—the context in which rhetoric occurs as described by the theorist. Some theorists offer discussion of both the world of the dominant paradigm and an alternative feminist paradigm or world, others describe the world of the dominant culture alone, and still others attend primarily to the world they wish to see created and pay little attention to the current world.

A third section in each chapter provides discussion of the definition of feminism offered by the theorist. As with the biography section, we include this material because each theorist conceptualizes feminism in her own way; this points to the multiple feminisms that exist as starting points for theorizing from feminist perspectives. Some of the theorists clearly articulate their own definitions of feminism, whereas for others, the definitions are implicit in their work. These definitions shape and inform the theories offered by these women and the transformations of rhetoric that result.

Each chapter also includes a section on the nature of the rhetor or the kind of agent the theorist sees as responding to and acting in the world described. Rhetors are those individuals who produce rhetoric, and the conceptualizations of who does so vary across the theorists. All nine of the women included in this book agree that women are particularly important rhetors, who deserve theoretical attention. In addition, some describe men as rhetors, and some include within their conceptualizations of the rhetor women who support the dominant culture.

The description of the rhetor is followed by a discussion of the theorist's rhetorical options or her description of the means available to the rhetor for acting in the world. Options include the tools rhetors use to negotiate the dominant culture and to act in a feminist world. We have chosen the term *options* over *strategies* in order to avoid the traditional connotation of adversarial, combative, goal-directed, ends-oriented efforts at persuasion. We conceptualize this component as the symbolic actions rhetors use to engage their worlds.

The final section in each chapter is a discussion of some of the transformations of rhetorical theory that might result from the theorist's work. We offer this discussion as a way of suggesting possible re-visions of rhetoric that the theories might produce and to encourage a dialogue on the ways in which the boundaries of the rhetorical discipline can be expanded as a result of feminist perspectives on rhetoric. We define *transformation* as the process of expanding a familiar construct—changing its composition, structure, or function—in order to enable it to accommodate or explain new material. We suggest that transformation occurs in two ways: through an approach to a construct from a different standpoint or ideological frame and through the use of new data with which to begin the conceptualization process. A construct may retain some of its previous identity or content, or it may look altogether different as a result of the process of reconceptualization and transformation. In the retention of some of its previous content, however, what gets carried over often is integrated or woven into the construct in very new ways.

Our discussion of possible transformations of rhetorical theory in this final section is deliberately general. We want to encourage others to engage in transformational work and do not want individuals to be confined by our ideas. We hope we provide enough detail to model the reconceptualization of rhetorical theory from feminist perspectives that is possible but not so much as to constrain thinking on any particular transformative possibility. We also realize that our readers have different levels of knowledge about rhetorical theory, and we attempt to address this situation by presenting sufficient detail to enable all readers to understand the proposed transformation but not so much that the description is tedious for those with a greater knowledge of rhetoric. Our goal in this section is not necessarily to reject traditional conceptualizations of rhetoric but to place them in a context that suggests their limitations when applied to less accepted or familiar forms of rhetoric. In keeping with our philosophy of inclusion, we wish to open up the possibilities for rhetoric rather than replace one paradigm with another.

We have organized the nine theories in a particular way in this book, one that aligns with our thinking about the various aspects of feminist transformations of rhetoric. We see the first two theorists—Cheris Kramarae and bell hooks—as offering systematic and somewhat comprehensive descriptions of the difficulties feminists see with the dominant culture and with rhetoric as it operates within that culture. Thus, they lay a foundation for the theories that follow. The theories of Gloria Anzaldúa, Mary Daly, Starhawk, and Paula Gunn Allen that follow describe two worlds or systems—one patriarchal and one feminist. In presenting two worlds or systems, these theorists explicate an alternative to the dominant culture, calling into question that culture as natural and normal. The last three theories—those of Trinh T. Minh-ha, Sally Miller Gearhart, and Sonia Johnson—involve descriptions of new systems or worldviews infused with feminist principles and practices. Trinh calls for a disruption of the existing system, although she does not articulate what a new system might look like (her philosophical orientation precludes her from doing so). Gearhart's and Johnson's theories offer descriptions of alternative worlds and how individuals might create such worlds.

We see this book as part of an evolution of rhetorical scholarship in which feminist perspectives re-vision many traditional constructs and theories. We hope that the ideas presented here will challenge, stimulate, encourage, and empower individuals to think about feminism, rhetoric, and theory in new, more humane ways. We hope, too, that this book facilitates the process described by Adrienne Rich of looking back, seeing rhetoric with fresh eyes, and ultimately generating a more comprehensive body of rhetorical theory.

CHAPTER 2

Feminist Perspectives in Rhetorical Studies

A History

The contributions to rhetoric of the nine theorists featured in this book best can be understood in the context of the history of feminist scholarship in rhetorical studies. Our focus is on rhetorical studies for two principal reasons. First, the nine women we include theorize largely in this area; second, space limitations preclude us from dealing with the influence of feminist perspectives on the entire communication discipline. Thus, we concentrate here on the area of the discipline that has contributed most directly to the development of the feminist rhetorical theories that are the focus of this book.

The developments we identify as part of the rhetorical history of the communication discipline include a variety of events and projects that have advanced feminist scholarship. Some of these are scholarly essays and books that have had significant impacts on the direction of feminist perspectives on rhetoric. A few of these works deal with the communication discipline as a whole and not only with rhetorical studies, but their impacts have been such that rhetorical theory has been affected. Other events are structural developments—the initiation of a journal or a conference, for instance—that proved pivotal to the emergence or direction of feminist agendas in rhetorical studies and, sometimes, influenced the discipline as a whole.

We suggest that five dimensions or threads have contributed in significant ways to the development of feminist perspectives in rhetorical studies: (1) radical beginnings; (2) efforts to include women as communicators and women's topics in the discipline; (3) critiques of the discipline from feminist perspectives; (4) labeling and refining of feminist perspectives; and (5) reconceptualizations of constructs and theories in rhetorical studies from feminist perspectives. Although this list of dimensions suggests discrete, chronological categories in the intersection of feminism and rhetoric, they are not clearly distinguishable from one another, nor did they occur in chronological order. Rather, they all have overlapped continually, and they all still are research areas in the discipline that continue to generate new studies that expand our knowledge of rhetorical practices.

Radical Beginnings

Pinpointing the time at which feminist perspectives began to enter the discipline of communication is difficult, but three essays and a book are among the works that clearly stand out as important initiating texts. Karlyn Kohrs Campbell's essay "The Rhetoric of Women's Liberation" is the earliest; it was published in 1973 in the major rhetorical journal in the field, the *Quarterly Journal of Speech.*[1] In this article, Campbell suggested that the rhetoric of the contemporary women's movement is an oxymoron in that it "wavers between the rhetorical and the non-rhetorical, the persuasive and the non-persuasive."[2] The rhetoric of the women's movement, she suggested, consists of substantive and stylistic components so distinctive that it constitutes a unique genre with special rhetorical features. Consequently, traditional definitions of persuasion, rhetorical situations, and rhetorical movements prove unsatisfactory when applied to the women's liberation movement. Campbell's article constituted the first effort to reconceptualize rhetorical constructs from a feminist perspective, a focus of feminist scholarship that would not appear again for many years.

Campbell's essay was followed in 1974 by an essay by Cheris Kramarae (formerly Kramer) titled "Women's Speech: Separate but Unequal?" In this essay, published in the *Quarterly Journal of Speech,* Kramarae raised the possibility of "systems of co-occurring, sex-linked, linguistic signals" that point to linguistic sex differences between women and men.[3] She argued that actual differences need to be studied to test the "sizeable amount of information that can be called folk-view," which she defined as "how people think women speak or how people think women should speak."[4] Kramarae also called for women as language users to be considered individually rather than as part of a general category: "Researchers interested in studying the speech of women as women . . . must be careful not to make the error of grouping all women together."[5] Thus, her essay foreshadowed the development of an emphasis on differences among women in the feminist movement and the development of standpoint theory, a recognition of the various positions from which individuals perceive the world. Kramarae's work is the focus of Chapter 3, and we will return to her ideas in greater depth there.

The year after Kramarae's essay appeared, a book was published that dealt specifically with the linguistic concerns she raised. Robin Lakoff's *Language and Woman's Place,* based on anecdotal evidence, suggested various ways in which women tend to use language. In particular, Lakoff asserted, women's language reinforces the belief that women are not powerful; yet, when women shift to masculine linguistic modes, they still are denied access to power because they are violating appropriate norms for women.[6] This work not only pointed to a paradox that repeatedly has been demonstrated to hold true for women's communication but laid the groundwork for discussion of the power relations undergirding talk that later became important in studies of gender and communication.

Sally Miller Gearhart's "The Womanization of Rhetoric," published in 1979 in *Women's Studies International Quarterly,* also contributed to the beginnings of feminist rhetorical theory.[7] Gearhart challenged a fundamental tenet of rhetorical studies—the definition of rhetoric as persuasion. She indicted this definition on the grounds that "any intent to persuade is an act of violence" and proposed instead a female model of communication as an antidote to the violence that currently characterizes life on planet Earth.[8] Gearhart described this model as "a mutual generation of energy for purposes of growth" in which neither party seeks to change the other but both contribute to an atmosphere in which change for all can occur.[9] Gearhart is the focus of Chapter 10, and we explore these ideas in more detail there.

The works of these four scholars are important because of the transformative shifts they foreshadowed for the discipline of rhetorical studies. Campbell's and Gearhart's essays were significant because, for the first time in print in the communication discipline, the argument was offered that feminism necessarily transforms rhetorical constructs and theories. These authors questioned fundamental assumptions about rhetoric, suggesting reconceptualizations of rhetorical studies grounded in the influence of feminist perspectives.

The contributions made by Kramarae and Lakoff foreshadowed the emergence of another major focus of feminist work in communication—efforts to incorporate, value, and legitimate the study of women's communication practices in the discipline. The emphasis they placed on the process of incorporating women's language and rhetorical practices as data—on simply making women's linguistic practices a subject of research in the discipline—laid the groundwork for the study of women's communicative practices from perspectives generated by women themselves. These essays, then, were radical in that they articulated—or at least anticipated the articulation of—some of the fundamental shifts that resulted when feminist perspectives were brought to bear on the rhetorical tradition and on the entire communication discipline.

Inclusion of Women in the Discipline

A second major development in terms of feminist perspectives in rhetorical studies was the incorporation of studies about women and topics concerning women into rhetorical studies. This effort at inclusion encompassed primarily three categories of studies: studies of women orators, studies of social movements about or of concern to women, and subject matters that affect or are particularly significant to women.

Studies of women rhetoricians were an early thrust of efforts to include women in the discipline. On the surface, studies of women orators appear to be traditional rhetorical studies; in virtually all of the initial essays on great women speakers, women's communication strategies and practices are described within traditional frameworks and approaches to rhetoric. In a typical study of this kind, for example, Francis Wright's speaking was examined according to Longinus's notion of eloquence.[10] The women speakers studied were, for the most part, political and social activists, not unlike men in positions of political and/or social power whose rhetorical practices were investigated by rhetorical scholars. They included, for example, Anita Bryant,[11] Abigail Duniway,[12] Ella Grasso,[13] Martha Griffiths,[14] the Grimké sisters,[15] Barbara Jordan,[16] Elizabeth Morgan,[17] Lucretia Mott,[18] and Harriet Beecher Stowe.[19] In addition, if the women studied were not from the United States, they were from the United Kingdom—Bernadette Devlin,[20] Emmeline Pankhurst,[21] Margaret Thatcher,[22] and Mary Wollstonecraft,[23] for example—in keeping with the preoccupation with American and British public address that dominated the early days of rhetorical studies.[24]

The inclusion of women as subjects of study, however, was noteworthy because the discipline had been built upon and privileged the speaking of men—especially those who were noteworthy for their political contributions in the public sphere.[25] The study of women not only pointed the way for considerations of gendered speaking styles, but, more important, once studies moved beyond white, middle- or upper-class men in positions of power, the study of diverse forms of expression, rhetors, and contexts became possible.[26]

In the studies of women rhetors, too, equal attention was given to historical and contemporary women speakers. Thus, these studies suggested a valuing of contemporary discourse that had not been present in rhetorical studies. Again, this shift in focus away from strictly historical figures and events may not seem especially noteworthy by today's standards now that virtually every rhetorical experience is available for investigation. But against the belief that greater objectivity and a more complete accounting of a life and work are possible if a speaker is no longer living, the study of contemporary individuals was radical.

A second kind of study that brought women into the discipline was the social movement study that focused on movements of particular relevance to women. The introduction of these studies into the discipline facilitated a rethinking of women's position in society generally and a reconsideration by rhetorical scholars of what counts as important communication. The challenge that women's movements posed to the status quo set in motion a series of challenges that ultimately extended to the discipline as a whole.

One of the earliest social movement studies of this type was Brenda Robinson Hancock's "Affirmation by Negation in the Women's Liberation Movement."[27] Hancock argued that feminists in the contemporary stage of the women's liberation movement affirmed their identities by negating the identities of men, thus facilitating catharsis, unity, and positive self-images for women. Other examples of social movement studies were Martha Solomon's and Sonja K. Foss's studies of the Equal Rights Amendment (ERA), which became a prevailing concern of the mainstream women's movement in the United States in the 1970s. Solomon examined the myth that ERA opponent Phyllis Schlafly created for her followers—a myth difficult for her opposition to counter.[28] Foss identified this same difficulty by outlining the different rhetorical visions of the proponents and opponents of the ERA, demonstrating the different motivations of each side.[29]

Feminist scholars also explored the origins of the women's rights movement in order to account for its range of concerns and strategies. Susan Zaeske's examination of the emergence of the early women's rights movement explored the implications of women's reliance on gendered morality as a strategy.[30] Campbell analyzed texts of two of the earliest known public speeches by women in the United States—speeches given by Priscilla Mason and Deborah Sampson Gannett—to suggest the special difficulties they faced given the masculine nature of rhetorical action.[31] Similarly, Cheryl Jorgensen-Earp showed how Emmeline Pankhurst, a spokesperson for the Women's Social and Political Union, deviated strategically from most movement rhetoric by using the very discourse the movement hoped to change for her own ends.[32] Examining the rhetoric of leaders across time and space, Susan Schultz Huxman suggested that, when taken together, Mary Wollstonecraft, Margaret Fuller, and Angelina Grimké offered a shared rhetorical vision of women's rights founded on the natural rights of women as autonomous individuals—rights granted by God at birth.[33]

The inclusion of women speakers and women's movements in rhetorical studies gave rise to numerous anthologies of the oratory of women speakers. These books codified the presence of women as rhetors, deserving of ongoing attention in the discipline. *This Great Argument: The Rights of Women,* edited by Hamida Bosmajian and Haig Bosmajian, included historical treatises by women and men about women's roles, contemporary issues about women as "the second sex," statements from U.S. Senate hearings on the ERA, and statements from contemporary women's liberation groups.[34] In 1982, Patricia Scileppi Kennedy and Gloria Hartmann O'Shields published *We Shall Be Heard,* a survey of important women public speakers from 1828 to 1976 that revealed the "tensions and conflicts fundamental to American progress as well as the ways in which women heralded their advent in American culture."[35]

Judith Anderson's *Outspoken Women* was published in 1984 and focused on American women reformers between 1635 and 1935.[36] Victoria L. DeFrancisco and Marvin D. Jensen added another volume to the contemporary literature on women as communicators with their book *Women's Voices in Our Time,* published in 1994. They documented the voices of women who achieved "legitimate" power as well as those who "emerged in spite of tradition," beginning in 1974, the year Barbara Jordan addressed the U.S. House Judiciary Committee at its impeachment inquiry of Richard Nixon.[37]

In 1989, Campbell contributed to the effort to anthologize women's rhetoric with her two-volume set *Man Cannot Speak for Her.* In the first volume, she provided critical analyses of pivotal discursive events in women's history, including women's rights conventions, significant speeches by such movement rhetors as Susan B. Anthony and Elizabeth Cady Stanton, and speeches by African American women.[38] The second volume is a collection of "key works in the history of the movement that reflect its origins and growth and represent the diversity of issues and styles that characterized it."[39] Speeches by Maria Stewart, Elizabeth Cady Stanton, Sojourner Truth, Susan B. Anthony, and Carrie Chapman Catt are among those included.

Campbell edited another two-volume set that chronicles women activists before and after 1925, providing background information, critical analyses of their rhetorical texts, and reference lists of their works. Written by various rhetorical scholars, the essays in this text provide scholars in rhetorical studies with significant data about many women rhetors who largely had been unknown to the rhetorical tradition and whose work had not been treated critically before.[40]

Two different kinds of anthologies expanded conceptions of women as communicators beyond public oratory, thus laying the groundwork for reconceptualizations of traditional rhetorical considerations. Barbara Bate and Anita Taylor edited a compilation of original research about women's communication with other women titled *Women Communicating: Studies of Women's Talk,* published in 1988. They noted that research on women talking with women was "striking in its absence" from the communication discipline[41] and included in their book chapters on women's use of humor; storytelling in mother-daughter interactions; and talk among women in a weavers' guild, a feminist bookstore, a women's clinic, and a women's music company.

Women Speak: The Eloquence of Women's Lives, by Karen A. Foss and Sonja K. Foss, published in 1991, also provided the discipline with an anthology that expanded and reconceptualized notions of women as communicators. Foss and Foss compiled 30 examples of texts produced by women, ranging from architecture to baking to gardening to holiday greetings to mothering to shopping, to expand what counts as significant forms of communication in the discipline.[42] Their focus was on forms of expression produced by ordinary women, more often than not in private realms.

In addition to anthologies of women's communication, women were included in the discipline in yet another way—through the study of subject matter of particular interest to women that traditionally had not been the focus of scholarly investigation. Making topics of special concern to women the subject of scholarship also suggested an expansion of interests on the part of rhetorical scholars as well as a legitimation of women that had not been seen earlier.

One such topic that has been investigated widely is the abortion debate. Randall Lake, in his essay "Order and Disorder in Anti-Abortion Rhetoric," described the descent-ascent metaphor that informs antiabortion discourse.[43] Celeste Condit (formerly Condit Railsback) described seven stages in the abortion controversy in the United States between 1960 and 1980 and elaborated on their implications in her book *Decoding Abortion Rhetoric*.[44] Condit showed how public discourse has produced changes in attitudes toward abortion and in the development of public policy about and private practice regarding abortion. Mari Boor Tonn also examined abortion rights rhetoric and concluded that the "topos of moral agony adopted by some abortion rights rhetors . . . to allay public discomfort with abortion, is rhetorically and politically self-defeating."[45] In addition, Nathan Stormer analyzed the photography in the video *The Miracle of Life* to show how it posits a social order focused on reproductive habits exemplary of antiabortion discourse.[46]

Motherhood—literally and figuratively—was another topic that began to receive attention in the communication discipline as scholars began to study issues of importance to women. Tonn examined the use of symbolic motherhood by Mary Harris "Mother" Jones to empower audiences of coal miners.[47] Mary M. Lay, Billie J. Wahlstrom, and Carol Brown's study of the rhetoric of midwifery provided another example of a study of motherhood—this time involving actual rather than metaphoric births—that focused on strategies that emerged within the Midwifery Study Advisory Group in Minnesota.[48]

Sexual harassment also became the subject of several studies that suggested attention to, a valuing of, and thus the normalizing of topics that once would have been ignored or marginalized because they are viewed as women's topics. One such study with particular relevance to the communication discipline appeared in 1992, when Julia T. Wood served as guest editor for a special section on sexual harassment in an issue of the journal *Applied Communication Research*. As part of this special section, Wood collected and published stories of sexual harassment from faculty members in the communication field.[49] Shereen

Bingham's edited volume *Conceptualizing Sexual Harassment as Discursive Practice* also contributed to the normalization of the topic of sexual harassment. Bingham offered an assessment of research on sexual harassment to date, focusing on the discursive practices that constitute the phenomenon, in order to suggest alternative frameworks for understanding and studying sexual harassment.[50]

Yet another focus of scholarly inquiry that brought women's concerns to the forefront was the notion of feminine style—characteristics of discourse associated with women speakers. First articulated by Campbell, *feminine style* refers to a discursive mode that emerges out of the experiences of women and is "adapted to the attitudes and experiences of female audiences," although it is not "a style exclusive to women, either as speakers or as audiences."[51] A feminine style is characterized by a personal tone, a heavy reliance on personal experience, an inductive structure, audience participation, and a goal of empowerment.[52] Bonnie J. Dow and Tonn extended the concept by suggesting that this style can be used not only as a strategy for audience empowerment but also "to promote an alternative political philosophy reflecting traditionally feminine values."[53] Dow later elaborated on the place of feminine style in rhetorical studies, suggesting that the limitations of this perspective have not been as fully acknowledged as they should be, particularly in terms of race and class.[54]

Jane Blankenship and Deborah C. Robson contributed to the exploration of feminine style by examining the political discourse of 45 contemporary women politicians. From their analysis, they concluded that a feminine style exists, characterized by, among other features, a grounding of political judgments in lived experience, a valuing of inclusivity, and a conceptualization of public office as the capacity to "get things done." They also asserted that a feminine style was gaining legitimacy through its use by both women and men in positions of power.[55]

Shawn J. Parry-Giles and Trevor Parry-Giles also examined feminine style in contemporary political discourse, focusing on five presidential campaign films. They argued that although these films employ a "feminine" style of presentation, such a style "works hegemonically to mask the 'masculine' themes embedded in them."[56] The body of research on feminine style, then, provides yet another example of efforts to situate women's interests in the disciplinary mainstream and to theorize from those interests.

Articles in which authors grapple with the intersections of personal identity, scholarship, and the academy suggest another form of recognition and valuing of the personal dimension as part of feminist scholarship by the mainstream. In "Listen Up. You Have To: Voices from 'Women and Communication,'" Elizabeth Bell reflected on the dilemmas, questions, and possibilities for feminist scholars who teach courses on women and communication.[57] The personal tone and content of Bell's essay, which likely would not have been published earlier, suggest that shifts instigated by the inclusion of women in the discipline are affecting the discipline as a whole. Foss and Foss also addressed the use of personal experience as part of a symposium titled "The Dialogue of Evidence," published in the *Western Journal of Communication* in 1994;[58] Dow extended this discussion with her essay "Politicizing Voice," in which she focused on issues involved in politicizing social location in the academy.[59] In each of these essays, the authors articulated the significance of integrating the personal into the teaching, research, and publishing practices of the academy. These efforts at inclusion initiated a gradual process of acceptance of feminist ideologies and practices, helped create space for feminist perspectives, and expanded the possibilities for rhetorical studies generally.

Critiques of the
Communication Discipline

The recognition that women had been neglected by rhetorical studies led to various critiques of disciplinary traditions and practices. One of the first such comprehensive critiques was provided by Kathryn Carter and Carole Spitzack's edited volume *Doing Research on Women's Communication*, published in 1989. In the introductory essay in this volume, Spitzack and Carter addressed what they referred to as the *blind spot* in the discipline—the impact of gender on research practices.[60] Two essays are particularly exemplary of the critique of the discipline's blind spot. Katherine Hawkins's "Exposing Masculine Science," the second essay in the book, challenged the unspoken masculine bias in research—a bias that negatively affects gender research.[61] Hawkins offered an alternative approach to communication research characterized by "dynamic, as opposed to static objectivity, a research goal of understanding, as opposed to control, and a conceptualization of the focus of study as active and sensitive, as opposed to passive and insensitive, to chosen modes of inquiry."[62]

In their essay in Carter and Spitzack's volume, Foss and Foss described the dilemma that feminist scholars face in attempting to gain visibility and legitimacy for a feminist perspective. To gain acceptance for a feminist perspective, they suggested, "scholars must find a way to present this perspective in the accepted publishing outlets of the field."[63] Foss and Foss identified seven accommodations feminist scholars make to the dominant research paradigm in order to increase the chances of publication, including using nonfeminist methods, citing nongender literature as a theoretical base, and suggesting limitations of gender research.[64] Carter and Spitzack's volume, then, was significant because of the comprehensiveness of its critique. Contributors questioned taken-for-granted assumptions about communication scholarship, identified publishing norms and practices that function to contain and subvert the radical nature of feminist research, and opened the way for rethinking communication concepts and scholarly practices.

A book devoted to a critique of traditional areas of study within speech communication, edited by Sheryl Perlmutter Bowen and Nancy Wyatt and published in 1993, was the first systematic effort to examine and critique various context areas of the discipline from feminist perspectives. Chapters were devoted to small group communication, organizational communication, performance studies, theater, rhetorical criticism, mass communication, and intercultural communication, as analyzed from feminist perspectives.[65] These chapters constituted strong critiques of the patriarchal assumptions embedded in the various content areas of the discipline and suggested the growing acceptance of feminist scholarship.

An effort on the part of three women scholars to publish an essay that dealt with methodological practices in regard to women reminded the communication discipline that considerable antagonism still exists toward feminist scholarship and that masculinist research biases still govern the publication process. Carole Blair, Julie R. Brown, and Leslie A. Baxter provided a critique of an article by Mark Hickson III, Don W. Stacks, and Jonathan H. Amsbary, published in 1992, that ranked women in the discipline according to the number of journal articles they had published.[66] Their essay was rejected for publication, but the rejection letters themselves seemed "sufficiently important as ideological fragments" that Blair, Brown, and Baxter wrote another essay, published in 1994 in the *Quarterly Journal of Speech,* about the masculinist ideology of those reviews.[67] They revealed how reviewers questioned their status as scholars, accused them of being antiscience, and declared them to be members of an "extremist fringe of the so-called feminist movement" because of their critique.[68] Blair, Brown, and Baxter used these reviews to highlight the problematic nature of the review process in communication journals: As privileged discourse, "typically exempt from public scrutiny and always protected by anonymity," reviews of essays submitted to journals "function to control and censor what is said in this discipline."[69]

The need for ongoing critique of the discipline in terms of its response to feminist scholarship was highlighted by the recency of Blair, Brown, and Baxter's experience. Much ambivalence—and sometimes hostility—remains concerning feminist scholarship, thus making feminist critiques of disciplinary practices regarding women and other marginalized groups a continuing necessity.

Labeling and Refining Feminist Perspectives

Efforts to define, clarify, and integrate feminist perspectives into the discipline as a whole and into rhetorical studies in particular began almost as soon as efforts at inclusion of women's rhetoric as data and critiques of the discipline

began. The emergence of rhetorical studies about women and women's movements and research on gender in all communication contexts raised the question
of what constitutes a feminist perspective. Various institutional mechanisms—
from conferences to caucuses to exchanges in journals—provided the space in
which such definition and clarification could occur.

The instigation of women's caucuses in the national organizations of the
communication discipline was one of the first signs of the nascent interest in
women's and feminist concerns and provided a space in which feminist perspectives could receive validation. The Women's Caucus of the Speech Communication Association (SCA; now the National Communication Association)
held its first business meeting at an SCA convention in 1971 and began offering
programs at the national convention the following year. The Organization for
Research on Women and Communication (ORWAC), affiliated with the Western
States Communication Association but national in scope, was started in 1976;
in 1977, ORWAC began publishing the journal *Women's Studies in Communication.*

The effort to include *Women's Studies in Communication* in SCA's *Index to
Journals in Communication Studies,* a volume that essentially designates the
important journals in the communication discipline, illustrated the growing
recognition of, but continuing ambivalence toward, feminist perspectives. Requests for inclusion in the 1985 and 1987 editions of the *Index* were denied on
the basis of small numbers of subscribers to ORWAC's journal. *Women's Studies
in Communication* coeditor Karen A. Foss addressed the political implications
of the failure to index the journal in a presentation at the 1988 SCA convention
in New Orleans, suggesting that the relatively small subscription numbers might
be due, at least in part, to the journal's lack of sanction by the national
association.[70] In 1989, James Chesebro, who had been chair of the Publications
Board when the decision was made not to include *Women's Studies in Communication* in the *Index,* reversed his position. He argued that the large number of
institutional subscriptions to the journal provided wide access to the publication
and that SCA's affirmative action statement should have applied in decisions
about the journal's inclusion. As a result of Chesebro's efforts, the journal was
included in the *Index* beginning with the 1990 edition, evidence that feminist
perspectives and scholarship were beginning to be recognized, supported, and
legitimated by the national organization of the discipline.

Several conferences designed specifically to address issues germane to
feminist scholarship also played a role in clarifying and refining feminist
perspectives in rhetorical studies. Although not all of these conferences dealt
with the nature of feminist scholarship in particular, they furthered feminist
scholarship by creating arenas in which feminist scholars could exchange ideas,
learn about what others were thinking and writing, and generally push the
boundaries of feminist scholarship.

The first conference to grapple with issues at the heart of feminist perspectives occurred as a result of an essay written by Kramarae about what she saw happening with language and sex research in England during her stay there in 1976-77.[71] In this essay, she suggested a "Prairie Pajama Party" for researchers in the Midwest interested in issues of language and gender. Cynthia Berryman-Fink and Virginia Eman Wheeless responded by organizing a conference on gender at Bowling Green State University in 1978. Not only did the conference become an annual tradition, but it spawned the Organization for the Study of Communication, Language, and Gender (OSCLG), created at the 1981 conference. In addition to sponsoring an annual conference, OSCLG also publishes the journal *Women and Language,* which began publication in 1976.

Another effort to define feminist perspectives occurred at the first Conference on Researh on Gender and Communication, held in 1984 at Pennsylvania State University. The conference was designed to address three general areas of inquiry: (1) "What do we currently know and believe about gender and communication?"; (2) "What methods are appropriate for research on gender and communication?"; and (3) "What are the priorities for research on gender and communication?"[72] This conference also became an annual event (later called the Conference on Gender and Communication) at which participants address current issues of concern to feminist scholars in communication.

Two programs at the Speech Communication Association convention in 1986 and 1987 further addressed the questions posed at the first Conference on Research on Gender and Communication and helped refine understandings of feminist perspectives. In 1986, a seminar titled "Feminist Theory and Criticism in the Study of Communication" was held at the SCA convention in Chicago to provide what seminar leader Lois Self called "a pulse check on feminist scholarship in our discipline and to share the insights and implications many of us individually were gathering from reading feminist writings in a variety of fields."[73] In addition, a forum on feminist scholarship was presented at the 1987 SCA convention in Boston to address a recurring question that was raised by participants at the forum the year before: "What makes scholarly or critical work in our discipline feminist?"[74]

Papers from both conventions were compiled in a special issue of *Women's Studies in Communication,* published in 1988, in which various feminist scholars offered their perspectives on what distinguishes feminist scholarship. Wood, serving as one respondent to this collection of essays, identified four major issues that concerned feminist scholars at that juncture: (1) "Is the concern of feminist scholarship women or gender or oppression?"; (2) "What is the 'unit of study' for feminist scholars?"; (3) "How salient are questions about method to the conduct of feminist scholarship?"; and (4) "To what extent should our scholarship be concerned with human symbolic processes?"[75]

Conference programs at national conferences, conferences devoted to gender and communication, and publishing outlets for feminist scholarship provided a collective space in which feminist scholars could gain access to one another's ideas and begin to construct collaboratively the perimeters of feminist scholarship for the discipline. In addition, these early organizational and institutional outlets facilitated the growth of feminist scholarship by generating opportunities to grapple with issues central to feminist research and to reflect on that research, thus ensuring increasing clarity and sophistication about feminist perspectives.

One of the outcomes of the early efforts to define feminist perspectives was the publication of essays and books that summarized the current status of feminist scholarship, providing feminist scholars with common and shared reference points. An early effort to synthesize the research about gender and communication that was emerging in a variety of disciplines into a feminist theoretical framework was Kramarae's *Women and Men Speaking: Frameworks for Analysis,* published in 1981. Kramarae identified four frameworks evident in research on gender and communication—muted group, reconstructed psychoanalysis, speech styles, and strategy—as a way of conceptualizing "the social factors involved in women's and men's language use and attitudes."[76]

A speech given by Brenda Dervin as president of the International Communication Association in Chicago in 1986 also provided a benchmark of the state of feminist scholarship.[77] Dervin summarized the origins, definitions, and characteristics of feminist scholarship; pointed to the contributions of feminist scholarship to other fields and to communication research; and provided some reasons feminist scholarship is needed. She noted: "Feminist scholarship, which sees potential transformation as a core of its focus, itself has transformative potential—to transform the discipline and the disciples, not by acting on but by being available to be interacted with."[78]

The work of Lana F. Rakow also has been instrumental in monitoring and registering the state of feminist scholarship. In 1987, Rakow published an essay designed to summarize and clarify the nature and status of feminist scholarship for the discipline.[79] She began by pointing out the schizophrenic nature of gender research: "On one hand, research is being conducted that is business as usual," including experimental studies and surveys of women's and men's attitudes and behaviors in different communication contexts.[80] On the other hand "is a growing new approach to studying gender and communication—feminist scholarship. This is research with a commitment to feminist theory, research that challenges old methodologies and assumptions and openly asserts its politics."[81] Rakow proposed five questions scholars interested in moving in the direction of feminist scholarship might consider: "Why am I doing this research? Is my research informed by feminist theory? What are my assumptions? What is the best methodology for me to use? What are my own subjectivities?"[82]

In 1992, Rakow published *Women Making Meaning,* a compilation of current thinking about feminist perspectives in communication scholarship. Part I dealt with "some of the most significant political questions that feminist scholars in the field of communication face," including the theoretical positions that have defined feminism and the deficiency of theories that universalize women.[83] Part II suggested ways in which feminist scholarship reconceptualizes the study of communication, and Part III brought together examples of feminist research that featured a wide range of methodologies, including textual analysis and ethnography.

As they clarified the nature of feminist scholarship, scholars began to recognize differing perspectives or standpoints within feminist scholarship and to move away from essentialist approaches that describe women as similar to each other and different from men based on innate characteristics. In 1992, Wood summarized the evolution from essentializing perspectives to standpoint epistemology in her essay "Gender and Moral Voice: Moving from Woman's Nature to Standpoint Epistemology."[84] Maureen A. Mathison expanded on Wood's ideas in an essay titled "Complicity as Epistemology," in which she discussed various approaches used by feminist scholars in rhetoric to address issues raised by standpoint theory. She suggested that the reliance on "experience" as the basis for epistemology on the part of some feminists carries the risk of "reifying observations into abstract categories much like androcentric epistemology."[85] She concluded by offering ways to proceed that open up possibilities for talking about situated knowledge and experience. Mark P. Orbe further developed standpoint theory in a 1998 article, in which he proposed a "co-cultural communication theoretical model that focuses on how persons traditionally marginalized in society communicate within dominant societal structures."[86]

Feminists of color were instrumental in creating awareness that all women do not share the same standpoint and that feminist perspectives need to take into account differences among women in terms of race, ethnicity, class, sexual preference, and age. In fact, such efforts largely were responsible for the linguistic shift from speaking about *the feminist perspective* and *a feminist perspective* to speaking about *feminist perspectives.*[87] A recognition emerged, in other words, that many feminist perspectives exist, grounded in different standpoints.

Marsha Houston has been a major contributor to the communication discipline in terms of identifying and exploring the standpoints and perspectives of African American women. She has provided not only data about black women's communicative experiences but theoretical and practical discussions about differences between black women's and white women's communication, thus offering continual reminders of the need to contextualize feminist theory.[88] Lisa A. Flores's explication of the stages by which Chicana feminists build a space for themselves through discourse contributed a Chicana rhetorical perspective that takes into account those "who carry the baggage of their border existence and who often find themselves straddling different cultures."[89] Dana L. Cloud's essay on Oprah Winfrey's biographies suggested an increasing interest in the intersections among identity standpoints. She analyzed racial and gendered dimensions of Winfrey's biographies to suggest how tokenism functions as a mechanism of liberal hegemony.[90]

Efforts to clarify the boundaries and types of feminist perspectives in the discipline led to a series of exchanges among scholars in the 1990s that provided further definition of various kinds of feminisms and diverse feminist agendas. One such exchange was between Barbara Biesecker and Campbell about the reasons for and approaches to incorporating women's texts into rhetorical history.[91] Biesecker cautioned against an "affirmative action approach" to the study of women's speeches, suggesting that the danger to such an approach is that "while we may have managed to insert women into the canon (and, again, this is no small thing), we . . . have not yet begun to challenge the underlying logic of canon formation and the uses to which it has been put that have written the rhetorical contributions of collective women into oblivion."[92] Dow offered another approach by summarizing some basic stances within rhetorical studies, approaches grouped loosely around those that value and focus on women's differences and those that label almost any analysis of women's public address *feminist*. She argued for a middle ground, developed as feminist scholars become more self-reflexive about the arguments they make, and urged scholars to begin to use the terms *feminism* and *feminist* in a more critical fashion.[93]

Condit also sought to advance the delineation of feminist perspectives in the discipline in her essay "In Praise of Eloquent Diversity," in which she outlined two perspectives she sees as characterizing current feminist work in rhetorical studies: the gender dichotomy and the gender diversity perspectives.[94] She labeled those who highlight women's experiences and rhetorical practices as *gender dichotomists,* preferring for herself the position of *gender diversity.* The goal of feminist scholarship in this perspective is to implement a multiplicity of genderings, and its advocates do not see a masculine bias as a primary characteristic of rhetorical studies.

Foss and Foss, writing with Cindy L. Griffin, responded by outlining yet a third position—what they call a *feminist reconstruction position*—in which the goal of feminist scholarship is the eradication of the ideology of domination that permeates Western culture. In this view, feminism is used to reconceptualize and reconstruct rhetorical concepts and theories that contribute to the ideology of domination.[95] Sharon D. Downey responded to the exchange and used the two essays as a starting point to argue for dialectical feminism as a viable perspective on the relationship between gender and rhetoric.[96] This exchange helped to define various feminist perspectives and encouraged scholars to consider a continuum rather than a polarity of feminist positions in the communication discipline.

With the emergence, labeling, and clarification of feminist perspectives, rhetorical studies and the field of communication generally began to exhibit signs of acceptance of feminist scholarship. Feminist criticism became an established method studied in rhetorical criticism classes; increasing numbers of theses, dissertations, and articles employed feminist methods; and feminist scholars began to include the word *feminist* in the titles of their dissertations and essays without fear of negative responses from dissertation and search committees. Special issues devoted to feminist scholarship appeared in communication journals, and the Feminist and Women Studies Division was formed in 1990 within SCA, an important step because divisions represent core content areas of the discipline.[97] There was a growing—albeit cautious—sense that feminist scholarship was not only tolerated but accepted as a legitimate perspective from which to approach communication. This emerging acceptance of feminist scholarship set the stage for still greater challenges to rhetorical studies.

Reconceptualizations

Calls for rhetorical studies—and the discipline as a whole—to reflect the different assumptions and research methods of feminist scholarship were present from the first stirrings of feminist perspectives in communication. Scholars recognized that incorporating feminist perspectives could do nothing less than transform the discipline. Foss and Foss, in their summary article in 1983, pointed out that, at that time, most of the research consisted of "building on accepted assumptions and findings by contributing additional data in these same directions." They argued that what was needed instead was "growth by revolution," whereby scholars question their presuppositions, replace them as appropriate, and create new conceptualizations that incorporate women's perspectives.[98]

In their 1987 typology of women in communication research, Spitzack and Carter similarly argued that feminist scholars need to do more than fill in the gaps in existing research categories of women as communicators if women truly are to be integrated into the communication discipline. The process of reconceptualization, they suggested, will produce "novel theories, investigative strategies and topic areas" that will transform the discipline.[99]

The recognition that feminist scholarship has transformative potential—that it can facilitate a rethinking or reconceptualizing of virtually every aspect of the communication discipline—can be found throughout the literature dealing

with the emergence and development of feminist perspectives. Reconceptualization was slow to occur, however, perhaps because such a process demands a
complete rethinking of disciplinary assumptions and practices.

Social movement literature is one area in which early interest in reconceptualization was visible. Katherine Kurs and Robert S. Cathcart, for example,
examined the reformist, radical, and lesbian-feminist rhetorics in the women's
movement and suggested that only lesbian feminism confronts both "the political order and the social hierarchy," thus creating "the dialectical enjoinment"
necessary for the ongoing development and success of the women's movement.[100] Their work suggested not only that there are several ideologies within
the women's movement but that only its most radical dimension truly qualifies
as a social movement.

Belle A. Edson also examined social movement theory from a feminist
perspective, showing that many traditional dimensions of movements—such as
leadership, group membership, and stages—are characterized differently
through a feminist lens.[101] Mary Rose Williams examined protest rhetoric, using
quilts as her data, to construct a subversive rhetorical theory at odds with much
of traditional social movement literature.[102] Williams identified movement
strategies designed to establish common ground and sustain ambiguity, which
suggest change through "affirmation rather than imposition."[103]

A comprehensive effort at reconceptualization was *A Feminist Dictionary,*
edited by Cheris Kramarae and Paula A. Treichler, with Ann Russo. This volume
was designed to "illustrate forms of expression through which women have
sought to describe, reflect upon, and theorize about women, language, and the
world."[104] The entries are multiple, sometimes contradictory, evolutionary, and
self-reflexive about women's experiences with language and with the world that
language names. The entry *home,* for example, includes among its definitions
"the location of known others and assumptions of shared values about social
behaviour," "a place to be ourselves," "a comfortable concentration camp," and
"[w]here the revolution begins."[105] The editors not only reconceptualized what
a dictionary is and who has the power to define, but they also brought to the
forefront the ways in which women make sense of and contribute to the world
linguistically.

Sonja K. Foss and Griffin have engaged in reconceptualizations of the
boundaries and nature of rhetorical theory in several essays. Beginning with a
comparison of the rhetorical theories of Kenneth Burke and feminist theorist
Starhawk (the subject of Chapter 7), they enlarged the boundaries of rhetorical
theory beyond the Burkean system that often is taken for granted in an essay
titled "A Feminist Perspective on Rhetorical Theory: Toward a Clarification of
Boundaries."[106] They suggested that Burke's theory describes the processes that
characterize a rhetoric of domination, but that it does not explain another type
of rhetoric—a rhetoric of inherent value—that Starhawk's theory explicates. In

a second essay, "Beyond Persuasion: A Proposal for an Invitational Rhetoric," Foss and Griffin also questioned and reconceptualized the definition of rhetoric as persuasion in their notion of an invitational rhetoric grounded in the feminist principles of equality, immanent value, and self-determination.[107]

In her essay "Women as Communicators: Mary Daly's Hagography as Rhetoric," Griffin also reconceptualized rhetorical strategies on the basis of the work of Mary Daly (the subject of Chapter 6). These strategies reach beyond traditional rhetorical boundaries by articulating a rhetorical duality—a foreground that oppresses women and a Background in which women can live self-determined lives.[108]

In another essay, "Rhetoricizing Alienation," Griffin advanced a "rhetoricized" concept of alienation, relying on the work of Mary Wollstonecraft to suggest a reconceptualization of Karl Marx's notion of alienation. Whereas Marx relied on a material notion of alienation, Wollstonecraft, writing approximately 50 years before him and taking gender into account, offered a rhetorical notion of alienation.[109] Griffin also used Wollstonecraft's *A Vindication of the Rights of Woman* to generate a web form of reasoning—a reconceptualization of standard notions of appropriate rhetorical form.[110] Yet another reconceptualization project by Griffin focused on the public sphere. In "The Essentialist Roots of the Public Sphere," she argued that the public sphere, as it has been constructed, is dependent on an essentialist view of women and men.[111]

Revisions in specific content areas in the communication discipline are another form the feminist work of reconceptualization has taken. In addition to rhetorical theory and its dimensions, the field of public address has been the site of several efforts at reconceptualization. Foss and Foss reconceptualized public address in the introduction to their book *Women Speak*.[112] They summarized several assumptions that characterize the area of public address, including the ideas that significant communication is produced by noteworthy, historical, generally male individuals in the public realm; that speechmaking is the most significant form of communication; that significant communicative acts are finished products; and that significant frameworks for analysis are derived from male perspectives. Their compilation of 30 forms of women's expression illustrated other significant communication formats that have been neglected by the communication discipline as a result of these assumptions.

Douglas Thomas reconceptualized both public speaking and American public address in a 1991 essay in which he proposed a new structure for the study of rhetoric that helps "re-create the rhetorical canon, re-define criteria for rhetorical masterpieces, and empower students of public address to heighten their awareness of the political dimensions of both their ability to speak and criticize popular discourse."[113] Thomas challenged not only the rhetorical canon, which largely has privileged the speaking of white establishment males, but also the assumptions behind the canon itself: "that there are ideal techniques of persuasion and/or style which students of public speaking should strive to imitate or incorporate."[114]

Foss and Foss's textbook *Inviting Transformation: Presentational Speaking for a Changing World,* rooted in feminist principles, transformed the standard perspectives on public speaking.[115] The model of presentational speaking suggested in the book reconceptualized such notions as the role of the speaker, audience analysis and adaptation, the three primary types of speeches, and the definition of *communication.* The focus of the book is on ways to create an environment in which both the audience and the speaker can choose to change, rather than on how to change the audience in the direction advocated by the speaker.

A symposium on the notion of a women's university provided models for reconceptualizing or re-visioning the place of communication in the university and the very nature of the university itself.[116] In an issue of *Communication Education* in 1996, five feminist scholars imagined the issues and possibilities that a women's university would provide, often moving outside of disciplinary boundaries to develop their ideas. They envisioned, for instance, tackling difficult communication issues such as abusive language and gendered racism in settings where "asking difficult questions is not perceived as a threat but as the norm."[117] They re-visioned diversity as "a *process* of learning new knowledge rather than a static *condition* of some students or faculty whose skin tone, culture, or nationality is not considered normal on campus."[118] These scholars reconceptualized communicative practices related not only to education but, ultimately, to the entire university structure.

The reconceptualization process, which necessarily calls into question rhetorical assumptions and suggests alternative rhetorical options and practices, simultaneously is grounded in and extends the other dimensions that contributed to the emergence and development of feminist perspectives—influential early works, efforts to include women in the discipline, feminist critiques of the discipline, and the refinement of feminist perspectives. Each of these contributions has been important to the ways that perspectives have developed in rhetorical studies. We see this volume as rooted in the groundbreaking work of early feminist scholars in communication and as another reconceptualization effort that we hope will lead to further transformations in rhetorical studies.

CHAPTER 3

Cheris Kramarae

"Feminists consider most theories of communication inadequate, misleading, and dangerous because they distort women's experiences, ideas, and concerns."[1] With this summary of her view of the treatment of women in communication theory and research, Cheris Kramarae suggests the commitment that guides her personal and professional life. Through her work in the areas of language, power, and technology as they relate to gender, Kramarae works to develop communication theory that more accurately reflects women's communicative experiences.

NOTE: Excerpts from "Shaking the Conventions of Higher Education or Appropriate and Appropriated Technology," presented by Cheris Kramarae at the Women, Information and Technology in Industry and Education Conference, Queensland University of Technology, Brisbane, Australia (December 5, 1997); and from *A Feminist Dictionary,* edited by Cheris Kramarae and Paula A. Treichler, with Ann Russo (Boston: Pandora, 1985), are reprinted by permission of Cheris Kramarae.

33

Born Cheris Rae Gamble on March 10, 1938, in Brookings, South Dakota, Kramarae grew up with her four siblings as part of the "House of the Seven Gambles," an affectionate play on the title of Nathaniel Hawthorne's *The House of the Seven Gables.* Her mother, Deda Rae Smits Gamble, was a creative speaker and writer who published hundreds of witty newspaper columns on topics ranging from writing to parenthood to means for achieving happiness. The money she earned by winning writing contests of the sort "In 25 words or less, tell us why Scrub-a-Dub soap is the best" paid for a complete remodeling of the family's house.[2] Kramarae's father, William H. Gamble, was head of the Electrical Engineering Department at South Dakota State University and served several times as the interim mayor of Brookings.

Two major influences on Kramarae's childhood presaged her later research interests. Her participation in a Brownie/Girl Scout troop, beginning in the third grade and continuing until her graduation from high school, enabled her to experience the joys and benefits of women working together and of female friendship. In high school, the Scouts taught themselves how to run a campaign to elect the first female to be president of a local senior class and to secure media coverage of their activities. Because of her strong Scout troop, Kramarae was "protected from many of the miseries that high school . . . can bring girls. The parties the Girl Scouts organized on high school dance nights were more lively and less fraught with insecurities than the proms."[3]

A second early influence on Kramarae was the "technological privilege" her family enjoyed.[4] Kramarae attributes some of her interest in using and assessing new technologies to the fact that her father's engineering talents provided the family with many new communication and transportation technologies during her childhood. She grew up, for example, with homemade electric tricycles, scooters, and sidewalk cars. Because the family was large, with many of the children's friends coming to the house, her father installed an intercom system (before such systems were available commercially) so that her mother could answer the doorbell without opening the door. One winter, Kramarae's father installed "an intercom in a snowperson built next to the sidewalk" that Kramarae used to address surprised passersby from the "comfort and security of the house."[5] Her family was the first in town to own a television set (her "mother had hopes that TV would provide in-depth programs which would enrich her children's education"),[6] and Kramarae became a ham radio operator with equipment "cobbled together from discarded electrical parts."[7]

The family's participation in technologies extended to flying. By the time she was in the third grade, Kramarae, along with her brothers and sisters, was learning to fly the airplane her family shared with several other families in town. Her official flying lessons, however, which resulted in her pilot's license, began when she was in college. Her mother, who believed flying was dangerous, refused to let Kramarae use the family car to drive to the airport for her lessons, so Kramarae borrowed a motorcycle to get herself there, "which made the entire expedition just the much more fun."[8]

Kramarae earned a B.S. degree in journalism and English from South Dakota State University in 1959. Following her graduation, she became city editor of the *Huron Daily Plainsman* in Huron, South Dakota, winning a job interview only because the publisher and editor thought the name on her resume was a typo: "They expected a (male) Chris to appear for the interview, and expected on the basis of the resume they had received to hire him." The publisher and editor kept Kramarae waiting for half an hour "before finally calling her in from the reception area, to explain the 'difficulty'" and to ask her if she thought she would be able to do the job even though there were "'no female city editors.'"[9]

Kramarae married Dale Kramer in 1960, when he was a doctoral student in English at Western Reserve University (now Case Western Reserve University) and she was a junior high school teacher in Cleveland, Ohio. Her husband accepted a teaching position at Ohio University in Athens, Ohio, the university at which Kramarae wanted to pursue an M.S. degree in journalism and English; she completed her degree in 1963. Kramer was an assistant professor and Kramarae an instructor in the English Department at Ohio University when their daughter, Brinlee, was born in 1965. When her husband accepted a teaching position at the University of Illinois in Urbana, Kramarae was hired as an instructor to teach four sections each semester of a course in verbal communication (a combination of composition and literature). Their second daughter, Jana, was born in 1967.[10]

Kramarae's commitment to feminism is, as her daughter Brinlee explains, "a part of her personality. Other people are generous, cheerful, shy; she is a feminist."[11] Her feminism was the impetus for Kramarae's return to graduate school in 1972: "Trying to provide a nourishing environment for a husband with a career and for two young children eager to grow up and out had many good moments, and teaching (as a 'faculty wife') several sections of the same course on a yearly temporary basis gave me some income along with valued time with students." But Kramarae worried that she would not find her life to be very fulfilling years hence if she were still "teaching the same course over and over again."[12]

Kramarae chose to pursue a Ph.D. in speech communication with a focus on sociolinguistics at the University of Illinois but kept her full-time teaching job because she feared she might have no job opportunities once she had completed her degree. Her feminist perspective led her to approach her doctoral studies with attention to the intersection between gender and language. She critically examined "the assumptions of the lecturer and assigned authors about the characteristics of women's and men's thought and talk, and assumptions about whose talk is worth studying in what settings."[13]

Kramarae's feminist critiques during her graduate studies "were continually at odds" with the male-centered research questions and standards of academia, and she was told that "several male professors regularly 'gossiped and prattled'" about what they called her "'hysterical' ideas. It was not a particularly support-ive atmosphere." Nevertheless, she was able to turn her "dissatisfaction with the curriculum into critiques" that gave her "intellectual satisfaction, university credit, and eventually a degree and publications."[14]

Kramarae changed her last name from her husband's name of *Kramer* to *Kramarae* in 1978. At the time she married in Ohio, state laws did not allow married women to retain their own names. When those laws were changed, Kramarae created a new name for herself, according to her "own wishes and directions,"[15] reordering the sounds of *Cheris Rae Kramer* to *Cheris Kramarae.* Her middle name, *Rae*, was the same as the middle name chosen by her mother when she left home for college; Kramarae chose to feature this name in her new surname.[16]

Following the completion of her doctorate, Kramarae was granted regular faculty status in the Speech Communication Department at the University of Illinois. At the time of her retirement in 1996, she held joint appointments in the Departments of Speech Communication, Women's Studies, Sociology, and Linguistics. She also served as the director of Women's Studies between 1993 and 1996 and was a cofounder, in 1991, of the colloquium Women, Information Technology, and Scholarship (WITS) at the Center for Advanced Study at the University of Illinois, an interdisciplinary group of faculty and academic professionals "working to help insure that new communications technologies will be structured and used in ways beneficial and equitable for all."[17]

Kramarae has held visiting faculty appointments around the world, including at the University of Natal-Durban in South Africa, the University of Baroda in India, the Universiteit van Amsterdam in the Netherlands, Birkbeck College of the University of London, and the Universität Konstanz in West Germany. While a visiting scholar at the Center for the Study of Women in Society (CSWS) at the University of Oregon in Eugene in 1988, Kramarae became enamored of the environment, intellectual atmosphere, and alternative interests that charac-terize the city of Eugene. When she was offered the position of acting director of CSWS in 1988, she accepted it, and when she and her husband retired, they moved to Eugene.

Kramarae's academic contributions to feminist scholarship concerning lan-guage began in 1974 with her article "Women's Speech: Separate but Unequal?" published in the *Quarterly Journal of Speech.* One of the earliest efforts to incorporate, value, and legitimate the study of women's communication in the communication discipline, it was the first of many articles and books Kramarae has written and edited on language and gender and their manifestations in areas such as technology, education, and women's studies. Many of these works were written with others, and the process of coauthoring, explains Kramarae, "has been an important aspect of much of my interest, ideas, and enjoyment of writing." The theories she has developed about language and gender, she is quick to point out, are not hers alone but are the results of collaborative relationships of "strength and joy" with other women.[18]

Many of Kramarae's books deal specifically with the intersections of gender, language, and power. Her edited volume *The Voices and Words of Women and Men* (1980) deals with how language and talk function differently for women and men. The authors of the various chapters examine subjects such as women's and men's expectations for female-male interaction, women's use of narrative chaining, interactional goals in women's friendship groups, and the relationship between language change and social change. In *Women and Men Speaking: Frameworks for Analysis* (1981), Kramarae considers ideas about the use of language by women and men from the perspectives of four theoretical frameworks: the muted group framework, the reconstructed psychoanalysis framework, the speech styles framework, and the strategy framework. *Language, Gender and Society* (1983), coedited with Barrie Thorne and Nancy Henley, and *Language and Power* (1984), coedited with Muriel Schulz and William M. O'Barr, are compilations of research studies on the topics of language, gender, and power.

Some of Kramarae's work involves the assessment of the processes of knowledge construction in general. *For Alma Mater: Theory and Practice in Feminist Scholarship* (1985), coedited with Paula A. Treichler and Beth Stafford, is an exploration of theoretical and methodological issues in feminist research. The various contributors, "representing a wide range of fields, address the language of feminist scholarship, its disciplinary and interdisciplinary practices, its boundaries, and its resources."[19] In *The Knowledge Explosion: Generations of Feminist Scholarship* (1992), coedited with Australian feminist scholar Dale Spender, the authors of the chapters document the problems and possibilities in various academic disciplines from feminist perspectives and address the resistance to women's initiatives, authority, and autonomy. *The Knowledge Explosion* also includes essays on such topics as pornography, reproductive technologies, the concept of originality, and sisterhood and friendship as feminist models.

Three of Kramarae's books are devoted to capturing and preserving women's words. *The Radical Women's Press of the 1850s* (1991), coedited with Ann Russo, is a compilation of excerpts, with annotations and analysis, from six feminist newspapers of the 1850s. Kramarae also compiled a similar book with Lana Rakow, *The Revolution in Words: Righting Women 1868-1871* (1990). Focused on one feminist newspaper, this book contains excerpts, annotations, and analyses of the nineteenth-century feminist newspaper *The Revolution*. By providing historical context for contemporary feminist work, Rakow and Kramarae reveal that nineteenth-century feminists had experienced and written "critiques of sexism, sexual harassment, male chauvinism and racism" not unlike those of twentieth-century feminists, a parallel that is both "exhilarating and depressing."[20]

The book that preserves women's words most extensively is *A Feminist Dictionary* (1985), reprinted as *Amazons, Bluestockings, and Crones: A Feminist Dictionary* (1992), which Kramarae coedited with Paula A. Treichler (and Ann Russo). This dictionary is designed "to document words, definitions, and conceptualizations that illustrate women's linguistic contributions" and "to illuminate forms of expression through which women have sought to describe, reflect upon, and theorize about women, language, and the world."[21] It provides definitions for terms relevant to women's experiences from the point of view of "people who are concerned about women's exclusion from the creation of meaning and from accounts of that creation."[22] Entries are included for terms such as *atomic widows, housewifing, I'm not a feminist but, marital rape, mammy, obey, phallic morality, sisterhood,* and *witch persecutions.* Most entries have multiple definitions from the perspectives of many women, ranging from "Aunt Jane of Kentucky" to feminist scholars and activists to Kramarae's daughters.[23]

Kramarae's continuing interest in technology is reflected in two of her books. *Technology and Women's Voices: Keeping in Touch* (1988) is a compilation of essays by scholars analyzing technology as women have participated in and been affected by it, including washing technology, public transportation, feminist computer networks, the typewriter, sewing circles, and the telephone. *Women, Information Technology, and Scholarship* (1993), coedited with H. Jeanie Taylor and Maureen Ebben, is an introduction to the WITS working colloquium. The book is a compilation of essays and bibliographies that deal with how the new information technologies are reconstituting race, sex, and class hierarchies in universities.

Kramarae continues to do research, write, and speak on feminism, communication, and technology; works with the faculty and students at CSWS, where she is a visiting professor; enjoys walking in the rhododendron park near her home; studies herbology and drumming; and builds houses with Habitat for Humanity. Committed to the celebration, inclusion, and legitimation of women's voices and experiences, Kramarae has served as a persistent voice in the communication field and related disciplines on behalf of the study of women and women's communication. She serves as a reminder, both in her works and in her life, that women can refuse "to be silent" and "that language and women are powerful."[24]

Nature of the World

A primary feature of the world for Kramarae is its linguistic nature, and the structure and use of language are the focus of her rhetorical theory. Language constructs the world according to the "words and syntax available,"[25] imposing "a structure on people's thinking and on their interaction."[26] "The labels and descriptions we use," explains Kramarae, "help determine what we experience."[27] They constrain how individuals within a particular linguistic structure think about the world and construct the meanings of that world in particular ways. No "human experience [is] 'free' from accompanying language."[28] Because language is implicated in all human activity, the study of language provides a great deal of information about society: "If we can discover the principles of language usage . . . we will at the same time discover principles of social relations."[29]

Much of Kramarae's work centers on the explication of social relations as they relate to gender. She seeks to understand how women are treated in language and the kinds of worlds created by the English language as it operates in the United States—the language system with which she is most familiar. One world she identifies is the mainstream world, created by language practices rooted in the "widely spread, and enduring hierarchical relationship between women and men."[30] Existing simultaneously with this mainstream world, however, is a world that is more hospitable to women and is created according to women's preferred values and ways of interacting.

Mainstream World

Kramarae's study of language structure and use suggests that the mainstream world most individuals experience on a daily basis is hostile toward women. The starting place for the establishment of this world is the social construction of gender through various communication practices. The constructs of male and female are not as natural as they seem, Kramarae suggests; rather, "the categories 'women' and 'men' are *ideas* that must be learned and reinforced" through language: "[W]e are trained to see two sexes. And then we do a lot of work to continue to see only these two sexes, which we call male and female, boys and girls, men and women."[31]

The language system creates not only two categories of differently gendered individuals but also an asymmetry in power relations between them. Language contains, communicates, and "perpetuates the ideologies of those in power," privileging their perceptions, experiences, and modes of expression.[32] The power relations established in the language system determine whose version of the communication situation will prevail; whose speech style will be seen as normal; who will be required to learn the communication style, and interpret the meaning, of the other; whose language style will be seen as deviant, irrational, and inferior; and who will be required to imitate the other's style in order to fit into the society.[33]

Gender—as well as race, age, class, and other characteristics of identity—is not simply an individual characteristic but also a dimension of existence created through language to which power is differentially assigned.

Because the English language is "a male-oriented symbolic system" or a "man-made language,"[34] it constructs a very different "relationship to the language structure" for women than it does for men.[35] Thus, "language has not served equally the needs of women and men."[36] Language dictates that "mainly WHIMMs, the white, heterosexual, inside, middle-class men . . . have the power to pronounce on what will be validated and valued,"[37] with the result that men's meanings are sanctioned and women's are not. Kramarae admits that "not all men have controlled language," but she also recognizes that "all men benefit from this control and all women suffer."[38]

The result of the construction of gender through the language system is a mainstream world "uncomfortable for women and sometimes even danger-ous,"[39] a world in which "women's creative and intellectual spirit" often is "ignored, denied or ridiculed as part of the general oppression of women."[40] Although many feminists label this world *patriarchy*, Kramarae avoids "men-tioning patriarchy, even when giving documentation of enduring restrictions, inequalities, and oppressions."[41] A primary reason for her reluctance to use the term is the racism and classism it may conceal: "Discussions of patriarchy can lead to talking about women as an undifferentiated mass" and may efface "other oppressions" that various women and men may face, such as exploitation based on "class, caste, religion, and race."[42] Many men, for example, such as men of color and economically disadvantaged men, face many of the same restrictions and are subject to the same kinds of oppression and feelings of discomfort to which women are subjected in the mainstream world. The term *patriarchy* encourages individuals to overlook this fact.

Instead of creating and applying one overarching label to the mainstream world, Kramarae is "most interested in using the particular word or phrase which asks for critical thinking" about the mainstream world so that the various forms of control that characterize it can be resisted.[43] She sees the essential feature of the mainstream world as "men's domination including the power relationships (many and varied) underlying women's oppression."[44] This world involves domination of various kinds, "which often work together" and are manifest in particular qualities, including inequality; violence; hierarchies of race, class, and gender; a feeling of separation and alienation from others; homophobia; competition; violence; and conquest.[45] Kramarae sometimes uses the term *beer groups* in an effort to capture the spirit of the mainstream world; she sees the "competitive gathering of men-dominated groups" for the purpose of drinking beer as embodying some of its primary values and characteristics.[46]

Although the mainstream world is "heavily controlled by men interested in heavy control of women," women often are active participants in the construction and maintenance of this world. As Kramarae explains, "Some women are sometimes involved in some of the creation of dominance, even though they are in general the subjects of much of the dominance." This is the case because "the values and goals of this culture affect all of us"; women are as subject to adopting and expressing the values and behaviors rewarded in the dominant culture as are men.[47]

Kramarae identifies some of the linguistic features of the mainstream world that operationalize its values, making it an uncomfortable, unfriendly place for women. Included are the normalization of white men's perspectives, control of interaction by men, and the threat of violence against women.

Normalization of White Men's Perspectives

The mainstream language system features white men and their perspectives, thus constructing them as the standard or norm. Because the English language does not adequately encompass their experiences, women constitute a "subordinate 'muted' group in the society":[48]

> Women (and members of other subordinate groups) are not as free or as able as men are to say what they wish, when and where they wish, because the words and the norms for their use have been formulated by the dominant group, men. So women cannot as easily or as directly articulate their experiences as men can.[49]

The result is a mainstream world that features white men and neglects women, in which women have problems "trying to use standard languages and standard usage to express their ideas and experiences."[50]

Kramarae provides a number of examples of the encoding of male interests and experience as the norm in language. Men's interest in the relational availability of women is evident in the titles for women "that distinguish them on the basis of their martial status"—*Mrs.* versus *Miss,* for example, whereas *Mr.* offers no such information. Men are assumed to be the standard and women the aberration in "distinctive occupational terms" such as *waiter* versus *waitress* and *sculptor* versus *sculptress.* Furthermore, words associated with men tend to remain neutral or positive, whereas "words associated with women tend to pejorate over time (for example, *woman* came to mean *mistress* or *paramour* in the nineteenth century," leading to the need for the term *lady* to refer to women generally).[51]

White males' perspectives are featured not only in language itself but in linguistic resources such as dictionaries, thus codifying the standardization of white men's viewpoints. Most dictionaries are constructed using processes that systematically exclude women's usages and "any notion of women as speakers, as linguistic innovators, or as definers of words":[52]

> Definitions for many dictionaries, for example, are constructed from usages found in works of the "best authors"; though the equation has been challenged in recent years, this designation usually means "male authors." Similarly, one criterion for the inclusion in a dictionary of a "new word" is the number of times it is found cited in print; given current cultural practices, not only are men's words more likely to be cited in the mainstream press, but also few dictionary editors seek out print media where women's words would predominate (such as feminist periodicals).[53]

The standard dictionary, then, constitutes "the cultural authority for meaning and usage"[54] that sets "forth a category system, a way of knowing ourselves and our relationships with the rest of the earth."[55] It features white men's perspectives as if they are natural and the only perspectives possible.

The systems and structures that derive from and are related to language reflect the same bias against women that language itself does. The same normalization of white men's perspectives found in the language pervades institutions, including academia. Until the advent of women's studies, little was known and taught about women in most academic disciplines, including the communication field. Although research on women in communication is increasing, there still "is very little explicit, serious attention paid to the ways women's communication networks are structured and function." In fact, Kramarae notes, there often "appear to be no women imagined in the communication models." Communication theories tend to suggest "links among the large, policy-making bodies and men's interaction," but typical women's interactions—such as women's informal associations or talk within the home setting —"are usually not even mentioned as social activity which needs to be understood."[56] Women's modes and realms of interaction are not seen as important to study because white men's communication is considered the standard.

Pedagogical practices reflect a similar pattern; the language used to construct its many dimensions imbues all facets of institutional education with a white male bias. Many female students suggest "not only that their classroom experiences are different from males' but also that their experiences are often unsatisfactory." A primary reason for women's experience of this "'chilly climate' in academic settings"[57] is the content of the curriculum, which features white men:

There is a lot of attention to wars of various kinds, and to victories and defeats. But seldom do schools lead discussions on sexual harassment, child abuse, violence against women, the growing economic plight of women and men of color, homophobia, or reproductive rights.[58]

When women are part of the curriculum, the materials that document their perspectives often are inadequate: "[T]here is little authentic knowledge about their existence available on the library shelves, and . . . what is there is not necessarily considered appropriate curriculum material."[59] The normalization of white men's perspectives allows such omissions to be seen as appropriate and acceptable.

The typical styles of learning preferred and used by white men are featured over women's in typical classroom interactions, again establishing the white male perspective as standard. White men tend to place a "priority on interaction based on individual expertise and presentation and elaboration of abstract concepts. The valuing of this kind of knowledge acquisition is compatible with a commitment to relatively nonpersonal, hierarchical classroom interaction."[60] In contrast, women are more likely to enjoy "classes in which students and teacher talk in a collaborative manner, rather than in student-to-teacher and teacher-to-student monologues."[61] They "report more ease and more discovery in settings where learning is a communal activity shared fairly equally by students and teacher."[62] Women also "feel more at ease with teachers who do not impose their views on others," and they "consider the openness and supportiveness of the instructor the salient factor in determining whether they feel comfortable about talking in class."[63] The kinds of interactions that create more comfortable learning environments for women, however, are not those featured in most schools and universities.

Just as the perspectives of white men are featured in the educational system, so technological systems feature their perspectives. "In fact," Kramarae points out, "one way of describing what has been traditionally considered as technology is to say it consists of the devices, machinery and processes which men are interested in. (This is a reason why we do not find discussions of child care devices in men's books on technology.)"[64] Women's involvement with technology often is not recognized as participation in technology, as Kramarae points out, because the nature of their participation does not fit the use of the term *technology* that has been normalized by mainstream society. She uses her own experiences as an example, citing her uses of technology during one day alone:

I had done the very customary activities of using, in a building constructed of wood, metals and plastics, the running water fixtures, heating system, refrigerator, toothbrush, ready-made clothing (which I had slightly altered by use of needle, thread

and scissors), telephone, electric lights, pen, typewriter, tampon and lotion. . . . I
rode an elevator and during the day I used hundreds of other items or processes
which are not just heaven- or hell-sent outgrowths of the soil. I and all other women
I know around here are heavily "involved" with technology.[65]

The definition of *technology*, then, provides another example of the normalization of white men's perspectives. As the term tends to be used, it refers to the
almost complete absence of major means of technology used by women (as well
as by many men).

Just as the English language excludes women and allows them virtually no
place in which to see themselves represented, so, too, are women missing from
the manifestations of that language in social structures and institutions of all
kinds. The normalization of the white male perspective in language, institutions, and technology, in summary, creates a mainstream world where women
often feel as though they are invisible, ill prepared, or simply do not fit.

Conversational Control by White Men

White men's control of interaction also is a feature of the mainstream world.
White men often use subtle ways of silencing women's talk in conversations,
resulting in interactions in which men's interests and opinions prevail. This
construction of "women's silence in mixed-sex talk"[66] is accomplished in a
variety of ways: "When women and men converse, in intimate and more formal
settings, men usually talk more, both in amount and time and number of turns
at talk. Men exert conversational control not only through sheer quantity of
speech, but also through interruptions."[67] In addition, the topics men raise are
"much more often developed than those women" raise, "largely because of
women's greater 'interaction work' (answering and asking questions, providing
active conversational support, for example, by inserting *ahuh* and *mhm* while
the men [talk])." When women do raise topics in conversation, men often make
"only minimal responses."[68] These behaviors suggest that "there is a clear
pattern for language style associated with men to be that of power and dominance, and that associated with women to be that of powerlessness and submis-
siveness."[69]

Kramarae provides an example of how white men's control of interaction
looks. She attended a meeting of an organization of college students and faculty
members interested in ecology issues, a session at which a male graduate
student and a female faculty member presented papers. She recounts what
happened in the interaction after the presentations:

In the discussion which followed the presentations, the two speakers talked, as did
a number of graduate students. Only one woman in the audience, a graduate student,

spoke; the male speaker, who had been addressed, retook the floor, ignored her words and turned his eye contact and words to the comments of the previous discussant, another male graduate student. I felt embarrassed for the woman who had offered the comments, who must have felt some humiliation. And I decided not to offer a question I had been considering.

After the meeting, Kramarae mentioned her concern to two of the men who had attended the meeting. She reports that neither "of them were conscious that there had been only one brief comment from a woman in the audience of about equal number of women and men, and none of them had noticed that her comments received no attention from the speaker." The perceived naturalness of such conversational control creates interactions in which "there is often danger, discomfort, risk for women. Women who try to participate often say afterwards, 'Why do I bother?'"[70]

Even in the supposedly more democratic world of the Internet, similar means of control often create situations in which white men's perspectives prevail, and women are left out. For women, "gaining the 'floor' in an electronic discussion can be as problematic" as gaining the floor in a meeting.[71] Various "methods by which women are made to feel relatively uncomfortable or unwelcome in many mixed-sex discussion groups"—ignoring the topics raised by women or introducing pornographic material or references offensive to women, for example—often have the effect of reducing women's contributions and increasing those of men.[72] One study of a discussion group—and even one in which feminism enjoyed considerable influence—showed "that women contributed only 30% of the messages, and the women's messages were shorter and were not responded to as often as the men's."[73]

Although greater participation by women is changing the nature of the Internet and making it a less hostile, more equitable place for women, the presumption still exists that men have the right to control conversations with women. Their communication practices often make women's contributions to conversations between women and men difficult and suggest why the mainstream world is not a comfortable and friendly place for women.

Threats of Violence

Male violence against women, the "ultimate exercise of personal and political power," is another feature of the mainstream world for women. Although violence long has "been an issue for feminists concerned with the victimization of women through rape and domestic abuse," Kramarae asserts that "the threat of male violence, implicit or explicit, restricts women's activities in every sphere and thus underlies all aspects of human communication."[74] *Street harassment* and *sexual harassment* are terms used to describe several ways in which the threat of violence is enacted. Both constitute means by which men violate the physical and psychological worlds of women, reminding them that they have the power to keep women from accomplishing their goals.

Street harassment involves the subjection of women to verbal and nonverbal remarks from men in public spaces. These "remarks typically comment on the woman's physical appearance or her presence in public, and are often sexual in nature."[75] They include wolf whistles, leers, catcalls, and street remarks that range from the offensive "Hey, cunt, answer me" to the seemingly benign "Great legs."[76]

The asymmetry of street harassment—its availability as an option to men but not to women—contributes to the feelings of danger that women experience in the mainstream world. Politeness norms dictate that strangers in public do not stare at others or comment on their appearance or actions. Men, however, are permitted to violate this norm of civil inattention when the stranger is a woman. As Kramarae points out, "Women do evaluate men they see and hear in public, of course, but they don't publicly announce the evaluation to them. Yet women in public often receive men's evaluations—compliments or insults—because they are in men's public."[77]

Street harassment teaches "women that they belong to the private sphere of the home, not the public world of the street."[78] Public places, "inaccurately described as areas open to the community or the people as a whole," are, in fact, often unfriendly environments for girls and women. Many public places and most public streets in the United States "are actually places governed primarily by males." The unquestioned assumption that men and their contributions belong in public even receives support from those who are responsible for protecting individuals in public spaces. "Even police," Kramarae notes, "employed to help maintain justice, often caution women that for their own safety they should not be in some 'public' places when it is dark; harassment of women is so pervasive and still so accepted that the idea of a curfew *for men* is still an outrageous idea for many people."[79]

Sexual harassment is another mechanism by which men exercise personal and political power over women. With the practice of sexual harassment, men remind women that their femaleness is their most salient characteristic in a situation that, ostensibly, has nothing to do with sex and gender. Sexual harassment includes the telling of offensive sexual jokes, persistent requests for dates, nonreciprocal compliments, demeaning references to women, sexual remarks, suggestive sounds such as whistling and sucking, and the use of terms of endearment such as *honey* and *dear* in professional settings. Sexual harassment is designed to "coerce and intimidate" women by reminding them of their "place in society" and of "the possible use of economic sanctions and physical force" against them.[80]

Although some women and men consider street remarks and sexual harassment to be complimentary, they have "little to do with physical attraction, provocative appearance, or sex," nor are they "about boys' and men's attempts to be 'nice' to girls or women."[81] These "compliments" are part of a system of sexual terrorism that aims to frighten and, by frightening, to dominate and control, reminding "women of their vulnerability to violent attack in American urban centers and to sexual violence in general."[82]

The English language and usage norms create a mainstream world in which women and men are treated asymmetrically, with women denied access to the same power men have to influence this world. Marked by the normalization of white men's perspectives in language and the systems it creates, men's control of interaction, and threats of violence, a world is created in which many women are silenced, devalued, and uncomfortable.

Women's World

Although Kramarae's focus is on explicating the ways in which the linguistic system—both in structure and in usage—creates a largely hostile mainstream environment for women, she also recognizes and articulates the dimensions of a world that is more hospitable to women and that exists concurrently with the mainstream world. This is a "more comfortable world/word structure" for women,[83] a world in which women gather together, learn from one another, work cooperatively and creatively, and play together in spaces they create themselves according to their own needs and wishes. Although Kramarae does not give this world a label, it might be called *women's world* because it is a world that is created when women interact in ways other than those sanctioned by the mainstream. Men may participate in these gatherings, but women are the ones who are more likely to be socialized into and committed to nonmainstream communication practices.

The defining characteristic of woman-created spaces is that they provide relief from and alternatives to the mainstream world. In women's world, women do not have to resist and cope with the mainstream world and can construct themselves and their relationships in ways different from those normalized by the mainstream. Kramarae sometimes uses the term *food groups* in an effort to capture the spirit of these "more cooperative gatherings of women";[84] for her, a representative scenario for women's world is a group of women talking and drinking herbal tea around a "table laden with carob brownies and whole-wheat muffins."[85]

The supportive, hospitable world women create together is not restricted to private spaces where women gather, although it is created most easily in such settings as "the kitchens of homes." Such a world can be created within environments in the dominant culture, whenever women "find ways to talk 'out of order'" from that culture to create a different space—in "the bathrooms and hallways of offices" and "in the lunch areas of factories," for example.[86] Many women live in both mainstream and women's worlds, going back and forth between them, enacting the values and communicative practices of the dominant culture in their professional lives, for example, and enacting support and affirmation in interactions with close women friends.

Not all gatherings of women create hospitable and humane environments, however. Such environments may not be created because women often have critical differences among them in terms of ideas and experiences. In addition, just as men tend to be socialized into the mainstream culture, so do women; thus, the values of domination of the mainstream world (including biases and hierarchies not only of gender but of race, class, and sexual orientation) often are brought into interactions among women, preventing the construction of a more supportive, woman-identified world. In fact, Kramarae acknowledges, women's relationships "are often painful, in part because we expect so much of each other, and in part because even when we are with women, we are also in the larger world which is heavily controlled by men interested in heavy control of women; their values and goals infect all of us."[87] Because women are encouraged to be competitive in the mainstream world, for example, that competition sometimes carries over into and affects their relationships in women's world.

Kramarae suggests some of the qualities that tend to characterize the world created by women to reflect their perspectives and ways of interacting. She recognizes that each woman probably would characterize this world differently, but, for her, it includes interconnection, safety, holism, trust, mutuality, adaptability, and equal access to information.

Interconnection

Interconnection is one of the traits that tends to mark the hospitable world women create for themselves. In this world, an understanding exists "of the interdependency of *all* Earth's life-forms,[88] an understanding that all "is relationships."[89] Consequently, women in this world experience connection not only among themselves but with all forms of life. We "are only just beginning to understand," Kramarae asserts, "the many connections all of us have with the other living elements on earth."[90] As a result of this awareness of interconnection, communities are created where psychological and physical "'distance' is reduced" and where there is "the potential for making real connections."[91]

Safety

Another feature of the world women create apart from the mainstream world is safety, characterized as a "safe home base"[92] in which women experience "'feelings of well being' with the languages they use" and the environments those languages engender.[93] Kramarae's vision of safety, however, does not involve a reluctance to confront and deal with "difficult issues." Safety is not a "'happy ever after' feminine utopia" that simply affirms women's perspectives or total agreement with one another.[94] Rather, it is a place where difficult questions can be asked, where uncomfortable issues can be discussed, and where "critical self-analysis" can occur.[95] These discussions take place in a context of "respect for the emotional, physical, social and cognitive needs" of others,[96] in which women "speak freely without fear of punishment."[97] In this world, "the words, ideas, opinions of others" are welcomed, nurtured, and accorded respect, even if they are different from the individual's own.[98]

Holism

A third feature of women's world is holism—women's commitment to the development of themselves and others as whole, balanced human beings. In professional settings, for example, holism means acknowledgment that women are complete human beings whose lives consist of more than their occupational commitments. Kramarae illustrates this holism in her description of a professional retreat for the members of the Women, Information Technology, and Scholarship colloquium:

> Our environment makes a difference to us. Campuses often aren't very thoughtful places to be, so WITS members held a retreat [off campus]. . . . We did not leave our bodies or spirits behind as we discussed. Our talk included references to food, eating, cooking, meditation, and human comfort as we talked about how intellectual engagement can best work.[99]

The holism that marks women's world includes attention to dimensions of women's lives such as spirituality; play; the nourishing of hearts, minds, and bodies; and social justice.[100]

Trust

In the supportive world constructed by women, interactions are characterized by trust. The participants trust one another with their ideas, feelings, dreams, and material possessions. Thus, the interactions are not efforts on the parts of individuals to convince others of their own value but are ones in which participants share and grow together. Participants freely admit their lack of knowledge or their need for help and trust that others will not take advantage of the vulnerabilities they reveal.

Kramarae illustrates the trust such communities engender with a group called *Digital Dames*, composed of women CEOs of on-line companies in California who meet every six weeks to share ideas, advice, and food. The women report that they talk quite openly about problems and possible solutions. One participant in the group noted: "You could never have a similar group of male computer CEOs. Never. They wouldn't share their ideas and weaknesses and their fears. We share our problems. Whereas with men, they tend to gloat and tell you about their victories."[101]

Kramarae explains that "some amount of self-censorship of speech" always is present "if we want approval from others, but in women's supportive conversations, there is usually less self-censorship than when in locations and events which are male dominated." Such is the case because of the level of trust that characterizes women's world. There can be a sharing of "experiences, hopes, visions, pleasure, space and sometimes finances."[102]

Mutuality

The world created by women is also a place of mutuality, where relationships among individuals are democratic, equal, and reciprocal. This world involves a rejection of all the forms of domination that mark the mainstream world, where people "of color serve white people, women serve men, nature serves culture, animals serve humans" and where there is "the strange notion of a God who gave man dominion over the Earth and women."[103] "If we start thinking about our relationships to the rest of the planet," Kramarae asserts, "we start thinking about how authoritarian, controlling linguistic policies are related to social political policies throughout the world."[104] In the women's world Kramarae describes, practices that exploit and oppress are not the norm and are not welcome.

Adaptability

In the world created by women, the devices and technologies created in the mainstream world to fit white men's experiences and interests are adapted to women's needs in order to improve their lives and the environment. In women's world, women "know that the latest, most expensive, and fastest model isn't always the model [they] need or want." Instead, women use the "resources they have and [adapt] what is around them for what they need. Not adoption, as much as adaptation."[105]

Adaptability is particularly evident in women's approach to technologies: "What we want is *appropriate* technology, which means we often have to make adjustments in what is available." Kramarae explains, "[T]he major reason [women] have been slower to embrace the new technologies, such as the Internet, is that we had to figure out how they could benefit rather than drain our energies; we had to adapt what was out there and invent new uses and forums." Women in this world are likely to ask questions about new technologies, such as "What are the problems in our lives—what are important issues in our experiences with work, safety, families, education? Can the Internet help with any of these problems? Or does the hype about the Internet divert our attention from these problems? Could some characteristics of the current Internet be altered to help solve the problems?" Women then "use their own knowledge to develop the new technologies for their own use," adapting "the new technologies to make them appropriate" for their lives.[106]

Equal Access to Information

The community created by and for women is marked by another quality that distinguishes it from the mainstream world: the accessibility and availability of information that improves women's lives. The information that is available in these communities is shared by and with all. Useful information is readily accessible to unemployed, disabled, and elderly women and to women from all racial and ethnic groups. It also is accessed "without need of intermediary, who may be unavailable, expensive, oppressive."[107]

Access to information through new communication delivery systems is particularly important for women. Kramarae asserts: "If the future of information is electronic, we need to ensure access for everyone, not just an elite. We imagine computer terminals connected to community systems in laundromats, homeless shelters, daycare centers, etc.—with sufficient support so that most people have access to the Internet."[108] Poor is the "community that knowingly allows whole segments of our real world to be excluded from the Internet."[109]

Kramarae delights in the fact that the interactive nature of the Internet is beginning to create the access she sees as characteristic of women's world. She sees cyberspace as having the potential to be a humane place for women simply because the technology is interactive: "Since the Internet is an interactive technology this means that [women] have some say in what it contains and how it works," she suggests. She continues:

This makes it different in critical ways for women from some of the other recent communication technology tools. From radio, for example. . . . [Women] *could have* made marvelous uses of the radio as a place to exchange information on housekeeping, health, economics, and the thousands of other topics in which they had an interest. Instead, they were fed the talk, news, and entertainment that men in the managerial offices determined. . . . It was much the same with television. . . . The earlier invention, the telephone, designed primarily for the use of business and businessmen, was something else, however. Once it was in homes, women found it a wonderfully interactive tool.[110]

The potential to have equal access to and influence on information processes and systems is a dimension that marks women's world. No one person or group establishes norms or policies for the others; instead, all have equal input into the norms and practices of the community, ideally beginning with the design stages of information systems.

Although Kramarae exposes some of the ways in which the linguistic system is involved in the creation and maintenance of the mainstream world that is hostile to women, she recognizes the existence of an equally powerful, if sometimes less visible, women's world. This hospitable world, created whenever and wherever women cooperate to create spaces of resistance to the mainstream world, incorporates women's perspectives and experiences and is characterized by qualities that enable women to feel comfortable and valued—interconnection, safety, holism, trust, mutuality, adaptability, and equal access to information.

Definition of Feminism

Kramarae's discussion of feminism begins with a recognition of the negative connotations of the term. The source of these negative connotations, she explains, is the assumption that maleness is the standard:

> And while male is the norm, and as such is assumed to be unproblematic, it is those who are critical of this state who can be seen to constitute the problem. Hence the tendency to discredit feminists who critique male power (with all the names of embittered, uppity, strident, nags, even unattractive) rather than to discredit male power and its uses and abuses.[111]

In an ironic reversal, feminists who initiate discussions about "the dominance and power of males" are criticized and chastised, whereas those who claim dominance and power—men—are not.[112] The result is that feminists, who are "thinking, courageous women," become inaccurately portrayed as "nasty" women "who should not be allowed to participate in discussions with men or hold jobs men hold dearly."[113] By "locating the problem in the women who protest, rather than in their own privilege, men can deny their own agency and further frustrate and exacerbate the position of women."[114]

Kramarae's definition of feminism is designed to disrupt the systems and processes that allow such negative associations with the term to develop. Feminism, for Kramarae, is the practice of challenging the linguistic system as well as all of the structures and institutions it produces, including education, politics, religion, and the economic system. It is "a renouncement of obedience to the systems erected by men"[115] that is accomplished through "a *critical* analysis of the ideas, practices and institutions of men, yesterday and today."[116] With its focus on disrupting mainstream linguistic structures, feminism is characterized by "rethinking" and "restructuring"[117] in a process Kramarae summarizes as "equilibrium busting."[118]

Feminism, then, is not "a single fixed state"[119] but an ongoing process of disruption of the linguistic and other structures that create a hostile environment for women: "Men have often put women in very constraining boxes," Kramarae explains, "and one of the goals of feminism is not to replace these boxes with others but to encourage more free roaming, including encouraging more linguistic innovations and movement."[120]

For Kramarae, the goal of feminism is not equality with men. Kramarae finds the concept of equality, as it is traditionally conceptualized, to be problematic:

> Equality in this system means that women and minority men are to be raised, from their position nearer the lower animals, to men's elevated position. Accepting a "women are as good as men" argument not only leaves unquestioned the patriarchal arrogance of the concept of equality but also the claim that humans are separate from, and better than, other animals that are subject to our control.[121]

Instead of seeking equality, Kramarae seeks to disrupt systems, including the language system, that are responsible for establishing concepts and values that are hostile to women. She hopes instead to create a world in which all beings are affirmed and valued and are given the opportunity for growth and fulfillment.

Nature of the Rhetor

Kramarae's rhetor is the feminist who challenges current structures of domination, including the linguistic system. When a woman articulates her experiences and perspectives through language, she speaks in ways not sanctioned by the patriarchy—she is "linguistically creative."[122] The rhetor Kramarae envisions, then, need not be exceptional in ways recognized by the dominant culture. She is an authority simply because she speaks on the basis of her "own experience as a valid source of truth and [upholds] the authority of experience and 'conscious subjectivity' as grounds for determining truth and making decisions."[123]

Kramarae sees rhetors working to disrupt linguistic structures primarily in two realms—inside and outside of academia. Feminists who work within the academy are "brave people . . . who have used a variety of research and analytical techniques to contribute to an explosion of inquiry on and magnificent writing about women and language."[124] They are activists who challenge patriarchal linguistic structures through their research, writing, teaching, and advocacy work within the university system.

Rhetors who work outside of academia, however, do equally important feminist work: "Those who are engaged in political activity outside the academy have a crucial contribution to make" in that "they can provide the perspectives which allow for the necessary and more comprehensive forms of knowledge making."[125] Many of the challenges to the knowledge produced in the academy have "come from the alternative visions of theorists not formally associated with any of the university research or teaching centers."[126] The "terminology and category systems" of linguistic systems and their related structures "are challenged and changed not primarily because of academicians' questions and critiques but because of activists' questions, critiques, and demands."[127] In short, Kramarae sees feminist activists outside of the academy as those who are able to "suggest new problems, methodologies, and interpretations."[128] Academic women, Kramarae believes, "would be severed from these sources at their peril."[129]

The distinction between rhetors within and outside of academia is not always clear: These "states are not mutually exclusive . . . sometimes the academic woman *is* also the activist in the community."[130] A reciprocal, dialogic relationship exists between the two types of rhetors who work to disrupt and transform the mainstream world, and, at various times, one type of rhetor is more effective than the other: "Sometimes women outside the university [are] making gains while women with similar training and concerns in the academy [are] having more difficulty."[131] Working together, feminist activists in academia and in the larger community have the capacity to challenge the construction of the mainstream world.

Rhetorical Options

Just as the patriarchal world is constructed linguistically, so, too, can it be dismantled in part through the transformation of language systems: "Since language systems are social constructions, they *are* open to alterations to fit" women's needs.[132] Everyday patterns of dominance can be transformed through linguistic change so that women are more fully self-determining and less cut off from communicative resources of talk, information, movement, and space. Through linguistic choices, rhetors "can either tacitly accept and thereby help perpetuate the status quo, or challenge and thereby help change it."[133]

Kramarae chooses to challenge the status quo, and her suggested rhetorical options allow rhetors to be "thieves of language,"[134] thereby emancipating linguistic structures from mainstream constraints. Her rhetorical options involve creating and using language "to undermine, unmask, and overturn ruling definitions and paradigms."[135] Only by using a greater variety of linguistic strategies can women create, on a more regular, sustained basis, the world they enjoy with other women.

Kramarae suggests three primary rhetorical options for disrupting the present language structure. The first focuses on the status quo and involves the analysis of linguistic structures to discover whether they contribute to the domination of women and, if so, how they do their work of domination. Kramarae's second rhetorical option is the study of women's communication in order to develop new models for communication practices. Her third option is enactment, where the knowledge gained as a result of the analysis and research produced in the first two options is put into practice in new linguistic modes.

Critique of Linguistic Practices

The critique of linguistic practices Kramarae advocates is focused on the "revelation of the patriarchal aspects of our language and speech."[136] Understanding and explicating the mainstream world requires considering "what our world is,"[137] a process that, for Kramarae, involves exploring the ways in which women's perceptions of and contributions to linguistic systems and their products are omitted or distorted. Critique involves conceptualizing linguistic products such as constructs, definitions, and histories from the experiences, perceptions, and insights of women and using the information gathered to identify the inadequacies and distortions in the mainstream versions. "Like many (most) feminists," she explains, "I'm interested in pushing on words and their definitions, questioning and often mocking traditional practices in order to make possible new meanings and practices."[138]

Kramarae provides numerous examples of the critique of linguistic practices. In a discussion of the term *technological progress,* for example, Kramarae suggests that it leaves out important information concerning women, and she supplies some of what has been omitted: "What men call technological progress often turns out to be more exploitation of 'Third World' workers, women in particular." She elaborates: "I am typing this on a computer, parts of which were assembled in other countries, most likely by women. Communication technology 'progress' is built on the lives of women working as 'factory girls' in assembly lines, at very low pay in bad conditions."[139] Although these facts constitute aspects of *technological progress,* they usually are not considered when the term is used.

Kramarae's assessment of the notion of freedom of speech as it is used on the Internet provides another example of the rhetorical option of critique. She notes that women and working class men have seldom had freedom of speech, which has traditionally required political and economic clout, printing presses, machinery, distribution resources. We're calling for some thoughtful discussions about what "freedom" is and for whom. There are many freedoms not talked about in most of the cyberspace literature. For example, freedom from hunger, and from sexual harassment. The concept of freedom as discussed by most on the Internet is quite limited.[140]

Kramarae also often corrects histories by adding women's words and women's contributions to them, thus challenging the choices and pointing to the omissions of many historians' accounts. She reports, for example, on a history of the sewing machine published in a national newsmagazine that dealt with the uses of the sewing machine by men such as Mahatma Gandhi and Richard Byrd. Kramarae corrects the omissions in the article: In "the two-column report, women (who have, of course, run up many more millions of hours on Singers and its competitors than have men) are not mentioned except for a reference to Isaac Singer's 'two wives and at least three mistresses.'"[141] Discovery of the contributions of women left out of histories brings "exhilaration at the discovery of foremothers and anger at the erasure of their work and the loss of their company at earlier times in our education."[142]

Kramarae recommends that the option of analysis of current linguistic practices be undertaken with a particular attitude—a "liberating, healthy" laughter that emphasizes the "absurdity of male prejudices."[143] This kind of humor recognizes common oppression and identifies its agents, producing laughter that "can reach the heart, give insight and sight, create a sense of community among diverse people, and validate a world-view." This humor has "the potential of splitting the world apart" in its generation not of "wisecracks" but "whys cracks."[144]

The rhetorical option of analyzing linguistic practices not only identifies omissions and distortions concerning women, but it has the effect of invalidating the notion of a "single, fixed truth, revealed by objectivity." Critique of linguistic practices makes clear that the concept of a single explanation must be abandoned in favor of "many *fixed* truths" or of "the plurality of shifting interpretations derived from different experience."[145]

Creation of New Linguistic Knowledge

The creation of new linguistic knowledge through research is a second rhetorical option suggested by Kramarae. In this option, the rhetor conducts research either formally (through academic research procedures) or informally (through experiences with women's language processes). The focus of this option is not on mainstream linguistic systems but on those that are more likely to be used in the environments women construct. This option involves putting "women at the center of analysis"[146] and "attending as much as possible to the words, ideas, and culture of women."[147]

The study of women's communication begins with asking questions that allow for the discovery of the characteristics and qualities of women's linguistic practices. Kramarae suggests some questions about women's communication in the United States and in other countries that researchers might want to ask: Who talks with whom about what in the household? What are the patterns of seating and conversation during meals? About what issues are women considered qualified to give information and advice? To whom do women in the area talk about their relationships and problems with husband, child care, birth control, household work, income, and national events? Who or what do women consider the most accessible or best source of information for each issue? Who holds confidences? Who talks with women about their problems and solutions? Of what organizations are women a part? Where do women not talk? What are women's and men's perceptions of women's talk in terms of style and content?[148]

The study of women's communication requires not only that researchers ask new questions but also that they answer those questions using particular kinds of data. They "must look for women's language and communication in new ways and in new places,"[149] which means that their data often are "the forms of women's discourse that men have labeled trivial."[150] A variety of sources are available for such study:

> We need to look in such places as gynecological handbooks passed between women for centuries; in women's art; in folklore and oral histories; in graffiti and gossip; in journals; in letters and diaries; in songs, billboards and posters; in the cant and chant of witchcraft and voodoo; in slogans; in parodies and humor; in poetry; in graphics; in comics and symbols; and in the mass of work by "noncanonized" writers whose richness and diversity we are only just beginning to comprehend.[151]

Women's forms of expression such as sewing, weaving, and embroidery also should be studied as legitimate communicative forms, Kramarae suggests: "These are often called 'alternative means of expression', which means that talk and writing are considered more prestigious methods of expression. . . . Rather than call them 'alternative means of expression' let's call them expression."[152]

In the selection of data for study, Kramarae cautions that the researcher should be as inclusive of multiple perspectives as possible and not assume that women are "an undifferentiated mass": "We need to listen well to women who talk about multiple identities and oppressions. We need to exercise caution that we don't make quick invocations of *women* as a category."[153] The study of women by white, middle-class scholars often privileges white, middle-class women by making them the paradigmatic examples of women. This practice makes women who are "not from the dominant classes . . . invisible or else placed at the periphery of the circle in spoken and written descriptions and analyses."[154] In the kind of research that Kramarae advocates, researchers must consider the perspectives of all women to understand women's linguistic practices. Kramarae acknowledges that a commitment to such integration "requires a great deal of work, including . . . being willing to see ourselves not as sisters to all others, but as often alien and oppressive rulers ourselves, as well as users of terminology that helps maintain divisions among women."[155]

Research on women's communication is done to provide data for constructing new models of communication that provide a greater array of rhetorical options for everyone. They "open up language and communication research to the full range of communicative experiences of which people are capable"[156] to create "a more sane and just world."[157] Such insights and models resulted, for example, from the study of women's consciousness-raising groups:

> Since early reports from consciousness-raising groups, feminists have focused on the social interaction of women in small groups as offering a different model of human communication. . . . Out of this work a paradigm is emerging which emphasizes co-operation rather than competition, a dialogue of complementary alternatives rather than a dialectic of opposing forces.[158]

In the creation of linguistic knowledge as a rhetorical option, women's communication is used heuristically to develop new ways of theorizing and practicing communication—forms that Kramarae believes can produce a more humane and hospitable world for both women and men. A close examination of "talk among women suggests that daily life can be structured in more cooperative and mutually empowering ways."[159]

Enactment of New Linguistic Practices

Kramarae's third rhetorical option involves the enactment of new linguistic practices, rooted in feminist assumptions and values, that disrupt the mainstream world. Enactment is the practice of creating new words and redefining words as a means to "redefining and reconceptualizing controlling norms and language." Through enactment, rhetors "use and invent words and definitions that offer new possibilities in the way we think and deal with gender, race, class, and earthly resources."[160] This option generates new language that features and values women's perspectives and experiences in ways that mainstream language does not.

Creation of New Words

Until women themselves name their experiences and the phenomena of the world, many of their experiences will remain invisible and thus difficult to think about, even for women. With the development of words for previously unnamed phenomena of the world, women begin to assume control of naming and to create a world that fits their perceptions and experiences. Naming involves "recovering and inventing ways of defining, speaking, and writing female experiences and perceptions"[161]—the formulation of "new woman-defined categories to more accurately reflect their own knowledge making."[162] Kramarae sees three important reasons for rhetors to engage in this practice: "First, having an 'established' word means that there is no need for a personal narrative to explain the concept to others. Second, having a word legitimates the concept. Third, having a shared word helps establish a bond, a link with others for whom the concept is meaningful."[163]

Kramarae provides various examples of the new words feminists have created using this rhetorical option. The term *non-women,* for example, referring to men, places not men but women at the center of language and mocks the commonly used generic *man* as a reference to men and women. The term is "a reversal, of course, of the category scheme which has been used by non-women. Most women do not regard this as a . . . permanent solution to sexism, but it nevertheless highlights the imposed category system which begins with the assumption that there are two hierarchical categories of humans."[164]

Other feminist coinages include *spinster's degree,* instead of *master's degree,* and *men's toilet syndrome* to "describe the tactic of keeping women out of power by conducting real . . . business" not at formal meetings "but informally among the men only."[165] Similarly, *mainstream thought* "becomes *malestream* thought, a term coined by philosopher Mary O'Brien when she was describing political philosophy that includes production but not reproduction as a key concept."[166] Some of the new words feminists have created are now widely known and used, including *male chauvinist, sexism, Ms., herstory,* and *sexual harassment.*

New naming practices extend to women's names, with many feminists creating new last names for themselves rather than retaining their husbands' or fathers' names. Kramarae explains: "Some women rename themselves by discarding their 'married name' and retaking their 'birth name' or another name of their choice, such as an important symbolic last name (e.g., Judy Chicago or Olivia Freewoman) or the first name of their mother or other close woman friend as a new last name (e.g., Sarah Elizabeth)."[167]

Naming as a means of enactment of a new linguistic system also includes giving others the freedom to make their own naming choices, thus honoring the labels they select for themselves. Kramarae points out that allowing others to name themselves is as important as feminists' creation of new words for women's experiences: "[W]e need to listen respectfully to the labels used by members of various groups, and we need to look very carefully and critically at how geographical areas and the people who live in them have been cut up by our politics, including our labels."[168]

Kramarae provides as an example the term *aborigine,* which was "one of the words that the English colonizers used in Australia to describe the people they pushed around and killed when they invaded." The term, however, actually "refers to an indigenous group of any country, not the name of a group of people with shared languages and culture." The alternative to *aborigine* preferred by those who live in New South Wales, Victoria, and Tasmania is *Koorie*; those who live in Queensland prefer *Murri*; and *Nyunga* is the preferred West Australia term.[169] Enactment through naming involves, then, not simply the rhetor's practice of naming but respect for others' choices in terms of naming.

Other feminists go beyond the creation of new words in their native languages to create entirely new languages. Kramarae provides as one example Suzette Haden Elgin's creation of the language Láadan:

> More recently, Suzette Haden Elgin, a linguist, has created a women's language to incorporate women's concerns; the Láadan lexicon includes many words about, for example, the complexities of and feelings toward pregnancy, menstruation, the failure of published histories to record accomplishments of women, the varieties of love—concepts which exist at present only through lengthy explanations.[170]

Through the creation of new words for objects, events, and qualities in their worlds that previously were unnamed and the creation of entirely new languages, naming practices allow rhetors to enact a world different from that produced and maintained by the mainstream language system.

Redefinition

A second option available to feminists for the enactment of new linguistic practices is redefinition, in which new definitions for mainstream words are created. In redefinition, rhetors make "traditionally negative words positive. That is, words traditionally associated with women, and therefore pejorative, [are] reclaimed and redefined as positive."[171] In many instances, this practice involves "etymological searches to resurrect old meanings of these terms. This can be done successfully with most of the words men use to describe women because the majority of these words have slid semantically to a derogatory sexual meaning."[172]

Kramarae provides examples of such new definitions created and used by feminists: Feminist theorist Mary Daly "calls herself a *hag,* which formerly meant 'an evil or frightening spirit.' She asks, evil and frightening to whom?"[173]

Similarly, a new definition of *construction* is "a well-paying field of human endeavor not open to women," and *tipping* is redefined as "a fantasy that allows our society to justify less than minimum wages for waitresses."[174]

Redefinition is a form of linguistic enactment, then, that enables rhetors to recast words that are irrelevant or hostile to women so that they assume a new role in feminists' linguistic practices and the environments they create. By making words affirm and validate women's experiences, rhetors using redefinition empower themselves through alteration of words that once ignored or devalued them.

The critique of linguistic practices, the creation of new linguistic knowledge from the study of the communication of women, and the enactment of new linguistic practices—the rhetorical options Kramarae suggests—may not appear to have the capacity to disrupt mainstream language and the structures it helps support. Kramarae, however, is optimistic about their impact: "Small fluctuations can grow as they interact with the rest of the system."[175] The rhetorical options available for rhetors for "breaking out of silence" create "momentous communicative change, a revolution in the way women and men speak and write." As a result, they contribute to the development of "a language appropriate for living" for all human beings.[176]

Transformations of Rhetorical Theory

Kramarae's rhetorical theory, focused on the assessment and disruption of mainstream linguistic structures to create a more hospitable environment for women, challenges the definitions of a number of fundamental rhetorical constructs. Primary among them are the rhetor, ethos, the public sphere, and criteria for assessing rhetoric.

Rhetor

Kramarae's work with the language system suggests that the traditional notion of the rhetor as an individual who has the power to use the resources of the world to claim positions, to create arguments in support of them, and to use symbols to move freely and confidently about the world does not hold true for all rhetors. The kinds of resources available to the rhetor, the credibility the rhetor is accorded, and the nature of the rhetor's agency all differ according to the rhetor's sex and race. White men are more likely to have agency, credibility, and access to the resources necessary to have their views prevail in the world. Women and men of color generally do not. As rhetors in the mainstream world, they tend to be muted, ridiculed, and denigrated and speak from positions that are very different from those held by white men.

Ethos

Closely related to Kramarae's reconceptualization of the traditional rhetor is her challenge to the traditional construct of ethos. White male rhetors may be accorded the kind of ethos described in traditional rhetorical theory—a demonstration of intelligence, moral character, and goodwill—but this kind of ethos is not always available to women in the mainstream world. Kramarae suggests a new conception of ethos for women—one in which ordinary women have ethos simply by speaking their experiences through a language they construct and mold to fit them, an act that challenges patriarchal linguistic structures. The distinguishing characteristic of this transformed ethos is the ability to use language creatively to suggest and create alternatives to the mainstream world that is hostile to women.

Realm for Rhetoric

Kramarae challenges the notion of the public sphere as it is viewed in traditional rhetorical theory—a place where citizens engage in rhetoric to affect policy in the public realm as an enactment of their civic responsibilities. Threats of violence to women in the form of street harassment and sexual harassment, however, often make the public sphere a hostile space for women. Such threats teach women that the public sphere is not open to everyone and that they, in fact, do not belong there. To locate rhetoric in the public sphere, then, means that women are not expected to be equal contributors to public processes and institutions, whereas many of the men who are responsible for keeping women away are. The public sphere, then, is not an ideal realm for rhetoric that facilitates the exercise of democracy and civic responsibility; rather, it is an oppressive, exclusionary, silencing, and even dangerous realm for some rhetors.

Assessment of Rhetoric

In her conceptualization of the new world, Kramarae implicitly suggests alternative criteria for the assessment of rhetoric. Instead of being judged by its effectiveness in accomplishing the rhetor's goals or its meeting of a particular set of ethical criteria, rhetoric, in Kramarae's view, is judged by whether it contributes to the development of particular qualities in the environment. Whatever its content or subject matter, rhetoric, according to these new criteria, should create a feeling of safety for those involved and emphasize and foster connection and interdependency. It also should be evaluated by its accessibility—it must be available to as many people as possible, without the need for intermediaries between rhetor and audience. These criteria for assessing and evaluating rhetorical practice are substantially different from those found in traditional rhetorical theory.

Kramarae's rhetorical theory provides several important alternatives to traditional rhetorical constructs. From the reconceptualization of ethos to the nature of the rhetor, the appropriate realm for rhetoric, and the criteria for assessing rhetoric, her transformations of rhetorical theory contribute to the development of new modes of communication. These new communicative forms facilitate the construction of women's "own house of words"—a new language and a new world in which women "will finally be at home."[177]

Bibliography

Books

Kramarae, Cheris, ed. *Technology and Women's Voices: Keeping in Touch.* New York: Routledge & Kegan Paul, 1988.

Kramarae, Cheris, ed. *The Voices and Words of Women and Men.* Oxford: Pergamon, 1980.

Kramarae, Cheris. *Women and Men Speaking: Frameworks for Analysis.* Rowley, MA: Newbury, 1981.

Kramarae, Cheris, and Dale Spender, eds. *The Knowledge Explosion: Generations of Feminist Scholarship.* New York: Teachers College, 1992.

Kramarae, Cheris, Muriel Schulz, and William M. O'Barr, eds. *Language and Power.* Beverly Hills, CA: Sage, 1984.

Kramarae, Cheris, and Paula A. Treichler, with Ann Russo, eds. *A Feminist Dictionary.* Boston: Pandora, 1985. Rpt. as *Amazons, Bluestockings, and Crones: A Feminist Dictionary.* Boston: Pandora, 1992.

Rakow, Lana, and Cheris Kramarae, eds. *The Revolution in Words: Righting Women 1868-1871.* New York: Routledge, 1990.

Russo, Ann, and Cheris Kramarae, eds. *The Radical Women's Press of the 1850s.* New York: Routledge, 1991.

Taylor, H. Jeanie, Cheris Kramarae, and Maureen Ebben, eds. *Women, Information Technology, and Scholarship.* Urbana: Board of Trustees, U of Illinois, 1993.

Thorne, Barrie, Cheris Kramarae, and Nancy Henley, eds. *Language, Gender and Society.* Rowley, MA: Newbury, 1983.

Treichler, Paula A., Cheris Kramarae, and Beth Stafford, eds. *For Alma Mater: Theory and Practice in Feminist Scholarship.* Urbana: U of Illinois P, 1985.

Articles

Ebben, Maureen, and Cheris Kramarae. "Women and Information Technologies: Creating a Cyberspace of Our Own." *Women, Information Technology, and Scholarship.*

Ed. H. Jeanie Taylor, Cheris Kramarae, and Maureen Ebben. Urbana: Board of Trustees, U of Illinois, 1993. 15-27.

Henley, Nancy M., and Cheris Kramarae. "Gender, Power, and Miscommunication." *"Miscommunication" and Problematic Talk*. Ed. Nikolas Coupland, Howard Giles, and John M. Wiemann. Newbury Park, CA: Sage, 1991. 18-43.

Hilpert, Fred P., Cheris Kramer, and Ruth Anne Clark. "Participants' Perceptions of Self and Partner in Mixed-Sex Dyads." *Central States Speech Journal* 26 (1975): 52-56.

Houston, Marsha, and Cheris Kramarae. "Speaking from Silence: Methods of Silencing and of Resistance." *Discourse and Society* 2 (1991): 387-99.

Jenkins, Lee, and Cheris Kramer. "Small Group Process: Learning from Women." *Women's Studies International Quarterly* 1 (1978): 67-84.

Jenkins, Mercilee M., and Cheris Kramarae. "A Thief in the House: Women and Language." *Men's Studies Modified: The Impact of Feminism on the Academic Disciplines*. Ed. Dale Spender. New York: Pergamon, 1981. 11-22.

Kissling, Elizabeth Arveda, and Cheris Kramarae. "Stranger Compliments: The Interpretation of Street Remarks." *Women's Studies in Communication* 14 (1991): 75-93.

Kramarae, Cheris. "Backstage Critique of Virtual Reality." *CyberSociety: Computer-Mediated Communication and Community*. Ed. Steven G. Jones. Thousand Oaks, CA: Sage, 1995. 36-56.

Kramarae, Cheris. "Censorship of Women's Voices on Radio." *Gender and Discourse: The Power of Talk*. Ed. Alexandra Dundas Todd and Sue Fisher. Norwood, NJ: Ablex, 1988. 243-54.

Kramarae, Cheris. "Centers of Change: An Introduction to Women's Own Communication Programs." *Communication Education* 45 (1996): 315-21.

Kramarae, Cheris. "Changing the Complexion of Gender in Language Research." *Handbook of Language and Social Psychology*. Ed. Howard Giles and W. Peter Robinson. New York: John Wiley, 1990. 345-61.

Kramarae, Cheris. "Chronic Power Problems." *Toward the Twenty-First Century: The Future of Speech Communication*. Ed. Julia T. Wood and Richard B. Gregg. Cresskill, NJ: Hampton, 1995. 209-17.

Kramarae, Cheris. "Classified Information: Race, Class, and (Always) Gender." *Gendered Relationships*. Ed. Julia T. Wood. Mountain View, CA: Mayfield, 1996. 20-38.

Kramarae, Cheris. "The Condition of Patriarchy." *The Knowledge Explosion: Generations of Feminist Scholarship*. Ed. Cheris Kramarae and Dale Spender. New York: Teachers College P, 1992. 397-403.

Kramarae, Cheris. "Electronic Gender: Attitudes and Practices on the Internet or Year 2007: Looking Ahead to Look Back at Women and the Internet." *Kommunikation von Geschlecht [Communication of Gender]*. Ed. Friederike Braun and Ursula Pasero. Pfaffenweiler, Ger.: Centaurus-Verlagsgesellschaft, 1997. 200-21.

Kramer, C. K. "Experimentation in Technique: Frank O'Connor's 'Judas.'" *Dublin Magazine* 8 (1969): 31-38.

Kramarae, Cheris. "A Feminist Critique of Sociolinguistics." *Journal of the Atlantic Provinces Linguistic Association* 8 (1986): 1-22.

Kramarae, Cheris. "Feminist Theories of Communication." *International Encyclopedia of Communications*. Ed. Erik Barnouw. Vol. 2. New York: Oxford UP, 1989. 157-60.

Kramer, Cheris. "Folklinguistics: Wishy-Washy Mommy Talk." *Psychology Today* 8 (1974): 82-85. Rpt. in *Messages: A Reader in Human Communication.* Ed. Jean M. Civikly. 2nd ed. New York: Random, 1977. 90-98; *Messages: A Reader in Human Communication.* Ed. Sanford B. Weinberg. 3rd ed. New York: Random, 1980. 312-21; *Exploring Language.* Ed. Gary Goshgarian. Boston: Little, Brown, 1977. 142-51; *Exploring Language.* Ed. Gary Goshgarian. 2nd ed. Boston: Little, Brown, 1980. 144-53; *Exploring Language.* Ed. Gary Goshgarian. 3rd ed. Boston: Little, Brown, 1983. 253-64; *Exploring Language.* Ed. Gary Goshgarian. 4th ed. Boston: Little, Brown, 1986. 226-35; *Words and the Writer: A Language Reader.* Ed. Michael J. Hogan. Glenview, IL: Scott, Foresman, 1983. 190-99; and *Gender Images: Readings for Composition.* Ed. Melita Schaum and Connie Flanagan. Boston: Houghton Mifflin, 1992. 105-12.

Kramarae, Cheris. "Gender and Dominance." *Communication Yearbook 15.* Ed. Stanley A. Deetz. Newbury Park, CA: Sage, 1992. 469-74.

Kramarae, Cheris. "Gender: How She Speaks." *Attitudes towards Language Variation: Social and Applied Contexts.* Ed. Ellen Bouchard Ryan and Howard Giles. London: Edward Arnold, 1982. 84-98.

Kramarae, Cheris. "Gotta Go Myrtle, Technology's at the Door." *Technology and Women's Voices: Keeping in Touch.* Ed. Cheris Kramarae. New York: Routledge & Kegan Paul, 1988. 1-14.

Kramarae, Cheris. "Harassment and Everyday Life." *Women Making Meaning: New Feminist Directions in Communication.* Ed. Lana F. Rakow. New York: Routledge, 1992. 100-20.

Kramarae, Cheris. "Introduction." *Communication, Language and Sex: Proceedings of the First Annual Conference.* Ed. Cynthia L. Berryman and Virginia A. Eman. Rowley, MA: Newbury, 1980. 1-7.

Kramarae, Cheris. "The Language of Multicultural Feminism." *CSWS [Center for the Study of Women in Society] Review* [U of Oregon] 1989: 3-5.

Kramarae, Cheris. "Language, Women's." *The Oxford Companion to Women's Writing in the United States.* Ed. Cathy N. Davidson and Linda Wagner-Martin. New York: Oxford UP, 1995. 469-71.

Kramarae, Cheris. "Nachrichten zu sprechen gestatte ich der Frau nicht: Widerstand gegenüber dem öffentlichen Sprechen von Frauen." *Gewalt durch Sprache.* Ed. Senta Trömel-Plötz. Frankfurt: Fischer Taschenbuch Verlag, 1984. 203-32.

Kramer, Cheris. "One Review of U.S.A. Language and Sex Research." *Osnabrücker Beitrage zur Sprachtheorie* 8 (1978): 93-01.

Kramer, Cheris. "Parallel Motives in *Lord Jim.*" *Conradiana* 2 (1970): 58.

Kramer, Cheris. "Perceptions of Female and Male Speech." *Language and Speech* 20 (1977): 151-61.

Kramarae, Cheris. "Present Problems with the Language of the Future." *Women's Studies* 14 (1987): 183-86.

Kramarae, Cheris. "The Problem of Orientation in Sex/Language Research." *Proceedings of the Conference on the Sociology of the Languages of American Women.* Ed. Betty Lou Dubois and Isabel Crouch. San Antonio, TX: Trinity U, 1976. 17-27.

Kramarae, Cheris. "Proprietors of Language." *Women and Language in Literature and Society*. Ed. Sally McConnell-Ginet, Ruth Borker, and Nelly Furman. New York: Praeger, 1980. 58-68.

Kramarae, Cheris. "Punctuating the Dictionary." *International Journal of the Sociology of Language* 94 (1992): 135-54.

Kramarae, Cheris. "Redefining Gender, Class and Race." *Beyond Boundaries: Sex and Gender Diversity in Communication*. Ed. Cynthia M. Lont and Sheryl A. Friedley. Fairfax, VA: George Mason UP, 1989. 317-29.

Kramarae, Cheris. "Response to Perry: 'Sex Stereotypes, Social Rules and Education: Changing Teaching and Teaching Change.'" *Theoretical and Critical Perspectives on Teacher Change*. Ed. Phyllis Kahaney, Linda A. M. Perry, and Joseph Janangelo. Norwood, NJ: Ablex, 1993. 40-44.

Kramer, Cheris. "Sex-Related Differences in Address Systems." *Anthropological Linguistics* 17 (1975): 198-210.

Kramarae, Cheris. "Shere Hite as Sociological Theorist." *Women as Revolutionary Agents of Change: The Hite Reports and Beyond*. By Shere Hite. Madison: U of Wisconsin P, 1993. 445-49.

Kramarae, Cheris. "Speech Crimes Which the Law Cannot Reach or Compliments and Other Insulting Behavior." *Proceedings of the First Berkeley Women and Language Conference*. Ed. Sue Bremner, Noelle Caskey, and Birch Moonwomon. Berkeley, CA: Berkeley Women and Language Group, 1986. 84-95.

Kramer, Cheris. "Stereotypes of Women's Speech: The Word from Cartoons." *Journal of Popular Culture* 8 (1974): 624-30. Rpt. in *Language Power*. Ed. Carol J. Boltz and Dorothy U. Seyler. New York: Random, 1982. 195-202.

Kramarae, Cheris. "Talk of Sewing Circles and Sweatshops." *Technology and Women's Voices: Keeping in Touch*. Ed. Cheris Kramarae. New York: Routledge & Kegan Paul, 1988. 147-60.

Kramarae, Cheris. "Talk, Sex, and Self-Help: Hite and Men's Power Anxiety." *Women's Studies in Communication* 18 (1995): 229-44.

Kramarae, Cheris. "Technology Policy, Gender, and Cyberspace." *Duke Journal of Gender Law and Policy* 4 (1997): 149-58.

Kramarae, Cheris. "Timely Moves from 'Missionary Girls' to Radicals." *CSWS [Center for the Study of Women in Society] Review* [U of Oregon] 1990: 14-17.

Kramarae, Cheris. "A Visiting Scholar." *CSWS [Center for the Study of Women in Society] Review* [U of Oregon] 1998: 13-16.

Kramarae, Cheris. "We Regret the Omissions." *CSWS [Center for the Study of Women in Society] Review* [U of Oregon] 1990: 2-3.

Kramer, Cheris. "Women's and Men's Ratings of Their Own and Ideal Speech." *Communication Quarterly* 26 (1978): 2-11.

Kramer, Cheris. "Women's Speech: Separate but Unequal?" *Quarterly Journal of Speech* 60 (1974): 14-24. Rpt. in *Language and Sex: Difference and Dominance*. Ed. Barrie Thorne and Nancy Henley. Rowley, MA: Newbury, 1975. 43-56.

Kramarae, Cheris, and Mercilee Jenkins. "Liberating Language: Women's Speech at a Feminist Conference." *Proceedings of the Second and Third Conferences on Com-*

munication, Language, and Gender. Ed. Larry E. Larmer and Mary Kenny Badami. Madison: U of Wisconsin—Extension, 1982. 79-92.

Kramarae, Cheris, and Mercilee Jenkins. "Women Changing Words Changing Women." *Sprachwandel und feministische Sprachpolitik: Internationale Perspektiven.* Ed. Marlis Hellinger. Wiesbaden, Ger.: Westdeutscher Verlag, 1985. 10-22.

Kramarae, Cheris, and Mercilee M. Jenkins. "Women Take Back the Talk." *Women and Language in Transition.* Ed. Joyce Penfield. Albany: State U of New York P, 1987. 137-56.

Kramarae, Cheris, and Jana Kramer. "Legal Snarls for Women in Cyberspace." *Internet Research: Electronic Networking Applications and Policy* 5 (1995): 14-24.

Kramarae, Cheris, and Jana Kramer. "Net Gains, Net Losses." *Women's Review of Books* 12 (1995): 33-35.

Kramarae, Cheris, Muriel Schulz, and William M. O'Barr. "Introduction: Toward an Understanding of Language and Power." *Language and Power.* Ed. Cheris Kramarae, Muriel Schulz, and William M. O'Barr. Beverly Hills, CA: Sage, 1984. 9-22.

Kramarae, Cheris, and Dale Spender. "Exploding Knowledge." *The Knowledge Explosion: Generations of Feminist Scholarship.* Ed. Cheris Kramarae and Dale Spender. New York: Teachers College P, 1992. 1-24.

Kramer, Cheris, Barrie Thorne, and Nancy Henley. "Perspectives on Language and Communication." *Signs: Journal of Women in Culture and Society* 3 (1978): 638-51.

Kramarae, Cheris, Barrie Thorne, and Nancy Henley. "Sex Similarities and Differences in Language, Speech, and Nonverbal Communication: An Annotated Bibliography." *Language, Gender and Society.* Ed. Barrie Thorne, Cheris Kramarae, and Nancy Henley. Rowley, MA: Newbury, 1983. 153-331.

Kramarae, Cheris, and Paula A. Treichler. "Power Relationships in the Classroom." *Gender in the Classroom: Power and Pedagogy.* Ed. Susan L. Gabriel and Isaiah Smithson. Urbana: U of Illinois P, 1990. 41-59.

Kramarae, Cheris, and Paula A. Treichler, with Ann Russo. "Words on a Feminist Dictionary." *A Feminist Dictionary.* Ed. Cheris Kramarae and Paula A. Treichler, with Ann Russo. Boston: Pandora, 1985. 1-22.

Kramer, Dale, and Cheris Kramer. "James's 'The Marriages': Designs of Structure." *University Review* [U of Missouri, Kansas City] 33 (1966): 75-80.

Kramer, Jana, and Cheris Kramarae. "Gendered Ethics on the Internet." *Communication Ethics in an Age of Diversity.* Ed. Josina M. Makau and Ronald C. Arnett. Urbana: U of Illinois P, 1997. 226-43.

Taylor, H. Jeanie, and Cheris Kramarae. "Women and Men on Electronic Networks: A Conversation or a Monologue?" *Women, Information Technology, and Scholarship.* Ed. H. Jeanie Taylor, Cheris Kramarae, and Maureen Ebben. Urbana: Board of Trustees, U of Illinois, 1993. 52-61.

Thorne, Barrie, Cheris Kramarae, and Nancy Henley. "Imagining a Different World of Talk." *Women In Search of Utopia: Mavericks and Mythmakers.* Ed. Ruby Rohrlich and Elaine Hoffman Baruch. New York: Schocken, 1984. 180-88.

Thorne, Barrie, Cheris Kramarae, and Nancy Henley. "Language, Gender and Society: Opening a Second Decade of Research." *Language, Gender and Society.* Ed. Barrie Thorne, Cheris Kramarae, and Nancy Henley. Rowley, MA: Newbury, 1983. 7-24.

Treichler, Paula A., and Cheris Kramarae. "Women's Talk in the Ivory Tower." *Communication Quarterly* 31 (1983): 118-32.
Treichler, Paula A., Richard M. Frankel, Cheris Kramarae, Kathleen Zoppi, and Howard B. Beckman. "Problems and *Prob*lems: Power Relationships in a Medical Encounter." *Language and Power.* Ed. Cheris Kramarae, Muriel Schulz, and William M. O'Barr. Beverly Hills, CA: Sage, 1984. 62-88.
West, Candace, Michelle M. Lazar, and Cheris Kramarae. "Gender in Discourse." *Discourse as Social Interaction.* Ed. Teun A. van Dijk. Thousand Oaks, CA: Sage, 1997. 119-43.

bell hooks

"Passionately concerned with education for critical consciousness, I continually search for ways to think, teach, and write that excite and liberate the mind . . . to live and act in a way that challenges systems of domination."[1] This statement summarizes the commitment that characterizes the life and work of Gloria Jean Watkins, who writes under the name *bell hooks*.[2] Born on September 25, 1952, in Hopkinsville, Kentucky, hooks was one of seven children born to Veodis Watkins, a custodian employed by the U.S. Postal Service, and Rosa Bell Watkins, a homemaker.

Hooks's childhood was characterized by an appreciation for various forms of music and art, but her particular interest was poetry. She memorized poems for special events at her church and school, and when storms caused power

NOTE: Excerpts from *Feminist Theory: From Margin to Center,* by bell hooks, and from *Talking Back: Thinking Feminist, Thinking Black,* by bell hooks, are reprinted with permission from the publisher, South End Press, 116 Saint Botolph Street, Boston, MA 02115.

outages, her family would light candles and stage impromptu talent shows, at which hooks would recite the poetry of William Wordsworth, Langston Hughes, Elizabeth Barrett Browning, and Gwendolyn Brooks.[3] For hooks, memorizing poetry "was pure enchantment": "[W]e learned by listening and reciting that words put together just so, said just so, could have the same impact on our psyches as song, could lift and exalt our spirits, enabling us to feel tremendous joy, or carrying us down into that most immediate and violent sense of loss and grief."[4]

Equally important lessons for hooks came as a result of growing up with five sisters and one brother. She saw her brother given "greater rights and privileges" than the girls in the family and learned, along with her sisters, to cater to her brother.[5] Hooks also learned in childhood to appreciate differences among women: "Sexist stereotypes were disrupted by the nature of our bodies and beings. Some of us were strong of body, athletic, and others were weak. Some of us were seen as sexy and cute, and others just plain. Some of us were brainy and others more interested in creative work."[6]

When hooks became involved in feminism, her experiences with so many women already had given her experience with sisterhood: "While many of my peers talked about sisterhood, they were not as committed to the practice of sisterhood. Practicing sisterhood was work I had done for years in my family." The understanding "that females could bond together in constructive ways even in the midst of sexism" strengthened her faith that "feminist sisterhood could be realized."[7]

During her childhood, hooks learned as well about the domination and control that characterize life under patriarchy: "Our daily life was full of patriarchal drama—the use of coercion, violent punishment, verbal harassment, to maintain male domination."[8] Male domination particularly was evident in her family's daily communication, for her family

> lived as though in two social spaces. One was a world without the father, when he would go to work, and that world was full of speech. . . . We could express ourselves loudly, passionately, outrageously. The other world was a male-dominated social space where sound and silence were dictated by his presence. . . . We would turn our volumes down, lower our voices; we would, if need be, remain silent. In this same childhood world we witnessed women—our grandmothers, mothers, aunts— speak with force and power in sex-segregated spaces, then retreat into a realm of silence in the presence of men.[9]

Male domination was manifest in her family in even more brutal ways. She remembers her father yelling and screaming, pushing and hitting her mother. One night, he threatened to kill her mother and threw her out of the house after hitting her. Hooks witnessed her mother, a person she knew as strong, as someone who could get things done, "a woman of ways and means, a woman of action," sitting "still, paralyzed, waiting for the next blow, pleading."[10] Hooks could not "bear the silent agreement that the man is right, that he has done what men are able to do."[11] Her "keen sense that inequity in [her] household was gender based"[12] led her, at the age of 16, to announce to her mother, "I will never marry. I will never be any man's prisoner."[13] Her mother's marriage made marriage "seem like a trap, a door closing in a room without air."[14]

Talking back, or "speaking as an equal to an authority figure . . . having an opinion" became a characteristic way in which hooks responded to such inequities. She felt that "black women spoke in a language so rich, so poetic, that it felt . . . like being shut off from life, smothered to death if one were not allowed to participate."[15] She "could not stop the words, making thought, writing speech."[16] "To make my voice," she explains, "I had to speak, to hear myself talk—and talk I did—darting in and out of grown folks' conversations and dialogues, answering questions that were not directed at me, endlessly asking questions, making speeches."[17]

Because she was not silent, as children (especially girls) were supposed to be, hooks was punished constantly for her verbosity. She was punished so often, in fact, that she began to feel persecuted, and when she learned the word *scapegoat,* she felt it accurately described her role in her family.[18] Persecuted, ridiculed, and punished, she "did not feel truly connected to these strange people, to these familial folks who could not only fail to grasp [her] worldview but who just simply did not want to hear it."[19] Childhood was a "constant experience of estrangement"[20] spent "dreaming of the moment" when she would find her way home: "In my imagination, home was a place of radical openness, of recognition and reconciliation, where one could create freely."[21]

The punishment and persecution hooks experienced as a child pushed her "in the direction of critical analytical thought."[22] "[P]sychologically wounded and at times physically hurt," hooks explains, "the primary force which kept me going, which lifted my spirits was critical engagement with ideas."[23] She "found the life of the mind a refuge, a sanctuary," where she "could experience a sense of agency and thereby construct" her "own subject identity."[24] She kept a daily diary or journal while growing up and found that it was a space of critical reflection for her—a place where she struggled to understand herself and the world around her, "that crazy world of family and community, that painful world."[25] As she explained in one journal entry, "Writing eases the anguish. It is my connection. Through it and with it I transcend despair."[26] This lived recognition of how critical thought can be used in the service of survival led hooks to value intellectual work "not because it brought status or recognition but because it offered resources to enhance survival and . . . pleasure in living."[27]

One childhood experience in particular gave hooks the courage to take risks—"to assert transgressive critical thoughts that may or may not be popular without debilitating fear."[28] Her grandmother's death in the family's home was "what the old folks would call 'a very easy death,'" one "full of tenderness and peace." This experience liberated hooks and "changed forever" her relation to living because it banished "all fear of death and dying." Whenever she was punished for speaking her beliefs, she was able to hold to her principles and beliefs by reminding herself that death was not to be feared: "It was an inner secret that enabled me to bear pain and suffering yet hold on to the conviction that I could rebel and resist whenever necessary."[29]

Following graduation from high school, hooks earned a B.A. in English at Stanford University, completing her degree in 1973. Her years at Stanford were difficult ones, and her desire to do intellectual work was not affirmed by her experiences there. She encountered racism, sexism, and classism and continually wondered why she was working to be an academic when she "did not see people in that environment who were opposing domination."[30]

Despite hooks's ambivalence about the academy, she went on to graduate school, earning an M.A. degree in English from the University of Wisconsin at Madison in 1976 and a Ph.D. in English from the University of California at Santa Cruz in 1983. Once again, she found life in the academy to be difficult: "During my graduate years I heard myself speaking often in the voice of resistance."[31] She was told that she "'did not have the proper demeanor of a graduate student'"; she refused to accept and assume the subordinate role that was required because the "forms of exploitation and domination" of graduate school evoked "images of a lifetime spent tolerating abuse."[32]

Despite her ambivalence about academic life, hooks embarked on a teaching career, serving as an instructor between 1976 and 1984 at the University of Southern California, the University of California at Riverside, the University of California at Santa Cruz, Occidental College, and San Francisco State University. She accepted a joint position as an assistant professor in the African-American Studies and English Departments at Yale University in 1985, and in 1988, she moved to Oberlin College in Ohio as an associate professor of American literature and women's studies. In 1994, she accepted the position of distinguished professor of English at City College of the City University of New York.

Hooks remains in academia primarily for a pragmatic reason: it gives her time to do her work.[33] She is disappointed, however, that the academic profession generally is not a place where the kind of intellectual work she values can take place. She entered academia "assuming it would be a place where a life of the mind would be affirmed"[34] and because she felt "moved, pushed, even, in the direction of intellectual work by forces stronger than that of individual will."[35] She discovered, however, that academia is a far different place from what she had imagined. Instead of being a place of open-mindedness and critical thinking, she found that it serves "basically a conservatizing function."[36] She also experienced it as a place where the "connection between theory and practice" is not respected[37] and where "our most urgent need, the most important of our work—the work of liberation"—is not valued.[38]

Discouraged at the lack of spiritual and emotional health and wholeness that characterizes many individuals in the academy, hooks describes the university as "a haven for those who are smart in book knowledge but who might be otherwise unfit for social interaction."[39] "To this day," hooks explains, "I feel as imprisoned in the academic world as I felt in the world of my growing up."[40] "People have this fantasy (as I did when I was young) of colleges being liberatory institutions, when in fact they're so much like every other institution in our culture in terms of *repression* and *containment*—so that now I feel like I'm trying to break out."[41] She clings "to the dream of a radical visionary artistic community that can sustain and nurture creativity" but has yet to find it in the academy.[42]

Hooks's commitment to intellectual work is demonstrated in her prodigious output. Her first literary efforts were plays and poetry; a chapbook of poems, *And There We Wept*, published in 1978, was her first book. She turned to nonfiction when she felt she had "received this 'message from the spirits,' that [she] really needed to do feminist work which would challenge the universalized category of 'woman.'"[43] Several books followed that deal with the relationship between feminism and black women. The first, *Ain't I a Woman: Black Women and Feminism*, was written when hooks was 19 years old and an undergraduate at Stanford University,[44] although she was not able to get the book published until 1981. It is "an examination of the impact of sexism on the black woman during slavery, the devaluation of black womanhood, black male sexism, racism within the recent feminist movement, and the black woman's involvement with feminism."[45]

In hooks's next book, *Feminist Theory: From Margin to Center* (1984), she proposes new directions for feminist theory from the perspective of black women. She calls for a new kind of women's movement, grounded in a recognition of the diversity of women's backgrounds and experiences. In *Talking Back: Thinking Feminist, Thinking Black* (1989), hooks continues to develop feminist theory from this perspective, providing an analysis of such issues as pedagogy, violence, militarism, and homophobia.

Hooks not only theorizes about feminist theory and its intersection with race, but she applies her theoretical perspective to cultural texts in a series of books. *Yearning: Race, Gender, and Cultural Politics* (1990) is an analysis of contemporary culture that focuses attention on cultural phenomena such as Malcolm X, advertising, the anthropology of Zora Neale Hurston, and films such as Spike Lee's *Do the Right Thing*.

Black Looks: Race and Representation (1992) deals both with the way African Americans are depicted in film, television, advertisements, and literature and with what hooks feels is the need for blacks and others to "see" the persistent hold of racism on the American imagination. In this book, hooks continues her analysis of cultural texts, assessing whether they constitute revolutionary intervention in the area of race and representation.

In *Outlaw Culture: Resisting Representations* (1994), hooks continues to engage in cultural criticism as a means for "educating for critical consciousness in liberatory ways."[46] In this book, hooks analyzes cultural texts such as Christopher Columbus, Camille Paglia, and films such as *The Crying Game*. In *Art on My Mind: Visual Politics* (1995), hooks imagines new ways to think and write about visual art as a contribution to the process of cultural transformation. Her topics range from photography's place in black life to women artists to architecture.

Hooks's *Reel to Real: Race, Sex, and Class at the Movies* (1996), another book of cultural criticism, is based on the premise that movies "change things." Hooks asserts that movies "take the real and make it into something else right before our very eyes. . . . They give the reimagined, reinvented version of the real. . . . That's what makes movies so compelling."[47] In this book, hooks analyzes films such as *Pulp Fiction* and *Waiting to Exhale* from feminist and black perspectives and interviews filmmakers such as Wayne Wang and Camille Billops.

Hooks also has written books designed to intervene in specific cultural practices of oppression. *Sisters of the Yam: Black Women and Self-Recovery* (1993) is a self-help book that combines individual efforts at self-actualization with the larger world of collective struggle. Hooks draws connections among psychological trauma, mental disorders, and the madness of forming self and identity in white supremacist capitalist patriarchy and shares strategies for self-recovery that she and other black women have used to heal their lives. In *Teaching to Transgress: Education as the Practice of Freedom* (1994), hooks turns her attention to teaching. She sees the classroom as a site in which the opportunity exists "to labor for freedom" and constructs a theory of "education as the practice of freedom."[48]

Killing Rage: Ending Racism (1995) is hooks's effort to intervene in practices of racism through an examination of the experiences of domination of all Americans. Hooks suggests that all individuals must move away from a psychology of blame around the issue of race. That such a move is possible is affirmed in hooks's belief that "our many cultures can be remade, that this nation can be transformed, that we can resist racism and in the act of resistance recover ourselves and be renewed."[49]

Four of hooks's books are more personal in nature and are grounded in her own experiences as guides for others in the effort to disrupt oppression. *Breaking Bread: Insurgent Black Intellectual Life* (1991), written with Cornel West, an African American writer, educator, and activist, is about black intellectual life and the ways in which hooks and West have chosen to lead such lives. *A Woman's Mourning Song* (1993) consists of an essay and a collection of poems in which hooks examines the way in which death serves as a guide for her in the liberation of the spirit. *Bone Black: Memories of Girlhood* (1996) is an autobiography of critical moments in hooks's childhood. She describes the lessons she learned about gender roles, domination, and education while growing up and the choices she made on the basis of those experiences. In *Wounds of Passion: A Writing Life* (1997), hooks documents the context that prepared her to become a writer and links "childhood obsessions about writing and the body to the early years of young adulthood" in which she worked "to establish a writing voice and create sustained work."[50]

In addition to her books, hooks has contributed dozens of essays to such publications as *Callaloo, Emerge, Utne Reader, Z Magazine, Artforum,* and *Catalyst.* She also founded a literary magazine, *Hambone,* with the poet Nathaniel Mackey, whom she met while she was an undergraduate at Stanford University and with whom she lived for more than 10 years.

In all of her works, hooks writes "with the intent to share ideas in a way that makes them accessible to the widest possible audience."[51] In particular, she is concerned with moving people with her work and believes that lack of accessibility "diminishes our work's power to make meaningful interventions in theory and practice."[52] She made a conscious decision not to use footnotes in her first book, *Ain't I a Woman,* because she believes that footnotes set class boundaries for readers, determining who a book is for: "I went into various communities and asked non-academic Black people if they read books with footnotes. The majority responded by saying that when they open a book with footnotes they immediately think that book isn't for them, that the book is for an academic person."[53] Although she acknowledges that her accessibility jeopardizes how seriously she is taken in academic circles, accessibility is "a political matter and a political decision" for her.[54]

Hooks's use of the name of *bell hooks* constitutes a similarly conscious political decision. The name under which she writes is the name of her great grandmother on her mother's side, a "sharp-tongued woman, a woman who spoke her mind, a woman who was not afraid to talk back."[55] She sees the self that is Gloria Watkins as contemplative and nonpublic, and publishing under a different name allows her to claim an identity that affirms her "right to speech."[56] She also sees a pseudonym as deflecting attention from personality and focusing it on ideas[57] and as a constant reminder not "to become over-identified with these ideas, so attached to them" that she "would be unable or unwilling to change perspectives" or to admit errors in her thinking.[58] Most important, however, the name is a way for hooks to claim a "legacy of defiance, of will, of courage," affirming a "link to female ancestors who were bold and daring in their speech."[59] The lowercase spelling of the name that hooks prefers is "about ego." She wants this stylistic practice to communicate that the substance of her books, "not who is writing them," is what is important.[60]

Nature of the World

The world with which hooks is concerned is the culture of domination that characterizes Western culture. This world is marked by oppression and exploitation and the devaluation of "reciprocity, community, and mutuality."[61] It features a "belief in a notion of superior and inferior, and its concomitant ideology—that the superior should rule over the inferior."[62] This ideology is so pervasive, hooks asserts, that "most citizens of the United States believe in their heart of hearts that it is natural for a group or an individual to dominate over others."[63] Acceptance of the naturalness of domination is manifest in the various crises that currently plague the planet: "Systematic dehumanization, worldwide famine, ecological devastation, industrial contamination, and the possibility of nuclear destruction are realities which remind us daily that we are in crisis."[64]

Hooks calls the current system that promotes domination and subjugation *white supremacist capitalist patriarchy,* a label that suggests interlocking structures of sexism, racism, class elitism, capitalism, and heterosexism. These systems all share the ideological ground of "a belief in domination, and a belief in notions of superior and inferior."[65] In them, values are assigned to differences and are ranked hierarchically, fostering hatred, vicious competition, alienation from others, elitism based on position in the hierarchy, and individualism rather than cooperation.

Because the various forms of oppression are interrelated and share the same foundation, hooks asserts that movements to free oppressed people must work for the freedom of all oppressed peoples and not just particular ones. What often happens, however, is that various movements begin to compete with one another:

> As a black woman interested in feminist movement, I am often asked whether being black is more important than being a woman; whether feminist struggle to end sexist oppression is more important than the struggle to end racism and vice-versa. . . . Rather than see anti-racist work as totally compatible with working to end sexist oppression, they are often seen as two movements competing for first place.[66]

"One would like to think that the more aware you become of one form of institutionalized domination and oppression," hooks suggests, "the easier it would be for you to see connections. But what we see instead is the capacity of humans to deny the connection of all these."[67] She concludes, as a result of her analysis of the ideology of domination, that the oppressed need to work together:

It is our collective responsibility as people of color and as white people . . . to help one another. . . . If I commit myself politically to black liberation struggle, to the struggle to end white supremacy, I am not making a commitment to working only for and with black people; I must engage in struggle with all willing comrades to strengthen our awareness and our resistance.[68]

Just as all individuals bear responsibility for working to end all kinds of domination, the "system of white-supremacist capitalist patriarchy is not maintained solely by white folks. It also is maintained by all the rest of us who internalize and enforce the values of this regime"[69] and who "act unconsciously, in complicity with a culture of domination."[70] Because all people within a culture of domination are socialized to embody its values and attitudes, all individuals are agents of domination, helping to perpetuate and maintain its systems. The process of colonization has made the oppressed "participants in daily rituals of power where we, in strict sado-masochistic fashion, find pleasure in ways of being and thinking, ways of looking at the world that reinforce and maintain our positions as the dominated."[71] Hooks elaborates:

I understand that in many places in the world oppressed and oppressor share the same color. I understand that right here in this room, oppressed and oppressor share the same gender. Right now as I speak, a man who is himself victimized, wounded, hurt by racism and class exploitation is actively dominating a woman in his life—that even as I speak, women who are ourselves exploited, victimized, are dominating children. It is necessary for us to remember, as we think critically about domination, that we all have the capacity to act in ways that oppress, dominate, wound.[72]

Although hooks sees racism, sexism, classism, capitalism, and heterosexism as interlocking systems, grounded in the same ideology of domination, she does suggest that sexism and the struggle to end patriarchal domination "should be of primary importance to women and men globally."[73] This is not because, as some feminists argue, sexist oppression "is the basis of all other oppressions." "Suggesting a hierarchy of oppression exists, with sexism in first place," asserts hooks, "evokes a sense of competing concerns that is unnecessary." Instead, hooks sees the struggle to end sexism as primary because sexist oppression "is the practice of domination most people experience, whether their role be that of discriminator or discriminated against, exploiter or exploited."[74]

Sexism is also the practice of domination most people are socialized to accept before they ever experience other forms of oppression because "most people witness and/or experience the practice of sexist domination in family settings." Usually, individuals experience and learn to accept domination within the family, whether the experience is one of domination of parent over child or man over woman. In contrast, individuals tend to witness and experience racism and classism as they "encounter the larger society, the world outside the home."[75] Hooks cites her own experience to support her perspective: "Growing up in a black, working-class, father-dominated household, I experienced coercive adult male authority as more immediately threatening, as more likely to cause immediate pain than racist oppression or class exploitation."[76]

Because the world of interlocking systems of domination is intense and pervasive, many people, hooks laments, believe "that nothing will ever change."[77] Hooks suggests otherwise; oppressed people must believe that people can change because "what we can't imagine, can't come to be."[78] She asks those who are discouraged to notice the individual incidents of people changing daily[79] and to "bear witness to the reality that our many cultures can be remade, that this nation can be transformed, that we can resist . . . and in the act of resistance recover ourselves and be renewed."[80]

Definition of Feminism

Hooks is optimistic about challenging and transforming the culture of domination because of the existence of what she calls *feminist movement.* The term *feminism* often is used in the United States as synonymous with *women's liberation,* suggesting "movement that aims to make women the social equals of men."[81] This definition of feminism, however, raises a number of questions for hooks: "Since men are not equals in white supremacist, capitalist, patriarchal class structure, which men do women want to be equal to? Do women share a common vision of what equality means?"[82]

Hooks asserts that the positive political significance and power of the term *feminism* must be recovered and maintained, a recovery that can be facilitated with a broader definition. Although hooks defines feminism as "the struggle to end sexist oppression,"[83] she explains that "to be 'feminist' in any authentic sense of the term is to want for all people, female and male, liberation from sexist role patterns, domination, and oppression."[84] Thus, feminism "directs our attention to systems of domination and the inter-relatedness of sex, race, and class oppression."[85] It is "a struggle to eradicate the ideology of domination that permeates Western culture on various levels"[86] and constitutes movement that challenges "an entire structure of domination of which patriarchy is one part."[87]

For hooks, feminist movement aims not only at eradicating the ideology of domination but also functions as a constructive, proactive force. It seeks to transform relationships and the larger culture "so that the alienation, competition, and dehumanization that characterize human interaction can be replaced with feelings of intimacy, mutuality, and camaraderie."[88] Although feminism begins with a commitment to end sexist oppression, it is not for women only. Feminism constitutes a basis for collective struggle among and on behalf of all oppressed people because it "challenges each of us to alter our person, our personal engagement (either as victims or perpetrators or both) in a system of domination."[89]

Hooks prefers the statement "I advocate feminism" to the more typical "I am a feminist." The new phrase, she believes, discourages a focus on stereotyped perspectives on feminism, with the speaker "plugged into preconceived notions of identity, role, or behavior." In contrast, the phrase "I advocate feminism" often prompts the question "What is feminism?" and encourages exploration of and discussion of feminist movement. Her preferred phrase also avoids linguistic structures that give primacy to one particular group; it "does not suggest that by committing oneself to feminism, the possibility of supporting other political movements is negated."[90]

Feminism has not achieved its transformative potential, according to hooks, because it has been a reformist, conservative movement, "mainly concerned with gaining equal access to domains of white male privilege."[91] The reforms many feminists have sought have been designed "to improve the social status of women within the existing social structure."[92] This kind of feminism

> offers women not liberation but the right to act as surrogate men. . . . The women's movement . . . gives women of all races, who desire to assume the imperialist, sexist, racist positions of destruction men hold . . . a platform that allows them to act as if the attainment of their personal aspirations and their lust for power is for the common good of all women.[93]

Feminism, then, must be a radical and revolutionary movement and not a reform movement. It must be committed to the "formation of an oppositional world view" and to "the establishment of a new social order."[94] "We must be willing," hooks urges, "to restore the spirit of risk—to be fast, wild, to be able to take hold, turn around, transform."[95] Hooks acknowledges that the kind of revolutionary feminism she seeks usually is initiated by "violent overthrow of an existing political structure," but "this cannot be the basis for feminist revolution in this society." She explains: "Our emphasis must be on cultural transformation: destroying dualism, eradicating systems of domination. Our struggle will be gradual and protracted."[96]

Not only the reformist stance of feminism but its racism and classism have kept it from achieving its transformative potential. The women who began the contemporary feminist movement in the United States in the 1960s "did not invite a wholistic analysis of woman's status in society that would take into consideration the varied aspects of our experience."[97] Because they "ignored the complexity of woman's experience,"[98] they were not able to create "theory that speaks to the widest audience of people."[99]

Hooks points to Betty Friedan's *The Feminine Mystique,* published in 1963, as a prime example of the racism and classism of much contemporary feminism. Heralded "as having paved the way for contemporary feminist movement," "the one-dimensional perspective on women's reality presented in [Friedan's] book became a marked feature of the contemporary feminist movement."[100] Writing as though her experiences reflected the norm without testing her assumptions to see if they were true across class and race, Friedan assumed that feminism was primarily for and about materially privileged white women. The women Friedan saw as victimized by sexism were "a select group of college-educated, middle and upper class, married white women—housewives bored with leisure, with the home, with children, with buying products, who wanted more out of life."[101] Although the "problems and dilemmas of leisure class white house-wives were real concerns that merited consideration and change," hooks suggests, "they were not the pressing political concerns of masses of women."[102]

The treatment of the issue of work by Friedan and other founders of contemporary feminism exemplifies its exclusive and narrow focus. When white, middle-class women assumed that liberation would be achieved by work outside the home, they ignored the fact that a vast majority of women already were working outside the home—women who "knew from their experiences that work was neither personally fulfilling nor liberatory—that it was for the most part exploitative and dehumanizing."[103] These working women were saying they wanted "to leave the world of alienated work" to have more time to spend with their families.[104] Feminists "should have been challenging the idea that *any* work would liberate women and demanding that feminist movement address the concerns of working women."[105] If feminism had focused on issues such as "improving conditions in the workplace for women," obtaining "better paying jobs for women," and "finding jobs for unemployed women of all classes," it would have been seen as a movement addressing the concerns of all women.[106] The treatment of work by feminists such as Friedan led many white, middle-class feminists to conclude that women who worked were already liberated; as a result, these feminists effectively said to the majority of working women, "[F]eminist movement is not for you."[107]

The treatment of the issue of motherhood in early feminist movement also reflected the race and class biases of its founders. Although early feminists demanded respect and acknowledgment for housework and child care, they did not attribute enough significance and value to parenting and motherhood. They often identified motherhood and child rearing as the locus of women's oppression and "argued that motherhood was a serious obstacle to women's liberation, a trap confining women to the home, keeping them tied to cleaning, cooking, and child care." But poor women and women of color did not see motherhood as "a serious obstacle" to their "freedom as women."[108] Motherhood did not prevent them from entering the world of paid work because they always had worked, and they often found in "parenting one of the few interpersonal relationships" where they were "affirmed and appreciated."[109]

Responsibility for the exclusivity that has tended to mark feminist movement, however, does not rest solely with the white, middle-class women who founded it. Many black women do not see feminism as relevant because they do "not see 'womanhood' as an important aspect" of their identity: "Racist, sexist socialization had conditioned us to devalue our femaleness and to regard race as the only relevant label of identification." These women see sexism as "insignificant in light of the harsher, more brutal reality of racism" and view involvement with feminism as a gesture of betrayal of black men and of the black race in general.[110]

Although feminist movement currently lacks "wholeness, lacks the broad analysis that could encompass a variety of human experiences,"[111] hooks is optimistic that feminism can be expanded and that a feminist movement can be advanced "that folks will long—yes, yearn—to be a part of."[112] To create such feminist movement requires as a starting point the "acceptance of difference."[113] A "liberatory ideology that can be shared with everyone . . . can be created only if the experiences of people on the margin who suffer sexist oppression and other forms of group oppression are understood, addressed, and incorporated."[114] Hooks acknowledges that her critique of the current state of feminism is harsh, but she engages in such a critique to help it realize its potential: "Though I criticize aspects of feminist movement as we have known it so far, a critique which is sometimes harsh and unrelenting, I do so not in an attempt to diminish feminist struggle but to enrich, to share in the work of making a liberatory ideology and a liberatory movement."[115]

Nature of the Rhetor

Rhetors in hooks's rhetorical theory—those persons who have the capacity to address the exigence of domination—are critical thinkers or intellectuals. For hooks, these rhetors are individuals who transgress "discursive frontiers" to examine "ideas in their vital bearing on a wider political culture."[116] Critical thinking is the principal quality of these rhetors because it is "the primary element allowing the possibility of change." Without "the capacity to think critically about our selves and our lives, none of us would be able to move forward, to change, to grow."[117] Because these rhetors explore ideas in the service of challenging and transforming an ideology of domination, they are necessarily feminists in hooks's use of the term—individuals who struggle to eradicate oppression and domination.

Hooks is particularly interested in the contributions that can be made by critical thinkers who are positioned in the margins. Marginality, for hooks, is a "site of radical possibility, a space of resistance . . . a central location for the production of a counter-hegemonic discourse."[118] "Understanding marginality as position and place of resistance is crucial for oppressed, exploited, colonized people,"[119] she asserts, because those critical thinkers who are located in the margin look "both from the outside in and from the inside out";[120] they focus their attention on both the center and the margin and understand both. This is a particularly significant standpoint for hooks because it provides "an oppositional world view—a mode of seeing unknown to most . . . oppressors."[121] For hooks, then, marginality is not a standpoint "one wishes to lose—to give up or surrender as part of moving into the center—but rather . . . a site one stays in, clings to even, because it nourishes one's capacity to resist. It offers to one the possibility of radical perspective from which to see and create, to imagine alternatives, new worlds."[122]

Marginalized rhetors—and black women in particular—are at the speaking center of hooks's theory. Her focus on black women is not an action designed to exclude others but an invitation to "listen to the voice of a black woman speaking [as] subject and not as underprivileged other."[123] She sees a "special vantage point" for black women because they are in an unusual position in society.[124] Not only are they "collectively at the bottom of the occupational ladder," but their

> overall social status is lower than that of any other group. Occupying such a position, we bear the brunt of sexist, racist, and classist oppression. At the same time, we are the group that has not been socialized to assume the role of exploiter/oppressor in that we are allowed no institutionalized "other" that we can exploit or oppress.[125]

Black women's perspectives also are unique in that no "other group in America has so had their identity socialized out of existence as have black women." As hooks explains, "We are rarely recognized as a group separate and distinct from black men, or as a present part of the larger group 'women' in this culture."[126] She asserts:

> When black people are talked about, sexism militates against the acknowledgement of the interests of black women; when women are talked about racism militates against a recognition of black female interests. When black people are talked about the focus tends to be on black *men*; and when women are talked about the focus tends to be on *white* women.[127]

Although hooks privileges black women, she believes that all people can be critical thinkers and intellectuals, and she welcomes them into the work of critical thinking. She acknowledges, however, that the standpoints rhetors bring to the work of challenging domination are different according to their different identities; individuals from particular racial and ethnic groups, sexual orientations, and class positions bring different perspectives to their thinking. All are welcome to study and think critically about any subject, however, and not simply those explicitly related to particular dimensions of their own identities. As hooks explains, "I did not think that I needed to be a white man to understand Hemingway's *The Sun Also Rises* nor did I think I needed to be in a classroom with white men to study this novel." She believes, however, that "as a black woman reading this white male writer I might have insights and interpretations that would be quite different from those of white male readers who might approach the text with the assumption that the novel's depiction of white male social reality was one they shared."[128]

The "special insight"[129] that may be contributed by marginalized rhetors derives not from any "essential traits and characteristics"[130] but from experience. In "certain circumstances," hooks believes, "experience affords us a privileged critical location from which to speak."[131] Rhetors with particular identities make use of experience that "cannot be acquired through books or even distanced observation and study of a particular reality"; they bring with them a "passion of experience."[132] Sometimes, such direct experience is critical to understanding—it can be "the most relevant way to apprehend reality."[133] As hooks explains, imagine "we are baking bread that needs flour. And we have all the other ingredients but no flour. Suddenly, the flour becomes most important even though it alone will not do. This is a way to think about experience"[134] and its role in the critical thinking process of the rhetor. Although critical thinkers need "to engage multiple locations, to address diverse standpoints, to allow us to gather knowledge fully and inclusively,"[135] the experience afforded because of membership in a particular group has the potential to result in unique insights.

The nature of the rhetor, in hooks's theory, involves adoption of the role of critical thinker or enlightened witness. This role constitutes a way of thinking that allows individuals to examine the harmful effects of domination in their personal lives and the public world and to discover what they can do to facilitate change. What unites rhetors in her theory is a "longing, this deep and profound yearning, to just have this domination *end*. And what I feel unites you and me is: we can locate in one another a similar yearning to be in a more *just* world."[136]

Rhetorical Options

The rhetorical options featured in hooks's rhetorical theory are designed to intervene in practices of domination. All of her options involve the basic process of decolonization, or developing the critical consciousness necessary to challenge and transform the ideology of domination. Colonization is the conquering of "the minds and habits"[137] of oppressed people so that they themselves internalize and accept their "inherent inferiority."[138]

Decolonization, in contrast, is the "breaking with the ways our reality is defined and shaped by the dominant culture and asserting our understanding of that reality, of our own experience."[139] The process of decolonization is a "disruption of the colonized/colonizer mind-set," a letting go of white supremacist capitalist patriarchal assumptions and values.[140] It is an oppositional worldview—different from that of the exploiters and oppressors—that enables rhetors to look at themselves and the world around them critically and analytically. Hooks's primary rhetorical option is the development of theory that not only analyzes the ideology of domination but also suggests various ways to disrupt and transform it. The other rhetorical options she suggests are methods of disseminating the theory that is developed: enactment, confession, dialogue, cultural criticism, education, and community outreach.

Theory Development

Hooks's major rhetorical option is the conceptualization and dissemination of new theories and models that challenge and work to eradicate domination. By creating strategies, visionary models, and imaginative maps, rhetors "enable colonized folks to decolonize their minds and actions, thereby promoting the insurrection of subjugated knowledge."[141] "We must show the way," hooks asserts. "There must exist a paradigm, a practical model for social change that includes an understanding of ways to transform consciousness that are linked to efforts to transform structures."[142] Resisting oppression means more than simply reacting against one's oppressors; it also requires that rhetors envision and develop "new habits of being, different ways to live in the world."[143]

Hooks is interested in a particular kind of theory—not abstract speculation but theory that addresses "the particular circumstances" of oppressed people.[144] Hooks despairs at the absence of such theory:

> I continue to be amazed that there is so much feminist writing produced and yet so little feminist theory that strives to speak to women, men and children about ways we might transform our lives via a conversion to feminist practice. Where can we find a body of feminist theory that is directed toward helping individuals integrate feminist thinking and practice into daily life? What feminist theory, for example, is directed toward assisting women who live in sexist households in their efforts to bring about feminist change?[145]

Hooks tells of the moment when she realized that feminist theory often provides little assistance in concrete situations:

[O]ne of my sisters seeks my advice, tells me her husband orders her to shut up in front of the children, speaking with contempt and disrespect and she wants to know how to change this situation because I've told her one can resist. She says to me "you're the feminist, tell me what to do." And it takes days for me to come up with a plan of action, a strategy she can use to positively confront and change the situation.[146]

The "most visionary task of all," then, is that of theorizing for concrete situations so that "alternative, transformative models" are available for use in people's daily lives.[147] Hooks predicts that the development of this kind of practical theory greatly will increase interest in and support for feminist movement: "[M]any folks might want to convert to feminist thought if they knew firsthand the powerful and passionate positive transformation it would create in every area of their . . . lives."[148]

In order for theory to have the potential to intervene in structures of domination in people's daily lives, it must be accessible to audiences; it must be translated into forms understandable to audiences that vary in age, sex, ethnicity, and degree of literacy. "Difficulty of access has been a problem with much feminist theory," explains hooks. "A feminist essay with revolutionary ideas written in a complicated, abstract manner using the jargon of a specific discipline, will not have the impact it should have on the consciousness of women and men because it will probably be read by only a small group of people."[149]

An accessible style of writing is important not only because it allows useful ideas to be disseminated but also because it embodies an equality that challenges hierarchy and structures of domination. Work "that is difficult to comprehend" and "linguistically convoluted"[150] reinscribes the politics of domination and perpetuates elitism, for "it is indeed the purpose of such theory to divide, separate, exclude, keep at a distance."[151] If those who develop theory are sincere about wanting to reach as many people as possible, "they must either write in a more accessible manner or write in the manner of their choice and see to it that the piece is made available to others using a style that can be easily understood."[152]

Enactment

Among the rhetorical options hooks suggests for the dissemination of theory is enactment, a way in which domination is disrupted at a very personal level. Rhetors who choose the option of enactment act in nondominating, nonexploitative, nonoppressive ways of being in their own lives. Enactment is the "lived practice of interaction" in a "nondominating context"[153] so that one's life is "a living example" of one's politics:[154]

> I think that the breakthrough that came out of the feminist struggle was to actually
> see the personal, to see that if we really wanted to understand the evil of racism or
> the evil of sexism, then where we needed to see it was not just on some grand
> institutional level. We also needed to look at it right in our own lives in terms of
> who came in our doors. . . . We need to look at how we conduct ourselves in daily
> life. How we relate to other people.[155]

Thus, to arrive at a "just, more humane world," hooks asks that rhetors "be willing to courageously surrender participation in whatever sphere of coercive hierarchical domination [they] enjoy individual and group privilege."[156] She asserts: "Our lived practice, every moment of the day," should be "saying 'No!'" to the culture of domination "in some way or another."[157]

Enactment of nondomination means, for example, that individuals, particularly those from oppressed groups, "practice speaking in a loving and caring manner" to acquaintances, friends, and family members. Such "an action makes it evident to all observers" that they "deserve care, respect, and ongoing affirmation."[158] Rhetors using enactment must "create new models for interaction . . . ways of being that promote respect and reconciliation,"[159] for these new ways of being constitute acts of "political resistance" that challenge the hierarchical, competitive system that seeks to have individuals "work against one another."[160] Hooks laments those occasions when she does not practice her commitment to a nondominational way of living, as was the case in an interaction with one of her sisters:

> One day I was talking to my sister who had been having some difficulties in her life
> and I said: "I think you should get your Ph.D. and you should do this and that . . ."
> Then she said: "wait a minute, look how you are talking to me!" I then realized that
> I was trying to impose my values and my agendas on her in a way that was very
> aggressive. . . . I feel that I have to constantly work against taking in the values of
> domination and hierarchy, because they are there in every part of our mind.[161]

Confession

Confession is the telling of one's personal experience, speaking the truth of one's life, or giving testimony,[162] and it constitutes another means by which theory can be disseminated. In confession, rhetors name and give voice to their experiences and "to personal sorrow and anguish, rage, bitterness, and even deep hatred."[163] As hooks explains, confession involves telling "the past as we have learned it mouth-to-mouth, telling the present as we see, know, and feel it in our hearts and with our words."[164]

The "confessional moment"[165] has the potential to intervene in structures of domination, however, only if it is connected to a larger political framework that situates the shared experiences in a context of "structures of domination and how they function."[166] There must be a connection between the transformation of consciousness that results from the confession and the process of politicization. The self-awareness that results from the confession, hooks asserts, must be linked to "knowledge of how we must act politically to change and transform the world."[167] Without this crucial step of relating one's experience to a critical framework or using one's experience strategically, the confession is simply a narcissistic act that turns the voices and beings of rhetors into "commodity, spectacle."[168] Without the connection to the political, the self "stays in place, the starting point from which one need never move."[169]

Anita Hill's testimony at the hearings on Clarence Thomas's suitability to be a U.S. Supreme Court justice in 1991, hooks suggests, was a confession that was not linked to a larger political agenda. Hill gave detailed testimony about Thomas's sexual harassment, but she never stated an agenda for her disclosure—she did not say how his sexual harassment affected his suitability for the Court or what she wanted to have happen as a result of her confession.[170] Confession, then, can provide an important means by which rhetors can decolonize their minds only if the connection between the personal experience recounted in the confession and a larger political agenda is articulated.

Dialogue

Another option hooks sees for disseminating theory that facilitates the decolonization of the mind is dialogue, discussion, or debate. By engaging in dialectical struggle with others, rhetors are able to engage in critical self-examination, reflect on and explore their beliefs, and come to new understandings. This growth happens because others provide "concrete counter-examples" that "disrupt the seemingly fixed (yet often unstated) assumptions" that individuals hold.[171] Dialogue also facilitates growth because it allows rhetors to test out their emerging beliefs and theories on others: "In hearing responses, we come to understand whether our words act to resist, to transform, to move."[172]

If dialogue is to prompt individuals to question their own beliefs and to think more critically, it must be characterized by constructive "critical interrogation";[173] censorship has no place in the process of dialogue. Often, oppressed people who are engaged in dialogue attempt to censor dissenting voices or criticism by other oppressed individuals because they believe such dissent "will play into the hands of dominating forces and undermine support for progressive causes."[174] Others avoid dissent or criticism because they believe it constitutes betrayal of their colleagues in struggle.[175] Hooks believes, however, that criticism of the ideas of others and a willingness to accept criticism of one's own ideas are essential in dialogue because any "movement grows and matures only to the degree that it passionately welcomes and encourages, in theory and practice, diversity of opinion, new ideas, critical exchange, and dissent."[176] Repression and censorship of others' ideas simply reinscribe hierarchy and elitism by privileging some voices over others; censorship silences every bit as much as the structures of domination that silence those who challenge them. "We remember the pain of silence," hooks notes, "and work to sustain our power to speak—freely, openly, provocatively."[177]

Dialogue must occur not only with colleagues and comrades in struggle but also with "those who exploit, oppress, and dominate."[178] Engaging in dialogue with those in privileged positions opens up spaces for greater understanding of the structures of domination and how they function. Such dialogue has a function for people of privilege, as well, in that it allows them to examine their own racism, sexism, and participation in various forms of oppression. Another advantage hooks sees of such dialogue is that it is a way for oppressed people to show those who oppress what they can do to help in the struggle. Often, when oppressed people are asked by those in positions of privilege what the privileged can do to resist oppression, the oppressed respond that they "are not willing to teach them . . . to show the way."[179] Hooks responds: For the oppressed to demand "that those who benefit materially by exercising white supremacist power, either actively or passively, willingly give up that privilege in response . . . and then to refuse to show the way, is to undermine our own cause."[180] The oppressed willingly must make "contact with all who would engage [them] in a constructive manner."[181]

Hooks's admonition that the oppressed must engage in dialogue with their oppressors does not mean that people of privilege have no responsibility for examining their own beliefs or actions or for doing their own work of changing consciousness. People of privilege should not "give up their *power of knowing*" in such dialogues and ask the oppressed to do the work for them.[182] The willingness to change on the part of the privileged should be reinforced by the oppressed, who can "show the way by [their] actions, by the information [they] share."[183]

The dialogue hooks envisions as enabling growth and transformation for its participants is best practiced through the mediating force of love. By *love,* hooks does not mean a sentimental longing for another person or the domination and possession that often are linked to love. Rather, love is a politicized force that enables movement "against dehumanization, against domination."[184] It is "the idea of being able to let fear go so you can move towards another person who's not like you."[185] It is *"mutual recognition . . .* the 'subject-to-subject' encounter, as opposed to 'subject-to-object'"—a mutual give-and-take in which the individuals involved "learn to understand, appreciate, and value" the worlds and perspectives of the others.[186]

Cultural Criticism

Hooks sees the practice of cultural criticism as another rhetorical option for critical thinkers who wish to disrupt domination. Particularly powerful is criticism that focuses on issues of representation in various forms of mass media. Hooks asks that rhetors "actively enter the terrain of popular culture"[187] because the "politics of domination inform the way the vast majority of images we consume are constructed and marketed."[188] She sees representation as "a crucial location of struggle for any exploited and oppressed people asserting subjectivity and decolonization of the mind."[189]

For hooks, television and film are central texts for such analysis because they, more than any other media, determine how oppressed peoples are seen and how other groups respond to them "based on their relation to these constructed and consumed images."[190] Television and film also are critical texts for cultural criticism because they are primary tools used to socialize oppressed peoples to internalize the thoughts and values of white supremacist capitalist patriarchy. Through these media, the thoughts and values of the ideology of domination are "projected into our living rooms, into the most intimate spaces of our lives." These thoughts and values "are always with us, their voices, values, and beliefs echoing in our brains. It is this constant presence of the colonizing mindset passively consumed that undermines our capacity to resist."[191] Hooks advocates cutting "down the number of hours we watch television so that we are not subjected to forms of subliminal socialization shaping how we see the world."[192] "The time has come," she asserts, "to interrupt, intervene, and change the channel."[193]

To engage in cultural criticism of media texts requires that rhetors develop a critical gaze, moving "beyond passive consumption" to "be fiercely confronting, challenging, interrogating."[194] The kind of critique hooks envisions in the practice of cultural criticism goes beyond the "question of positive or negative representation" or whether the oppressed are portrayed in the media through good or bad images.[195] The primary tasks of the rhetor who engages in cultural criticism are to "interrogate these messages coming to us"[196] and to analyze "the complexity of what is taking place."[197] Simply because a text was created by a black person, for example, does not mean "the representations will automatically have integrity beyond anything a white person can produce";[198] such a text is not "intrinsically counter-hegemonic."[199] Nor does the mere visibility of an oppressed group in a cultural product or text "mean that images are inherently radical or progressive."[200] Simply "to portray marginalized . . . subculture is not necessarily to be giving a portrait of subversion and oppositional life."[201]

Cultural criticism involves not simply challenging and resisting particular forms of representation but also inventing new images. It must be rooted in "much deeper bases than 'in reaction to.'"[202] It also must be concerned with

> transforming the image, creating alternatives, asking ourselves questions about what types of images subvert, pose critical alternatives, and transform our worldviews and move us away from dualistic thinking about good and bad. Making a space for the transgressive image, the outlaw rebel vision, is essential to any effort to create a context for transformation.[203]

For hooks, the visual arts play a particularly important role in the process of creating new, nondominating images. Hooks acknowledges that "art does not have much of a place" in the lives of many blacks and other oppressed peoples and that many of them simply do not think about art.[204] She also recognizes that in "the cultural marketplace," art usually mirrors "institutionalized systems of domination."[205] But she believes that art created and engaged outside of formal, institutional structures of domination—art that is created and enjoyed by the oppressed in their places of work and everyday life—can function "as a force that promotes the development of critical consciousness and resistance movement."[206] Art occupies a radical place in the freedom struggle precisely because it provides a means for imagining new possibilities; it "serves as the foundation for emerging visions."[207]

Hooks provides an example of the need for art to serve as the source of new images: "It's disturbing to me that practically every black woman I know, from every social class, from all walks of life, can talk about the stereotypes of black womanhood. But when I ask these same women to name what types of images they'd like to see, they can't answer that question. That's scary."[208] Cultural critics "have to be about the business of inventing all manner of images and representations that show us the way we want to be and are," hooks asserts.[209] We "need more than merely 'positive' images—we need *challenging* images." She continues: "[W]e need some wholesale reenvisioning that's outside the realm of the merely reactionary!"[210] If "one could make a people lose touch with their capacity to create, lose sight of their will and their power to make art," hooks suggests, "then the work of subjugation, of colonization, is complete."[211]

Art is oppositional in yet another way. Aesthetic images have healing power, a healing that is oppositional for oppressed peoples in that it makes whole what the white supremacist capitalist patriarchal culture sees as inferior and inadequate. Hooks explains that

> among the traditional Southern black folks I grew up around there was a shared belief in the idea that beautiful things, objects that could be considered luxurious, that were expensive and difficult to own, were necessary for the spirit. The more

downtrodden and unfortunate the circumstances, the more "beauty" was needed to uplift, to offer a vision of hope, to transform.[212]

Art can serve as "a balm to a depressed and wounded spirit," a function that is "in every way oppositional."[213]

Cultural criticism, then, involves the rhetor in two basic processes. The first is the development of "an oppositional perspective"[214] that moves "against and beyond boundaries"[215] to provide a "critique of conventional expectations and desires,"[216] contesting all dominant forms and structures. But opposition is not enough. As hooks explains, "In that vacant space after one has resisted there is still the necessity to become—to make oneself anew." This requires the second step of inventing "new, alternative habits of being"—of presenting possibilities for a transformed future.[217]

Education

Theory dissemination also occurs through education, and hooks believes that formal education at all levels has the potential to be a site where individuals can unlearn the ideology of domination and where critical thinking can take place in the service of decolonization. Hooks sees education as "one of the few locations" where people can be inspired "to have conversion experiences away from their allegiances to the oppressive norms."[218] But "education as the practice of freedom"[219] occurs only when pedagogical practices do "not reinforce structures of domination: imperialism, racism, sexism, and class exploitation."[220] She suggests that "many professors who are progressive in their politics . . . have resolutely refused to change the nature of their pedagogical practice" and thus "perpetuate those very hierarchies and biases they are critiquing."[221]

The rhetorical option of revolutionary pedagogy requires that teachers relinquish "traditional ways of teaching that reinforce domination."[222] Such revolutionary practices might include teachers' encouragement of students to influence the agendas of their classrooms, interacting with students according to their individual needs,[223] positioning themselves as learners along with their students, and electing not to assume postures of omniscience.[224] This kind of pedagogy also means that all voices are heard in the classroom[225] and that teachers genuinely value everyone's presence.[226] The potential of education to serve as a site at which the ideology of domination can be disrupted, then, is realized only if education is practiced in nondominating ways.

Community Outreach

Hooks suggests that critical thinkers who develop theory designed to end domination engage in specific actions in the community to "concretely empower" individuals in their "everyday lives."[227] She suggests "offering women's studies courses at a local community center, YWCA, YMCA, church, etc." to disseminate information on feminism and to allow it to alter "perspectives on reality."[228] She suggests that students in women's studies at universities "go into communities and discuss feminist issues door-to-door," working to "bridge the gap between their educational experiences and the educational experiences of masses of women."[229]

Hooks would like to see institutes formed "for the study of gender and relationships in every state of the union . . . to contribute to the rebuilding of a national reality where people live more compassionately and humanely with one another."[230] Such institutes might "have workers for freedom who would go door to door and evaluate the needs of individual households and communities." A team of researchers "would then devise a plan for each household to be educated for critical consciousness in ways that would allow them to gain access to the knowledge and skills necessary to change their circumstances."[231] Hooks also advocates literacy programs as an important activity for community outreach efforts. Critical thinkers must "organize literacy training programs"[232] because the "process of decolonization and radical politicization requires literacy."[233]

Hooks is confident about the effectiveness of the various options for the development and dissemination of theory she advocates and employs to facilitate decolonization: "The programs for change sketched here are the ones that those of us who have come from the bottom, who have decolonized our minds, who have gained economic self-sufficiency, have used. We know they work. They changed our lives so that we can live fully and well."[234]

Transformations of Rhetorical Theory

Hooks's rhetorical theory is designed to disrupt and transform the white supremacist capitalist patriarchal system of domination through rhetorical options that focus on decolonization. Her efforts to emancipate through her rhetorical theory suggest alternative conceptions to a number of traditional rhetorical assumptions and constructs, including the purpose of rhetoric, the assumption of hierarchy at the heart of rhetoric, and ethos. Along with other feminist theorists, hooks introduces to traditional rhetorical theory a new rhetorical option, enactment, and lends support to the importance of the visual arts as a rhetorical option—one undertheorized and devalued in traditional rhetorical theory.

Purpose for Rhetoric

Hooks's proposed purpose for rhetoric—the function she would like rhetoric to serve for those who use it—is to facilitate the eradication of the ideology of domination that pervades Western culture. She asks that rhetoric be used to transform the culture of domination into a culture characterized by equality, mutuality, and respect. This purpose contrasts dramatically with the primary goal assumed for rhetors in traditional rhetorical theory, which is to have their own perspectives prevail—or dominate—and to accomplish their own goals, often at the expense of the achievement of the goals of others.

Thus, hooks's rhetorical options revolve around the development of critical consciousness for decolonization, which enables rhetors to recognize the ideology of domination in practice and to commit themselves to its disruption. All of the rhetorical options hooks recommends are ones that enact and embody a commitment to nondominating and nonexploitative communication as a means of creating a more humane world.

Hierarchy

Many basic rhetorical constructs and processes are built on an assumption of hierarchy as both natural and desirable. Rhetoric is to be used, for example, to ascertain which positions on issues are superior to others in the marketplace of ideas. It is used by rhetors to assert their superiority over others through such means as superior rhetorical skill; rankings of rhetors by degree of ethos or credibility they are accorded; and arguments that, because they win or prevail over other arguments, are seen as superior. In some theories of rhetoric, hierarchy is seen as the motivating principle for rhetoric, encouraging the use of rhetoric to attain higher positions on the various hierarchies in which rhetors are involved.[235] Hooks, however, rejects hierarchy as a natural, unchangeable condition and seeks to eliminate the hierarchic principle from rhetoric. She asserts that although this principle appears natural, it is not; it can be replaced with an alternative, equally viable ideology of reciprocity, community, and mutuality. A rhetoric built on these values, hooks suggests, would look significantly different from a rhetoric rooted in hierarchy.

Ethos

Hooks is particularly interested in marginal rhetors—those who produce counterhegemonic discourse from positions of marginality. Such rhetors, however, are not accorded ethos from a traditional perspective in that they do not have the qualifications that would allow them to claim mainstream credibility. But hooks sees them as possessing ethos nonetheless—a transformed ethos—in that they have insights others do not because of the dual vision afforded by their marginal status. Their ethos is not determined by the degree to which they exhibit intelligence, moral character, and goodwill but by the insights they are able to offer derived from their personal experiences. They are not underprivileged or disqualified as rhetors but, instead, are able to imagine alternatives and to create nondominating relations and cultures most easily. They are thus at the forefront in terms of their capacity to create change.

Enactment

Hooks not only transforms traditional constructs of rhetorical theory, but she proposes a rhetorical option not included in the traditional repertoire of options for rhetors: enactment. This option allows rhetors to disrupt domination at a very personal level simply by acting and engaging in rhetoric that is nondominating, nonexploitative, and nonoppressive. Enactment involves making one's life a living example of one's commitment to reciprocity and equality. It is directed not at other rhetors explicitly—although others may observe the rhetor's behavior and choose to imitate it—but primarily at rhetors' own thoughts and actions as they try to live in ways that are nondominating.

Importance of the Visual Arts

Although rhetorical theorists have been slow to study and theorize visual imagery as rhetoric, they are beginning to accept visual symbols as rhetorical, with as much influence on audiences as verbal symbols. Hooks reinforces this trend in rhetorical theory by paying particular attention to the visual arts as symbolic forms. She sees them as important because they allow oppressed individuals to imagine new possibilities and alternatives. They help rhetors move from critique and resistance to the creation of new forms and thus new worlds. They also serve the function of healing and making whole what mainstream ideology defines as inferior and inadequate, suggesting that marginalized rhetors *are* capable, wise, and competent and have the capacity to affect the world in which they live.

Hooks's transformations of rhetorical theory revise traditional constructs, offer new ones, and extend still others. Her rhetorical theory embodies her commitment to emancipation from a dominating, oppressive world and to the creation of a more humane world. Hers is a rhetorical theory that provides means for emancipation for all rhetors: "That is why we want to share the liberatory power of . . . self-determination. Our freedom is sweet. It will be sweeter when we are all free."[236]

Bibliography

Books

hooks, bell. *Ain't I a Woman: Black Women and Feminism.* Boston: South End, 1981.
hooks, bell. *Art on My Mind: Visual Politics.* New York: New Press, 1995.

hooks, bell. *Black Looks: Race and Representation.* Boston: South End, 1992.

hooks, bell. *Bone Black: Memories of Girlhood.* New York: Henry Holt, 1996.

hooks, bell. *Feminist Theory: From Margin to Center.* Boston: South End, 1984.

hooks, bell. *Killing Rage: Ending Racism.* New York: Henry Holt, 1995.

hooks, bell. *Outlaw Culture: Resisting Representations.* New York: Routledge, 1994.

hooks, bell. *Reel to Real: Race, Sex, and Class at the Movies.* New York: Routledge, 1996.

hooks, bell. *Sisters of the Yam: Black Women and Self-Recovery.* Boston: South End, 1993.

hooks, bell. *Talking Back: Thinking Feminist, Thinking Black.* Boston: South End, 1989.

hooks, bell. *Teaching to Transgress: Education as the Practice of Freedom.* New York: Routledge, 1994.

hooks, bell. *A Woman's Mourning Song.* New York: Harlem River, 1993.

hooks, bell. *Wounds of Passion: A Writing Life.* New York: Henry Holt, 1997.

hooks, bell. *Yearning: Race, Gender, and Cultural Politics.* Boston: South End, 1990.

hooks, bell, and Cornel West. *Breaking Bread: Insurgent Black Intellectual Life.* Boston: South End, 1991.

Articles

Barlow, John Perry, and bell hooks. "An Intimate Conversation." *Shambhala Sun* 4 (1995): 60-67, 72.

Galas, Diamanda, and bell hooks. "Standing at the Crossroads: A Conversation between Diamanda Galas and bell hooks." *Village Voice* 20 Sept. 1994: 15-18.

hooks, bell. "Aesthetic Intervention." *Emma Amos: Changing the Subject: Paintings and Prints, 1992-1994.* By Emma Amos. New York: Art in General, 1994. 5-12. Rpt. as "Aesthetic Interventions." *Art on My Mind: Visual Politics.* By bell hooks. New York: New, 1995. 163-70.

hooks, bell. "An Aesthetic of Blackness: Strange and Oppositional." *Women, Creativity, and the Arts: Critical and Autobiographical Perspectives.* Ed. Diane Apostolos-Cappadona and Lucinda Ebersole. New York: Continuum, 1995. 75-86. Rpt. from *Yearning: Race, Gender, and Cultural Politics.* By bell hooks. Boston: South End, 1990. 103-13.

hooks, bell. "Altars of Sacrifice: Re-membering Basquiat." *Art in America* 81 (1993): 68-75, 117. Rpt. in *Outlaw Culture: Resisting Representations.* By bell hooks. New York: Routledge, 1994. 25-37; and *Art on My Mind: Visual Politics.* By bell hooks. New York: New, 1995. 35-48.

hooks, bell. "Bell Hooks Speaking about Paulo Freire—the Man, His Work." *Paulo Freire: A Critical Encounter.* Ed. Peter McLaren and Peter Leonard. New York: Routledge, 1993. 146-54. Rpt. in *Teaching to Transgress: Education as the Practice of Freedom.* By bell hooks. New York: Routledge, 1994. 45-58.

hooks, bell. "Black Is a Woman's Color." *Bearing Witness.* Ed. Henry Louis Gates Jr. New York: Pantheon, 1991. 338-48.

hooks, bell. "Black Woman Artist Becoming." *Life Notes: Personal Writings by Contemporary Black Women*. Ed. Patricia Bell-Scott. New York: W. W. Norton, 1994. 181-89.

hooks, bell. "Black Women: Constructing the Revolutionary Subject." *An American Half-Century: Postwar Culture and Politics in the USA*. Ed. Michael Klein. Boulder, CO: Pluto, 1994. 172-91.

hooks, bell. "Black Women Writing: Creating More Space." *Sage* 2 (1985): 44-46. Rpt. in *Talking Back: Thinking Feminist, Thinking Black*. By bell hooks. Boston: South End, 1989. 142-47.

hooks, bell. "Breaking the Silence between Mothers and Daughters." *Sage* 1 (1984): 28-29.

hooks, bell. "Carrie Mae Weems: Diasporic Landscapes of Longing." *Inside the Visible: An Elliptical Traverse of 20th Century Art: In, of, and from the Feminine*. Ed. M. Catherine de Zegher. Cambridge: MIT P, 1996. 173-78. Rpt. in *Art on My Mind: Visual Politics*. By bell hooks. New York: New, 1995. 65-73.

hooks, bell. "Challenging Men." *Sparerib* 217 (1990): 12-15.

hooks, bell. "Challenging Patriarchy Means Challenging Men to Change." *Z Magazine* 4 (1991): 33-36.

hooks, bell. "Choosing the Margin as a Space of Radical Openness." *Women, Knowledge, and Reality: Explorations in Feminist Philosophy*. Ed. Ann Garry and Marilyn Pearsall. 2nd ed. New York: Routledge, 1996. 48-55. Rpt. from *Yearning: Race, Gender, and Cultural Politics*. By bell hooks. Boston: South End, 1990. 145-53.

hooks, bell. "Critical Reflections." *Artforum* 33 (1994): 64-65, 100.

hooks, bell. "Critical Reflections: Adrienne Kennedy, the Writer, the Work." *Intersecting Boundaries: The Theatre of Adrienne Kennedy*. Ed. Paul K. Bryant-Jackson and Lois More Overbeck. Minneapolis: U of Minnesota P, 1992. 179-85.

hooks, bell. "Culture to Culture: Ethnography and Cultural Studies as Critical Intervention." *Rhetoric: Concepts, Definitions, Boundaries*. Ed. William A. Covino and David A. Jolliffe. Boston: Allyn & Bacon, 1995. 328-35.

hooks, bell. "Dissident Heat: Fire with Fire." *"Bad Girls," "Good Girls": Women, Sex, and Power in the Nineties*. Ed. Nan Bauer Maglin and Donna Perry. New Brunswick, NJ: Rutgers UP, 1996. 57-64. Rpt. from *Outlaw Culture: Resisting Representations*. By bell hooks. New York: Routledge, 1994. 91-100.

hooks, bell. "Doing It for Daddy." *Constructing Masculinity*. Ed. Maurice Berger, Brian Wallis, and Simon Watson. New York: Routledge, 1995. 98-106. Rpt. as "Doing It for Daddy: Black Masculinity in the Mainstream." *Reel to Real: Race, Sex, and Class at the Movies*. By bell hooks. New York: Routledge, 1996. 83-90.

hooks, bell. "Eating the Other: Desire and Resistance from *Black Looks: Race and Representation*." *Forbidden Passages: Writings Banned in Canada*. Ed. Pat Califia and Janine Fuller. San Francisco: Cleis, 1995. 130-47. Rpt. from *Black Looks: Race and Representation*. By bell hooks. Boston: South End, 1992. 21-39.

hooks, bell. "Ending Female Sexual Oppression." *Women's Studies: Essential Readings*. Ed. Stevi Jackson, Karen Atkinson, Deirdre Beddoe, Teri Brewer, Sue Faulkner, Anthea Hucklesby, Rose Pearson, Helen Power, Jane Prince, Michele Ryan, and Pauline Young. Washington Square: New York UP, 1993. 245. Rpt. (shortened version) from *Feminist Theory: From Margin to Center.* By bell hooks. Boston: South End, 1984. 147-56.

hooks, bell. "Eros, Eroticism and the Pedagogical Process." *Cultural Studies* 7 (1993): 58-63. Rpt. in *Teaching to Transgress: Education as the Practice of Freedom.* By bell hooks. New York: Routledge, 1994. 191-99.

hooks, bell. "Expertease: Bell Hooks on Cultural Interrogations." *Artforum* 27 (1989): 18-20.

hooks, bell. "Feminism and Black Women's Studies." *Sage* 6 (1989): 54-56.

hooks, bell. "Feminism and Racism: The Struggle Continues." *Z Magazine* 3 (1990): 41-43.

hooks, bell. "Feminism: A Transformational Politic." *I Am Because We Are: Readings in Black Philosophy.* Ed. Fred Lee Hord (Mzee Lasana Okpara) and Jonathan Scott Lee. Amherst: U of Massachusetts P, 1995. 329-37. Rpt. from *Talking Back: Thinking Feminist, Thinking Black.* By bell hooks. Boston: South End, 1989. 19-27.

hooks, bell. "Feminism: Crying for Our Souls." *Feminist Foremothers in Women's Studies, Psychology, and Mental Health.* Ed. Phyllis Chesler, Esther D. Rothblum, and Ellen Cole. New York: Haworth, 1995. 265-71.

hooks, bell. "Feminism Inside: Toward a Black Body Politic." *Black Male: Representations of Masculinity in Contemporary American Art.* Ed. Thelma Golden. New York: Whitney Museum of American Art, 1994. 127-40.

hooks, bell. "From Scepticism to Feminism." *Women's Review of Books* 7 (1990): 29.

hooks, bell. "Future Feminist Movements." *Off Our Backs* 20 (1990): 9.

hooks, bell. "Girls Together: Sustained Sisterhood." *Sister to Sister: Women Write about the Unbreakable Bond.* Ed. Patricia Foster. New York: Anchor-Doubleday, 1995. 161-69.

hooks, bell. "The Hill-Thomas Hearing." *Artforum* 31 (1992): 13-14.

hooks, bell. "In Our Glory: Photography and Black Life." *Picturing Us: African American Identity in Photography.* Ed. Deborah Willis. New York: New, 1994. 42-53. Rpt. in *Art on My Mind: Visual Politics.* By bell hooks. New York: New, 1995. 54-64.

hooks, bell. "Keeping a Legacy of Shared Struggle." *Blacks and Jews: Alliances and Arguments.* Ed. Paul Berman. New York: Delacorte, 1994. 229-38. Rpt. in *Killing Rage: Ending Racism.* By bell hooks. New York: Henry Holt, 1995. 204-14.

hooks, bell. "Keeping Close to Home: Class and Education." *Working-Class Women in the Academy: Laborers in the Knowledge Factory.* Ed. Michelle M. Tokarczyk and Elizabeth A. Fay. Amherst: U of Massachusetts P, 1993. 99-111. Rpt. from *Talking Back: Thinking Feminist, Thinking Black.* By bell hooks. Boston: South End, 1989. 73-83.

hooks, bell. "Let Freedom Ring." *Why L.A. Happened: Implications of the '92 Los Angeles Rebellion.* Ed. Haki R. Madhubuti. Chicago: Third World, 1993. 241-46.

hooks, bell. "Lorna Simpson: *Waterbearer.*" *Artforum* 32 (1993): 136-37. Rpt. (expanded version) as "Facing Difference: The Black Female Body." *Art on My Mind: Visual Politics.* By bell hooks. New York: New, 1995. 94-100.

hooks, bell. "Marginality as Site of Resistance." *Out There: Marginalization and Contemporary Cultures.* Ed. Russell Ferguson, Martha Gever, Trinh T. Minh-ha, and

Cornel West. New York: New Museum of Contemporary Art; Cambridge: MIT P, 1990. 341-43.

hooks, bell. "Men in Feminist Struggle: The Necessary Movement." *Women Respond to the Men's Movement: A Feminist Collection.* Ed. Kay Leigh Hagan. San Francisco: HarperCollins, 1992. 111-17.

hooks, bell. "Micheaux: Celebrating Blackness." *Black American Literature Forum* 25 (1991): 351-60. Rpt. as "Micheaux's Films: Celebrating Blackness." *Black Looks: Race and Representation.* By bell hooks. Boston: South End, 1992. 133-43.

hooks, bell. "The Oppositional Gaze: Black Female Spectators." *Black American Cinema.* Ed. Manthia Diawara. New York: Routledge, 1993. 288-302. Rpt. from *Black Looks: Race and Representation.* By bell hooks. Boston: South End, 1992. 115-31; and in *Reel to Real: Race, Sex, and Class at the Movies.* By bell hooks. New York: Routledge, 1996. 197-213.

hooks, bell. "Performance Practice as a Site of Opposition." *The Politics of Black Performance.* Ed. Catherine Ugwu. Seattle: Bay, 1995. 210-21.

hooks, bell. "Plantation Mistress or Soul Sister?" *Signs of Life in the U.S.A.: Readings on Popular Culture for Writers.* Ed. Sonia Maasik and Jack Solomon. 2nd ed. Boston: Bedford, 1997. 223-30.

hooks, bell. "Point of View: Black Students Who Reject Feminism." *Chronicle of Higher Education* 13 July 1994: A44.

hooks, bell. "Postmodern Blackness." *A Postmodern Reader.* Ed. Joseph Natoli and Linda Hutcheon. Albany: State U of New York P, 1993. 510-18. Rpt. from *Yearning: Race, Gender, and Cultural Politics.* By bell hooks. Boston: South End, 1990. 23-31; in *Colonial Discourse and Post-Colonial Theory: A Reader.* Ed. Patrick Williams and Laura Chrisman. New York: Columbia UP, 1994. 421-27; and *The Truth about the Truth: De-Confusing and Re-Constructing the Postmodern World.* Ed. Walter Truett Anderson. New York: Jeremy P. Tarcher/Putnam, 1995. 117-24.

hooks, bell. "Power to the Pussy: We Don't Wannabe Dicks in Drag." *Madonnarama: Essays on Sex and Popular Culture.* Ed. Lisa Frank and Paul Smith. San Francisco: Cleis, 1993. 65-80. Rpt. in *Outlaw Culture: Resisting Representations.* By bell hooks. New York: Routledge, 1994. 9-23.

hooks, bell. "Pulp the Hype: On the QT: Cool Tool." *Artforum* 33 (1995): 63. Rpt. (expanded version) as "Cool Cynicism: *Pulp Fiction.*" *Reel to Real: Race, Sex, and Class at the Movies.* By bell hooks. New York: Routledge, 1996. 47-51.

hooks, bell. "Reading and Resistance: *The Color Purple.*" *Alice Walker: Critical Perspectives Past and Present.* Ed. Henry Louis Gates Jr. and K. A. Appiah. New York: Amistad, 1993. 284-95.

hooks, bell. "Reflections of a 'Good' Daughter." *Double Stitch: Black Women Write about Mothers and Daughters.* Ed. Patricia Bell-Scott, Beverly Guy-Sheftall, Jacqueline Jones Royster, Janet Sims-Wood, Miriam DeCosta-Willis, and Lucie Fultz. Boston: Beacon, 1991. 149-51.

hooks, bell. "Representing Whiteness in the Black Imagination." *Cultural Studies.* Ed. Lawrence Grossberg, Cary Nelson, and Paula A. Treichler. New York: Routledge, 1992. 338-46. Rpt. as "Representations of Whiteness in the Black Imagination." *Killing Rage: Ending Racism.* By bell hooks. New York: Henry Holt, 1995. 31-50.

hooks, bell. "Roundtable Discussion: Christian Ethics and Theology in Womanist Perspective: Bell Hooks." *Journal of Feminist Studies in Religion* 5 (1989): 102-04.

hooks, bell. "Seduced by Violence No More." *Transforming a Rape Culture.* Ed. Emilie Buchwald, Pamela R. Fletcher, and Martha Roth. Minneapolis: Milkweed, 1993. 353-56. Rpt. in *Outlaw Culture: Resisting Representations.* By bell hooks. New York: Routledge, 1994. 109-13; and *Debating Sexual Correctness: Pornography, Sexual Harassment, Date Rape, and the Politics of Sexual Equality.* Ed. Adele M. Stan. New York: Delta, 1995. 231-35.

hooks, bell. "Seductive Sexualities: Representing Blackness in Poetry and on Screen." *American Feminist Thought at Century's End: A Reader.* Ed. Linda S. Kauffman. Cambridge, MA: Blackwell, 1993. 65-72. Rpt. from *Yearning: Race, Gender, and Cultural Politics.* By bell hooks. Boston: South End, 1990. 193-201.

hooks, bell. "Sisterhood: Political Solidarity between Women." *Feminism and Community.* Ed. Penny A. Weiss and Marilyn Friedman. Philadelphia: Temple UP, 1995. 293-315. Rpt. from *Feminist Theory: From Margin to Center.* By bell hooks. Boston: South End, 1984. 43-65.

hooks, bell. "Sorrowful Black Death Is Not a Hot Ticket." *Sight and Sound* 4 (1994): 10-14.

hooks, bell. "Subversive Beauty: New Modes of Contestation." *Felix Gonzalez-Torres.* Ed. Russell Ferguson. Los Angeles: Museum of Contemporary Art, 1994. 45-49. Rpt. in *Art on My Mind: Visual Politics.* By bell hooks. New York: New, 1995. 49-53.

hooks, bell. "Talking Back." *Discourse* 8 (1986-87): 123-28. Rpt. in *Talking Back: Thinking Feminist, Thinking Black.* By bell hooks. Boston: South End, 1989. 5-9; *Making Face, Making Soul/Haciendo Caras: Creative and Critical Perspectives by Feminists of Color.* Ed. Gloria Anzaldúa. San Francisco: Aunt Lute, 1990. 207-11; and *Out There: Marginalization and Contemporary Cultures.* Ed. Russell Ferguson, Martha Gever, Trinh T. Minh-ha, and Cornel West. New York: New Museum of Contemporary Art; Cambridge: MIT P, 1990. 337-40.

hooks, bell. "Theory as Liberatory Practice." *Yale Journal of Law and Feminism* 4 (1991): 1-12. Rpt. (shortened version) in *Ms.* July/Aug. 1992: 80-82; (shortened version) as "'Out of the Academy and into the Streets.'" *Getting There: The Movement toward Gender Equality.* Ed. Diana Wells. New York: Carroll & Graf/Richard Gallen, 1994. 191-97; and *Teaching to Transgress: Education as the Practice of Freedom.* By bell hooks. New York: Routledge, 1994. 59-75.

hooks, bell. "'This Is the Oppressor's Language/Yet I Need It to Talk to You': Language, a Place of Struggle." *Between Languages and Cultures: Translation and Cross-Cultural Texts.* Ed. Anuradha Dingwaney and Carol Maier. Pittsburgh: U of Pittsburgh P, 1995. 295-301. Rpt. in "Language: Teaching New Worlds/New Words." *Teaching to Transgress: Education as the Practice of Freedom.* By bell hooks. New York: Routledge, 1994. 167-75.

hooks, bell. "Violence in Intimate Relationships." *Family Matters: Readings on Family Lives and the Law.* Ed. Martha Minow. New York: New, 1993. 200-05. Rpt. from *Talking Back: Thinking Feminist, Thinking Black.* By bell hooks. Boston: South End, 1989. 84-91.

hooks, bell. "Waking Up to Racism." *Tricycle: The Buddhist Review* 4 (1994): 42-45.

hooks, bell. "Wounds of Passion." *Ms.* Mar./Apr. 1998: 56-60.
hooks, bell. "Writing from the Darkness." *Tri-Quarterly* 75 (1989): 71-77.
hooks, bell, Gloria Steinem, Urvashi Vaid, and Naomi Wolf. "Let's Get Real about Feminism: The Backlash, the Myths, the Movement." *Ms.* Sept./Oct. 1993: 34-43.
hooks, bell, and Cornel West. "Insurgent Black Intellectual Life: bell hooks and Cornel West Break Bread." *Off Our Backs* 23 (1993): 1-3.
West, Cornel, and bell hooks. "Breaking Bread: A Dialogue among Communities in Search of Common Ground." *The New American Crisis: Radical Analyses of the Problems Facing America Today.* Ed. Greg Ruggiero and Stuart Sahulka. New York: New, 1995. 224-38.

Interviews

Carroll, Rebecca. "Bell Hooks Unplugged." *Elle* Dec. 1994: 78, 80, 81.
Cooper, Desiree. "Bourgeois Feminism: Bell Hooks on Why We Aren't All Sisters under the Skin." *Columbus Guardian* [Ohio] 8 Sept. 1994: 15.
Gilroy, Paul. "A Dialogue with Bell Hooks." *Small Acts: Thoughts on the Politics of Black Cultures.* Ed. Paul Gilroy. New York: Serpent's Tail, 1993. 208-36.
Jones, Lisa. "Sister Knowledge." *Essence* May 1995: 187, 188, 190, 256, 258.
Juno, Andrea, and V. Vale. "Bell Hooks." *Angry Women* 13 (1991): 78-97.
Lutz, Helma. "Feminist Theory in Practice: An Interview with Bell Hooks: Encounter with an Impressive Female Academic Fighter against Multiple Forms of Oppression." *Women's Studies International Forum* 16 (1993): 419-25.
Olson, Gary A. "Bell Hooks and the Politics of Literacy: A Conversation." *Journal of Advanced Composition* 14 (1994): 1-19. Rpt. in *Philosophy, Rhetoric, Literary Criticism: (Inter)views.* Ed. Gary A. Olson. Carbondale: Southern Illinois UP, 1994. 81-111; and (expanded version) Olson, Gary A., and Elizabeth Hirsh. "Feminist *Praxis* and the Politics of Literacy: A Conversation with Bell Hooks." *Women Writing Culture.* Ed. Gary A. Olson and Elizabeth Hirsh. Albany: State U of New York P, 1995. 105-37.
Sischy, Ingrid. "Bell Hooks." *Interview* 25 (1995): 122-27.
Trend, David. "Representation and Resistance: An Interview with Bell Hooks." *Socialist Review* 24 (1994): 115-28. Rpt. as "Representation and Democracy: An Interview." *Radical Democracy: Identity, Citizenship, and the State.* Ed. David Trend. New York: Routledge, 1996. 229-36.

CHAPTER 5

Gloria Anzaldúa

I am a wind-swayed bridge, a crossroads inhabited by whirlwinds. Gloria, the facilitator. Gloria the mediator, straddling the walls between abysses. "Your allegiance is to La Raza, the Chicano movement," say the members of my race. "Your allegiance is to the Third World," say my Black and Asian friends. "Your allegiance is to your gender, to women," say the feminists. Then there's my allegiance to the Gay movement, to the socialist revolution, to the New Age, to magic and the occult. What am I? *A third world lesbian feminist with Marxist and mystic leanings.* They would chop me up into little fragments and tag each piece with a label.[1]

NOTE: Excerpts from *Borderlands/La Frontera: The New Mestiza,* © 1987 by Gloria Anzaldúa, and from *Making Face, Making Soul/Haciendo Caras: Creative and Critical Perspectives by Feminists of Color,* © 1990 by Gloria Anzaldúa, are reprinted by permission of Aunt Lute Books.

Gloria Evanjelina Anzaldúa's purpose for writing is to understand and articulate her experiences as a *mestiza,* situated between cultures. Efforts to define her own place within this space have led her to theorize living in the margins or Borderlands, a location that offers various "crossings" or possibilities for communicating across boundaries and cultures.

Anzaldúa was born in Hargill, a Mexican community on the Rio Grande in South Texas on September 26, 1942, to a Mexican mother, Amalia García Anzaldúa, and an Anglo father, Urbano Anzaldúa. Her mother was only 16 when she gave birth to Anzaldúa, the first of four children. Her father was a sharecropper, working a succession of corporate farms, and Anzaldúa carries especially strong memories of the chicken farm, with "the white feathers of three thousand Leghorn chickens blanketing the land for acres around."[2] As a sharecropper, her father was loaned seed and living expenses to be repaid "at harvest time," when her father "forked over 40% of the earnings. Sometimes we earned less than we owed," Anzaldúa explains, "but always the corporations fared well."[3]

Always subsisting, the family found that survival became even more tenuous after Anzaldúa's father died of a heart attack at the age of 38. Anzaldúa was 15 years old at the time, and her father's death was a transformative experience for her; it shattered not only her innocence but "the myth that there existed a male figure" to look after her:

> Nobody's going to save you
> No one's going to cut you down
> cut the thorns around you.
> No one's going to storm
> the castle walls nor
> kiss awake your birth,
> climb down your hair,
> nor mount you
> onto the white steed.
>
> There is no one who
> will feed the yearning.
> Face it. You will have
> to do, do it yourself.[4]
>
> (used by permission of Gloria Anzaldúa)

Growing up, Anzaldúa felt as if she were "not of this earth. An alien from another planet—I'd been dropped on my mother's lap."[5] Her feelings of difference stemmed from several sources. She started menstruating at the age of three months and had breasts by the age of seven, a source of embarrassment and shame to both Anzaldúa and her mother: "This, the deep dark secret between us, her punishment for having fucked before the wedding ceremony, my punishment for being born."[6] Her dark skin was another sign of difference; Anzaldúa remembers the refrain of her fair-skinned grandmother and mother: "Don't go out in the sun. . . . If you get any darker, they'll mistake you for an Indian."[7] Furthermore, she was highly intelligent—"a dumb Mexican who was smart"[8]—which also set her apart because such intelligence was not expected by her Anglo teachers.

But perhaps most important as a source of difference was Anzaldúa's behavior. She was rebellious, a quality her mother had not anticipated: "What my mother wanted in return for having birthed me and for nurturing me was that I submit to her without rebellion. . . . She objected not so much to my disobedience but to my questioning her right to demand obedience from me."[9] Anzaldúa remembers having a strong sense of who she was from a very early age: "I had a stubborn will." She describes trying "constantly to mobilize my soul under my own regime, to live life on my own terms no matter how unsuitable to others they were. . . . Every bit of self-faith I'd painstakingly gathered took a beating daily. Nothing in my culture approved of me."[10] That Anzaldúa made a deliberate choice to become a lesbian was additional evidence of her rebelliousness and further separated her from her culture of origin:

> I knew who was getting the strokes and who was getting the slaps; the boys would always be privileged. . . . As a thinking woman, I looked at the model of the heterosexual couple. I would never be able to stand putting up with that kind of shit from a man. Or if I did put up with it I would be very ashamed of myself and feel very bad about myself.
> So the only viable choice for me was lesbianism.[11]

Reading and storytelling were Anzaldúa's mechanisms for coping with her differences as a child. She recalls that from the moment her father dropped a 25-cent pocket Western into her lap, "the act of reading forever changed me."[12] She retreated into books and stories, reading in bed under the covers and making up stories to tell her sister to keep her from revealing Anzaldúa's "self-imposed insomnia."[13] This retreat into books proved the starting point of her life's work as a writer, poet, teacher, and cultural theorist.

The first person in six generations to leave the valley in which she was raised,[14] Anzaldúa attended the Pan-American University at Edinburg, Texas, where she earned a B.A. in English, art, and education in 1969. She received her M.A. in literature and education in 1973 from the University of Texas at Austin, and she currently is pursuing a Ph.D. in literature at the University of California at Santa Cruz. Anzaldúa's academic career has included teaching high school English in migrant, adult, and bilingual programs in Texas. She also has taught creative writing, Chicana/o studies, and feminist studies at the University of Texas at Austin; at San Francisco State University; at Vermont College of Norwich University in Montpelier, Vermont; and at the University of California at Santa Cruz.

Anzaldúa's primary identity, however, is as a writer: "I cannot separate my writing from any part of my life. It is all one."[15] She sees writing as a means of "managing the universe and its energies" and believes that writing transforms "the storyteller and the listener into something or someone."[16] This transformative function of writing is the subject of much of her work. Her first book, *This Bridge Called My Back* (1981), coedited with Cherríe Moraga, won a Before Columbus Foundation American Book Award. It addresses issues of feminist revolution from the perspectives of women of color and includes sections on the roots of radicalism for women of color, how women of color derive feminist political theories from their racial and cultural backgrounds, and the use of writing as a tool for self-preservation and revolution by women of color. Anzaldúa and Moraga also identify the destructive and demoralizing effects of racism in the women's movement and the cultural, class, and sexual differences that divide women of color, offering "an uncompromised definition of feminism by women of color in the U.S." as part of a process of creating a feminist future.[17]

Anzaldúa is also the author of *Borderlands/La Frontera: The New Mestiza* (1987), in which she describes the historical, mythic, and personal journey of generations who, like herself, inhabited and continue to inhabit the border between Mexico and the United States. She explores the Borderlands, using her own experiences as a starting point—as part of an "almost instinctive urge to communicate, to speak, to write about life on the borders, life in the shadows."[18]

Anzaldúa's next book, *Making Face, Making Soul/Haciendo Caras: Creative and Critical Perspectives by Feminists of Color* (1990), is an edited volume that Anzaldúa considers an extension of the theorizing that began in *This Bridge Called My Back*. Designed to explore the masks others have imposed, it serves to make "accessible to others our struggle with all our identities, our linkage-making strategies and our healing of broken limbs."[19] For Anzaldúa, this anthology operationalizes ways in which women of color "see through the disguises we hide behind and drop our *personas* so that we may become subjects in our own discourses."[20] Ultimately, *Making Face* is designed to "deepen the dialogue between all women" and to "take on the various issues—hindrances and possibilities—in alliance-building."[21]

Anzaldúa's poetry, which she integrates throughout her prose, also has appeared in numerous anthologies and journals. In addition, she is the author of two bilingual children's stories. *Friends from the Other Side/Amigos del otro lado* (1993) is the story of a Mexican American girl, Prietita, and Joaquin, a Mexican boy who crosses the Rio Grande into Texas in search of a better life. Prietita protects Joaquin from the taunts of *mojado* by neighborhood children as well as from the Border Patrol. *Prietita and the Ghost Woman/Prietita y La Llorona* (1995) is the tale of Prietita and her encounter with the historical and mystical figure La Llorona, who haunts the night in search of her lost children.

Anzaldúa's writing has been acknowledged formally in a variety of ways, including a National Endowment for the Arts Award for Fiction in 1991, a Lesbian Rights Award in 1991, and the Sappho Award of Distinction in 1992. In addition, she has served on the editorial boards of various journals, including *Sinister Wisdom, Frontiers,* and *Bridge.* Anzaldúa also has been a writer-in-residence at the Loft in Minneapolis, Minnesota, and was granted a MacDowell Artist Colony Fellowship in 1982. More recently, she was an artist-in-residence at Pomona College in California, where she collaborated with four other Latina artists and writers from Mexico and the United States—Santa Barraza, Cristina Luna, Liliana Wilson Grez, and Isabel Juárez Espinosa—to produce a series of public programs and an exhibition. Called "Entre Américas: El Taller Nepantla," the exhibition was mounted in 1995 at the San José Center for Latino Arts.

Anzaldúa's work continues to be concerned with the boundaries constructed by and the bridges across cultures. She is a personal witness to the Borderlands as well as a voice for the full expression of the contradictions that constitute every Borderlands identity: "I will no longer be made to feel ashamed of existing. I will have my voice: Indian, Spanish, white. I will have my serpent's tongue—my woman's voice, my sexual voice, my poet's voice. I will overcome the tradition of silence."[22]

Nature of the World

The nature of the world Anzaldúa envisions consists of a continuum from Borderlands to *nepantla* to *mestiza* consciousness. Starting with a literal geographic Borderlands—the border between the United States and Mexico—she first describes a world of cultural tension and clash. Next is *nepantla,* an Aztec word that means "torn between ways"; this term emphasizes Borderlands as an ongoing, evolving process rather than a static state, condition, or place. Third is the *mestiza* consciousness, a perspective ideally suited to a world in which everyone lives in Borderlands. At the same time that she describes each of these layers or states of being, she also suggests stances that inhabitants of the Borderlands take toward that world—various means of *haciendo caras,* or making face, that move from coping with cultural clash to negotiating face in interaction with the dominant culture to assuming self-defined agency.

The Borderlands

The impetus for the notion of the Borderlands—the first dimension in Anzaldúa's continuum—was her own experiences as a *mestiza,* or a woman of mixed blood, living literally on the border between the Mexican and Anglo cultures. The collision of cultures led her to formulate the concept of the Borderlands as an in-between state in which there is pain but also the possibility for synthesis: "The U.S.-Mexican border *es una herida abierta* [an open wound] where the Third World grates against the first and bleeds. And before a scab forms it hemorrhages again, the lifeblood of two worlds merging to form a third country—a border culture."[23]

Anzaldúa does not limit her consideration of Borderlands only to the literal U.S.-Mexican border, however. She enlarges the concept beyond its geographic meaning by distinguishing between *borderlands* with a small *b* and *Borderlands* with a capital *B*. Written lowercase, the word refers to a geographic site—the "actual southwest borderlands or any borderlands between two cultures." When she capitalizes it, however, she is using it as "metaphor, not actuality" to refer to a state that exists whenever cultural differences exist, whether those cultures involve physical differences such as race, class, or gender or differences that are less tangible—psychological, social, or cultural.[24] Anzaldúa's own Borderlands are not limited, for example, to her Mexican and American identities; she describes herself as caught as well between the worlds of lesbian and straight, between First World and Third World, between working class and middle class, and even between literary genres, combining as she does poetry and prose.

For the inhabitants of Borderlands—whether geographic, cultural, or psychological—the most salient feature is disorientation caused by the constant clash of different cultures, which often are the result of arbitrary boundaries: "Borders are set up to define the places that are safe and unsafe, to distinguish *us* from *them.* A border is a dividing line, a narrow strip along a steep edge. A borderland is a vague and undetermined place created by the emotional residue of an unnatural boundary. It is in a constant state of transition."[25] Anzaldúa uses the image of living on the equator to explain how oppositional competing cultures can be: "North of the equator the water flows clockwise, south of the equator it flows counterclockwise—two radically different perspectives, two different conocimientos, two different world views. We on the equator are pulled in different directions."[26]

For Anzaldúa, the constant disorientation of the Borderlands—and its accompanying ambivalence, indecisiveness, insecurity, and perplexity—is captured in the phrase *psychic restlessness.*[27] Life at the borders and in margins is characterized by efforts to keep "intact one's shifting and multiple identity and integrity"; it is like "trying to swim in a new element, an 'alien' element."[28] The metaphor she uses for the feeling of disorientation is a wound:

> 1,950 mile-long open wound
> dividing a *pueblo,* a culture,
> running down the length of my body,
> staking fence rods in my flesh,
>   splits me   splits me
>   *me raja*   *me raja*
> This is my home
> this thin edge of
>   barbwire.[29]

The psychic restlessness imposed by the Borderlands is compounded by the silencing of its inhabitants. Several processes work together to deny or inhibit the voices of those who reside in the Borderlands. Inhabitants often silence themselves by their own processes of self-abnegation. The conflicting demands of the Borderlands, combined with the tendency to internalize the conflicts they produce, often result in feelings of worthlessness. Anzaldúa summarizes this feeling when she says, "I have so internalized the borderland conflict that sometimes I feel like one cancels out the other and we are zero, nothing, no one."[30]

Another form of silencing imposed upon those in the Borderlands results from the refusal of the dominant culture to take seriously the perspectives of those marginalized; their voices are like faint echoes, always submerged within dominant culture. Anzaldúa selects the image of an abyss to describe this form of silencing:

> We cross or fall or are shoved into abysses whether we speak or remain silent. And when we do speak from the cracked spaces, it is *con voz del fondo del abismo* [with a voice from the depths of the abyss], a voice drowned out by white noise, distance and the distancing by others who don't want to hear. We are besieged by a "silence that hollows us."[31]

Inhabitants of the Borderlands, then, are denied authentic voice by the dominant culture.

That those in the Borderlands must choose a singular identity from which to speak—to privilege only one of their multiple identities—probably constitutes the most powerful means of silencing them, however: "When we come into possession of a voice, we sometimes have to choose with which voice (the voice of the dyke, the Chicana, the professor, the master), in which voice (first person, third, vernacular, formal), or in which language (Black English, Tex-Mex, Spanish, academese) to speak and write in."[32] Anzaldúa suggests that the need to compartmentalize or dichotomize the self is a characteristic of the dominant culture that is particularly problematic for those at the borders: "Who, me confused? Ambivalent? Not so. Only your labels split me."[33]

Anzaldúa constructs a stance for those struggling with the tensions of the Borderlands with the phrase *haciendo caras* (making faces).[34] Those in the Borderlands are asked to construct faces that make accommodations to the dominant culture. In this sense, *haciendo caras* suggests a process of putting on a mask to hide true identity, buying into the social structures inscribed by the dominant culture—structures "marked with instructions on how to be *mujer, macho,* working class, Chicana."[35] Anzaldúa cites Mitsuye Yamada to summarize the accommodation process of coping with the dominant culture: "Over my mask/is your mask of me. . . . My mask is control/concealment/endurance/my mask is escape/from my/self."[36] Those in the margins have had to learn how to "'change' faces"—to "acquire the ability, like a chameleon, to change color when the dangers are many and the options few." They have been forced "to adopt a face that would pass."[37]

Anzaldúa's discussion of the Borderlands as the starting point for her worldview focuses largely on the tensions, distortions, accommodations, and denials of identity that characterize inhabitants of the Borderlands. At the same time, she suggests that paradigms that demand a unified identity no longer are workable for anyone. The Borderlands condition is, in fact, an analogue of the entire planet, and its contradictions are universal. It confronts humans whenever they choose to recognize the multiple identities that constitute their own selves or enter contexts in which several cultures coexist. In one way or another, all human beings inhabit the Borderlands or experience facets of their lives and identities that involve cultures that "edge each another."[38]

Nepantla

The suggestion that the Borderlands is a universal state gives rise to Anzaldúa's next dimension in her worldview—*nepantla.* An Aztec word meaning "torn between ways,"[39] *nepantla* emphasizes not only the full range of dimensions that can exist in the Borderlands but also psychic, emotional, and supernatural states. There is an interface between the different realities suggested by the term *nepantla* that extends the notion of the Borderlands into something more inclusive of multiple realities of all kinds. Anzaldúa elaborates: "[W]ith *nepantla* there's more of a connection to the spirit world. There's more a connection to the world after death and to psychic spaces like between air and water."[40]

Nepantla also is distinguished from the Borderlands by an emphasis on notions of process as well as of space. As a literal and figurative space, *nepantla* is "capable of accommodating mutually exclusive, discontinuous and inconsistent worlds"; it shows how seemingly contradictory realities can fit together. At the same time, it is a process, "a journey into both the interior and exterior of the self."[41] Anzaldúa describes it as "an in-between state, that uncertain terrain one crosses when moving from one place to another . . . when traveling from the present identity into a new identity."[42] *Nepantla*, then, is a philosophy that involves learning how to access different kinds of knowledge alongside or behind consensual reality—the reality agreed upon by a culture—and to create new meanings or realities as well.

Anzaldúa envisions the *nepantla* state to be more inclusive than the term *Borderlands*. Not only is *nepantla* a less static term, without reference to actual boundaries, but it encompasses space and process in a new paradigm for managing conflicted identities. Because it is not an English term, it also has fewer associations and connotations to limit how it is understood among English speakers, thus allowing it broad applicability. It contains in-between spaces as well as the borders of those spaces and agreed-upon realities and those that lie behind them; it involves the process of moving through these spaces from the unknown to new understandings and identities.

Nepantla can be equated with yet another nuance of *haciendo caras*—that of *making a face at*. One can make a face or distort the face into any number of grimaces for a variety of reasons—to challenge, to subvert, to confuse, to mock, or simply to have fun. That the act of making a face can be motivated by many different intentions is not unlike the *nepantla* state; it, too, contains a range of contradictory processes, conditions, and actions that enable individuals to cope with and manage the world's contradictions in creative ways.

Mestiza Consciousness

Anzaldúa adds as a final realm in her worldview a consciousness that lies beyond and transcends the Borderlands and *nepantla* conditions. She labels this "a new *mestiza* consciousness, *una consciencia de mujer,*" which is an outcome, an extension, and a synthesis of the features she sees as characterizing any Borderlands culture.[43]

The notion of synthesis is crucial to Anzaldúa's description of the *mestiza* consciousness. It is not simply a place where separate cultural pieces are assembled or where a balancing of opposing powers occurs—the features of the Borderlands and *nepantla* states. Rather, it entails an effort at synthesis so that the self "has added a third element which is greater than the sum of its severed parts. That third element is a new consciousness—a *mestiza* consciousness."[44] Although it is disorienting and painful in the making, this consciousness is energizing and transforming because it "comes from a continual creative motion that keeps breaking down the unitary aspect" of each paradigm of culture and identity.[45] As a result, the *mestiza* consciousness can serve as a model or prototype because "the future depends on the breaking down of paradigms, it

depends on the straddling of two or more cultures."[46] The *mestiza* leads the way
to the new consciousness by balancing at the edge of contradiction and change:
"That focal point or fulcrum, that juncture where the *mestiza* stands, is where
phenomena tend to collide. It is where the possibility of uniting all that is
separate occurs."[47]

The new *mestiza* consciousness Anzaldúa envisions relies on the biological,
racial, ideological, and cultural advantages of cross pollination. She uses Jose
Vasconcelos's notion of the cosmic race—"a fifth race embracing the four major
races of the world"—as a starting point to suggest the strengths and possibilities
of a *mestiza* culture: "At the confluence of two or more genetic streams, with
chromosomes constantly 'crossing over,' this mixture of races, rather than
resulting in an inferior being, provides hybrid progeny, a mutable, more malle-
able species with a rich gene pool."[48] The strengths of the new culture are not
simply biological, however. They touch every aspect of culture, providing for
myriad possibilities of disrupting traditional ways of seeing, acting, and constructing cultural identities.

By putting "history through a sieve" and looking at "the forces that we as a
race, as women, have been a part of," the perspective provided by a *mestiza*
consciousness suggests a conscious rupturing and reinterpretation of history by
"using new symbols" to shape "new myths." Increasingly tolerant of ambiguity,
the inhabitant of the Borderlands becomes "vulnerable to foreign ways of seeing
and thinking," "surrenders all notions of safety," and learns to transform the
self according to new conceptions: "*la concepción que tiene de sí misma, asi
sera* [the conception she has of herself, thus will she be]."[49]

The connotation of *haciendo caras* that corresponds to the *mestiza* dimension of Anzaldúa's continuum is making face as a form of agency. To make face
is to assume a stance that says, "'Don't walk all over me,' the one that says, 'Get
out of my face.'"[50] In this way, *haciendo caras* means the process of articulating,
displaying, and enacting identity—acquiring, as Anzaldúa describes it, "the
agency of making our own *caras*," of constructing identity on one's own terms.[51]
Anzaldúa uses herself and her own life to suggest how the perspective offered
by the *mestiza* consciousness can be the impetus for agency:

> I want the freedom to carve and chisel my own face, to staunch the bleeding with
> ashes, to fashion my own gods out of my entrails. . . . I will have to stand and claim
> my space, making a new culture—*una cultura mestiza*—with my own lumber, my
> own bricks and mortar and my own feminist architecture.[52]

Anzaldúa's continuum of the world—from the Borderlands through *nepantla*
to the *mestiza* consciousness—suggests not only a progression from literal to
increasingly symbolic and inclusive but also a shift from problematic to positive
and creative. She begins with the struggles that characterize the Borderlands—

the need to come to terms with the tangible contradictions and uncertainties of the in-between, where "[h]atred, anger and exploitation are the prominent features of this landscape."[53] As she describes the more psychological and symbolic aspects of the *nepantla* condition, the negative is mitigated by a sense of perspective, "a piece of ground to stand on, a ground from which to view the world."[54] The sense of perspective gained is fully realized with the *mestiza* consciousness, where, despite ongoing discomforts and tensions, possibilities exist for synthesis and transformation—for devising a culture suited to a world that is necessarily composed of multiple cultures and identities.[55] Anzaldúa's metaphor of *haciendo caras* reinforces these various components of her continuum, suggesting how perspectives and agency change in the progression from literal to more metaphoric conceptualizations of the conditions that make up the Borderlands.

Definition of Feminism

The *mestiza* is at the heart of Anzaldúa's vision of feminism, which addresses all forms of oppression in the Borderlands: "As long as woman is put down, the Indian and the Black in all of us" are put down. "The struggle of the mestiza is above all a feminist one."[56] But it is a struggle that will transform all cultures: "Our movements, like the wind, sweep through the sea of grass in California, cut swaths in Texas, take root in Maine, sway public opinion in North Dakota, stir the dust in New Mexico. Now here, now there, *aquí y alla,* we and our *movimientos* are firmly committed to transforming all our cultures."[57]

For Anzaldúa, women are the primary agents who will take action against or respond to oppressions, and women's responses to and assumption of responsibility for what happens in their lives is at the core of feminism. The image of hands captures her notion of feminism as response:

> I hear a movement of hands doing ground-root work. Women, alone, in groups, in whole *pueblos,* no longer feeling impotent. Women responding, taking care of each other, the taking care a constant no matter how busy she is scrambling, getting through the living. . . . Women with the patience of the marginated, the perseverance of the turtle, woman who won't let go until the monster reforms or bleeds to death. Woman who wants to change *norte america,* who has already begun to change the world.[58]

Although Anzaldúa does not see feminism as a single movement, she sees a common center of healing that unites the various feminisms: "Though the particulars of each woman's *responding* differ, though their values, political views, and color of their skins differ, though some pull in different directions, there is a common movement: The reaching out to heal."[59] The notion of healing is another way of expressing Anzaldúa's notion of moving across borders to create new forms of consciousness; healing involves working together across divisions to effect a positive outcome.

Critics of the women's movement may condemn the splintering and loss of a single goal they see in feminism, but Anzaldúa does not. For her, feminism simply has "changed its rhythm, trekked across plateaus, climbed over peaks, slid down abysses. Moving always. . . . Our throats now partially free, we shout sing film tape paint write laugh dance act our alternative responses, make up our own anthems."[60] Like all cultures that exist in the Borderlands, feminism exhibits a diversity and a plurality that provide it with possibilities for paradigm-changing visions. The myriad forms the movement assumes mean only that it can reach more individuals and have more wide-ranging impact.

Nature of the Rhetor

The rhetor that Anzaldúa makes central to her rhetorical theory is the *mestiza,* the woman of mixed blood who straddles multiple cultural boundaries. The choice of the *mestiza* captures the progression of worlds Anzaldúa constructs— from someone who deals with literal borders to a consciousness that encompasses and transforms the border experience into a prototype for interaction. By using the feminine ending and feminine pronoun for *mestiza,* Anzaldúa privileges women as rhetors; they are the catalysts for change who will produce "a massive revolution in attitudes, beliefs, in the very nature of 'reality.'"[61] Anzaldúa's starting point for defining this rhetor is her own experiences: "I am a border woman. I grew up between two cultures, the Mexican (with a heavy Indian influence) and the Anglo (as a member of a colonized people in our own territory). I have been straddling that *tejas*-Mexican border, and others, all my life."[62]

The choice of the term *mestiza* is an important one. Often viewed negatively from the standpoint of the dominant culture, the term forces an immediate inversion of thinking about the Borderlands. Typically viewed as the home of "*los atravesados*" (border crossers), which Anzaldúa describes as "the squint-eyed, the perverse, the queer, the troublesome, the mongrel, the mulato, the half-breed, the half dead," she invites a reversal of the marginalization of these inhabitants of the Borderlands.[63] Anzaldúa gives centrality, legitimacy, and agency to these "strangers" or "others" who have been denigrated by the dominant culture.

Ultimately, then, although women may be at the forefront of the new consciousness, Anzaldúa's notion of the rhetor expands to include anyone who is an outsider. She notes especially the role of lesbians and gay men as "supreme crossers of culture" in creating a new consciousness.[64] Because gay men and lesbians "come from all colors, all classes, all races, all time periods," they "link people with each other" and "transfer ideas and information from one culture to another."[65] Like the *mestiza,* Anzaldúa explains, "the queer" exists "at this time and point on the evolutionary continuum for a purpose. We are a blending that proves that all blood is intricately woven together, and that we are spawned out of similar souls."[66]

In a continuation of her reversal of the traditional images of those at the margins, Anzaldúa conceptualizes the *mestiza* rhetor as especially tenacious, visionary, and active precisely because of her experiences in multiple cultures. Beset with contradictory versions of reality, the *mestiza* has a sense of perspective and flexibility: "She has discovered that she can't hold concepts or ideas in rigid boundaries. The borders and walls that are supposed to keep the undesirable ideas out are entrenched habits and patterns of behavior; these habits and patterns are the enemy within."[67] Having to juggle cultures, manage contradictions, and present multiple personalities, the *mestiza* is a rhetor who is, in fact, highly skilled. She is always ready to take on the multiple and contradictory conditions that confront her and is resourceful in creating new and even stronger ways of being in the world. Drawing on images from her own Chicana heritage, Anzaldúa uses the metaphor of corn to capture the *mestiza*'s strength:

> Indigenous like corn, like corn, the *mestiza* is a product of crossbreeding, designed for preservation under a variety of conditions. Like an ear of corn—a female seed-bearing-organ—the *mestiza* is tenacious, tightly wrapped in the husks of her culture. Like kernels she clings to the cob; with thick stalks and strong brace roots, she holds tight to the earth—she will survive the crossroads.[68]

The *mestiza*'s strength derives from her ability to maintain her ties to her original identities but also to create new structures and possibilities. The *mestiza* makes "'sense' of it all" by "kicking a hole out of the old boundaries of the self and slipping under or over, dragging the old skin along, stumbling over it."[69] Anzaldúa adopts the image of the rattlesnake to illustrate the process by which understanding is enlarged in this fashion. When the serpent sheds its skin, a little piece of skin is always left that forms the rattle, keeping part of the old; similarly, the shedding of an old structure or identity always involves adding new knowledge, new consciousness.[70] The *mestiza* rhetor must be willing to reach for the other side—to expand the boundaries of the self—because "only when she is on the other side" can she see things "in a different perspective. It is only then that she makes the connections, formulates the insights. It is only then that her consciousness expands a tiny notch, another rattle appears on the rattlesnake tail."[71]

The *mestiza* rhetor works in a "pluralistic mode," using all there is to use on the way to a world that values the cross-fertilization available from the *mestiza* worldview; "nothing is thrust out, the good, the bad and the ugly, nothing rejected, nothing abandoned. Not only does she sustain contradictions, she turns the ambivalence into something else."[72] The *mestiza* continually must "shift out of habitual formations; from convergent thinking, analytical reasoning that tends to use rationality to move toward a single goal (a Western mode), to divergent thinking, characterized by movement away from set patterns and goals and toward a more whole perspective, one that includes rather than excludes."[73]

The rhetor, by virtue of her own struggles with identity, comes to view the world from a larger perspective than that of the individual, singular self. She is able to step outside of herself and her history to view the world in new ways: We no "longer stand outside nor behind the frame of the painting. We are both the foreground, the background and the figures predominating."[74] The *mestiza* rhetor assumes a transcendent stance—one that takes into account the contradictions of her own identity and translates those into a larger perspective; consequently, she is "of the herd, yet not of it."[75] Anzaldúa elaborates, using her own life as illustration:

> As a *mestiza* I have no country, my homeland cast me out; yet all countries are mine because I am every woman's sister or potential lover. (As a lesbian I have no race, my own people disclaim me; but I am all races because there is the queer of me in all races.) I am cultureless because, as a feminist, I challenge the collective cultural/religious male-derived beliefs of Indo-Hispanics and Anglos; yet I am cultured because I am participating in the creation of yet another culture, a new story to explain the world and our participation in it, a new value system with images and symbols that connect us to each other and to the planet.[76]

Anzaldúa uses her own approach to writing to provide another example of how the *mestiza* rhetor contains but also transcends the contradictions of the Borderlands. In her writing, she refuses to dichotomize her presentation of self—to privilege any part of her identity—and demands that all facets be recognized and valued. Thus, she juxtaposes the Spanish and English languages to present her Anglo and Chicana identities simultaneously. She often moves between the two languages in midsentence, sometimes translating a Spanish phrase and sometimes letting it stand without translation. The Spanish functions to mark the specificity of the Chicana contribution, while the English moves the narrative along in more generic ways.[77] At the same time, Anzaldúa transcends the dichotomy created by the presence of the two languages by generating her own meanings that stand beyond either language in particular.

Rhetorical Options

Anzaldúa's rhetorical options are centered on metaphor; she suggests that we "perceive ourselves through metaphor" and that metaphors are, in fact, the way that change occurs. Anzaldúa terms the metaphoric process *la facultad,* or the "capacity to see in surface phenomena the meaning of deeper realities, to see the deep structure below the surface." *La facultad* is the process of communicating through metaphor "in images and symbols which are the faces of feeling."[78] Metaphor, then, is "a bridge between evoked emotion and conscious knowledge; words are cables that hold up the bridge. Images are more direct, more immediate than words, and closer to the unconscious."[79]

Resistance to change in a person, according to Anzaldúa, is in direct proportion to the number of dead metaphors that person carries. The "cure" consists of either removing those metaphors or "adding what is lacking—restoring the balance and strengthening the physical, mental, and emotional states of the person." Extracting "the old dead metaphors" can be a way of changing consciousness and of empowering an individual: "This 'cure' leads to a change" in the belief system such that the person snaps "out of the paralyzing states of confusion, depression, anxiety, and powerlessness" and is "catapulted into enabling states of confidence and inner strength."[80] Similarly, the provision of new metaphors to individuals offers them different perspectives from which to view the world, and when they have choices about their worldviews—choices provided by metaphor—the outcome is empowerment: "People in possession of the vehicles of communication are, indeed, in partial possession of their lives."[81]

The basic rhetorical option Anzaldúa advocates, then, is shifting metaphors. Shifting metaphors means changing perspectives—making new connections and seeing in new ways—through the creative use of language. Such shifts ultimately can change the world. Anzaldúa summarizes:

> My "awakened dreams" are about shifts. Thought shifts, reality shifts, gender shifts: one person metamorphoses into another in a world where people fly through the air, heal from mortal wounds. I am playing with my Self, I am playing with the world's soul, I am the dialogue between my Self and *el espíritu del mundo.* I change myself, I change the world.[82]

In whatever form such metaphoric shifts occur, they contribute to the possibility of changing worldviews by offering others new perspectives: "If we've done our job well we may give others access to a language and images with which they can articulate/express pain, confusion, joy, and other experiences thus far experienced only on an inarticulated emotional level."[83] Metaphors, then, have the power to affect both the creator of and the audience for the metaphor.

Anzaldúa's own writing contains numerous examples of metaphoric shifts, suggesting how central this concept is to her view of change. One such example occurs when she shifts the metaphors associated with the term *bearing*: "Haven't we always borne jugs of water, children, poverty? Why not learn to bear baskets of hope, love, self-nourishment and to step lightly?"[84] Anzaldúa exemplifies such shifts as well when she takes a traditionally female image—that of kneading bread—and transforms it into an image that encompasses the contradictions of the Borderlands: *"Soy un amasamiento,* I am an act of kneading, of uniting and joining that not only has produced both a creature of darkness and a creature of light, but also a creature that questions the definitions of light and dark and gives them new meanings."[85]

Also illustrative of the process of shifting metaphors is Anzaldúa's transformation of the term *Aztlán* from place to metaphor. The legendary place of origin of the Aztecs in Mexico, Aztlán often is seen as a symbol of a desired homeland, a site of return or rediscovery of Chicano/a culture.[86] Anzaldúa, however, suggests that the contemporary Aztlán is the U.S. Southwest, and this time, "the traffic is from south to north."[87] For Anzaldúa, the history of migration and immigration across the border constructs the concept of Aztlán not as a utopian land but a subjective one that shifts as Borderlands shift. No longer a physical space that someday will be transformed into the center of a national identity, Aztlán comes to mean identity itself. What Anzaldúa calls the "tradition of long walks,"[88] then, leads not back to a mythical Aztlán and a dream of origin but to engagement with various cultural identities at all kinds of borders. Aztlán is a movable border within the self, where the self comes to terms with fluctuating positionalities.[89]

Anzaldúa outlines three general categories or contexts in which metaphoric shifts can occur—in the intrapersonal, interpersonal, and public arenas. The intrapersonal level deals with using metaphors to change self-perceptions, the interpersonal with shifts that affect interactions with others, and the public arena covers activities in public contexts that promote shifts in consciousness among larger audiences.

Intrapersonal Realm

Changing oneself is a basic means of helping create *mestiza* culture; it is a process in which rhetors can engage at any time because it concentrates on and works on the self: "I believe that by changing ourselves we change the world." This process involves both "going deep into the self and expanding out into the world, a simultaneous recreation of the self and a reconstruction of society."[90]

According to Anzaldúa, any intrapersonal change is a process of selecting and incorporating into consciousness new ways of seeing. Anzaldúa explains how she uses this kind of metaphoric shift to change herself:

I choose words, images, and body sensations and animate them to impress them on my consciousness, thereby making changes in my belief system and reprogramming my consciousness. This involves looking my inner demons in the face, then deciding which I want in my psyche. Those I don't want, I starve; I feed them no words, no images, no feelings. I spend no time with them, share not my home with them. Neglected, they leave.[91]

For Anzaldúa, then, a basic way of creating change is by making changes at the intrapersonal level—in the words used and the energy devoted to the concepts behind those words—in order to affirm a different vision of the world from the inside out.

Interpersonal Realm

Anzaldúa chooses four metaphors to summarize various interpersonal options for connecting with others across cultural differences: island, drawbridge, bridge, and sandbar.[92] Anzaldúa recognizes that there are many "ways of being, of acting, and of interacting in the world"; for her, these options cluster around the metaphor of a bridge. This process, which Anzaldúa refers to as "'chusando' movidas" (choosing moves),[93] relies on a metaphoric shift—on selecting the kind of bridge that will guide a particular interaction: Every "step forward is a *travesía,* a crossing. I am again an alien in new territory. And again, and again. But if I escape conscious awareness, escape 'knowing,' I won't be moving."[94]

Like the process of self-change, Anzaldúa's bridge metaphors offer new ways of organizing perceptions; thus, they offer rhetors options for connecting with others across cultural differences. They suggest not only how to cope with the cultural clash that is the basis for the Borderlands but also how to move from such a coping stance to a stance of agency, which is crucial to the attainment of the *mestiza* consciousness.

Island

Anzaldúa's first rhetorical option in terms of the interpersonal realm is the island. The island mode implies that there are "no causeways, no bridges, maybe no ferries, either" that can connect or cross between individuals of differing identities or standpoints.[95] In a sense, then, this option does not contain the possibilities for connection. Because it involves a deliberate choice not to connect, however, it represents a perspective or approach that is available within the interpersonal domain.

For Anzaldúa, the options suggested by the island mode are short-term because totally closing the self off from dealing with difference—staying forever on an island apart from others—is impossible: "Yet being an island cannot be a way of life—there are no life-long islands because no one is totally self-sufficient."[96] The island, however, does provide a place where rhetors can come to terms with the contradictions of the Borderlands and prepare for action. It allows for the process of building defenses to insulate the self from the attacks that inevitably accompany efforts to reach out from the Borderlands. The island, in a sense, is a "way station" that allows individuals the time and space necessary to assimilate, explore, and process the meanings of the Borderlands.

The possibilities of the island as a way station and place for integration are accompanied by potentially more dangerous options as well: anger and rage. Such emotions are often a part of the island mode, helping provide a sense of self that can resist the demands of the dominant culture.[97] Anzaldúa suggests, however, that many women and people of color get stuck in this state of resistance—reacting to and raging against what others do or have done, "proudly defiant" in their refutation of the dominant culture's views and beliefs. When rage is the only response selected, the island becomes a hiding place on which rhetors close themselves off from others. Anzaldúa, then, acknowledges the appeal of the island mode, but, at the same time, she is not tolerant of those who get stuck in the resistance and rage that often accompany a stance of isolation. She believes such resistance is, ultimately, a limiting response: "All reaction is limited by, and dependent on, what it is reacting against."[98]

For Anzaldúa, the island is not a productive long-term option, and she prefers to see it as a "path/state to something else" rather than as a way of life.[99] The resistance, anger, and withdrawal of the island perpetuate the dichotomies from which she is trying to escape: "At some point, on our way to a new consciousness, we will have to leave the opposite bank, the split between the two mortal combatants somehow healed so that we are on both shores at once."[100] Anzaldúa elaborates: "We can no longer withdraw. To rage and look upon you with contempt is to rage and be contemptuous of ourselves. We can no longer blame you, nor disown the white parts, the male parts, the pathological parts, the queer parts, the vulnerable parts."[101]

The term *responsibility* is central to Anzaldúa's approach to the three other interpersonal rhetorical modes she describes—the drawbridge, the bridge, and the sandbar. Responsibility is "the ability to respond," which means being accountable for and proactive in terms of options.[102] Thus, her next three options for interaction require a move out of the reaction that characterizes the island mode—which Anzaldúa associates with victimage—into a sense of agency and choice: "And there in front of us is the crossroads and choice: to feel a victim where someone else is in control and therefore responsible and to blame . . . or to feel strong, and, for the most part, in control."[103] For Anzaldúa, the *mestiza* rhetor can use her strength and agency advantageously and creatively to develop new rhetorical options rather than be at the mercy of the crossing strategies themselves: "We are learning to depend more and more on our own sources for survival, learning not to let the weight of this burden, the bridge, break our backs."[104]

Implicit in Anzaldúa's remaining three options is also the need to form alliances with those whose interests are similar. Anzaldúa believes that a sense of responsibility includes watching out for and working with others to promote change: "We have come to realize that we are not alone in the struggle nor separate nor autonomous but that we—white black straight queer female male—are connected and interdependent. We are each accountable for what is happening down the street, south of the border or across the sea."[105]

Anzaldúa sees the process of coalition building as important because, when they form alliances, individuals and groups must come to terms with their differing approaches and styles. The process of forming coalitions offers a model for how communicating across differences can occur:

> In alliance we are confronted with the problem of how we share or don't share space, how we can position ourselves with individuals or groups who are different from and at odds with each other, how we can reconcile one's love for diverse groups when members of these groups do not love each other, cannot relate to each other, and don't know how to work together.[106]

Forming alliances is another way of taking responsibility for the construction of a new culture and new consciousness across cultural differences.

Drawbridge

One possibility for interpersonal exchange grounded in responsibility is suggested by the metaphor of the drawbridge. It represents a course of action with alternating possibilities: Rhetors can choose to be up (separated from contact with others) or down (willing to connect with those different from themselves). When the drawbridge is in the up position, rhetors pull back physically and emotionally from connecting in order to rest, to preserve the self, and to clarify positions. When the drawbridge is down, the self is more vulnerable; there is a "partial loss of self" that comes from making oneself available to others, and there is the risk of "being 'walked' on, being 'used.'"[107] The drawbridge, then, allows for connection without giving up entirely the safety of the island.

Bridge

Adopting the option of the bridge is yet another possibility for shifting metaphors in the interpersonal realm. This option means being available to others at all times—serving as the mediator among self, community, and other cultures whenever necessary. By being constantly willing to work with others in managing and moving beyond the tensions of the Borderlands, the rhetor who selects this option does the most to further *mestiza* consciousness. Being a bridge is draining, however, because "being 'there' for people *all the time, mediating all the time*" means there is little respite from connection and interaction.[108] This is the option Anzaldúa most often chooses in her own life; she refers to herself as a "persistent bridge."[109] She inserts herself into the dominant culture, willing to engage in the struggles necessary to facilitate the growth of *mestiza* consciousness.

Sandbar

Connecting interpersonally can be accomplished as well through the metaphor of the sandbar, a submerged or partially submerged ridge of sand constructed by waves offshore. This is an appealing metaphor for Anzaldúa, although she has not abandoned the metaphor of the drawbridge: The "infrastructures of bridge and drawbridge feel too man-made and steel-like for me. Still liking the drawbridge concept, I sought and found the sandbar."[110] Because it is an organic construction, the sandbar feels to her like a natural form of connection.

The fluidity of the sandbar is its primary defining characteristic; not only does the sandbar shift locations, thus suggesting the possibility of shifting emphases, but it is not always available for use as a bridge. It allows for choices about "who to allow to 'see' your bridge, who you'll allow to walk on your 'bridge,' that is, who you'll make connections with."[111] It also provides some of the opportunities of the island mode—ways of "getting a breather from being a perpetual bridge without having to withdraw completely."[112] Furthermore, the decisions about the kinds and amounts of interactions in which to engage are made fluidly, taking into consideration all of the other factors operating at any given moment: "The high tides and low tides of your life are factors which help decide whether or where you're a sandbar today, tomorrow."[113] The sandbar option, then, allows for "more mobility and more freedom" than the other options.[114] It enables rhetors to connect with others while also allowing for retreat and renewal, and it recognizes shifting concerns that necessarily affect how and when connections are made.

The island, drawbridge, bridge, and sandbar encapsulate Anzaldúa's interpersonal rhetorical options. Each of these options represents a choice available to rhetors for connection. Anzaldúa recognizes that different options may characterize "different stages of our process," but she encourages rhetors to choose "to connect, heart to heart, *con corazones abiertos*" (with open hearts).[115]

Public Realm

Yet another means exists by which to create different perceptual shifts, this time in the public arena—creative arts, performances, and presentations of various kinds. Any act of creativity functions to "rearrange or create 'new' patterns that will contribute to building, creating and being an integral part" of what Anzaldúa calls "the molding" in which we are encased.[116] She sees the arts in the tradition of her Indian ancestors, who "did not split the artistic from the functional, the sacred from the secular, art from everyday life."[117] Creative acts are not "inert and 'dead' objects (as the aesthetics of Western culture think of art works)."[118] Rather, each work of art "has an identity" and contains the "presences" or "incarnations" of persons, ancestors, gods, or natural and cosmic powers. Such works are living enactments that incorporate both "a physical thing and the power that infuses it." In this way, any form of creative expression functions metaphorically, spinning "its energies between gods and humans" in order to make people "hopeful, happy, secure."[119]

The fine arts provide new perspectives and patterns that promote movement outside of existing or traditional boundaries. Especially for those—like the *mestiza* rhetor—who traditionally have been denied access to "language, fine arts and literature," acts of creativity can be ways of forming new identities. Art is a way of moving between old patterns and new forms of agency: "We are forced to steal a bit of visual, oral or written language, to escape and hide out long enough so that with half a hand" we can create different patterns and perspectives.[120] Art, like Anzaldúa's other rhetorical options, provides a means of shifting between "the personal voice and language, with its apparatuses of culture and ideologies, and art mediums with their genre laws—the human voice trying to outshout a roaring waterfall."[121] Anzaldúa suggests that the arts are effective precisely because of the possibilities for bridging and for agency that they contain:

> Art is a sneak attack while the giant sleeps, a sleight of hands when the giant is awake, moving so quick they can do their deed before the giant swats them. Our survival depends on being creative. . . . By sending our voices, visuals and visions outward into the world, we alter the walls and make them a framework for new windows and doors.[122]

Anzaldúa's work is directed at bridging the contradictions of the Borderlands and using those contradictions in positive ways to create a world characterized by a new *mestiza* consciousness that is flexible and tenacious and encompasses diversity. Her frequent iterations of the bridge metaphor and her admonition to build bridges "as one walks"[123] reinforce her preference for rhetorical options that bridge rather than withdraw from the tensions of the Borderlands. She also recognizes that there are a wide range—perhaps an almost infinite number—of ways in which a new consciousness can emerge. She chooses to focus on modes of cultural interaction or cultural crossings grounded in self-responsibility, with individuals choosing those options that work best for them. To learn to "be a crossroads"[124] is both Anzaldúa's mission and the crux of her rhetorical theory; this objective captures the options she favors—options that encourage connection, creativity, and communication.

Transformations of Rhetorical Theory

Anzaldúa's rhetorical theory, created from a Borderlands identity, is used to construct a new *mestiza* consciousness suitable for the entire planet. The concepts that undergo the greatest transformation in Anzaldúa's writings are ethos, exigence, identification, opposition, and the nature of change.

Ethos

Anzaldúa recognizes that the traditional conception of ethos, in which audience members assign credibility to rhetors who demonstrate intelligence, moral character, and goodwill, in fact reproduces the cultural expectations of these qualities as credible. Her theory forces recognition that ethos is a privileged notion that ensures that a particular culture—the dominant one—will continue to flourish. She privileges instead the characteristics of marginalized rhetors—rhetors from the Borderlands—and finds in their diversity a special strength of character and vision that constitute a different conception of ethos. She also makes these rhetors special because they model the connections possible for all individuals—they have and can present a perspective not available within the confines of the dominant culture.

Anzaldúa reconceptualizes ethos in another way as well. In traditional notions of ethos, rhetors are accorded credibility for being truthful—speaking honestly and in ways that are consistent with the values of the audience. Anzaldúa suggests, however, that marginalized rhetors rarely can speak out of their authentic experiences in the dominant culture; to be credible in that culture, they must present falsehoods and "make faces" that are appropriate for and adjusted to those in control. Ethos, then, involves a splitting and compartmentalizing of the self, constructing a mask to accommodate the dominant culture, and hiding one's true face behind that mask. *Haciendo caras* is Anzaldúa's shorthand description for developing credibility. It involves constructing an appropriate face but also contains other possibilities for facework—making a face, making one's own face, or constructing one's own agency. Anzaldúa's approach to ethos is much more complex than the monodimensional conception found in traditional rhetorical theory. It recognizes the need to construct several layers of ethos—some authentic, some accommodating, and some that contain a new sense of agency.

Exigence

Anzaldúa's rhetorical theory also offers a challenge to the traditional notion of exigence. In traditional rhetorical theory, the exigence is a defect in a situation that a rhetor tries to address and resolve. If the rhetorical options selected are appropriate, the defect or lack is repaired or resolved. In Anzaldúa's conception of the exigence, however, the defect remains open by design. She talks of Borderlands as grating against each other, creating an open wound that scabs, breaks open, and continues to hemorrhage. Just as the Borderlands scab never completely heals, the exigence is never fully resolved. The options Anzaldúa advocates are designed not to provide closure but to keep the wound open and festering, preventing the synthesis that the scab represents. From this tension and lack of resolution come new, creative connections and new forms of healing.

Identification

With her metaphors of the island, drawbridge, bridge, and sandbar, Anzaldúa reconceptualizes the notion of identification. Identification often is seen as a primary means to persuasion, with rhetors able to persuade others of the value of their positions and to create sources of identification or shared substance between rhetor and audience.[125] Anzaldúa's conception of this construct suggests that identification is more complex than is the case with the traditional notion. With her crossing metaphors, Anzaldúa suggests that different degrees of identification are desirable between rhetor and audience; to seek consubstantiality with everyone at all times is not appropriate. Rhetoric may be used to create identification, but it also functions when individuals break all connections, take time for themselves, and make no attempt at identification whatsoever. There also may be situations in which rhetors alternatively choose to connect and to remove themselves from identification with an audience. The equation of rhetoric and identification is not always necessary or desirable for Anzaldúa.

Change

The nature of change also is transformed in Anzaldúa's rhetorical theory. Change happens not when rhetors present definite positions to audiences and argue for their acceptance on the basis of their presumed superiority. Instead, rhetors offer multiple options to audiences (including themselves)—multiple metaphors, images, and perspectives—and allow audience members to select those they feel are best for them. Anzaldúa's theory resists the settling and narrowing that characterize many change efforts with a rhetoric that provides abundant options both to rhetors themselves and to others.

Anzaldúa's rhetorical theory is founded on a commitment to multiplicity, instability, disorientation, insecurity, and conflicting demands. She resists the tendencies manifest in traditional rhetorical theory toward stability, rigidity, codification, and confinement in terms of meaning. As a result, she not only changes rhetorical theory in dramatic ways but suggests new options—"theories that overlap many 'worlds.'" She facilitates the articulation of new positions for "in-between" rhetors interested in realizing new perspectives and worldviews— realizing *mestiza* consciousness.[126]

Bibliography

Books

Anzaldúa, Gloria. *Borderlands/La Frontera: The New Mestiza*. San Francisco: Aunt Lute, 1987.

Anzaldúa, Gloria. *Friends from the Other Side/Amigos del otro lado*. San Francisco: Children's, 1993.

Anzaldúa, Gloria, ed. *Making Face, Making Soul/Haciendo Caras: Creative and Critical Perspectives by Feminists of Color.* San Francisco: Aunt Lute, 1990.

Anzaldúa, Gloria. *Prietita and the Ghost Woman/Prietita y La Llorona*. San Francisco: Children's, 1995.

Moraga, Cherríe, and Gloria Anzaldúa, eds. *This Bridge Called My Back: Writings by Radical Women of Color.* 1981. New York: Kitchen Table: Women of Color, 1983.

Articles

Anzaldúa, Gloria. "Afterword: A Movement of Women." *This Way Daybreak Comes: Women's Values and the Future*. Ed. Annie Cheatham and Mary Clare Powell. Philadelphia: New Society, 1986. 223-36.

Anzaldúa, Gloria. "Bridge, Drawbridge, Sandbar or Island: *Lesbians-of-Color Hacienda Alianzas*." *Bridges of Power: Women's Multicultural Alliances*. Ed. Lisa Albrecht and Rose M. Brewer. Philadelphia: New Society, 1990. 216-31.

Anzaldúa, Gloria. "Border *Arte: Nepantla, el lugar de la frontera*." *La Frontera/The Border: Art about the Mexico/United States Border Experience*. San Diego, CA: Centro Cultural de la Raza and Museum of Contemporary Art, 1973. 107-14.

Anzaldúa, Gloria. "*La conciencia de la mestiza*: Toward a New Consciousness." *Borderlands/La Frontera: The New Mestiza*. By Gloria Anzaldúa. San Francisco: Aunt Lute, 1987. 77-91. Rpt. in *Redefining Sexual Ethics: A Sourcebook of Essays, Stories, and Poems*. Ed. Susan E. Davies and Eleanor H. Haney. Cleveland, OH: Pilgrim,

1991. 207-19; *Rereading America: Cultural Contexts for Critical Thinking and Writing.* Ed. Gary Colombo, Robert Cullen, and Bonnie Lisle. 2nd ed. Boston: Bedford, 1992. 386-96; *Infinite Divisions: An Anthology of Chicana Literature.* Ed. Tey Diana Rebolledo and Eliana S. Rivero. Tucson: U of Arizona P, 1993. 81-83; *Ways of Reading.* Ed. David Bartholomae and Anthony Petrosky. 3rd ed. Boston: Bedford, 1993. 49-61; *Acoma: Revista Internazionale di Studi Nordamericani* 1 (1994): 19-30; *In Other Words: Literature by Latinas of the United States.* Ed. Roberta Fernández. Houston, TX: Arte Público, 1994. 266-79; and *The Woman That I Am: The Literature and Culture of Contemporary Women of Color.* Ed. D. Soyini Madison. New York: St. Martin's, 1994. 560-72.

Anzaldúa, Gloria. "En Rapport, in Opposition: Cobrando cuentas a las nuestras." *Making Face, Making Soul/Haciendo Caras: Creative and Critical Perspectives by Feminists of Color.* Ed. Gloria Anzaldúa. San Francisco: Aunt Lute, 1990. 142-44. Rpt. (shortened version) in *Feminist Frontiers III.* Ed. Laurel Richardson and Verta Taylor. New York: McGraw-Hill, 1993. 508-12; *Race, Class and Gender in the United States: An Integrated Study.* Ed. Paula Rothenberg. 2nd ed. New York: St. Martin's, 1994. 408-13.

Anzaldúa, Gloria. "Entering into the Serpent." *Borderlands/La Frontera: The New Mestiza.* By Gloria Anzaldúa. San Francisco: Aunt Lute, 1987. 25-39. Rpt. in *Ways of Reading: An Anthology for Writers.* Ed. David Bartholomae and Anthony Petrosky. 3rd ed. Boston: Bedford, 1993. 25-38; (shortened version) as "The Presences." *Keys to the Open Gate: A Woman's Spirituality Sourcebook.* By Kimberley Snow. Berkeley, CA: Conari, 1994. 323-25.

Anzaldúa, Gloria. "Foreword to the Second Edition." *This Bridge Called My Back: Writings by Radical Women of Color.* Ed. Cherríe Moraga and Gloria Anzaldúa. 2nd ed. New York: Kitchen Table: Women of Color, 1983. N. pag.

Anzaldúa, Gloria. "The Homeland, Aztlán/el otro México." *Borderlands/La Frontera: The New Mestiza.* By Gloria Anzaldúa. San Francisco: Aunt Lute, 1987. 1-13. Rpt. in *Aztlán: Essays on the Chicano Homeland.* Ed. Rudolfo A. Anaya and Francisco A. Lomelí. Albuquerque: U of New Mexico P, 1989. 191-204; as "The New Mestiza." *Social Theory: The Multicultural and Classic Readings.* Ed. Charles Lemert. Boulder, CO: Westview, 1993. 626-32.

Anzaldúa, Gloria. "How to Tame a Wild Tongue." *Borderlands/La Frontera: The New Mestiza.* By Gloria Anzaldúa. San Francisco: Aunt Lute, 1987. 53-64. Rpt. in *Out There: Marginalization and Contemporary Cultures.* Ed. Russell Ferguson, Martha Gever, Trinh T. Minh-ha, and Cornel West. New York: New Museum of Contemporary Art; Cambridge: MIT P, 1990. 207-15; (shortened version) *Braided Lives: An Anthology of Multicultural American Writing.* St. Paul: Minnesota Humanities Commission, 1991. 94-97; *Education for Democracy: A Sourcebook for Students and Teachers.* Ed. Benjamin R. Barber and Richard M. Battistoni. Dubuque, IA: Kendall/Hunt, 1993. 247-61; (shortened version) *Infinite Divisions: An Anthology of Chicana Literature.* Ed. Tey Diana Rebolledo and Eliana S. Rivero. Tucson: U of Arizona P, 1993. 180-82; *Ways of Reading: An Anthology for Writers.* Ed. David Bartholomae and Anthony Petrosky. 3rd ed. Boston: Bedford, 1993. 39-48; *Background Readings for Instructors Using the Bedford Handbook for Writers.* Ed. Glenn

B. Blalock. 4th ed. Boston: Bedford, 1994. 291-99; *Signs of Life in the U.S.A.: Readings on Popular Culture.* Ed. Sonia Maasik and Jack Solomon. Boston: Bedford, 1994. 431-39; *A Cultural Studies Reader: History, Theory, Practice.* Ed. Jessica Munns and Gita Rajan. New York: Longman, 1995. 402-11; *Encountering Cultures.* Ed. Richard Holeton. 2nd ed. Englewood Cliffs, NJ: Blair, 1995. 152-62; (shortened version) *Identities: Readings from Contemporary Culture.* Ed. Ann Raimes. Boston: Houghton Mifflin, 1995. 267-72; and (shortened version) *Latinas: Women's Voices from the Borderlands.* Ed. Lillian Castillo-Speed. New York: Simon & Schuster, 1995. 250-56.

Anzaldúa, Gloria. "Metaphors in the Tradition of the Shaman." *Conversant Essays: Contemporary Poets on Poetry.* Ed. James McCorkle. Detroit, MI: Wayne State UP, 1990. 99-100.

Anzaldúa, Gloria. "Movimientos de rebeldía y las culturas que traicionan." *Borderlands/La Frontera: The New Mestiza.* By Gloria Anzaldúa. San Francisco: Aunt Lute, 1987. 15-23. Rpt. in *Argument and Analysis: Reading, Thinking, Writing.* Ed. LynnDianne Beene and Krystan V. Douglas. Austin, TX: Holt, Rinehart & Winston, 1989. 294-302; as "The Strength of My Rebellion." *Issues in Feminism: An Introduction to Women's Studies.* Ed. Sheila Ruth. 3rd ed. Mountain View, CA: Mayfield, 1995. 269-73; and (shortened version) *Women: Images and Realities: A Multicultural Anthology.* Ed. Amy Kesselman, Lily D. McNair, and Nancy Schniedewind. Mountain View, CA: Mayfield, 1995. 43-45.

Anzaldúa, Gloria. "O.K. Momma, Who the Hell Am I? An Interview with Luisah Teish." *This Bridge Called My Back: Writings by Radical Women of Color.* Ed. Cherríe Moraga and Gloria Anzaldúa. 2nd ed. New York: Kitchen Table: Women of Color, 1983. 221-31.

Anzaldúa, Gloria. "La prieta." *This Bridge Called My Back: Writings by Radical Women of Color.* Ed. Cherríe Moraga and Gloria Anzaldúa. 2nd ed. New York: Kitchen Table: Women of Color, 1983. 198-209.

Anzaldúa, Gloria. "Speaking in Tongues: A Letter to 3rd World Women Writers." *This Bridge Called My Back: Writings by Radical Women of Color.* Ed. Cherríe Moraga and Gloria Anzaldúa. 2nd ed. New York: Kitchen Table: Women of Color, 1983. 165-73. Rpt. in *The Writer's Perspective: Voices from American Cultures.* Ed. Maria Cecilia Freeman. Englewood Cliffs, NJ: Prentice Hall, 1994. 289-95.

Anzaldúa, Gloria. "Talking Wild." *Et cetera* 52 (1995-96): 393-400.

Short Stories and Poetry

Anzaldúa, Gloria. "Border Crossings." *Trivia: A Journal of Ideas* 14 (1989): 46-51.

Anzaldúa, Gloria. "Cervicide." *Borderlands/La Frontera: The New Mestiza.* San Francisco: Aunt Lute, 1987. 104-05. Rpt. in *The Many Worlds of Literature.* Ed. Stuart Hirschberg. New York: Macmillan, 1994. 679-80; and *One World, Many Cultures.* Ed. Stuart Hirschberg. 2nd ed. Boston: Allyn & Bacon, 1995. 500-04.

Anzaldúa, Gloria. "Cihuatlyotl, Woman Alone." *Borderlands/La Frontera: The New Mestiza.* By Gloria Anzaldúa. San Francisco: Aunt Lute, 1987. 173. Rpt. in *Redefining Sexual Ethics: A Sourcebook of Essays, Stories, and Poems.* Ed. Susan E. Davies and Eleanor H. Haney. Cleveland, OH: Pilgrim, 1991. 203-04.

Anzaldúa, Gloria. "Cry from the Borderlands." *Crossroads* 31 (1993): 19-21.

Anzaldúa, Gloria Evanjelina. "Del otro lado." *Compañeras: Latina Lesbians.* Ed. Juanita Ramos. New York: Routledge, 1994. 2-3.

Anzaldúa, Gloria. "La historia de una marimacho." *Third Woman* 4 (1989): 64-68.

Anzaldúa, Gloria. "Holy Relics." *Conditions: Six* 2 (1980): 144-50. Rpt. in *Daughters of the Fifth Sun: A Collection of Latina Fiction and Poetry.* Ed. Bryce Milligan, Mary Guerrero Milligan, and Angela de Hoyos. New York: Riverhead, 1995. 90.

Anzaldúa, Gloria. "Horse." *Borderlands/La Frontera: The New Mestiza.* San Francisco: Aunt Lute, 1987. 106-07. Rpt. in *Legacies.* Ed. Carley Rees Bogarad and Jan Zlotnik Schmidt. Fort Worth, TX: Harcourt Brace, 1995. 909-11.

Anzaldúa, Gloria. "In the Name of All the Mothers Who Have Lost Children in the War/*En el nombre de todas las madres que han perdido hijos en la guerra.*" *Ikon: Creativity and Change* 4 (1985): 134-37.

Anzaldúa, Gloria. "Life Line." *Lesbian Love Stories.* Ed. Irene Zahava. Freedom, CA: Crossing, 1989. 1-3. Rpt. in *The Writer's Perspective: Voices from American Cultures.* Ed. Maria Cecilia Freeman. Englewood Cliffs, NJ: Prentice Hall, 1994. 73-76.

Anzaldúa, Gloria. "Ms. Right, My Soul Mate." *Lesbian Love Stories.* Ed. Irene Zahava. Vol. 2. Freedom, CA: Crossing, 1991. 184-88.

Anzaldúa, Gloria. "Nightvoice." *Chicana Lesbians: The Girls Our Mothers Warned Us About.* Ed. Carla Trujillo. Berkeley, CA: Third Woman, 1991. 64-66.

Anzaldúa, Gloria. "No se raje, Chicanita." *Borderlands/La Frontera: The New Mestiza.* San Francisco: Aunt Lute, 1987. 200-01. Rpt. in *Vouz avez dit Chicano: Anthologie thématique de poésie Chicano.* Ed. Elyette Benjamin-Labarthe. Aquitaine, Fr.: Editions de la Maison des Science de L'Homme D'Aquitaine, 1993. 154-57.

Anzaldúa, Gloria. "Old Loyalties." *Chicana Lesbians: The Girls Our Mothers Warned Us About.* Ed. Carla Trujillo. Berkeley, CA: Third Woman, 1991. 74-75.

Anzaldúa, Gloria. "El Paisano Is a Bird of Good Omen." *Cuentos: Stories by Latinas.* Ed. Alma Gómez, Cherríe Moraga, and Mariana Romo-Carmona. New York: Kitchen Table: Women of Color, 1983. 153-75.

Anzaldúa, Gloria. "People Should Not Die in June in South Texas." *Growing Up Latino: Memoirs and Stories.* Ed. Harold Augenbraum and Ilan Stavans. Boston: Houghton Mifflin, 1993. 280-87.

Anzaldúa, Gloria. "Reincarnation (for Julie)," "Birth," "Abstractions (for H. Michaux)," "Now Let Us Go (Tinuique)," "The Visitor," and "El pecado." *Tejidos* 3 (1976): 6-8.

Anzaldúa, Gloria. "Shadow," "Tres pajaros perdidos," and "Never, Momma." *Third Woman* 2 (1984): 5-9.

Anzaldúa, Gloria. "Sobre piedras con lagartijos." *Borderlands/La Frontera: The New Mestiza.* San Francisco: Aunt Lute, 1987. 121-22. Rpt. in *Vous avez dit Chicano: Anthologie thématique de poésie Chicano.* Ed. Elyette Benjamin-Labarthe. Aquitaine, Fr.: Editions de la Maison des Science de L'Homme D'Aquitaine, 1993. 236-39.

Anzaldúa, Gloria. "Sus plumas el viento." *Borderlands/La Frontera: The New Mestiza.* San Francisco: Aunt Lute, 1987. 116-19. Rpt. in *Redefining Sexual Ethics: A Sourcebook of Essays, Stories, and Poems.* Ed. Susan E. Davies and Eleanor H. Haney. Cleveland, OH: Pilgrim, 1991. 181-84.

Anzaldúa, Gloria. "Tlilli, Tlapalli: The Path of the Red and Black Ink." *Borderlands/La Frontera: The New Mestiza.* San Francisco: Aunt Lute, 1987. 65-75. Rpt. in *The Graywolf Annual Five: Multicultural Literacy.* Ed. Scott Walker and Rick Simonson. St. Paul, MN: Graywolf, 1988. 29-40; as "Bedtime Cuentos." *Writing about the World.* Ed. Susan McLeod, with Stacia Bates, Alan Hunt, John Jarvis, and Shelley Spear. New York: Harcourt Brace Jovanovich, 1991. 316-25; and *Patterns of Exposition 13.* Ed. Randall E. Decker and Robert A. Schwegler. New York: HarperCollins, 1992. 503-13.

Anzaldúa, Gloria. "To Live in the Borderlands Means You." *Borderlands/La Frontera: The New Mestiza.* San Francisco: Aunt Lute, 1987. 194-95. Rpt. in *Infinite Divisions: An Anthology of Chicana Literature.* Ed. Tey Diana Rebolledo and Eliana S. Rivero. Tucson: U of Arizona P, 1993. 293-95; *Borderlands and Barrios: Latina Cultures in the United States.* Ed. Denis L. Heyck. New York: Routledge, 1994. 400-02; *Celebrate America in Poetry and Art.* Ed. Nora Panzer. New York: Hyperion, 1994. 65; *Developing Writers: A Workshop Approach.* Ed. Pamela Gay. Belmont, CA: Wadsworth, 1994; *Legacies.* Ed. Carley Rees Bogarad and Jan Zlotnik Schmidt. Fort Worth, TX: Harcourt Brace, 1995. 1081-82; *A New Look at the American West: Lessons for Secondary History and Literature Classes.* Ed. Gloria Eastman and Barbara Miller. Boulder, CO: Social Science Education Consortium, 1996. 225-26.

Anzaldúa, Gloria. "To(o) Queer the Writer—*Loca, escritora y Chicana.*" *InVersions: Writing by Dykes, Queers and Lesbians.* Ed. Betsy Warland. Vancouver, BC: Press Gang, 1991. 249-63.

Anzaldúa, Gloria. "*Tres mujeres in el gabinete*/Three Women in the Closet." *Lesbian Poetry: An Anthology.* Ed. Elly Bulkin and Joan Larkin. Watertown, MA: Persephone, 1981. 172-73.

Anzaldúa, Gloria. "We Call Them Greasers." *Borderlands/La Frontera: The New Mestiza.* San Francisco: Aunt Lute, 1987. 134-35. Rpt. in *The HarperCollins World Reader: The Modern World.* Ed. Mary Ann Caws and Christopher Prendergast. New York: HarperCollins, 1994. 2496-97.

Anzaldúa, Gloria. "A Woman Lies Buried under Me." *Sinister Wisdom* 19 (1982): 2.

Anzaldúa, Gloria. "Woman," "Temple," "Guitarrera," "Helpless," and "Pesadilla." *Tejidos* 4 (1977): 15-17.

Anzaldúa, Gloria. "Yo no fuí, fue tete." *Quarry West* 26 (1989): 48-50.

Interviews

De la Peña, Terri. "On the Borderlands with Gloria Anzaldúa." *Off Our Backs* 21 (1991): 1-4.

Keating, AnnLouise. "Writing, Politics, and *las lesberadas: Platicando con* Gloria Anzaldúa." *Frontiers: A Journal of Women Studies* 14 (1993): 105-30.

Lotbiniere-Harwood, Suzanne. "Conversations at the Book Fair: Interview with Gloria Anzaldúa." *Trivia: A Journal of Ideas* 14 (1989): 37-45.

CHAPTER **6**

Mary Daly

> As I Re-member my own intellectual voyage as a Radical Feminist Philosopher, I
> am intensely aware of the struggle to stay on my True Course, despite undermining
> by demons of distraction that have seemed always to be attempting to pull me off
> course. These I eventually Dis-covered and Named as agents and institutions of
> patriarchy, whose intent was to keep me . . . within the stranglehold of the fore-
> ground, that is, fatherland. My True Course was and is Outercourse—moving
> beyond the imprisoning mental, physical, emotional, spiritual walls of patriarchy.[1]

These words, written by Mary Daly in the opening pages of her autobiography,
speak to the determination, spirit, and energy of this Radical Feminist Philosopher. Her voyage away from patriarchy and her journey into the Outercourse
have been the central focus of Daly's life, writings, and teaching.

Not content to begin recounting her life with the moment of her birth, Daly
remembers that she carried on "fascinating discussions" about her future with
her mother before birth. Her mother "deeply wanted to have just one child—
definitely a girl," but Daly herself needed to decide whether she wanted to enter

this world at all and then whether to live her life as a girl or boy. In this prebirth state, Daly explains, she "studied the situation more closely" and decided to be born.[2] The decision concerning her sex, however, was more difficult. Daly knew that exceptional men existed, although they rarely held institutional power. She noted the sexism against women in the world but saw that the problem was a systemic one, embodied in the life-hating system of patriarchy, "characterized by oppression, repression, depression and cruelty." She also recognized that neither men nor women had behaved particularly admirably under this system. After reflecting on the "extremely poor showing" and the "wretched record of the majority of males wielding patriarchal power on this planet," Daly decided to become a "woman-identified woman warrior and philosopher—to counter patriarchy and embark upon a Be-Dazzling Metapatriarchal Voyage."[3]

Daly knew she would be challenging the status quo and that being born into a life-hating, woman-hating society would make hers a rough voyage. Daly also knew that many people would perceive her as a "one-sided man-hater, a bitch."[4] Nevertheless, she was convinced that she should throw her small weight on the side of the oppressed, and she saw that her entry into the world would be at a "critical Moment—or series of Moments—in history," the time when the "Movement for the liberation of women would Re-surge."[5] She describes her "Original birthday," October 16, 1928, as follows:

> When my Original birthday came, I found mySelf sailing down the birth canal, enjoying the ride and raring to go on my Be-Dazzling Outercourse. The Moment I heard them say "It's a girl!" I squawked with Elemental Self-congratulation. I know that they believed I was crying but I continue to harbor the idea that I was in reality Be-Laughing and that in fact my first word when I saw the light of day was "be-ing."[6]

Daly's parents, Anna Daly and Frank Daly, were working-class Irish Catholics in Schenectady, New York. Her father, who sold ice cream freezers, was forced to leave school after the eighth grade to support his family. As an adult, he wrote a book on how to sell ice cream equipment that Daly believes may have given her the idea that one day she, too, would write a book. Her mother "passionately loved learning" and described as the "tragedy of her life" her being "yanked out of high school" as a sophomore to work for the telephone company. She worked there for "sixteen exhausting years" before she met and married her husband.[7]

Educated in small Catholic elementary and high schools, Daly felt that she was not like the other students there because of her love of books, desire to be a philosopher—an occupation not open to girls at that time—and early woman-identified ways. She always liked her name, for example, and knew early in her life that she "wouldn't sell it for anything" by marrying and becoming "'Mrs.' something or other"; such an act, she believed, would be a violation of her Self.[8]

After high school, Daly attended the College of Saint Rose, an all-women's college in Albany, New York, and took courses that challenged her intellectually. The women who taught these courses demonstrated for Daly that women could be college professors, something Daly wanted to be. In contrast to her women professors, she found the priests at Saint Rose to be amazingly dull and uninteresting, but they were the ones who taught the philosophy courses in which she was interested. Daly took these classes and "devoured the texts," but she "profoundly wanted more—much more."[9]

At Saint Rose, Daly directly confronted evidence of the stunting and taming of women as well as a strong undercurrent preventing deep friendships among women. She remembers the experience as intensely limiting, characterized by an insidious implicit message that women "were not destined for greatness."[10] Daly majored in English because no philosophy major existed and because she knew she wanted to be a writer. Looking for more than what she was offered by the courses required for her major, Daly took so many extra courses and amassed such an unusual number of credits on her transcript that the registrar told Daly she was an embarrassment.[11]

Nearing graduation, Daly knew she wanted to go on to graduate school, but this would be difficult to do because she had no money or connections.[12] Determined to get her master's degree in philosophy, Daly recognized that as "an inhabitant of the spiritual, intellectual, and economic catholic ghetto," her only option was Catholic University of America in Washington, D.C., which offered full-tuition scholarships for graduate students.[13] These scholarships were available, however, only in the fields in which students had majored as undergraduates, so Daly opted to pursue an M.A. in English and took philosophy courses on the side.[14]

At the close of her studies at Catholic University, Daly saw an ad for the School of Sacred Theology, offering a Ph.D. in religion for women, which was being started at St. Mary's College in South Bend, Indiana. She requested admission and received an immediate response with an offer of a scholarship plus a part-time job teaching English. Daly received her Ph.D. in religion from St. Mary's College at the age of 25.

Dissatisfied with her doctorate—she had wanted her Ph.D. to be in philosophy—Daly applied for admission to the University of Notre Dame, located across the road from St. Mary's. She was refused admission solely because she was a woman. At the same time, St. Mary's withdrew its offer of a teaching position, and Daly was without a job or academic program. After receiving rejections from more than two dozen colleges, she was offered and accepted a teaching position at Cardinal Cushing College in Brookline, Massachusetts, for the fall of 1954.

Daly characterizes her life between 1954 and 1959 as "surviving the grind of the grim fifties." During this period, however, she did audit some of Paul

Tillich's lectures at Harvard Divinity School, determine that she would like to write a book, and discover Simone de Beauvoir's *The Second Sex.*[15] This book helped her to make sense of her experiences and the feelings she had about women's position in society. She describes herself as drinking it "in great gulps like a woman who had been deprived of water almost to a point beyond endurance."[16]

Daly still yearned to be a philosopher, believing that this not only would satisfy her own intellectual needs but assist her in securing a teaching position "in a college which might be said to have an intellectually challenging atmosphere."[17] After more rejections from universities, Daly realized that the United States was not going to be the place where she could earn her degree in philosophy. When she discovered that Germany and Switzerland were the only two countries that would not permit the exclusion of women from academic programs on the basis of sex, she turned her attention abroad. In 1959, Daly was awarded a Swiss Exchange Scholarship to study at the University of Fribourg in Switzerland. She stayed abroad for seven years, feeling more at home there than in the United States. At the University of Fribourg, she earned two doctorates—one in philosophy and one in theology—taking her courses in Latin and French. During this time she published *Natural Knowledge of God in the Philosophy of Jacques Maritain* (1966) and began writing *The Church and the Second Sex.*

Daly would have liked to have stayed in Switzerland indefinitely, but she had to return to the United States in 1966 because she was no longer eligible for student status, and Switzerland would not let her remain in the country as a worker. After considering offers from several institutions, she accepted a position at Boston College as an assistant professor. She later realized that with her degrees and teaching experience, she easily could have negotiated for associate status with tenure at the time of her hiring.

In 1968, Daly published *The Church and the Second Sex,* a book that exposes the misogyny of Christianity, particularly that of the Roman Catholic Church. With the publication of the book, she requested tenure and promotion at Boston College but instead was offered a one-year contract that would terminate at the end of the year.[18] Even at this early stage of her career, Daly had extensive qualifications: She held seven degrees, including three doctorates; she had 16 years of teaching experience, with positive student evaluations; and she had published two books, as well as various articles in scholarly journals.

Denial of tenure for Daly resulted in a lengthy battle that involved media attention, the resignation in protest by two members of the college's promotion and tenure committee, a march of 1,500 students to the college president's house with a petition signed by 2,500 students (the students were mostly men—Boston College had not yet admitted women to the College of Arts and Sciences), a seven-hour teach-in, and the spraying of red graffiti on the side of the administration building ("faint traces of which remain to this day"). Finally, Daly explains, "the Jesuits could no longer hide behind their rosary beads," and a special review committee was established to investigate Daly's tenure case.[19]

No decision was made on Daly's tenure during that school year, but Daly was sent a telegram, without congratulations, from the president of Boston College, granting her tenure and promotion; she received the telegram while she was teaching summer classes at a small college in Oregon. When she returned to Boston College in the fall of 1968, she began to experience harassment of various kinds. Students were told at registration that Daly's classes were full when they were not and that she was extremely difficult as a professor.

Despite these obstacles, Daly continued to teach at Boston College and to write. In 1973, she published *Beyond God the Father: Toward a Philosophy of Women's Liberation.* In this book, Daly defines women as members of a sexual caste and argues for the potential of the women's revolution to transform human consciousness. Daly applied for promotion to full professor in 1974 and, as in her earlier battle for tenure, her request was denied. By this time, Daly had published three books; had seen her work reprinted in several languages; had published more than 30 articles in scholarly journals, other periodicals, books, and symposia proceedings; had engaged in extensive committee and advisory work; and had presented more than 70 addresses to professional and community groups, including keynote addresses to international symposia. The chair of her department at Boston College, however, noted that feminist studies did not serve her well in backing up her promotion request.[20]

When she received a grant from the Rockefeller Foundation, Daly used the funds to take an unpaid leave from Boston College from 1975 to 1978, spending the time writing her next book, *Gyn/Ecology: The Metaethics of Radical Feminism* (1978). A work about women's becoming, *Gyn/Ecology* offers a harsh critique of patriarchy in myriad forms and identifies and discusses the demons that prevent women from journeying into full lives. When she returned to Boston College, harassment continued. Some of Daly's classes were disrupted by individuals who were not enrolled in them, and other classes were officially monitored by college representatives. Students filed official complaints regarding the disruptions and the monitoring, and a letter of support signed by every member of Daly's monitored classes was sent to *The Heights,* the school newspaper. Daly explains part of her rationale for staying at Boston College despite the harassment: "Boston College had functioned as a laboratory and microcosm, enabling me to understand even more deeply not only the banal mechanisms of phallocratic evil but also possibilities of transcendence."[21]

Daly's next book, *Pure Lust: Elemental Feminist Philosophy* (1984), is a work that speaks to the Elemental powers of women and their abilities to realize these powers. Daly took three years of unpaid leave from Boston College to write the book and returned to teaching in the fall of 1983. In 1987, "in cahoots" with Jane Caputi, she published *Websters' First New Intergalactic Wickedary of the English Language.* A dictionary-like sourcebook of words, definitions, and concepts Daly has created in her writing over the years, the book is "Wicked" in the sense of "beyond patriarchal 'good' and 'evil'; characterized by Original Integrity; Originally Sinful; actively participating in the Unfolding of Be-ing as Good."[22]

In 1989, Daly again requested and was denied promotion to the rank of full professor at Boston College. Without even going through the two cartons of materials she had submitted, the promotion committee objected to her lack of refereed articles. When asked why she stayed at Boston College, Daly responded, "I will leave, if I choose to leave, on my own terms. I have every right to be here. I choose to stand my ground."[23]

In 1992, Daly published *Outercourse: The Be-Dazzling Voyage,* an autobiography of her life and her work. Her mantra as she wrote the book was, "'Keep Going Mary. Go!' Because they want me to stop. They want us to stop. The undead vampire men, the bio-robots gone berserk, the leaders. They want us to stop, because they are winding down."[24] In Daly's next book, *Quintessence . . . Realizing the Future: A Radical Elemental Feminist Manifesto,* she moves beyond *Outercourse* to develop her Elemental Feminist Philosophy. As Daly explains, she continues to work and to write not only because patriarchy would like her to stop but because "you see, I have arrived here, Now, and I can begin. Because I was born for this Time, and I am strong."[25]

Nature of the World

Since the publication of *Beyond God the Father,* Daly has been describing systematically and comprehensively an ethical, institutional, and ontological duality that exists in society. She labels the components of this duality the *foreground* and the *Background.* The foreground is misogynistic—antiwoman and oppressive—and Daly sees this misogyny as linked to the hatred of all life forms. The Background, in contrast, is the realm in which women move beyond oppression and hatred and journey into a life-loving and life-affirming state of Be-ing.

Foreground

The foreground is patriarchy—a sexist social system that is distinctly unnatural and constitutes a limiting and destructive realm for women. The foreground is "plastic, contrived," and "possessed," a place where women's identities, self-images, and experiences are so distorted that they rarely reflect the truths of women's lives. This realm is a "male-centered and monodimensional arena where fabrication, objectification, and alienation take place." It is the "zone of fixed feelings, perceptions, behaviors," the place where reversals and deception are common. Daly also labels this realm the *flatland,* where nothing is wild, free, or unpredictable.[26]

The foreground is marked by violence and aggression. So rooted is the system in the "fusion of obsession and aggression," Daly explains, that human potential, both male and female, is destroyed.[27] Daly describes the violence and aggression of the foreground as a "life-hating lechery that rapes and kills the objects of its obsession/aggression"—women—and a "Lecherous State" infused with evil. The foreground is a "sadosociety" and a "pseudosociety"—a society characterized by "unmitigated malevolence" that attempts to annihilate all life, to dismember spirit and matter, and to mold images of women for male purposes.[28]

Women (and men) have become so accustomed to the foreground that they simply do not see it as something that can be changed. As Daly explains, women "have screened out experience" and attended only to those issues "considered meaningful and licit within the boundaries of prevailing thought structures."[29] The foreground, then, is steeped in lies—in the "mental/spiritual deprivation" that prevents women from seeing beyond the dogma of foreground ideology.[30]

The lies of foreground ideology occur in numerous contexts, including science, theology, psychology, and biology, but one of the biggest lies of the foreground assumes the form of pornography. Daly explains that the "pornographic Lie . . . is that the normal female demands the force, the violence, the pain. . . . Every woman is affected by the basic pornographic message that 'women want it.'"[31] She elaborates: "Having been forced to swallow this Biggest Lie, the victims of such mental torture continue to argue for justice, rationality, and human liberation, and to be grateful for the slightest concessions, while remaining unable to see that their basic right to be-ing is denied by the sadosociety."[32] Pornography is but one example of the lies of the foreground, which inflicts deep damage on women by its myriad deceptive messages. The effects of such lies are to prevent women from listening to their Selves and to each other and to keep women focused on and believing in the fabrications of the foreground.

Another form the fabrications of the foreground assume is false images that reinforce women's subservient roles and perpetuate their lower status. Daly critiques religious symbols as one institutionalized source of these false images, arguing that institutionalized religion, particularly Catholicism and Christianity, offers women a "derivative status" in relation to men; it perpetuates a "planetary caste system" with women always at the bottom.[33] The result is the dehumanization of women in the eyes of many and an "alienated self," an "authentic being [who] struggles to say its own name."[34] Institutionalized religion causes women to internalize "the identity and roles imposed" upon them "so that what may seem to be an experienced identity is in reality a false identity."[35] The story of Adam and Eve, the image of "Mary kneeling before her own Son," and the "exalted" status of women on pedestals are but a few of the symbols of this false identity and dehumanization of women offered by the foreground Church.[36]

Daly exposes the institutionalization of fabricated images of women embedded in other social structures as well—structures that often are regarded as harmless cultural practices or historical events of the past. Women often are complicit in the perpetuation of these images because social structures deem the practices behind them natural and customary. A global foreground that facilitates and honors such practices as Indian suttee, Chinese foot binding, African genital mutilation, European witch burnings, and even American gynecology perpetuates the deceptive and deadly nature of these false female images and cultural practices. As the foreground world of misogyny becomes ritualized and performances are repeatedly enacted, women become emotionally complicit in their own murders and their own physical mutilation. In the foreground, "both victims and victimizers . . . perform uncritically their preordained roles" and forget that they are participating in deceptive and deadly myths.[37]

When women bind the feet of their own daughters to ensure their marriageability, when they willingly throw themselves on their husbands' funeral pyres because they have no means of support or survival, or when they submit to dangerous and unnecessary gynecological procedures because modern medicine deems them necessary or helpful, they are internalizing the lies of the foreground that sanction the "murder/dismemberment" of women. Daly explains that those who see racism and/or imperialism in "indictment of these atrocities can do so only by blinding themselves to the fact that the oppression of women knows no ethnic, national, or religious bounds."[38] These ritualized and socially sanctioned practices take on the image of normalcy as cultures—and women themselves—fail to recognize or appreciate the harms done as a result of them. The lies of women's willingness to be hurt, their pleasure in physical and emotional pain, and their passive acceptance of foreground dogma become so inscribed in the foreground mentality that to think otherwise is to challenge the very heart of this realm.

Concerned primarily with the manufacture of illusions—illusions that keep women locked into positions of inferiority and dependence—the foreground is pervasive and antifemale. Women conform to the destructive roles and accept carefully controlled definitions of themselves in the foreground, unable or unwilling to resist the messages perpetuated by the Church, society, and the institutional structures of culture. Because resistance of such messages is difficult, the foreground prevents individuals from achieving their "innately ordained Self-direction toward Happiness."[39]

Background

As pervasive and damaging as it is, the foreground is not the only realm in which women can function. In stark contrast to the foreground, in the Background, rules are broken, lies are dispelled, and life-affirming images are created for women. Whether or not men can inhabit the Background is unclear. Daly does not specifically say they cannot, but she also does not include them in her discussions. Her focus is on women and on creating woman-identified identities.

Daly defines the Background as the "Realm of Wild Reality; the Homeland of women's Selves and of all other Others; the Time/Space where auras of plants, planets, stars, animals and all Other animate beings connect."[40] The Background is the wild realm, the realm of "Hags and Crones. It is Hag-ocracy," where the demons of the foreground are reduced to ghosts and long-forgotten memories.[41]

The Background is a realm of affirmation and journey that functions in opposition to the foreground in almost every way. In the Background, individuals move the "Wrong Way" or "Contrary-Wise"—contrary to foreground logic and rules—to reverse the images presented in the foreground and to create new ways of thinking and living for women.[42] They engage in a process of rejecting foreground fabrications and creating alternative woman-identified Selves. Perhaps most important, the Background is a place where women search for Being, which Daly defines as "ontological self-affirmation" and a "qualitative leap of courage in the face of patriarchy."[43] Be-ing is participation in the "Ultimate/ Intimate Reality" and "the 'Final Cause,' the Good who is Self-communicating, who is the Verb from whom, in whom, and with whom all true movements move."[44] Be-ing requires action and movement and involves breaking through the fabrications of the foreground so that senses once dormant return to life.

The Background is rooted in an ethic of biophilia, "the Original Lust for Life"[45] or the "Pure Lust" of an "intense longing" to leave the foreground. Biophilic Pure Lust is "high humor, hope and cosmic accord/harmony of those women who choose to escape."[46] Biophilic Pure Lust involves connecting with the stars, animals, plants, and all life forms. Whereas the foreground is life violating and grounded in an ethic of violence, the Background is ethically oriented to the passionate involvement and connection of women to life and the elements.

Daly characterizes the Background as a process of ontological journeying that is not linear; rather, it requires that women spin past those who block them from the Background and through "their mazes . . . at multiple times in multiple ways."[47] The journey is a voyage in which Survivors of the foreground begin to reject the deception of patriarchy and define their own lives, defying the

deception of patriarchal history"[48] and discovering a world in which women
identify the sources of deception in all of their complex and simple forms and
create new identities, new Selves, and new frameworks for living.

Once the spiraling journey begins, women undergo a metamorphosis that
Daly identifies as "the succession of transformative moments/movements of
be-ing"[49] and "living the spiraling journey of integrity and transformation."[50]
The Otherworld of the Background is a call to participate in spiraling/metamor-
phosing moments/movements of be-ing, to remember the deception of patriarchy but to put it in the past, and to express "an Other way of understanding
ultimate/intimate reality."[51] The Background is a call to exhibit the courage to
name what once was unnameable, to move into the center of the Self, and to act
"out-wardly" to dis-cover life.[52]

The world of the Background encourages women to speak their own experiences and to articulate their own values and perspectives. Women reject
foreground identities and the "State of Possession" the foreground offers them.
They use "new words" and new structures that transform or re-call the "meanings of old words" to move into a different cognitive space.[53] Even while women
are caught in a physical space controlled by males, the Background allows them
to focus "upon different patterns of meaning than those explicitly expressed and
accepted" in the foreground.[54]

The Background, in contrast to the foreground, calls women to Life and
encourages them to take control of their histories, identities, and experiences.
It celebrates the woman-centered perceptions that have been denied in the
foreground and is grounded in a Biophilic ethic—a life-loving and life-affirming orientation to the world. The Background runs contrary to the foreground,
encouraging activities and actions that violate foreground assumptions about
and perceptions of women. It identifies and unravels the deceptions of the
foreground and offers, instead, be-ing—the ultimate, spiraling journey that
connects women with their Selves, one another, and the cosmos.

Definition of Feminism

Daly's feminism is a Radical Feminism that reflects her ontological orientation.
She defines the Radical Feminism of the Background as "the Cause of causes,
which alone of all revolutionary causes exposes the basic model and source of
all forms of oppression—patriarchy—and thus can open up consciousness to
active participation in Movement, Transcendence, and Happiness." Radical
Feminism requires be-ing "*for* women and all Elemental Life" and brings with
it the awareness of ways of living that do not conform to the foreground or
patriarchal norms. Individuals are Radical Feminists when they "aim at nothing
less than an entire subversion of the present order of society."[55] Grounded in a
"metaethics . . . of a *deeper intuitive* type," Radical Feminism is the means by

which the foreground's hidden agendas are exposed and mythic reversals are acknowledged and refused.[56]

Women who choose to be feminists of the kind Daly advocates—Radical Feminists—must be willing to reject the male God and all his fabrications and bond with other women. To be a Radical Feminist is to become a member of a minority, to place one's trust in other women, and to reclaim women's relationships with other women. To be such a feminist is to step into the Background, to embrace the cognitive and affective shift that takes place in the soul as a result, and to embark on the spiraling journey of female becoming that takes women into the Background.

Individuals in the foreground may call themselves *feminists,* Daly explains, but they advocate a plastic feminism that feeds on violence, guilt, and anxiety. Their information and perceptions are man-made, and the effect is to spread disillusionment about feminism among women. Plastic feminists argue that feminism has failed women and that women must turn to men or to "phallic sponsors for support in their crisis of feminist faith."[57] In the plastic feminism of the foreground, women are programmed to become consumers and propagators of male-mediated information. They become "walking, talking subliminal" messages, cajoling other women "to accept defeat."[58]

Nature of the Rhetor

Two very different kinds of rhetors exist in Daly's rhetorical theory. One group of rhetors perpetuates and reinforces the realm of the foreground, whereas the other participates in the journey of be-ing inherent in the realm of the Background. The rhetors in the foreground are characterized by their negative qualities, which Daly carefully articulates in order to expose their perspectives and their methods. Rhetors in the Background, in contrast, are characterized by their life-affirming and Contrary-Wise traits.

Foreground

The most common characteristic of foreground rhetors is their desire to control women and bully them into submission. Daly labels these individuals *snools,* and she offers a "Glossary of Snools" in which she identifies and discusses the qualities of these foreground rhetors. Snools are "the cast of characters governing and legitimizing bore-ocracy" or the foreground.[59] They are "cringing" and "mean-spirited" individuals who rule in the foreground; as a verb, *snool* means "to reduce to submission," to bully, to cringe, to cower.[60] Although snools may appear to be under the spell of the foreground and thus accept no responsibility for their actions, they are responsible for their actions and for keeping women from finding their way to the Background easily.

Daly explains that snools "appear and re-appear in various forms,"[61] including *fixers, plug-uglies,* and *wantwits.* Fixers, also known as *Fix-Masters,* make the foreground seem nonvolatile and solid; they "continually aim to freeze life." Plug-uglies are snools who are "often active in political pressure and intimidation" and who represent the brutality that is characteristic of the foreground. Plug-uglies "include everyday rapists, child-abusers, pimps, wife-beaters, maimers, murderers, dismemberers, as well as professional hatchet-men such as those physicians and surgeons, politicians, scientists, and military experts who kill in order to cure."[62] Wantwits are individuals who lack the "qualities of sense and intelligence"; they are necessary cogs "in the negatively spinning wheels of foolocracy."[63] Snools, then, assume many forms and engage in diverse—but always oppressive—activities.

Not all foreground communicators are male; women can be snools, and the common characteristic shared by these women is that they are *Totaled Women.* Daly uses as synonyms for these rhetors labels such as *Daddy's Girls* and *Fembots,*[64] suggesting that they have been taught to "cater compulsively to [their] master's 'special' quirks."[65] Daly identifies several kinds of Totaled Women. *Sadofeminists,* for example, advocate "a species of plastic feminism marked by malignant hatred of and/or indifference to women";[66] *Self-loathing ladies* "titter," suppressing their laughter so as not to offend males.[67] In general, Totaled Women are numb to the effects of patriarchy and conform to its standards with pleasure. Female foreground rhetors, like their male counterparts, seek to thwart and intimidate those women who wish to journey into the Background.

Background

Daly's typology of Background rhetors is equally as disrespectful to mainstream or foreground ears as is her list of foreground rhetors. Daly labels the rhetors of the Background *Hags, Crones,* and *Spinsters* as well as *Fates, Gnomes, Salamanders, Scolds, Shrews, Soothsayers, Virgins, Websters,* and *Weirds.*[68] She suggests that "as the crowd increases, the diversity intensifies," celebrating the various manifestations of "traveling companions" in the Background.[69]

The power of Background rhetors lies in their "astral force" and their "Lusty" spirits that voyage along and Name be-ing.[70] A Weird, for example, is a "FATE," a "SOOTHSAYER"; a Webster is "a weaver."[71] A Spinster is "a woman whose occupation is to Spin, to participate in the whirling movement of creation; one who has chosen her Self, who defines her Self by choice neither in relation to children nor to men."[72] Thus, both Websters and Spinsters are Virgin women who are "never captured: UNSUBDUED." Consequently, each type of woman is a Wanton, an individual who lacks "discipline: not susceptible to control:

UNRULY." Unruly women also are Shrews. A Shrew is "a person, especially (now only) a woman given to railing or scolding or other perverse or malignant behavior." Shrews, of course, are "*Scolds*: A Scold is 'in early use, a person (especially a woman) of ribald speech; later a woman . . . addicted to abusive language.'"[73] In the foreground, the language of women regularly is labeled *shrewish,* and Background scolding about foreground "phallic lust predictably will be called ribald and abusive."[74]

Nonhuman animals also constitute Background rhetors, and their traits are especially valued as characteristics women want to assume or on which they might rely. Gnomes are ageless creatures who often guard precious treasures, which they reveal "to mortals for whom they have friendship."[75] Undines are water nymphs who "represent the treacherousness of rivers, lakes, and torrents." Background rhetoric, Daly explains, often seems treacherous and even "wicked" to foreground inhabitants; undines are the source of this treacherousness as well as the guides who help women navigate through foreground resistance.[76] A Salamander is a "mythical and not clearly defined animal having the power to endure fire without harm." Background rhetors can borrow characteristics—such as those of the salamanders—from their nonhuman companions. When they do, they become Salamandrous, which means "living as it were in fire; fiery, hot, passionate." Salamandrous Background rhetors, then, are brave women who re-member "the nine million women who were massacred during the Witchcraze in Western Europe" by fire and who now are "fueled by Female Fury." They "inhabit the element Fire" and transform it into female energy or gynergy.[77]

As women enter the Background, they become Hags—haggard or untamed by foreground standards. Haggard women seem "evil" and "ugly" to those with a foreground mentality, but in the Background, these rhetors are recognized to be on "the journey of radical be-ing." The longer women remain haggard, the more they are seen as examples of "courage, strength, and wisdom." Thus, Hags become Crones—"the long-lasting ones" who live to record and create life outside of the foreground.[78]

Subverting the foreground and becoming woman identified requires that rhetors recognize both the strategic use of rhetoric in the foreground and the alternatives available to Background rhetors. Whereas foreground rhetors block Radical Feminist be-coming, Background rhetors facilitate this journey and transformation. Rhetoric in the two realms functions very differently and produces very different outcomes

Rhetorical Options

In the foreground, numerous rhetorical options exist to prevent women from recognizing their oppression and to keep them from challenging it once they do recognize its presence. In the Background, options exist to challenge this oppression and to create new ways of living.

Foreground

Daly identifies six rhetorical options for keeping women silenced, alienated, controlled, and contained in the foreground. The fabrications characteristic of the foreground are the options of ritualistic violence toward women, silencing and erasing women's voices, fixing women's images, refusing to see the problem, reversal, and elementary terms.

Ritualistic Violence toward Women

Ritualized violence toward women is violence that, when repeated in similar patterns over years or centuries, conditions individuals to perceive it as normal and even acceptable. Daly identifies several cultural practices that are or have been normalized but are or were highly destructive to women. Some are obvious, such as the practices of Indian suttee, Chinese foot binding, and African genital mutilation; these ritualized, symbolic acts illustrate the depth and scope of violent and oppressive foreground practices.[79]

Daly explains that the ritualized nature of these practices, as well as the confusing label of *cultural,* masks the concrete reality of murder in the lives of women. Suttee, the ceremonial burning alive of widows on the funeral pyres of their husbands, is grounded in a religious principle that forbids remarriage, in the cultural practice of marrying very young girls to much older men, and in the social reality that widows tend to lead lives of prostitution and to die from venereal disease after their husbands' deaths should they escape suttee.[80] The Chinese ritual of binding women's feet in very early childhood is rooted in the cultural and "familiar fixation on 'purity'"—women and girls should "never 'run around'"—as well as in the ideological belief in the beauty of a "courtesan's 'tiny feet.'"[81] Genital mutilation, as practiced in Africa and elsewhere, is designed to enhance male sexual pleasure. It ranges from the removal of the tip of a girl's clitoris to the removal of the entire clitoris, labia minora, and parts of the labia majora and then the sealing of the vaginal orifice so that it heals with only a small opening. This ritual leaves women, if they live through the operation, "debilitated for the rest of their lives" and certain that they will encounter the "little knife" repeatedly as they have to be cut open for intercourse and then again for the birth of a child.[82]

Although Western women may believe their cultures do not engage in ritualistic violence, such violence also occurs in Europe and the United States. The Sado-Ritual Syndrome is evident, for example, in European witch burnings and North American gynecological practices. Between the fifteenth and the seventeenth centuries, witches were accused of being sexually impure and possessing a "carnal lust which is in women insatiable."[83] As a result, women (and a few men) who were thought to be witches were burned alive or were tortured until they confessed their sins, after which they were burned. The punishment was designed to purify the women and to give the persecutors sanction to project "their fantasies upon the accused women."[84] Many of the women tortured and killed were those who lived "outside the control of the patriarchal family"; often, they were healers, midwives, or unmarried women, and the practice served as a form of foreground political and social control.[85]

Equally as controlling as witch burning is the foreground practice of North American gynecology and therapy, which Daly characterizes as the "'doctor knows best' . . . Ice Age of Gynocidal Gynecology." The "massacre of the wise women/healers during the witchcraze was followed by the rise of man-mid-wives who eventually became dignified by the name 'gynecologist.'"[86] Since that time, women have been reduced to little more than "sex organs," and gynecology has become the practice of "ruthlessly cutting up women's bod-ies."[87] Practices characteristic of this Ice Age are not only cesarean sections and mastectomies but the current epidemic of hysterectomies in the United States, chemical cures for female infertility, the unnecessary practices of cosmetic surgery, and the treatment of menopause as a sickness.[88] Again, Daly describes each as a form of political and social control and as embodying an ideology of foreground domination and violence toward women.

Silencing and Erasing Women's Voices

A second rhetorical option used by foreground rhetors is the silencing and erasure of women's voices. The strategy of silencing takes many forms, but it centers on the creation of fear in the minds of women should they speak out against the foreground. Calling women *sick, selfish, sexless,* or *man-haters* when they raise the issue of women's oppression and telling them that they lack a sense of humor when they challenge foreground jokes are rhetorical practices that are used to threaten women into silence.[89] Fear of the labels *spinster* or *lesbian* are other "boring and predictable" rhetorical practices that have "driven many into matrimony, mental hospitals, and—worst of all—numbing, dumbing normality."[90] Such labels effectively silence women because of their negative connotations in the foreground. Silenced, women then are prevented from speaking against foreground practices and policies and on behalf of their woman-identified Selves.

Silencing and erasure occur as well in "pseudo generic" terms such as *he* and *man.* The equally deceptive terms *people* and *person,* which supposedly include both women and men, represent more subtle modes of erasure. The debate over *he* and *man* is not new, and many women are aware of this form of erasure. Women, however, often are lulled into complacency with *people* until they hear a phrase such as "people and their wives."[91] This erasure also occurs in specific professions, exemplified in phrases such as "doctors and their wives" and "faculty and their wives." At this point, Background rhetors become aware of the linguistic manipulation in operation and the erasure of women as full participants in society. Both silencing and erasure, which typically occur together, constrain women and prevent them from recognizing their full powers and abilities.

Fixing Women's Images

The rhetorical option of fixing women's images is a third way that rhetoric is used in the foreground to keep women in positions of inferiority and submission. Daly articulates the ways in which women's identities become fixed so that they have very little sense of their Selves and very little control over constructing their identities. She argues that this rhetorical practice allows those in the foreground to construct powerful and "eminently forgettable images of women" in art, literature, religion, and the mass media.[92] In these arenas, women become *Cosmo* Girls, *Playboy* Bunnies, foxy ladies, chicks, and pussycats and are cast as bitches, beavers, old bats, biddies, cows, and nags.[93] In the realm of religion, women's images also are fixed, this time as one-dimensional beings—exalted yet in need of protection, discipline, and rule.[94]

The effects of fixing women's images to be consistent with foreground assumptions are profound. Daly explains that in "a patriarchal world, which is the only one known in recorded history, it has been impossible for women together to speak our own word."[95] Thus, the "naming of what it means to be human" has not been done by women, nor has it taken women into account.[96] Fixing women's images as something other than woman-identified, Self-identified human beings results in a "false identification" that saps women's energy and deflects their anger and hope.[97] In fixing women's images, strong women are labeled *ugly,* and resistance is difficult because options to foreground images rarely, if ever, are presented or supported.[98] The result is a state of "*robotitude,*" or "the reduction of life in the state of servitude to mechanical motion." Women, fixed into images not of their own making, are encouraged to follow "false molds" implanted in their minds during their "first months and years of existence."[99] To be fixed into robotitude is never to go beyond the state of maintaining these images, never "breaking the casts" of foreground existence into which women have been molded so that they can cast their "Selves into the world."[100]

Refusing to See the Problem

A fourth rhetorical practice Daly identifies as characterizing the foreground involves using discourse that hides the presence of a sexual caste system and clouds the issue of women's oppression. Daly labels these responses *depreciation, particularization, spiritualization,* and *universalization* and suggests that they function to hide the realities of women's situation in the foreground. The first possibility, depreciation, is used when the question is asked: "Are you on that subject of women again when there are so many important problems—like war, racism, pollution of the environment?" Daly explains that, upon hearing such a question, individuals would think that "there is no connection between sexism and the rape of the Third World, the rape of the blacks, or the rape of land and water."[101]

Particularization, a second response used to cloud the issue of women's oppression, is exemplified in the statement "Oh, that's a Catholic problem. The Catholic Church is so medieval." In this rhetorical option, individuals believe that "there is no patriarchy anywhere else"—that the foreground is limited to only a few institutions.[102] Spiritualization is "the refusal to look at concrete oppressive facts" and is used in the common response "In Christ there is neither male nor female." Spiritualization clouds the fact that "*even if* this were true, the fact is that everywhere else there certainly is." Moreover, given "the concrete facts of social reality and . . . that the Christ-image is male, one has to ask what meaning-content the passage possibly can have."[103] Universalization presents the issue of women's oppression as somehow naturally subsumed under human oppression. Universalization occurs when individuals remark, "But isn't the real problem *human* liberation?"[104] Perhaps it is, Daly responds, but when used as a foreground rhetorical option, universalization masks the specific problems of sexism.

All of the various responses to the problem of women's oppression effectively take the focus away from foreground practices and the oppression of women. As rhetorical options, they successfully deflect and prevent conversation and analysis from occurring and move women's energies away from challenging the foreground.

Reversal

The rhetorical option of reversal is inherent in all of patriarchy—its symbols, stories, politics, social structures, and behaviors. Reversal includes the attribution of female capacities to males, redundancy and contradiction, and the use of terms or phrases to mean the opposite of what they really mean. Daly suggests that reversals often are "blatantly silly."[105] The most famous example of a reversal is the case of the birth of Eve from Adam's rib, leading to the "insistence that a male was the original mother."[106]

Reversal also can be "deceptively innocuous sounding," exemplified in writer William A. Rossi's account of Chinese foot binding, which he describes as "one of the most persuasive examples of the foot's *natural* eroticism."[107] Daly suggests that Rossi's description is designed to link "sexual desire" with the "natural" mutilation of a woman's foot.[108] Equally as horrifying as reversal is the use of the adjective *curious* to mask the horror of the ritual. Reversals usually result in doublethink, a process in which individuals simultaneously hold in their minds opposing or incompatible ideas. Examples of doublethink are references to the MX missile as a *Peacekeeper* and to human bodies as *machines*. Doublethink, Daly explains, "is the perverted psychological mechanism which makes reversals acceptable and even invisible."[109]

Elementary Terms

Elementary terms are distinguished by their contrived nature and their capacity to dull the imagination and discourage critical thinking. Elementary is characterized by "artificiality, lack of depth, aura and interconnectedness with living be-ing." Elementaries, according to Daly, are artificial, evil, and destructive terms that grow out of foreground logic and influences. Terms, she continues, are "dead words that terminate thought." Elementary terms, then, distort and mediate experiences and events. Difficult to identify, "they are like poisonous fumes and radioactive emissions permeating the atmosphere."[110] Elementary terms fall into three categories: mummies, dummies, and anti-bodies.

Mummies are the most widespread of the elementary terms in the foreground and serve as the foundation or blueprint for all other elementary terms. Examples of mummy terms are *civilization, mystery, custom, forefathers,* and *history*.[111] These and other mummies are the terms commonly used in the foreground to legitimate as well as perpetuate the perspectives of the foreground. Mummy terms pretend a "depth that they do not possess" and, in their lack of depth, "leave no profound impression."[112] Mummy terms do not name reality; instead, they mystify and create emptiness and hollowness.

Mummies make way for *dummies*. A dummy is "an imitation, copy or likeness of something intended for use as a substitute: EFFIGY."[113] Dummy terms act as substitutes for phenomena that occur in nature. Examples of dummy terms are *plant* for "nuclear power plant," *daughter* to describe a decay product produced by radioactive matter, *Tide* to describe a laundry soap, and "the dummy of dummies" in the 1980s—*Star Wars*.[114] Dummy terms also demean what they label and copy. Examples of degrading dummy labels in the foreground are *witch, chick,* and *bitch*.[115]

Dummy terms suggest that life is not valued in the realm of the foreground; dummies are against life and thus foreshadow another category of terms: *anti-bodies*. Terms that are anti-biotic are antilife. As rhetorical options in the foreground, anti-biotic terms and phrases are so far removed from the thing in nature they name that they do not even resemble the object or entity they symbolize. Examples include SAINT, a 1960s' acronym for "Satellite Interceptor"; MAD, meaning "Mutual Assured Destruction"; and *AIDS,* the acronym for "Acquired Immune Deficiency Syndrome."[116]

Whether by word, ritual, or philosophy, the foreground is powerfully antilife, antiwoman, and antinature. Individually and together, the foreground options function to reinforce and perpetuate the foreground world and make it difficult to see and thus to resist. Daly, however, presents numerous rhetorical options for Background rhetors to use as they move out of the foreground and into the Other realm. Background rhetorical options are vastly different from foreground options, and their focus is on facilitating a recognition of the foreground and moving beyond it.

Background Options

Daly identifies several rhetorical options for Background rhetors: metaphor; redefinition; capitalization; Spelling/Be-Spelling; Grammar/Sin-Tactics; Pronouncing; Spooking, Sparking, and Spinning; and Be-Laughing. Daly explains that such options

> open up levels of reality otherwise closed to us and they unlock dimensions and elements of our souls which correspond to these hidden dimensions and elements of reality. . . . There is no way that Elemental feminist philosophy can speak adequately to the realms of Wild be-ing without symbols. In discovering these, we must pay particular attention to the task of "sounding out" symbols.[117]

Background rhetors can make use of all or any combination of these options to create a reality other than the foreground. There is no one right way to go about creating this reality. Daly encourages Background Prudes to heed their intuition about "which symbols ring true, listening to the sounds of their names and to the rhythms of the contexts in which this Naming occurs."[118]

Metaphor

Because the Background offers a "deviant philosophy," rhetors must use metaphors to move away from the norm of the foreground and to "express woman-identified thought."[119] Metaphors "Name/evoke a shock, a clash with the 'going logic' and they introduce a new logic." Metaphors elicit change because they name the desired change and suggest alternative visions, realities, and possibilities. Because metaphors help individuals see Other ways of being and be-ing, they can be used by Background rhetors to "cut through the mazes of man-made mystification" and to transform thought and action.[120]

Metaphors are particularly relevant to the process of Be-ing because the prefix *meta* suggests not only "transformation" but also "occurring later" and "situated behind."[121] Thus, metaphors allow rhetors to situate themselves beyond the foreground as they come to recognize its "insufferable" influences and behind the foreground as they recover archaic meanings and definitions of words and symbols. Metaphors of Metabeing are "times/spaces of continuing transcending of earlier stages of shedding the shackles of body/mind that fix women as targets of phallic lust."[122] These metaphors, then, transform and facilitate the journey and voyage that are the Background.

Redefinition

Redefinition is required for Background rhetors because "deception is embedded in the very texture" of words, a deception that the option of redefinition exorcises.[123] Using redefinition, Background rhetors can reclaim words that have been infected with foreground logic. Redefinition does not involve "an entirely different set of words . . . in a *material* sense. . . . Rather, words which, materially speaking, are identical with the old become new in a semantic context that arises from qualitatively new experience."[124] Redefinitions are verified "in the rising consciousness women have of ourselves and of our situation." Because this consciousness inevitably "contradicts the established sense of reality" reflected in foreground "social and linguistic structures, its verbal expressions sometimes involve apparent contradictions."[125]

Daly redefines terms throughout her work, modeling this rhetorical option. She suggests that the definition of *Spinster,* for example, is not an older, unmarried woman but instead "'a woman whose occupation is to spin.' There is no reason to limit the meaning of this rich and cosmic verb. A woman whose occupation is to spin participates in the whirling movement of creation."[126] Redefined, Spinsters, as well as Prudes, Hags, Crones, and the numerous others whose Background labels Daly recovers from archaic definitions, spin a new word world and realm of existence. Words in the Background regularly violate the rules for definition in the foreground as Spinsters journey past the boring holes of their foreground identities and spin new webs of Be-ing.

Capitalization

The rhetorical option of capitalization is used to distinguish Background words and phrases from foreground attempts at communication. Daly explains that the practice of irregular capitalization does not conform to standard use but to the meanings of words, and words "wear capital letters for a variety of reasons."[127] Sometimes, an irregular capitalization names a *Background* reality; at other times, it names foreground fabrications. Websters and Nag-Gnostics, for example, inhabit the Background, and the Corporate Big Brothers of

Boredom live in the foreground. At still other times, irregular capitalization adds emphasis—such as the difference between the *Background* and *fore-ground*—and/or expresses humor and irony. The rhetorical option of capitalization points to the fact that words are meant to be seen as well as heard, and the creation of a different visual reality leads to a different reality for women of the Background.

One exception Daly makes to her capitalization of Background words is the term *be-ing*. Daly uses the term to indicate the Background experience of participating "in the Ultimate/Intimate Reality—Be-ing."[128] She explains that the lowercase form signifies finite participation, whereas the capitalized form indicates the "Reality designated by *Be-ing*," which is continuous and unfolding.[129] The lowercase *be-ing*, then, reflects a finite state, a Background state in which individuals participate for brief moments. The state of *Be-ing* requires *be-ing*, or the constant movement of life.

Spelling/Be-Spelling

The option of Spelling/Be-Spelling involves changing the shape of a word in order to reveal its alternative Background meaning and to create a different visual reality with words. Daly labels this practice *Archimagical Shape-shifting*, and its purpose is to transform words physically so that Background meanings can become evident. A slash in a word, for example, changes an oppressive foreground term into a liberating Background one. *Gynecology*, for example, designates a misogynistic "branch of murderous modern medicine,"[130] but *Gyn/Ecology* names pro-woman, pro-environmental practices, assisting rhetors in recognizing and eliminating foreground efforts to destroy women and nature.

Spelling/Be-Spelling is "Spell-Craft," which results in the release of the ontological powers of a word. Background Websters who Spell/Be-Spell are aided by the "Spelling Bees," who are highly skilled at communicating in unconventional ways. Like the dancing and humming of Bees, Websters Weave "around rhythmically," altering "the environment in which a word is Heard, thereby releasing its powers of incantation."[131] The context for the rhetorical option of Be-Spelling is critical as Websters cooperate with words and use their suggestions and cues to weave together "a Biophilic context/atmosphere."[132] *Hag*, for example, although heard negatively in the foreground, is Be-Spelled in the Background, freeing it to "Name the fierce beauty, courage, and wisdom of Crones."[133]

A third aspect of Spelling/Be-Spelling involves combining parts of words or entire words. The Spelling of the title of *Wickedary*, for example, suggests that readers hear "*Wicked* in a Hag-identified context" and combine it "with the suffix *-ary* (meaning 'of or belonging to or connected with')." The combination, Daly explains, creates an image of a dictionary that belongs to "Wicked women."[134] Similarly, *Nag-Gnostic,* in the Background, identifies "a Nag who Senses with certainty" a world other than the patriarchy and who therefore practices the Virtue of Nagging" in order to resist the psychic numbing of the foreground.[135]

Redefinition, capitalization, and Spelling/Be-Spelling call attention to the fact that words are "alive"; they throw the old order out of order and Dis-cover New/Archaic Orders.[136] In the Background, words assist rhetors in escaping the foreground and creating an environment in which "women can really breathe."[137] Breathing fiery words and sounds, Background Spell-Casters recognize the importance of disturbing the prearranged foreground atmosphere, share that disturbance with one another, and create Background Spelling Disorder.

Grammar/Sin-Tactics

The term *grammar* commonly refers to the study of words as they are employed according to established usage. With the rhetorical option of Grammar/Sin-Tactics, rhetors recognize that grammar has been reduced to a focus on how words should be arranged in sentences according to foreground logic and has become devoid of *glamour,* its etymological twin, which holds magical and Be-witching qualities. Background rhetors must break this tidy and boring arrangement, and they do so by implementing Sin-Tactics.

To be Sin-Tactical is to ask who has the authority to dictate the placement of words in sentences. At issue in this rhetorical option are the politics of language and the challenging of those in control. Daly suggests that Background rhetors, or Wicked Grammarians, Unfix words and recognize that words "do not live in dictionaries; they live in minds."[138] Wicked Websters wield a Witches' Hammer and release the magical power of words, listening for their musical natures as they are put together in new ways, naming and highlighting new realities. Working with wording, pronoun choice, slashes, hyphens, and the orientation of Be-ing, Grammar-Hammering Hags release "words from male-ordered boxes and cages," enabling them to "Spin about freely," whirling "in New directions."[139]

Pronunciation

Daly's Background rhetors not only focus on the appearance and written arrangement of words, but they speak out against foreground practices and structures. Daly identifies three such ways of speaking out against the foreground: Denouncing, Pronouncing, and Announcing. Denouncing is the Pronouncing of "patriarchal ideologies, institutions, and practices to be blameworthy and evil."[140] It incorporates the refusal to be used by the patriarchy and the unwillingness to be gagged or stifled by foreground practices and tactics.

Pronouncing is the naming of words and experiences that Background inhabitants have not been able to name in the foreground. It means speaking out loud, which frees words from woman-identified mouths so that rhetors hear the possibilities of be-ing.

Announcing is the practice of declaring in public "the arrival, presence, or readiness of" something.[141] Background rhetors publicly announce their presence and call for the end of "mirrordom." Daly relies on Virginia Woolf's description of the relationship between women and men to explain the concept of mirrordom: *"For if she begins to tell the truth* the figure in the looking-glass shrinks; his fitness for life is diminished. How is he to go on giving judgment . . . making laws, writing books . . . unless he can see himself at breakfast and at dinner as at least twice the size he really is?"[142] Announcing cracks the foreground mirrors and proclaims the arrival of Weird women whose Time has come.

The rhetorical options described thus far focus on the ways in which rhetors can use language, both written and spoken, to create a Background reality. Daly offers other rhetorical possibilities, however, that involve relationships—rather than specific linguistic practices—that can create Background realities and knowledge. One option is Spooking, Sparking, and Spinning; another is Be-Laughing.

Spooking, Sparking, and Spinning

Women are spooked by patriarchal males in numerous ways; as a result, Spooking is a multilayered phenomenon that involves keeping women in the foreground occupied with false and anesthetized selves. Through means such as the vulgar names women are called, silencing and erasing through language, and the impossible images presented through the media and other institutions, women are Totaled and Tokenized in the foreground. This spooking by foreground rhetors creates a kind of "Painted Bird"—a woman who is someone else's creation on the outside and fearful of speaking against this creation on the inside.[143]

Spooking in the Background, in contrast, involves unpainting foreground images and roles and exorcising the demons of the foreground. To Spook back is to Dis-possess one's Self, to unwind the veils and to refuse the "frozen, reified, and fetishized" foreground self.[144] Spooking means learning to Speak back to the foreground. It involves re-calling "Self-confident styles of walking/standing/sitting/gesturing which express be-ing." Spooking creates a "different cognitive space" in which women notice "oppressive set-ups" and focus upon "different patterns of meaning than those explicitly expressed by the cognitive majority."[145] Spooking involves breaking the myths of the foreground, deviating from the natural or expected course, and asking wild questions—wild whys that take individuals away from fragmented "fathers' philosophies" and into the Background.[146]

Spooking requires energy; in Daly's theory, this energy takes the form of *Sparking,* defined as "Speaking with tongues of fire" or "igniting the divine Spark in women."[147] Sparking involves "lighting the Fires of Female Friendship; encouraging women to become sister Pyrotechnists; and building the Fire that is fueled by Fury," lighting "the place where we can Spin and Weave tapestries of Crone-centered creation."[148] Daly recognizes, however, that there is "no reason to think that sisterhood is easy" because women have "suffered a duality of consciousness" that keeps them separated from their Selves and one another.[149] The result is a kind of "paralysis of the will"[150] that can be overcome by building Gynergy, the fires of "female energy" that understands this paralysis and assists in the creation of identities free from foreground ideologies and practices.[151]

Sparking is one way to re-fuse the splintering of the foreground by "recognizing the divine Spark in the Self and in other Selves and *accepting* this Spark."[152] Sparking is Radically Self-affirming and threatening to foreground inhabitants. Although considerable efforts are made in the foreground to prevent both Spooking and Sparking, Hags and Crones must band together to create a place for Spinning.

Spinning, the work of Spinsters, is defined as turning around, "moving Counterclockwise; whirling away in all directions from the death march of patriarchy."[153] Having Spooked back at the foreground and fueled the Sparking Fires of Female energy, rhetors participate in Spinning past the foreground and into the Background. Spinsters spin out with an integrity that "must be intense enough to make possible spinning in more than one dimension, spanning through more than one environment."[154]

Spinning involves living on the boundary in order to weave a web of connections. Like Charlotte, the spider in *Charlotte's Web,* Spinster Spiders use whatever materials are at hand to save others from the butchering of the foreground.[155] They also spread themselves over wide areas, "ballooning" their way beyond the myriad foreground fabrications and connecting the threads of Sparking Sisters wherever they go. Like spiders, Spinning rhetors may seem a bit frightening but only because they are individuals who see in ways not familiar to many; they see/make "new patterns of perception as preparation for the later/deeper stages of Journeying."[156]

Be-Laughing

Be-Laughing expresses Background humor and carries rhetors into "ontological laughing."[157] Lusty Leapers/Laughers choose the option of Be-Laughing when they engage in the forbidden act of laughing at foreground myths and illusions. Be-Laughing moves laughing rhetors "into the Background. It is be-ing Silly together." Background rhetors "actually do the thing which mysterious men most dread":[158] They Laugh Out Loud, challenging the inflated views foreground rhetors have of themselves.

Be-Laughing, also called *Metafooling,* is a threefold process that begins with Nixing. *To Nix* is to "VETO, FORBID, PROHIBIT, BAN, REJECT, CANCEL."[159] Individuals who Nix are Nixes, and they forbid and ban foreground actions. They also recognize the emptiness of foreground practices and, as Daly explains, "say 'Nix!' to this nothingness."[160] Nixing leads to *Hexing,* which designates a "harpy, witch" or "hedge."[161] Because hedges are boundaries, in this rhetorical option, witches, or hexing rhetors, are engaged not only in Boundary Living but also in Boundary Breaking.

Hexing depends on Background pride, rage, laughter, and courage and is grounded in the opening of hidden gateways to the Background. Hexing implies a revolt, a movement away from and out of the foreground. This rhetorical option is *canny* in the sense of "supernaturally wise"; the rhetoric of Hexing is the "laughter of Seers who See the Other side of the hedge."[162]

The Boundary Breaking of hexing leads to the rhetorical option of X-ing, a metaphor for breaking out of the boundaries of the foreground. Witches long have been known as *contrary,* which means they do everything "'contrary' to" the customs of men. The option of X-ing, then, involves reversing the reversals of the foreground and looking, speaking, and acting "the Wrong Way, that is, Contrary to" tradition and custom.[163]

X-ing brings rhetors "Dangerously near to hidden truths," exposing long-forgotten memories.[164] These memories rise to the surface as words "catch the threads of Elemental Memory, that is, Deep Memory." This X-ing memory goes "beyond the fabricated elementary 'recollections' of the foreground" and offers instead life-affirming, elemental be-ing.[165] In using X-ing rhetoric, rhetors find "the Courage to Be, to See, to Live, to Grieve, to Rage, and to Laugh Out Loud."[166]

Foreground rhetorical options create a world that is male centered, monodimensional, and, above all, patriarchal. Women's existence within the foreground is spiritually and physically fractured, and the images held out to women reduce them to an objectified and alienated existence. Women's histories, perspectives, and experiences are eliminated from language and thought, and women remain in the traditional position of inferiority to men. The violence done to women in the foreground perpetuates doublethink, where women are exalted yet violated on multiple levels and in various ways. Foreground communication, in summary, robs women of their Be-ing and of life-affirming realities.

Background rhetorical options, in contrast, create a world in which reality is not fixed and in which "creative action in and toward transcendence" is necessary and celebrated.[167] The voyage of Be-coming that results from Background rhetoric grows out of the need for women to be Self-identified and for women to support others in their own efforts at Self-identification. Background rhetoric creates an ever-changing world of symbols, a world in which inter-relationships, passion, and irregular movement are privileged. Rhetoric takes individuals on a journey through time and space, a journey that breaks foreground rules for order and that encourages "new perceptions of reality—perceptions that come from being where one is."[168]

Daly's theory suggests that the two worlds of the foreground and the Background are in continual battle. Foreground rhetors seek to maintain this realm, while Background rhetors work furiously to disrupt the foreground and to allow the Background to flourish in its place. The rhetors in both realms are characterized by strong personalities. In the foreground, they are mean-spirited and plastic; in the Background, they are Self-affirming and centered. Change, for Daly, happens when women recognize the manipulations and oppression of the foreground, leave it, and find their way to the Background.

Daly recognizes the resistance individuals have to the seeming harshness of her theory, her confrontative explanations, and her fierce call to change. She acknowledges "that most men would prefer not to see. It is also understandable that many women would prefer not to see. Seeing means that everything changes: you can't go home again."[169] The world Daly creates is a new homeland, a home in which individuals use symbols to create life and to celebrate woman-identified ways.

Transformations of Rhetorical Theory

Daly's rhetorical theory is characterized by a duality not commonly acknowledged in studies of rhetoric. This duality encompasses the foreground—the realm of fabrication and destruction—and the Background—the realm of be-ing in a woman-centered reality. The duality featured by Daly leads to a reconceptualization of the constructs of exigence, the division between public and private spheres, the nature of the rhetor, and audience adaptation. Although Daly's theory prompts rhetorical scholars to reconsider these notions, she would advocate Nixing, Hexing, and X-ing traditional conceptions and Spinning into new realms of theorizing and be-ing.

Exigence

In traditional theories of rhetoric, the rhetor is confronted with a particular exigence, a situation that requires or suggests a particular response.[170] For Daly, however, the presence of the foreground and the Background suggests that the notion of a single exigence operating in any situation is inadequate. Although the foreground exists and must call a particular kind of rhetoric into being if it is to continue, the Background exists simultaneously, providing a very different condition to which the rhetor can respond. Not only one exigence exists; several do, and rhetors have the option of attending to one or all of them. In fact, rhetors in the Background often must attend to foreground fabrications as they begin the process of journeying into the Background. The notion of a single exigence, then, is inadequate to explain the journey, and the notion of exigence itself becomes much more complex than previously assumed.

Realm for Rhetoric

Daly also challenges the privilege accorded to rhetoric in the public sphere in traditional rhetorical theory. Her theory suggests that the emphasis on public rhetoric functions to erase the considerable rhetorical activity that occurs in what typically is labeled the *private realm*—what Daly calls the *Background.* It also reifies the perceived appropriateness of public discourse and masks the violent nature of foreground rhetoric, which, Daly suggests, actually is a rhetoric of lies and violence. When attention is paid only to foreground or public rhetoric, the oppressive nature of the rhetoric of the public realm is minimized. Private or Background rhetoric is seen to belong to private spaces and thus is deemed irrelevant to the important political issues of the public realm. Women's efforts to move out of states of oppression, in sum, are considered private matters and not worthy of rhetorical study. Daly reverses this perception, making the Background the vital site for rhetorical action.

Rhetor

With her notions of foreground and Background rhetors, Daly reconceptualizes the nature of the rhetor. In the spheres of the foreground and Background, rhetors occupy very different positions—snools and Sadofeminists in the foreground, journeying women on voyages of Self-creation in the Background. As a result, not only does Daly condemn foreground rhetors in no uncertain terms, but she describes in considerable detail their oppressive characteristics and methods. Once glorified as the preferred rhetors of greatest importance, foreground rhetors are cast as mean-spirited individuals who are insensitive to truly important rhetorical situations. Background rhetors, in contrast, engage in creative, meaningful rhetorical activity and thus constitute the rhetors of significance. Their rhetorical activity centers on be-ing and on Biophilic activities and processes—activities to which rhetorical scholars have yet to devote significant attention.

Daly's rhetors also are nonhuman entities, something rhetorical scholars only have begun to consider. In Daly's theories, entities other than people have important information to share and thus constitute important rhetors. Human rhetors secure critical information from their nonhuman peers, such as animals, insects, and astral beings, and often look to them for models of how to act. Gnomes who protect treasures and information and Salamanders who navigate through the fire of the foreground, for example, communicate with rhetors, transmitting valuable information and modeling new options for how human rhetors might behave and communicate.

Audience Adaptation

Daly's rhetorical theory also transforms the nature of audience analysis and adaptation in dramatic ways. Traditional theories suggest that rhetors adapt their messages carefully to suit particular audiences, a notion Daly rejects. Audience analysis and adaptation, as it traditionally is understood, is a means of silencing in that it constitutes an adaptation to and acceptance of the foreground. To adapt their messages to foreground ears means that rhetors remain in the realm of the foreground with its oppressive structures. Audience adaptation, then, is not a means to make a message more acceptable but a foreground method of constraint that silences, denigrates, and manipulates women.

Daly models her view of audience adaptation throughout her work. She alters language to suit her purposes and does not adapt it at all to the particular characteristics of her audiences. She violates basic assumptions of appropriateness by openly naming as negative that with which she disagrees throughout her work. She accuses foreground audiences of violence and lies, and her rhetorical options of Spooking and Spinning, Nixing, Hexing, and X-ing patently reject, dismiss, and ignore foreground audiences. In the Background, audience adaptation, if it is relevant at all, is the audience's ability to adapt to the rhetor's message; the act of adaptation is the responsibility of the listener and not the rhetor.

Daly's work expands rhetorical scholarship into areas that conventional scholars have avoided or minimized. Daly views many traditional constructs as more complex and multifaceted than the ways in which they traditionally have been constructed, and she exposes the problematic nature of many dimensions of these constructs for women. Daly moves Contrariwise, stepping out of the realm of the foreground, rejecting its fabrications and fixations. She encourages other rhetors to do the same—to move the Wrong Way—and to journey into the spiraling realms of Self-Centered be-ing.

Bibliography

Books

Daly, Mary. *The Problem of Speculative Theology.* Washington, DC: Thomist, 1965. Rpt. as "The Problem of Speculative Theology." *The Thomist* 29 (1965) 177-216.

Daly, Mary F. *Natural Knowledge of God in the Philosophy of Jacques Maritain: A Critical Study.* Rome: Officium Libri Catholici [Catholic Book Agency], 1966.

Daly, Mary. *The Church and the Second Sex.* Boston: Beacon, 1968; New York: Harper Colophon, 1975, issued with "Autobiographical Preface to the Colophon Edition" and "Feminist Postchristian Introduction"; Boston: Beacon, 1985, revised with "New Archaic Afterwords."

Daly, Mary. *Beyond God the Father: Toward a Philosophy of Women's Liberation.* Boston: Beacon, 1973, 1985.

Daly, Mary. *Gyn/Ecology: The Metaethics of Radical Feminism.* Boston: Beacon, 1978.

Daly, Mary. *Pure Lust: Elemental Feminist Philosophy.* Boston: Beacon, 1984; London: Women's Press, 1984; Boston: Beacon, 1992. Distributed in the United States by Trafalger Square Publishing.

Daly, Mary, in Cahoots with Jane Caputi. *Websters' First New Intergalactic Wickedary of the English Language.* Boston: Beacon, 1987; London: Women's Press, 1988; Boston: Beacon, 1993. Distributed in the United States by Trafalger Square Publishing. Rpt. (shortened version) as "Preliminary Web One: 'The Wickedary: Its History/Metamystery.'" *Rhetoric: Concepts, Definitions, Boundaries.* By William A. Covino and David A. Jolliffe. Boston: Allyn & Bacon, 1995. 425-32.

Daly, Mary. *Outercourse: The Be-Dazzling Voyage.* New York: HarperCollins, 1992; London: Women's Press, 1993. Distributed in the United States by Trafalger Square Publishing.

Articles

Daly, Mary. "Women and the Church." *Commonweal* 79 (14 Feb. 1964): 603.

Daly, Mary. "Catholic Women and the Modern Era." *Wir schweigen nicht länger! Frauen äussern sich zum II. Vatikanischen Konzil [We Won't Keep Silence Any Longer! Women Speak Out to Vatican Council II].* Ed. Gertrud Heinzelmann. Zurich: Interfeminas Verlag, 1965. 108-10.

Daly, Mary. "The Forgotten Sex: A Built-in Bias." *Commonweal* 81 (15 Jan. 1965): 508-11.

Daly, Mary. "Zeroing in on Freedom." *Commonweal* 86 (2 June 1967): 316-17.

Note: *At Mary Daly's request, the entries in this bibliography are listed in chronological rather than alphabetical order.*

Daly, Mary. "Antifeminism in the Church." *Information Documentation of the Conciliar Church.* No. 68-44. Rome: Information Documentation on the Conciliar Church, 1968.

Daly, Mary. "Christian Mission after the Death of God." *Demands for Christian Renewal.* Ed. William J. Wilson. New York: Maryknoll, 1968. 1-18.

Daly, Mary. "Dispensing with Trivia." *Commonweal* 88 (31 May 1968): 322-25.

Daly, Mary. "An Exchange of Views: Underground Theology." *Commonweal* 88 (9 Aug. 1968): 532-34.

Daly, Mary. "Hans Kung." *The New Day: Catholic Theologians of the Renewal.* Ed. Jerry Boney and Lawrence E. Molumby. Richmond, VA: John Knox, 1968. 129-42.

Daly, Mary. "Mary Daly on the Church." *Commonweal* 91 (14 Nov. 1969): 215.

Daly, Mary. "Return of the Protestant Principle. The Stakes: The Survival of Christianity." *Commonweal* 90 (6 June 1969): 338-41.

Daly, Mary. "The Problem of Hope: Can We Judge the Theology of Hope an Unmixed Blessing?" *Commonweal* 92 (26 June 1970): 314-17.

Daly, Mary. "Toward Partnership in the Church." *Voices of the New Feminism.* Ed. Mary Lou Thompson. Boston: Beacon, 1970. 136-51.

Daly, Mary. "Women and the Catholic Church." *Sisterhood Is Powerful: An Anthology of Writings from the Women's Liberation Movement.* Ed. Robin Morgan. New York: Vintage, 1970. 124-38.

Daly, Mary. "After the Death of God the Father: Women's Liberation and the Transformation of Christian Consciousness." *Commonweal* 94 (12 Mar. 1971): 7-11. Rpt. in *Womanspirit Rising: A Feminist Reader in Religion.* Ed. Carol P. Christ and Judith Plaskow. San Francisco: Harper & Row, 1979. 53-62.

Daly, Mary. "Abortion and Sexual Caste." *Commonweal* 95 (4 Feb. 1972): 415-19.

Daly, Mary. "A Call for the Castration of Sexist Religion." *Unitarian Universalist Christian* 27 (1972): 23-37.

Daly, Mary. "The Courage to See: Religious Implications of the New Sisterhood." *Christian Century* 22 Sept. 1972: 1108-11.

Daly, Mary. "The Spiritual Revolution: Women's Liberation as Theological Re-education." *Andover Newton Quarterly* 12 (1972): 163-76.

Daly, Mary. "The Women's Movement: An Exodus Community." *Religious Education* 67 (1972): 327-35. Rpt. in *Women and Religion.* Ed. Elizabeth Clark and Herbert Richardson. New York: Harper & Row, 1977. 265-71.

Daly, Mary. "Post-Christian Theology: Some Connections between Idolatry and Methodolarity, between Deicide and Methodicide." *Women and Religion 1973.* Ed. Joan Arnold Romero. Tallahassee: American Academy of Religion, Florida State U, 1973. 33-38.

Daly, Mary. "The Spiritual Dimension of Women's Liberation." *Notes from the Third Year: Major Writings of the Radical Feminists.* Ed. Anne Koedt and Shulamith Firestone. New York: Notes from the Second Year, 1971. 75-79. Rpt. in *Radical Feminism.* Ed. Anne Koedt, Ellen Levine, and Anita Rapone. New York: Quadrangle, 1973. 259-67.

Daly, Mary. "God Is a Verb." *Ms.* Dec. 1974: 58-62, 96-98.

Daly, Mary. "The Qualitative Leap beyond Patriarchal Religion." *Quest* 1 (1975): 20-40. Rpt. in *A World of Ideas: Essential Readings for College Writers*. Ed. Lee A. Jacobus. 3rd ed. Boston: Bedford, 1990. 605-29.

Daly, Mary. "A Short Essay on Hearing and on the Qualitative Leap of Radical Feminism." *Horizons* 2 (1975): 120-24.

Daly, Mary. "Femminismo radicale: Al di là della religione patriarcale." *Vecchi e nuovi dei: Stude e riflessioni sul senso religioso dei nostri tempi*. Ed. Rocco Caporale. Turin: Editoriale Valentino, 1976. 357-88.

Daly, Mary. "The Courage to Leave: A Response to John Cobb's Theology." *John Cobb's Theology in Process*. Ed. David R. Griffin and Thomas J. J. Altizer. Philadelphia: Westminster, 1977. 84-98.

Daly, Mary. "Pouvoirs elementaux des femmes: Re-Memoration/re-membrement." *L'émergence d'une culture au feminin*. Ed. Marisa Zavalloni. Montreal: Saint-Martin, 1987. 133-46.

Daly, Mary. "Be-Friending: Weaving Contexts, Creating Atmospheres." *Weaving the Visions: New Patterns in Feminist Spirituality*. Ed. Judith Plaskow and Carol P. Christ. New York: HarperCollins, 1989. 199-207.

Daly, Mary. "Spiraling into the Nineties." *Woman of Power* 17 (1990): 6-12.

Daly, Mary. "Sin Big." *New Yorker* 26 Feb./4 Mar. 1996: 76-84.

CHAPTER 7

Starhawk

We say that there are Four Sacred Things, and the fifth is spirit. And when you live in right relation to the four, you gain the power to contact the fifth. The four are earth, air, fire, and water. They live in the four directions, north, east, south, and west. No one can own them or put a price on them. To live in right relation is to preserve them and protect them, never to waste them, always to share what we have of them and to return all we take from them to the cycles of regeneration. Together they form the magic circle, which is the circle of life. And the understanding of that circle is the beginning of all healing.[1]

These words, spoken by the character Madrone in Starhawk's novel *The Fifth Sacred Thing,* reflect Starhawk's orientation toward the sacredness of the earth and the healing powers available through the magic circle of life. This orientation also informs her theory of rhetoric and her perspectives on human interaction.

Born Miriam Simos on June 17, 1951, to Bertha Goldfarb Simos and Jack Simos, Starhawk is one of two children. Her parents, second-generation immigrants, came from Orthodox Jewish backgrounds but rebelled against many of the traditions their parents had embraced. Her father was a political activist who embraced communism briefly in the 1930s and was one of the early pioneers of drama therapy. Starhawk explains: "There is a radical tradition in my family. In a funny way, I have followed in my father's footsteps," seeing "drama as a way of resolving difficulties." Her father's death when she was quite young affected her deeply: "Even though I was only five, his death taught me that nothing is permanent—to take life to its fullest because you might not have what you thought you did tomorrow."[2] After her husband's death, her mother earned a graduate degree, wrote a book on grief therapy, and worked professionally as a social worker at a time when most women did not work outside the home.

In the late 1960s and early 1970s, Starhawk attended the University of California at Los Angeles and earned a B.A. degree in fine arts. She then moved to San Francisco, attended Antioch West, and received a master's degree in psychology and feminist therapy in 1982. She spent considerable time during these years hitchhiking, bicycling, and camping along the California coast. As she traveled, Starhawk explains, she discovered an intimate connection to the world, seeing "everything as alive, erotic, engaged in a constant dance of mutual pleasuring, and myself as a special part of it all. But I didn't yet have a way to name my experience."[3]

Starhawk's growing awareness of her place in a connected world provided the impetus for a spiritual journey that led her to leave her Judaic spiritual heritage and to embrace the spiritual traditions of Paganism and Witchcraft. The word *Pagan* comes from a Latin word meaning country dweller. To Pagans, "nature is sacred" and "has an inherent value that supersedes human convenience or profit." The gods and goddesses of Paganism are "immanent: embodied in the living processes of nature and human culture."[4] *Wicca* or *Witchcraft* refers to "a Pagan tradition with the Goddess at center." Starhawk describes Witchcraft as "a mystery religion, based on ritual, on consciously structured collective experiences that allow us to encounter the immeasurable. It is the old, pre-Christian, tribal religion of Europe." As in other earth-based, tribal traditions, in Witchcraft, the earth is seen as sacred and the "cosmos as the living body of the Goddess . . . who encompasses us and is immanent within us."[5] The term *Wicca* "comes from the Anglo-Saxon root *wic,* meaning to bend or shape—to shape reality, to make magic. Witches bend energy and shape consciousness"; they weave new possibilities.[6]

In choosing the label *Witch* to describe herself, Starhawk asserts her "commitment to the Goddess, to the protection, preservation, nurturing, and fostering of the great powers of life as they emerge in every being."[7] Starhawk recognizes that the term invokes fear and conjures up images of women flying "around on brooms or brewing up noxious potions"—activities that are not part of her conception and practice of Witchcraft.[8] "Until we confront the fears and stereotypes evoked by the word," she explains, "we cannot contact the powers that are also embedded there."[9]

Starhawk's journey into Pagan spirituality and the practice of Wicca occurred "mostly alone . . . it was an accidental process, something I always felt, but didn't know others believed in."[10] When she moved to San Francisco, however, she became involved with others interested in Paganism and Witchcraft and studied these religious practices in a more systematic way. Wicca made sense to her because "as a young woman in the 1960s, the Jewish religion provided no role" for her "in leadership, no role of importance, no female role models with any power." In addition, Wicca was consistent with her own experiences of spirituality: "I had always had my most powerful spiritual moments in nature." Although she still identifies with the Jewish faith culturally, ethnically, and even "religiously, to some extent," Paganism and Witchcraft are where she feels most at home.[11]

Starhawk changed her name from her birth name, Miriam Simos, as a way of affirming her commitment to Witchcraft and the Goddess. She explains the rationale for the change:

> Naming affirms value. When we name ourselves, or take on a new name, we may be seeing an aspect of our power that is new. My own name came from a dream about a hawk who turned into a wise old woman and took me under her protection. The star came from the card in the Tarot that symbolizes hope and the deep self. Taking on the name Starhawk for me meant taking on a commitment to the Goddess and to new levels of my own power-from-within. The name itself became a challenge.[12]

As a partial response to this challenge, Starhawk has been involved in political activism and protest actions throughout her adult life. In the 1960s, she protested the Vietnam War, and in the early 1970s, she became involved in feminism, consciousness-raising groups, and women's organizations. During the 1970s, she embraced the spiritual aspects of the feminist movement; she explains that she "always saw feminism as political even though it wasn't seen as overtly political, and I have always made a connection between politics and spirituality."[13]

The turning point in Starhawk's activism came at a protest at the nuclear power plant in Diablo Valley, California, in 1981. She describes this event as "tremendously important" because, "for the first time, we were consciously attempting to use nonviolent means of protest." Participants had to undergo training in nonviolence and attend workshops that taught the principles of "solidarity and consensus decision making,"[14] and the blockade itself involved "affinity groups, consensus process, feminist processes," and attempts to ensure that "everybody's voice was heard."[15] The experience reinforced Starhawk's belief in and commitment to the interconnection of politics and spirituality.

In the 1980s, Starhawk continued to organize and participate in actions against nuclear weapons and was involved in protests at the Livermore and Vandenberg weapons facilities in California and the nuclear test site in Nevada. Beginning in 1980, when the United States was "waging war in Central America," Starhawk began to act as a witness for peace in that region, traveling to Central America to witness events taking place and to help develop sustainable agricultural practices there. These actions, she explains, called attention to the human and earth-based violations occurring as a result of U.S. activities: "If Americans are there, violations are less likely to occur because we come back and act as spokespeople in the U.S."[16] Starhawk also is involved in Amnesty International and Witness for Peace; organizes and participates in environmental protests against, for example, unsustainable logging practices; and helps coordinate a needle-exchange program in the San Francisco area, working to stop the spread of AIDS among drug users.

Recently, Starhawk has turned her attention to anti-intervention activities, a form of activism that seeks to offer "positive alternatives" to mere protest. Anti-intervention actions are based on the assumption that individuals need to protest, but they also must "work on the other side; they must work to offer positive solutions and models to the things they are attempting to change." In other words, individuals must do more than act against something; they must live in ways other than those they seek to change. This means living "off-grid"— becoming self-sufficient in alternative ways of living to those of the mainstream. For Starhawk, this means, for example, learning to "repair your own water lines, to grow your own food."[17] Starhawk and her husband, David, have purchased land in what she describes as "Boar Country" in her first novel, *The Fifth Sacred Thing* (1993), in which she incorporates her anti-intervention philosophy and practices.

Anti-intervention activity requires a thorough knowledge of the activity or condition being protested. It means that in order to protest logging, for example, "you must be able to recognize an old-growth redwood when you're standing in a grove of trees." Starhawk elaborates: "I didn't know the difference between an old-growth tree and a second-growth tree [until I realized that] if you want to protest the cutting of trees, you have to recognize the difference." Also required is an awareness of the larger context of the issue. "You can't just stop cutting all trees," she explains. "[S]ome trees need to be removed from a forest, it makes a healthier forest and assists in the balance of nature. We need to develop models of sustainable forestry."[18] Anti-intervention activism, then, requires that individuals have considerable knowledge of the conditions against which they are protesting and that they connect that knowledge to the solutions they advocate.

Starhawk's personal life has been marked by the collectivism that characterizes her activism. Since 1986, she has lived in a collective household in San Francisco. She defines family as "whatever association of people works in your life—that might be a heterosexual couple with a nuclear family, a lesbian couple, a gay couple, or a group of friends and partners that provide you with support." Starhawk's household consists of her "friend, Rose; [her] husband, David; Rose's husband and their adopted daughter; various stepdaughters at various times; and one other woman and her 15-year-old daughter."[19]

Starhawk also has been part of a coven—the Reclaiming Collective—since her move to San Francisco. Covens are "groups of Witches who practice ritual together," contain no more than 13 members (representing the 13 full moons in a year), and are said to be "closer than family."[20] The Reclaiming Collective is a group of women who "work on spirituality, politics, teach, and offer workshops . . . in the tradition of the Craft." The collective currently is in the process of articulating its core values, deliberately choosing a focus on values rather than beliefs: "We didn't want to define our beliefs because ultimately you crucify those who don't share them. We think it's healthier to identify our core values."[21]

Starhawk describes her writing career as beginning "the week I turned twenty-one," when her mother gave her a typewriter as a college graduation gift.[22] As soon as Starhawk received the typewriter, she realized she would be spending much of her life writing. She has written numerous books, beginning with *The Spiral Dance: A Rebirth of the Ancient Religion of the Great Goddess,* published in 1979 and updated in 1989. The book was rejected by many publishers before its publication; one reviewer stated: "I don't think this author knows what she's trying to say and I doubt that she has the intelligence to say it if she did."[23] A book of "poetic theology," *Spiral Dance* is an introduction to Witchcraft, rituals, invocations, and magic; it has sold more than 100,000 copies.[24]

Starhawk's second book, *Dreaming the Dark: Magic, Sex and Politics* (1982), is "about bringing together the spiritual and the political. Or rather, it is a work that attempts to move in the space where that split does not exist."[25] In *Dreaming the Dark,* Starhawk attempts to "know the dark, and dream it into a new image" and encourages her readers to do the same.[26] The book is rooted in her own journey from fear to hope and empowerment in terms of her commitment to and experiences with nonviolent resistance.

Truth or Dare: Encounters with Power, Authority, and Mystery (1987) is a book of "theory and practice," with the chapters introduced by stories that can be read separately or together to create a larger story. The book contains exercises that Starhawk has used in classes and workshops, with the Reclaiming Collective, and in her own life, and she offers them to her readers: "[N]ow the material is yours to use as is, change, or to inspire you to create your own."[27]

Starhawk's novel *The Fifth Sacred Thing* (1993) is a work of fiction that chronicles the lives of Madrone, Bird, and Maya as they struggle to live in life-sustaining, nonviolent ways amid tremendous violence and environmental abuse. Starhawk wanted to write fiction long before she wrote *The Fifth Scared Thing* but "never could get anything published," she explains, "until I published my other books. They say it's easier to publish fiction after you've published other things."[28] In 1997, Starhawk published *Walking to Mercury,* the prequel to *The Fifth Sacred Thing,* in which the life of Maya and her connection to the Goddess are explored.

Starhawk returned to nonfiction with *The Pagan Book of Living and Dying* (1997), a joint effort with M. Macha NightMare and the Reclaiming Collective. This book is a "collection of resources for those who are assisting a dying person, grieving a beloved, or planning a funeral or memorial service."[29] Motivated by the deaths of close friends, the death of Starhawk's mother, and the lack of coherent material on Pagan rituals for grieving and death, Starhawk and her coauthors compiled songs, prayers, and chants—adapting some and creating others—so that they could be shared with those who are experiencing loss. The book, NightMare explains, displays, "in the best setting possible, the vast talents, insights, spiritual depth, and richness of present-day Pagans and Witches."[30]

Starhawk's work as an activist and writer is grounded in her commitment to the immanent value of every aspect of the earth. As she explains:

> The earth is a living, conscious being. In company with cultures of many different times and places, we name these things as sacred: air, fire, water, and earth. . . .
>
> All people, all living things, are part of the earth life, and so are sacred. No one of us stands higher or lower than any other. Only justice can assure balance; only ecological balance can sustain freedom. Only in freedom can that fifth sacred thing we call spirit flourish in its full diversity.[31]

Nature of the World

In Starhawk's rhetorical theory, two worlds exist—the world of patriarchy and the world of the Goddess—with patriarchy the world that currently is pervasive. Starhawk defines patriarchy as an overarching social system or structure characterized by hierarchy, obedience, power-over, and fragmentation. Patriarchy is a "toxic" world, she asserts, and is becoming more polluted daily.[32]

Patriarchy

Patriarchy is, first and foremost, a hierarchical system maintained by "the belief that some people are more valuable than others."[33] In a hierarchical system such as patriarchy, those on the top command, and those below obey. Early systems of hierarchy included systems of land and property ownership, paternity, and status based on position, such as aristocracy, royalty, and clergy. More recent systems of hierarchy are found in social and political institutions, in religion and spirituality, and in the less obvious and seemingly benevolent structures of the classroom, workplace, and family. Each of these systems perpetuates the dominance of some individuals over others, and each is designed to make that dominance seem normal or natural. Although in some hierarchies, Starhawk recognizes, those with more power empower those with less, this rarely happens in a patriarchal system.

Value in the patriarchal world is judged according to external criteria. People are measured by such standards as money, material objects, titles, and accomplishments rather than for their inherent worth. In the world of power-over, human beings have no inherent worth—value must be earned through the acquisition of status and property. This view of worth is "modeled on the God who stands outside the world, outside nature, who must be appeased, placated, feared, and above all, obeyed."[34] Patriarchy, Starhawk explains, promotes insecurity and self-hate and "teaches us that our worth is not a given but must be earned and subordinated to the value of someone else whose status is higher than ours."[35]

Hierarchy in the patriarchal world requires obedience, which Starhawk describes as "the destruction of the self." To be obedient "is to be a slave, unfree. When we comply, when we aid the system in its ultimate disregard and destruction of us, we hate ourselves."[36] Consequently, obedience is not always easy to instill because it contradicts humans' natural self-love. In patriarchy, however, obedience becomes possible because it is "etched in the psyche, too deep to be questioned, and reinforced by training, religion, and ideology."[37] Starhawk uses the king as her model for obedience to authority; the king is an authority whom individuals internalize and who, ultimately, possesses them. Historically, individuals could look to a certain individual who represented this king, but currently, under patriarchy, "we internalize the image of the King, which becomes an entity within, a psychic structure that assures our obedience to authority."[38] The king, then, continues to live in the minds of those who participate in patriarchy, and they obey the messages produced by his internalized image.

Starhawk labels the dominant and oppressive type of power that reinforces obedience in patriarchy *power-over*. Power-over is an exploitative form of power that celebrates and encourages manipulation and a view of the world as mechanistic and disconnected; ultimately, it divides, manipulates, and controls individuals. In the structure of power-over, "good people obey the rules," and authority, which is dependent on one's position in the patriarchal hierarchy, is placed "in a realm beyond question, valued above reason or the evidence of the senses." Power-over allows individuals "to cause pain and suffering quite comfortably in defense of the rules."[39] It tears down rather than builds up and is "the story of the literal dismemberment of the world, the tearing apart of the fabric of living interrelationships that once governed human life."[40]

Power-over's most obvious manifestation is the power of the "prison guard, of the gun, power that is ultimately backed by force."[41] Starhawk suggests, however, that power-over exists in every institution in society—the workplace, schools, and even doctors' offices. Power-over rules not only with weapons but through its more subtle manifestations in language—"the language of law, of rules, of abstract, generalized formulations enforced on the concrete realities of particular circumstances."[42] Power-over dominates

> by controlling the resources we need to live; money, food, medical care; or by controlling more subtle resources: information, approval, love. We are so accustomed to power-over, so steeped in its language and its implicit threats, that we often become aware of its functioning only when we see its extreme manifestations. For we have been shaped in its institutions, so that the insides of our minds resemble the battlefield and the jail.[43]

Another quality of the patriarchal world is estrangement, a belief in fragmentation and disconnection. In the patriarchal system, the world is seen as "an object, made up of many separate, isolated parts."[44] In patriarchy, Starhawk explains, "we are raised separately—to the point of pain. We are trained to compete from our earliest years, taught that drives and desires and bodies are objects to be controlled." The thought forms that reinforce a belief in disconnection "can be enormously strong, they have all the force of Western culture behind them. They sustain their power with the constant mantra, the whisper in the ear that says, 'You are separated, isolated, alone.'"[45]

The patriarchal system is a human invention, however, and not an imperative of nature. Thus, patriarchy is not the only structure possible. Other possibilities are present because domination

> is a *system* and we *are* part of it, and in that lies hope. For any system is always in delicate balance, dependent for its stability on the feedback of its parts. When the feedback changes, so does the system. At first it reacts to regain its stability, but if the new feedback is sustained, the system will be transformed.[46]

Goddess System

In spite of the prevalence of the patriarchal world, an alternative system—a life-affirming system informed by the Goddess—also is present. In this system, the Goddess is manifest in many images and aspects. She is "a constellation of forms and associations—earth, air, fire, water, moon and star, sun, flower and seed, willow and apple, black, red, white, Maiden, Mother, and Crone."[47] The Goddess evokes "the divine—the moving energy that unites all being."[48] She is every being on the planet and is in each individual, element, animal, and life force. The Goddess does not rule the world, Starhawk explains: "She *is* the world."[49]

The Goddess image is both male and female and "does not symbolize female rule over men—but freedom from rule. She herself has male aspects. . . . [B]ut we call her 'she' because to name is not to limit or describe but to invoke. We call her in and a power comes who is different from what comes when we say 'he' or 'it.'" By naming the source of immanence female, "something arises that challenges the ways in which our minds have been shaped in images of male control."[50] Evoking the symbol of the Goddess can be profoundly liberating, especially for women, because the Goddess brings back power and authority to women, their bodies, and their life processes. Birth, growth, lovemaking, aging, and death in the Goddess system are processes to be valued and celebrated, not controlled and denied.

Starhawk suggests that most men are more disconnected from the earth than most women, but the Goddess makes possible a personal relationship with the earth for men. As Starhawk explains, "[A] man who embraces his own connection with the Goddess experiences the power of nurturing within himself, independent of his tie to a living woman." As a result of the Goddess, men no longer can "remain so comfortably split" from the earth.[51] Present in each being, the Goddess possesses an energy that reconnects individuals to the earth and to one another.

The world rooted in the Goddess is a world of inherent value—the value all individuals possess by virtue of being who they are. Starhawk defines *immanence* as the embodiment of the Goddess, the idea that "we are each a manifestation of the living being of earth, that nature, culture, and life in all their diversity are sacred." Immanence is based on the idea, she explains, that "your life is worth something. You need only be what you are. All that is, has its being in you."[52] The Goddess promotes the recognition that each "has something unique to bring into the world": "Powers exist that only you can bring to life; a perspective exists that is yours alone. No one else can speak your truth for you or give birth to your vision."[53] In fact, Starhawk frequently asks audiences, "Would you like to have a vision of the Goddess?" When they nod, she tells them "to turn and look at the person sitting next to them."[54]

Inherent value does not mean that "everyone is innately good or that nothing should ever be destroyed. What is valued is the whole pattern." Starhawk notes, for example, that in her garden, she pulls the "snails off the iris leaves and crush[es] them—they are out of pattern here. They have no natural predators and devour the diversity of the garden." Brought by a French immigrant to California 100 years ago, some snails escaped their fate as escargot and now "ravage plants all up and down the West Coast." Starhawk continues: "Yet I do not expect to completely kill them off. We will, at best, strike a balance, a new pattern. Nor will I put out poison, which disrupts larger patterns still. I will be predator, not poisoner."[55] Immanence, then, is not about dominating and ruling others but about patterns of being and the balance of life.

A second primary feature of Starhawk's alternate system is interconnection, "the understanding that all being is interrelated, that we are linked with all of the cosmos as parts of one living organism. What affects one of us affects us all."[56] She explains that although we are told that

> rape is an issue separate from nuclear war, that a woman's struggle for equal pay is not related to a black teenager's struggle to find a job or to the struggle to prevent the export of a nuclear reactor to a site on a web of earthquake faults near an active volcano in the Philippines, all these realities are shaped by the consciousness that shapes our power relationships.[57]

These relationships are just that—related—and as interconnected events, Starhawk asserts, they "shape our economic and social systems; our technology; our science; our religions; our views of women and men; our views of races and cultures that differ from our own; our sexuality; our Gods and our wars."[58] To be interconnected spiritually and materially, individuals must recognize that there is no division, no enemy, no difference between the Goddess and themselves: "All the beings of the world are in constant communication on many levels and dimensions. There is . . . a complex intertwined feedback system of changes that shape other changes."[59]

Starhawk sees the world of the Goddess as one way that the "lumbering" world of patriarchy can be overcome.[60] Society can unite around a spiritual and material sense of interconnection and immanence instead of adhering to the patriarchal values of hierarchy, obedience, power-over, and fragmentation. Starhawk's rhetorical theory is directed at replacing the patriarchal system with the Goddess system, and feminism is the means she chooses by which to enact it.

Definition of Feminism

Since the early 1970s, Starhawk has identified herself as a feminist. Her feminist thoughts began with the questions "What is femaleness?" and "What is maleness?", and the answers she discovered revealed that the definitions of *female* and *male* function only to oppress women and constrain men.[61] She now defines feminism as seeing with an "acrostic vision." To possess acrostic vision is to shift one's vision, to look at something—like femaleness and maleness—from a different angle. Feminism, then, involves looking "at our culture and our conditioning from another angle" and reading "an entirely different message."[62] Starhawk applies a feminist consciousness in areas sometimes seen as unrelated to one another: "Even in an analysis of our global economy, of coffee farmers, for example, a feminist consciousness shows us the connection between the domination of men over women and the economic domination of one country over another."[63]

Starhawk's feminism goes beyond acrostic vision to encompass a political analysis. Feminism involves attention to the power relations that characterize relationships. It is

> the political analysis that looks at how structures in society mirror the relationships of domination between women and men. Whole systems of power relations are connected to the domination of men over women. We can use women and men as the groundwork and model for domination and control because this model of power, of domination, can be found in systems of domination of all kinds. Feminism is about challenging this model of power on which our culture is based.[64]

Collectivity is another aspect of Starhawk's feminism, and she suggests that "we are created collectively and can only be changed collectively. One of the clearest insights of feminism is that our struggles are *not* just individual, and our pain is not private pain; it is created by [the] ways in which our culture treats women as a class." If feminism is to be successful, it "must stress that we are all responsible for each other."[65] The focus should not be on individual enlightenment but on interconnection and commitment to one another.

Starhawk's view of feminism contains a commitment to ecofeminism, the perspective that the domination of humans over the earth is integrally related to the domination of men over women. She explains that "the kinds of power relationships men and women have are very similar to the relationships we have with the earth. We can't really heal the earth unless we heal the relationships between men and women. Healing the relationships between women and men is pointless if we can't sustain the planet."[66] In contrast to many environmentalists, Starhawk does not see humans as "a blight" on the earth. Humans play an important role in nature, just as termites and fungi do. Humans need to learn to live in nature because "all of life and all of nature live in constant communication. What we need to be doing as humans is learning how to listen, how to communicate back." Humans are "not separate from nature, we're part of nature. We do not have the right to blanketly exploit and destroy nature."[67]

Feminism and ecofeminism are not essentialist perspectives for Starhawk, although they often are interpreted as being so. Essentialism is the view that women and men are biologically determined and that consequently, for example, women are more spiritually inclined or talented or are closer to nature than are men. Starhawk asserts: "I'm not an essentialist, I never have been. Anyone who has bothered to read my work would know that. I do not believe women are essentially more spiritual or closer to nature." Whether women and men are essentially or innately different from one another cannot be known at this time, Starhawk suggests, because of the sexist nature of society: "As long as the search for innate differences is framed in a sexist society," we never will know. "Our ideas will be conditioned by the sexist society we have been raised in."[68]

Starhawk suggests that for feminism to be effective, individuals must recognize and embrace both female and male dimensions. Feminist spirituality, for her, involves a recognition of the Goddess as, among other things, an energy field that contains both maleness and femaleness. Although the female aspects of the Goddess often are given special attention, both forces must be acknowledged in order for balance to be sustained. Although Western culture's continual focus on the male has upset the balance of life, feminism and feminist spirituality can guide individuals back to a place where "all life is a thing of wonder."[69]

Nature of the Rhetor

Starhawk's vision of two worlds—the world of patriarchy and the world of the Goddess—requires two very different kinds of rhetors. In the patriarchal world, rhetors are grounded in self-hate and estrangement. In the world of the Goddess, in contrast, rhetors function from the life-affirming position of power-from-within.

Patriarchy

Rhetors in patriarchy are self-haters, "the inner representation of power-over."[70] Starhawk suggests that patriarchy "has created us in its image," and self-hater rhetors have internalized the messages and images of power-over from "every institution in society with which we have contact."[71] They believe that people must dominate or be dominated and that hierarchy is inevitable and desirable. Self-hater rhetors assume they are bad when bad things happen to them and that their worth comes from their positions in the external world. The very "ground of self-love has been undermined" for these individuals; from a very young age, self-haters are told they do not have the right to be who they are, feel what they feel, or do what they want to do.[72] As a result, self-haters constantly censor and monitor their desires and impulses in order to conform to the patriarchal world.

Constantly on guard for inappropriate or unacceptable behaviors, self-haters are threatened easily by the loss of approval from others, and they continually seek the esteem of others in order to feel valuable. They keep steady the "inner gun that keeps us in an inner prison," Starhawk explains, in order to ensure their worth and value.[73] As a result of this continual negation of the self, isolation and loneliness prevail. Afraid to tell others who they are, self-haters keep their fears and their identities hidden inside, carrying with them the patriarchal traits of isolation and estrangement.

Goddess System

Although self-haters are common in the patriarchy, in the world of the Goddess, rhetors are grounded in an entirely different orientation. Rhetors who resist domination and act within the system of the Goddess come from a position of personal power, or what Starhawk labels *power-from-within.* Power-from-within resides within each individual and is rooted in integrity, immanence, and interconnection. By *integrity,* Starhawk means that humans act with "consistency; we act in accordance with our thoughts, our images, our speeches; we keep our commitments."[74] Individuals in the Goddess system possess not only integrity but a recognition of both the immanence of each individual and the interconnectedness of all things on the earth.

Power-from-within is not something individuals have; rather, it is something they do. The root of the word *power* is the Latin word *"podere* ('to be able')"; this suggests the ability of an individual to respond to a situation, "the power that comes from within."[75] When individuals act from a position of power-from-within, they have the "power to direct energy" to create change, and if this energy possesses integrity and balance, it "flows freely in the direction" individuals choose. Misdirected, the energy of power-from-within "gets blocked or mis-channeled." As Starhawk explains: "If I think and say that I hate pollution, and yet walk by and leave the beer cans lying at my feet, the energy of my feelings is dissipated. Instead of feeling my own power to do something, however small, about litter, I feel and become more powerless."[76]

Starhawk recognizes that the choices individuals make from a place of power-from-within have consequences. Individuals are responsible for their own actions and decisions and "must bear the consequences" of those decisions.[77] These consequences are based not on absolutes but on the ordering principles of nature that cannot be taken out of context: "[T]here are no *things* separate from context."[78] When the pope, Starhawk explains, makes a decision about birth control that affects millions of people, then the pope is responsible for the "poverty, starvation, [and] suffering" that his decision will produce.[79]

Power-from-within, then, is the orientation the rhetor assumes in the Goddess system. Power-from-within is the ability of individuals to act and direct their energies in responsible and proactive ways. It generates a sense of empowerment—individually and collectively—and is not something individuals earn, as they do power-over; rather, it is something individuals inherently have. Power-from-within is a position from which individuals can participate in the world, resist oppression, and enact change.

Rhetorical Options

Starhawk sees two unique sets of rhetorical options as available to rhetors. The first set, designed to perpetuate patriarchy, is grounded in the various positions available to the self-hater. These consist of the five roles of the Judge, the Censor, the Conqueror, the Master and Servant, and the Orderer. As rhetorical options, these positions offer various strategies and techniques for perpetuating patriarchy. In the world of the Goddess, in contrast, the rhetorical options are quite different. They consist of mystery, ritual, and power-with, options that perpetuate the values of the Goddess system and assist rhetors in the creation and maintenance of the world in which they wish to live.

Patriarchy

The rhetoric of the self-hater can be manifested in numerous ways, and Starhawk's five roles suggest the variety possible. Individuals who accept the patriarchal structure, consciously or not, regularly find themselves choosing one or more of these options. The result is a perpetuation of control, isolation, and the denial of individuals' inherent worth.

The Judge

When the role of the Judge is enacted, the self is experienced as an object—as a thing to be scrutinized and evaluated—with the power and right to treat others similarly. The Judge "demands obedience," and value is allotted or measured according to how individuals meet the standards of obedience. When individuals are possessed by the Judge, they are "obsessed with questions of good and bad, right and wrong, purity and impurity." Guilt—the "internalized hate of the self"—is the control mechanism of these rhetors, and it is "instilled through fear of punishment." As Starhawk explains, "Guilt is the way we punish ourselves."[80]

The Judge "sustains the power of every coercive institution" by observation, the incessant watching over of every activity and decision. Guilt is easy to induce for the Judge because individuals may be observed by any number of agencies or institutions. Such observations permeate the daily activities of virtually all individuals and take tangible form in "school records, credit records, criminal records, IRS records," and the like.[81] Even God and Santa Claus are "portrayed to us as the Big Judge, always watching us, knowing our every sin."[82]

The work of the Judge regularly occurs inside the individual, too. Punishment "becomes self-administered" because "it is a voice within" that is telling rhetors they "are bad." Possessed by the Judge, they "mount surveillance" on themselves, "carefully noting any failure to meet the standards," frequently punishing themselves before they even have committed the crime.[83] Judges, then, also act as self-monitors. "I cannot run naked into the ocean," an individual may say. "[T]he park police might see us."[84] Although they seem benign, these less tangible forms of observation prevent individuals from engaging in activities in which they would like to participate. Often, individuals "are not aware of being externally controlled," so they "are helpless to challenge that control." Guilt does not motivate individuals to change; "instead, it paralyzes us."[85] Constantly watched, individuals cannot celebrate or nurture themselves; they only can hide from the Judge, place restrictions on their activities, and devalue themselves and their experiences.

The Censor

In patriarchy, individuals are not able to think and speak freely. The Censor prevents them from doing so by controlling speech and action—by whispering in their ears: "Don't say that! You don't really think that. You're the only one that feels that way—don't tell anyone."[86] The Censor keeps individuals in isolation and prevents them from reaching out and making connections. As a result, individuals cannot trust their own thoughts and ideas; they are allowed to establish intimacy only by "establishing a mutual litany of insecurities and self-doubts."[87]

Censors are obsessed with questions of isolation and connection. They continually ask themselves, "Can I connect? Will I be heard? How much of myself must I conceal to be accepted?" Starhawk explains, however, that "the acceptance we buy through concealing ourselves leaves us feeling even more isolated, sure that should we reveal who we really are, our worthlessness will show."[88] The Censor's weapon is shame; shame prevents individuals from speaking out because they are afraid others will discover their faults. Once these faults are discovered, Censors believe, they will be rejected.

Censors also silence others by blaming those who do speak out for "making a scene" or by holding them responsible for the concerns they raise.[89] Issues of responsibility thus are clouded in the rhetoric of the Censor because the victimizer often is ignored, forgotten, or even serves as a source of sympathy, while the individual who speaks out is branded a troublemaker. Starhawk points to Freud's decision to abandon his theory that the emotional suffering adults feel often stems from sexual abuse in their childhoods as an example of the Censor at work. If Freud had made this information public, Starhawk suggests, a great deal of "rage and indignation" likely would have greeted him. Individuals would have rejected the man rather than the theory because everyone knew that "only fine, noble, valiant, and edifying deeds (subjects) ought to be talked about publicly."[90]

Although individuals are silenced regularly by the Censor, they also can be encouraged to keep talking when they "actually have nothing to say. 'Say something!' the voice whispers. 'Show the teacher how smart you are. Show the boss how on top of it all you are. Keep talking—don't let there be a silence that might reveal the real emptiness here.'"[91] Censors tend to speak about everything but the issues at hand. In pain, individuals discuss newspaper headlines rather than the suffering they feel at the moment.[92] Whether silenced or babbling, the Censor's primary tactic is to keep individuals from speaking out about their joys, pains, and fears.

When individuals adopt the role of the Censor, boredom often is the result. Starhawk explains that, in living with the Censor, individuals "become numb," do not act out or speak out, and are left with a kind of gray dullness that settles over them like a fog. The Censor's presence is an absence—an absence "of feeling, passion, energy."[93] Under the Censor's power, individuals withdraw, deny their feelings, and lose the power and motivation to change conditions. Censors experience a "shutting down," a disengagement from the world manifested in boredom that blocks and dissipates power.

The Conqueror, Defender, or Avenger

As a result of patriarchy, individuals learn to see the war leader as the model for safety. Starhawk labels this rhetorical option the *Conqueror*, the *Defender against Enemies*, or the *Avenger*, and the goal is to protect by destroying the enemy. Individuals who use the rhetorical option of the Conqueror "see enemies everywhere"; any problem, disagreement, or difference "becomes the occasion for defining the other as the enemy."[94] Friends, family, and coworkers all can become enemies at any moment. Whenever Conquerors or Defenders feel frightened or insecure, they look for and find an enemy. As Starhawk explains, when "we feel weak, unsupported, vulnerable, we are most susceptible to the Defender's threats and promises. The Defender paints the world around us as dangerous, and threatening. Death, violation, humiliation await us unless we comply. Fearful, we believe the Defender's vision."[95]

The Defender's protection, however, is not really protection, for in seeking it, rhetors already have lost themselves and "become complicit" in their own destruction.[96] In the rhetorical option of Defender, individuals "condone, comply with, and participate in the brutalization of the other."[97] There is yet another way in which the Defender creates unsafe conditions. When individuals possessed by the Defender become obsessed by the image of the enemy, they also begin to experience parts of their own selves as the enemy, which then become something to destroy. The act of brutalizing others only results in brutalizing the self, as Starhawk illustrates with an example:

> "Breathe deep," I say to Betty, a woman in her late twenties who has come for help. She feels depressed, uneasy in groups and fearful of people. "Follow your breath down to the place where it begins, to your place of power. Look to the center, to your own core. What do you see there?"
> Betty begins to cry. "I see a monster. It's ugly and cringing and sniveling. I hate it. It's me."
> "What do you want to do with it?"
> "Kill it. Hide it. I'm afraid people will see it. If I let anyone really know who I am, they'll find out I'm the monster."[98]

The Defender does not really keep anyone safe because the "very insistence on seeing enemies creates enemies" and keeps individuals "locked into battle."[99] The Defender also encourages a rhetoric that glorifies and magnifies struggle. No battle is unimportant; no struggle is too small for the Conqueror or Defender. Every disagreement becomes a battle, and every battle seems crucial. Through the eyes of the rhetor who selects this option, "everything becomes blown up in importance: slights and insults, issues and decisions."[100] In the role of the Defender, ordinariness becomes synonymous with death, the hero must be removed from the common ranks, and "survival is only for the special."[101]

The Master and the Servant

Patriarchy creates a world where only hierarchical models for giving and sharing are available. In patriarchy, one person's needs supersede another's—the Master's needs must be met, and the Servant is the one who meets those needs. In the option of the Master and the Servant, the "core issue is need." The Master believes that "[o]thers exist only to meet my needs," whereas the Servant holds that "I have no needs—I only exist to meet the needs of others."[102]

Women and children particularly are vulnerable to Servant roles, whereas men are prone to adoption of the role of the Master. Patriarchy teaches women to mold their needs and desires around those of men, and children often are "sacrificed to the needs of adults" through abuse, incest, alcohol, and the like.[103] Citing Sandy Butler, Starhawk explains that men, trained to "believe they should occupy positions of power in this society," expect "to be loved and cared for by parents and wives as they go about making their mark on the world."[104]

In both options, individuals continue to feel empty as their identities and inherent value are denied.

The Master and Servant option is rooted in a loss of identity. When individuals assume the role of Master, they "cannot see the being of others"; they lose sight of other people's individuality and unique identities as they recognize only their own needs. As Servants, individuals are invisible, simply filling a certain role. The loss of identity occurs in numerous ways—through the changing of women's names when they marry, specific behaviors of obedience that violate a person's own needs and wishes, and even physical control and possession. Starhawk suggests, for example, that those "possessed by the Master see the Servants' bodies as territory they are entitled to control and conquer." This control is reflected in "images of violent pornography," damaging views of sexuality, and unhealthy relationships between women and men.[105]

The rhetorical option of the Master and Servant destroys individuals' inherent value. Serving the Master may offer individuals a sense of worth, but the rewards are unpredictable. An individual's service may be valued, and Masters may promise to take care of their Servants, but Masters often are too busy ensuring that their own needs are met to follow through on their promises. The myth is that if an individual adopts the Servant option, worth and appreciation will follow. In reality, individuals become dependent on one another for worth and value rather than recognizing their own and others' inherent worth.

The Orderer

Starhawk's fifth rhetorical option is the one chosen by the Orderer, who, in the patriarchal world, "establishes order in the realm. He carves out the universe from chaos, parcels out the lands, determines who ranks high and who ranks low, makes the laws and enforces them."[106] Those who select this option must maintain control. The rhetoric of the Orderer imposes rigid patterns on the natural world, promoting the belief that "all can be known and controlled." There is no room for the wild in the rhetorical option of the Orderer—no place "for the mystery that cannot be analyzed, defined, contained."[107] Focused on control, Orderers are distracted from noticing how they "are controlled by others and what is really destroying" them.[108]

The promise of the Orderer is that if individuals gain enough control over themselves and the natural world, their value will increase. Bodies, as a result, are experienced as something to be controlled and "set in order"—they are not to be felt but to be "carved and shaped. . . . Our size, our shape, our sexuality, our level of fitness become qualities subject to will rather than need, desire, health, or inclination."[109] Selection of this option demands denial because Orderers must close their eyes to the reality around and within them, "to feelings, to interactions, to the needs of the body so as to accept the Orderer's arrangements."[110] Orderers see themselves as programmable computers and as dismembered machines that can be taken apart. The universe, too, is viewed mechanistically as a clock valued for its function rather than its immanent spirit. But because chaos and destruction are a part of nature, the Orderer's world is filled with the anxiety that results from trying to control what cannot be controlled. Orderers are perpetually nervous, for they know that disorder in all of its manifestations eventually will catch up with them.[111]

Creativity also is the nemesis of the Orderer because it "is a mystery: a work comes through the artist and takes on a life and will of its own."[112] The Orderer, however, attempts to control this mystery—to harness it and break it apart so that segments of it can be practiced or rehearsed. Because artists are rebels and creativity is not a mechanized process to be ruled, the Orderer sees fit to make the artist "suffer, especially women artists, who are doubly rebels."[113]

Starhawk's five self-hating rhetorical options enable individuals to do everything they can to promote and reinforce patriarchy through denial, obsession, guilt, shame, and dependence. Starhawk explains that to "heal the world and heal ourselves in the process, we must understand both how we internalize domination and how we can foster freedom. We must understand how we internalize each aspect of the self-hater and develop techniques for ridding ourselves of internalized domination."[114]

Goddess System

Because a different orientation to the world is possible, rhetors have available a different set of rhetorical options. Starhawk's rhetorical options for creating a world informed by the Goddess are grounded in the assumption that in order to resist domination, individuals must act in life-affirming ways. They do this through mystery, an orientation to the world that all rhetors in the Goddess system assume, and through collective action, which occurs in ritual and through power-with in various kinds of group structures.

Mystery

Rhetors in the Goddess system are grounded in mystery—the recognition of the Goddess and the creative powers of that realm. Mystery is "what is wild in us, what is never entirely predictable or safe."[115] Mystery involves paradox, patterns of time and the body, "a sense of place," the growth of plants and children, and "the knowledge that through us move forces older and stronger than human will."[116] Mystery existed before the domination and control of the patriarchal world and is the "arising of powers that are uncharted and untamed, that will not follow the logic of naked force, and so act in unexpected ways.

Mystery is surprise."[117] Although, by its very name, mystery seems abstract and far removed from concrete experience, it is "made up of the stuff of everyday life." It centers on "the most common of human experiences: birth, death, love, nurture, challenge, passion, time."[118]

Grounded in mystery, individuals change their perceptions, descriptions, and consciousness of where they are. In other words, they realize that the ideologies and dogmas of patriarchy do not provide the only answers. In *The Fifth Sacred Thing,* Starhawk gives an example of this use of mystery. Struggling to develop a plan to prevent a military invasion of their city, the people of the Bay Area in California realize that they simply can refuse to engage in violence. Taught that people must protect themselves from violence with violence, they realize that they can reject this dogma as the only solution. Instead, they develop a plan of noncooperation with and invitation to the invading soldiers to join them in their world, if they wish. Although some of the invading soldiers initially do respond with violence to this invitation, the city is protected by this action, and the war ends almost as soon as it begins.

Mystery, then, involves resistance through the creation of new ways of seeing and being in the world, accepting uncertainty and even randomness, and deciding to engage and act in the world. Mystery is not a passive state but a willingness to recognize, celebrate, and honor "the cycles, the patterns, the balance of the world, the arising of great forces that sustain life."[119] To embrace mystery is to "refuse to be boxed and suppressed. . . . We want to be out in the storm, not inside under fluorescent lights. We ask inconvenient questions. We awaken from the sleep-fog of compliance and move to a rhythm older and deeper than the laws of the King. We will not keep silent."[120] When individuals hold an orientation of mystery, Starhawk concludes, they "have a bad attitude" and "make trouble" for the ordered world of patriarchy.[121]

Starhawk identifies laughter and a love of the body as options that help rhetors open up to mystery. Laughter involves assuming the role of the trickster and the sacred clown, who exist "precisely to keep us from taking ourselves too seriously"—a consequence of patriarchy.[122] The use of humor of any kind— from making fun of things to seeing life's ironies to formal parody—functions to loosen patriarchy's grip. Rhetors who can laugh are more likely to see and appreciate new alternatives and thus to be open to mystery.

Loving one's body also is a way to open to mystery: "To open to mystery is to love the body, to marvel at the intensities of its pleasures," to allow oneself "to fully feel its sensitivity to pain."[123] Starhawk uses sexuality as one example of an aspect of the body that assists rhetors in engaging in mystery. She advocates a sexuality based on honesty, vitality, and pleasure rather than on control or procreation.[124] Loving one's body encourages a respect for diverse drives, cycles, rhythms, and passions. It produces an energy that Starhawk argues is erotic, sacred, and dependent on a "deep connection with others."[125] Laughter and loving one's body, then, are two ways to open up to mystery and to make trouble for patriarchy.

Ritual

Grounded in mystery, ritual is a second option Starhawk suggests for creating an alternative world to that of patriarchy. A ritual is a "patterned movement of energy to accomplish a purpose"; it is grounded in and focused on change.[126] Rituals develop out of the individual or community and reflect the needs and desires of those involved at the time. Rituals reshape not only individuals but the culture, creating "a culture of life" that makes new patterns for living.[127] Rituals are opportunities for transformation because they create a "free space, a hole torn in the fabric of domination."[128] They are an important rhetorical option because they wear away "control from below"; they change the individual consciousness, which then changes the larger social structure.[129]

Starhawk explains that change, whether personal or disciplinary, is "frightening, but Witches have a saying, 'Where there's fear, there's power.'" If, she continues, we can learn to "feel our fear without letting it stop us, fear can become an ally, a sign to tell us that something we have encountered can be transformed." Engagement in ritual means that an individual is open to change: "To do ritual, you must be willing to be transformed in some way. . . . If you aren't willing to be changed by the ritual, don't do it."[130] If individuals are not willing to confront themselves, they "risk reproducing the landscape of domination in the very structures" they create to challenge authority.[131]

Starhawk offers a general form or framework for rituals, developed out of her own community; she urges rhetors, however, to recognize that rituals are alive, and when they are written down, "we risk killing [them]."[132] In offering the basic structure of rituals, Starhawk hopes that rhetors will use their own imaginations and situations to create new rituals or variations of the ones she presents.[133]

The various steps Starhawk outlines for rituals incorporate discursive and nondiscursive rhetorical practices, and rhetors make use of a wide range of symbols as they progress through the various steps. The basic structure of a ritual begins with a cleansing and grounding. Cleansing involves letting go of concerns and stresses and can be done through the use of one or more of the elements of water, fire, movement, and sound. To cleanse, individuals can take a bath, burn sage, or use movements (such as stretching) or sound (such as breathing) to release tensions and preoccupations. The goal is to let go of concerns that might prevent individuals from being fully present at the ritual both mentally and emotionally.

Grounding is the establishment of "an energy connection with the earth" and involves connecting not only with the earth but with the forces that surround individuals, each individual's own center, and the other people involved in the ritual.[134] Grounding occurs in various forms, but it usually involves concentrated or purposeful breathing and visualization. The Tree of Life is one example of grounding. In this exercise, individuals imagine their spines as the trunks of trees, with their roots going deep into the earth. Energy flows from the tops of their heads through their bodies, into the earth, and back up into their bodies in a circular pattern. The goal is to connect with the earth and to feel the "energy flow up from the earth," filling the entire body.[135]

Rhetors then are ready to create a sacred space or cast a circle, which involves marking off from everyday activities the space being used for the ritual. Although some rituals take place in churches, temples, or cathedrals, they also may occur in living rooms, meadows, or public halls. In whatever setting the ritual occurs, participants must take the time to transform the space, which may include moving furniture, constructing some sort of altar, or even drawing or casting a circle around the space in order to mark its boundaries.[136]

When the space is formed, participants call the powers of the four directions and the center, and here flexibility is important. Calling the powers may involve locating the powers according to geographic bearings as well as negotiating respect for the different religious beliefs of those involved.[137] Starhawk suggests that on the West Coast, participants might identify East with the air, sunrise, and the mind; South with fire, noon, and energy; West with twilight and water; and North with midnight and earth. On the East Coast, however, the reversal of East and West might make sense. To avoid religious battles, she suggests that one person call out each direction and that other participants respond with images or qualities that come to mind.

The next step in the ritual is invocation of the Goddess in all her aspects, a process that reminds participants of the sacred and its powers. Because the Goddess resides in each individual, invocation of the sacred being may occur simply through the singing out of the name of each individual present and looking at that person as the name is being sung to honor the embodiment of the sacred in that person. Invocation of the Goddess also may be done through singing, chanting, drumming, the recitation of poetry, dancing, or quiet meditation.

After the Goddess is invoked, the heart of the ritual occurs—the step that constitutes the magic or the creation of energy with the capacity to transform. Starhawk describes magic as "the art of liberation, the act that releases the mysteries, that ruptures the fabric of our beliefs and lets us look into the heart of deep space where dwell the immeasurable, life-generating powers."[138] Magic is, in other words, *"the art of changing consciousness at will."*[139] It involves "directing energy through images" or the creation of "a mental image that represents the forces we want to generate or harmonize with."[140]

Participants may use chanting, storytelling, dancing, meditation, drumming, or visualization in the heart of the ritual to bring together the energy of group members to create magic. They may engage in creating a cone of power, for example, where the group's energy comes together in order to create a reality larger than each individual, or they may do a womb chant, touching the womb area of the person next to them in order to feel how individuals are linked. The choices for this part of the ritual are endless, and whether the ritual is performed individually or as part of a group, what is important is that individuals make or discover connections previously unmade, move energy, identify with other forms of being, and change their states of consciousness.

The ritual next moves toward its closing. The directing of energy "makes people hungry," and Starhawk recommends that rituals incorporate the sharing of food at their closing.[141] The sharing of food, or at least socializing and talking with one another about the ritual or other aspects of life, encourages the transition from ritual to the everyday and helps the boundaries of the space claimed return to their more fluid or mundane condition. Phrases such as "open the circle" can be used to "complete a transition of return and to say goodbye to all that has been invoked."[142]

Ritual, then, relies on the patterned movement of energy among individuals or within an individual. Although certain steps are recommended, rituals are flexible and can be developed to meet the needs of almost any situation.

Power-With

Starhawk's rhetorical option of power-with, practiced in the world of the Goddess, assists rhetors in their efforts to create change by working in groups. Starhawk believes that individuals alone cannot change the world: "To heal ourselves, to restore the earth to life, to create the situations in which freedom can flourish, we must work together in groups."[143] For Starhawk, groups are not only a naturally occurring part of human life but they are sites of transformation. As individuals leave the isolation of the self-hater and engage in mystery and ritual, they regularly do so in groups. In order for these collective efforts at transformation to be successful, however, individuals must work from a position of power-with.

Power-with is "the power of a strong individual in a group of equals, the power not to command, but to suggest and be listened to, to begin something and see it happen." The source of power-with is the willingness of others to listen to another's ideas so that the respect these ideas generate is accorded to the person and not the role occupied.[144] Power-with is grounded in influence rather than in patriarchal forms of leadership, and decisions are made not because one person suggests an option or persuades others but because the group, as a collective, believes a certain plan is good. Power-with is "more fluid and fragile than authority. It is dependent on personal responsibility, on . . . creativity and daring, and on the willingness of others to respond."[145] Rhetors who communicate using power-with may shape and guide a group but cannot force their will on it.

In order to assist rhetors in engaging in power-with, Starhawk identifies four types of groups that she sees as possible when individuals come together: intimate, task, support, and learning groups. These groups reflect a range of possibilities for transformation and, when rooted in mystery and power-with, enable change to take place. Ritual, too, can be a part of each of the four groups. Starhawk describes the purpose and characteristics of each group so that rhetors are aware of the strengths and weaknesses inherent in each.

In intimate groups, the primary purpose of group members simply is to be in the group. Intimate groups create community and form long-term, ongoing relationships; they often take years to develop. Examples are groups such as families, households, and covens. Intimate groups "demand long-term, open ended commitments and a high degree of openness and trust." A basic chemistry or attraction needs to exist in intimate groups; Starhawk asserts that "it's pointless trying to be intimate with someone whose company you don't enjoy."[146]

In contrast to intimate groups, the primary purpose of task groups is to get something done. Task groups may be involved in public actions or demonstrations, operating a collective business, or providing services to other individuals. They last, "ideally, just as long as they need to last to do what they are trying to do." Members of task groups may come and go; consequently, these groups are marked by varying degrees of openness and trust. Task-group members may not be "very attracted to each other's personalities," but they value one another because of their skills and experience.[147]

The primary purpose of support groups is change, which can take the form of "insight, healing, [or] recovery from external or internalized oppression."[148] They may focus on specific issues, such as discrimination or addiction, but they also can "generate the insights necessary for action," whether private or public. This third type of group varies in size and degree of intimacy and may last for a prearranged span of time or for as long as the support is needed. Trust is key for the effectiveness of the support group because "members need to trust that they will not be judged or condemned for speaking, and that their secrets will remain confidential."[149]

Learning groups occur in classes, workshops, seminars, and the like, and their purpose is to facilitate knowledge acquisition and understanding. For learning groups to be successful, Starhawk asserts, teachers must see themselves as learners. One person or several may act as teacher, or the group may direct its own learning process. In groups with teachers, the teacher's goal is to become "obsolete" because students usually have the potential to replace the teacher over time.[150] Size and intimacy vary greatly in learning groups, which also usually have a limited duration.

However gifted a group, conflict does and should occur in any of the four types of groups, and Starhawk acknowledges this very real phenomenon. Conflict "is not a sign of a group's failure but a necessary and potentially healthy aspect of its growth."[151] Conflict, Starhawk explains, "means that my needs, desires, or ideas run counter to yours."[152] The end result of conflict in groups, when it surfaces, is not for one side to overpower the other but for individuals to see the conflict as "information about differing needs and recognize those needs as valid."[153] Conflict often occurs during times of transition, when a group is confused about its primary purpose or path. This type of conflict is creative in that "each person in the group become[s] more aware of her or his own needs and purposes," and the group may gain clarity and vision as a result.[154] During times of conflict, members may leave the group, but groups can ease their transition by making sure those who leave are empowered to succeed outside the group in other ways.

Starhawk recognizes not only that groups experience conflict but that they also evolve. Groups progress through stages that correspond to the four directions and elements of the Wiccan magic circle: air, fire, water, and earth. Groups do not follow these stages in perfect order, but the directions are "a framework for thinking about group changes over time, as well as for identifying some of the dynamic polarities that exist in groups."[155]

The stage of air corresponds to the direction of the East and the quality of the mind and is a stage "of light, illumination, naming, differentiation."[156] In this stage, a group comes together "around a common vision or set of ideas." This stage often is the "honeymoon period, during which members feel close to each other and admire each other—because they don't really know each other."[157] The goal in this stage is to establish an identity and a primary purpose for the group. The "stronger that identity becomes as an independent force, the less amenable it is to any individual's control."[158]

Fire represents the second stage in a group's development and corresponds to the direction of the South and the quality of energy. This stage is the stage of "passion, courage, will, expansion," and in this stage, a group begins to expand rapidly and to feel its energy and power.[159] In the fire stage, events move quickly: "Conflicts are heated as people struggle around issues of power."[160] Rage and anger may be part of this stage but can be used creatively rather than destructively if individuals remember that conflict is a source of information and not a struggle for power-over.

Following the high-energy period of the fire stage is the third stage, represented by water, which is much more peaceful; in this stage, a group might appear to have collapsed after its fire period. Water corresponds to the West and emotion and is characterized by feeling, nurturing, sensuality, and introspection. At this stage, members "may resist new plans and projects," but this is because they need "time to turn inward."[161] Emotional and sexual involvements and attachments are common at this stage, and the group often "struggles with the feelings members have for each other."[162] In general, then, the individuals in a group test their connections and ability to trust one another at this stage, a difficult period in the group's evolution.

If a group survives the conflict of the water stage, "it tends to *crystallize,* defining itself and its boundaries more clearly."[163] This is the stage of earth, the direction of the North and the quality of body. This phase "represents growth, sustenance, the solidity of limits and boundaries, the ability to build lasting achievements."[164] At this stage, members are united by the trust built in the water stage and can work together to turn their visions into actual, tangible realities. By this time, group members have numerous skills and resources and are able to do many things well. They can expect to make lasting changes in this phase, but one of their biggest challenges is to bring new members in while simultaneously sustaining trust. A second challenge is not to let what the group "does become institutionalized, codified, rigid, or dogmatic, to stay open to change, creativity and new visions."[165]

In nonhierarchical groups such as those Starhawk advocates, there are numerous leaders, "people who are willing to look ahead, anticipate problems, suggest new directions, try out new solutions, keep track of information and decisions, who lead in the sense of stepping out in front and going first."[166] Even though she advocates that individuals operate from positions of power-with as they assume these roles, Starhawk encourages the rotation of individuals in these positions because any of them can lead to burnout if not handled carefully. Some roles are more pleasant than others, but even pleasant roles can be draining for individuals who are required to perform them too long. The various roles of nonhierarchical leaders also correspond to the four directions and four elements of the magic circle.[167] Starhawk names each of these roles according to the Wicca magic circle in order to move power out into the open, to reveal its "hidden structure," and to change the relationships among people in a group.[168]

In the East are the Crows. This is the direction of air, mind, and vision, and Crows keep "an overview of the group's tasks and progress."[169] Starhawk explains that "Crows fly high and see far. . . . They take the long view, see the long-term vision, keep in focus the group's goals." Crows attend to resources, future needs, and current strengths and weaknesses. In doing so, Crows "suggest new directions, make plans and develop strategies, and look ahead to anticipate problems and needs."[170]

Corresponding to the Wiccan direction of the South, leaders take the role of the Graces—individuals who help the group expand. Graces correspond to fire and continually monitor the energy generated by the group, "helping to raise it when it flags, and to direct and channel it when it is strong." Graces provide enthusiasm, "make people feel good," and welcome newcomers.[171] Women are trained well to be good Graces, Starhawk acknowledges, but they must work closely with the Dragon in the North in order to stay grounded.

In the direction of the West, or water, are the Snakes. As leaders, Snakes represent renewal, rebirth, and fertility, and they ensure that these qualities are a part of a group's process. Snakes attend to the underview of a group's feelings and emotions by gliding through the group, keeping "current with the group's gossip." They become aware of conflict early and bring it into the open, "where they may help to mediate or resolve problems."[172]

Dragons, corresponding to the North and to the body, are a fourth kind of leader. Dragons "keep the group grounded, in touch with the practical, the realistic." Dragons foster nurturing in such a way as to secure the longevity of the group and guard a group's resources and boundaries, articulating its limitations when others may not want to hear them.[173] Dragons are concerned with whether the work of the group is sustainable, whether resources are being replenished, and how people can nurture one another better. They attend to resource constraints and boundaries and to how, optimally, a person might leave a group. Dragons give a group a sense of safety, but they also "may be perceived as throwing a wet blanket on the fires of fresh enthusiasm." They also may "win great appreciation from those in the group who are feeling overwhelmed and can't buck the driving force of the Crows and Graces."[174]

A fifth kind of leader, the Spider, resides at the center of the four directions. "The spider spins a web that connects points across a stretch of empty space. Every circle needs a center," Starhawk explains, "a way in which people feel connected. A group's center may be a spiritual heart, a common goal or vision, or it may manifest in a person" who sits metaphorically at the center of the web.[175] When the task of the Spider is not assigned, the role may fall to the person everyone calls for information about meetings or events or the person in whom most group members confide.

Starhawk also suggests roles that do not correspond to the Wiccan circle and that are less visible and less leadership oriented. These roles, which should be rotated among a group's membership, are the coordinator, facilitator, vibeswatcher, priestess/priest, peacekeeper, and mediator. Starhawk notes that she dislikes "most of the names for these roles" but hasn't invented "any better ones."[176] The coordinator is similar to the Spider because the individual in this position serves "as a group center, a switchboard through which information is passed."[177] The facilitator observes the "*content* of the talk in a meeting" and assists in keeping the "meeting focused and moving."[178] The vibeswatcher "remains aware of the levels of tension and anxiety" in a meeting and may interrupt discussion to suggest that "people breathe, that feelings be acknowledged, that personal attacks be stopped."[179] The priestess/priest monitors the energy of the group, keeping it moving, channeling it, and sometimes "opening her/his own body to let it flow through."[180] The peacekeeper keeps order and deals with crises at meetings and demonstrations or whenever a group is together. The mediator is the individual who remains neutral and objective in order to help others "resolve conflict."[181]

Starhawk, then, recognizes the ongoing possibilities of groups as places of transformation in which her rhetorical options of mystery, ritual, and power-with can flourish. For Starhawk, individual change is reinforced through collective transformation, through rejection of the self-hater roles, and through the embrace of the mystery of the Goddess. Although the patriarchal world reifies hierarchy, power-over, self-hate, and estrangement, the world of the Goddess, in which immanence, connection, and community are central, reinforces the importance of the sacred in efforts to create change. Based on interconnection and immanence, the world of the Goddess constitutes an acknowledgment and celebration of the sacredness of all individuals and their places in the circle of life.

Transformations of Rhetorical Theory

Starhawk's rhetorical theory provides alternative conceptions of a number of rhetorical constructs and assumptions, informed as it is by the life-affirming system of the Goddess. The primary transformations she offers concern the realm for rhetoric, power, the change process, and the audience.

Realm for Rhetoric

A primary revision Starhawk makes in rhetorical theory concerns the perceived naturalness of the realm of the public for rhetoric. In traditional rhetorical theory, rhetoric is seen as occurring in and against a public backdrop that is natural, standard, and objective or neutral in the sense that it does not embody a particular set of values. What Starhawk makes clear, in contrast, is that although the public realm indeed may be an appropriate site for rhetoric, other options are available as sites in which rhetoric occurs. These may be private realms and can be chosen (and, in fact, constructed) by individuals or groups. The idea that there is only one possibility for the realm of rhetoric—the public realm that embodies patriarchy, with its characteristics of division, hierarchy, and power-over—is too limiting. An alternative realm for rhetoric exists, according to Starhawk, and is a life-affirming system rooted in the Goddess and characterized by such qualities as inherent value and interconnection. This alternate site, moreover, can and frequently does occur when individuals are not located in what has come to be known as the *public sphere.*

When the realm for rhetoric changes, new possibilities for rhetorical options also become available. The rhetorical options of judgment, censorship, conquest, defense, and domination, for example, which constitute ways of engaging in rhetoric in the traditional realm, no longer are seen as natural and normal, which they are when the realm for rhetoric is patriarchy. Rhetorical options such as mystery and ritual become possible, enabling rhetors to create and contribute to dramatically different kinds of worlds, rooted in different values, that have not, as yet, been explored fully.

Power

Starhawk's notions of power constitute a second challenge to traditional conceptions of rhetoric. Power traditionally is conceptualized in rhetorical theory as the rhetor's ability to dominate—to have the rhetor's beliefs prevail and to secure the adherence of audience members to the rhetor's point of view. Starhawk's constructs of power-with and power-from-within suggest that this concept is more complex than is indicated by the monolithic view of power found in traditional rhetorical theory. Power-from-within is an intrapersonal power that enables individuals to respond creatively and effectively in situations. Power-with is an interpersonal power rooted in creative ideas that others find valuable. By expanding the kinds of power available to be manifest through rhetoric, Starhawk expands the possibilities for rhetoric beyond those that express power-over and encourages scholars to consider other dimensions of power—dimensions that are equally effective at producing change.

Change

Starhawk reconceptualizes the nature of change in rhetorical theory as well. In the rhetorical system of the Goddess, rhetorical options rooted in change do not involve persuading others to change their beliefs or actions. Instead, they involve individual or collective rhetorical activity directed at the self. Options such as mystery, ritual, and power-with focus on changing the consciousness of the rhetor as a means for changing larger structures. These options involve changing the perceptions and descriptions of who and what individuals are and facilitating the development of a consciousness that enables them to live in life-affirming ways. They also involve connecting with the life force of the Goddess, which, again, facilitates a new consciousness for rhetors. Change, then, occurs not because others persuade an individual but because individuals are grounded in magic and mystery. Contrary to the rhetorical discipline's focus on change as the result of external forces, Starhawk suggests that change occurs as a result of internal factors rooted in a life-affirming interconnection with the Goddess.

Audience

Starhawk's notion of inherent value in the Goddess-based rhetorical system transforms yet another rhetorical construct: the conception of the audience. She sees all individuals as possessing immanent value by virtue of embodying the Goddess; they do not need to have the status of possessions, occupations, or external access to prestige to have value. Starhawk's view of the individual as having immanent value changes the traditional view of audience members as less competent and informed than the rhetor and who, as a result, need the ideas the rhetor can offer. For Starhawk, the audience is no less competent, informed, or expert than the rhetor; both rhetor and audience are unique, offering perspectives that are of interest and value and that are worthy of being shared with others. The relationship between the rhetor and the audience is one of reciprocity, with each individual embodying aspects of the Goddess. A hierarchy of speaker and listener, then, is nonsensical in Starhawk's theory—one manifestation of the Goddess never can be more correct than another. Engaged in the act of communication, individuals strive to recognize the inherent value of others and do not determine value based on external standards.

Starhawk's theory expands the perimeters of some of the most basic traditional assumptions about rhetoric. She suggests that much of what rhetorical scholars have assumed as given is arbitrary and certainly not inevitable. Her rhetoric functions to highlight and maximize the celebration and honor of the Goddess in all her aspects, resulting in options for rhetoric that facilitate the flourishing of life and spirit:

> For she is no longer sleeping but awake and rising, reaching out her hands to touch us again. When we reach for her, she reveals herself to us, in the stones and the soil beneath our feet, in the whitewater rapids and limpid pools of the imagination, in tears and laughter, ecstasy and sorrow, common courage and common struggle, wind and fire.[182]

Bibliography

Books

Starhawk. *Dreaming the Dark: Magic, Sex and Politics.* 1982. Boston: Beacon, 1988.
Starhawk. *The Fifth Sacred Thing.* New York: Bantam, 1993.
Starhawk. *The Spiral Dance: A Rebirth of the Ancient Religion of the Great Goddess.* 1979. San Francisco: HarperCollins, 1989.
Starhawk. *Truth or Dare: Encounters with Power, Authority, and Mystery.* San Francisco: Harper & Row, 1987.
Starhawk. *Walking to Mercury.* New York: Bantam, 1997.

Starhawk, M. Macha NightMare, and the Reclaiming Collective. *The Pagan Book of Living and Dying: Practical Rituals, Prayers, Blessings, and Meditations on Crossing Over.* New York: HarperCollins, 1997.

Articles

Starhawk. "Ritual as Bonding: Action as Ritual." *Weaving the Visions: New Patterns in Feminist Spirituality.* Ed. Judith Plaskow and Carol P. Christ. San Francisco: HarperCollins, 1989. 326-35.
Starhawk. "Roundtable Discussion: Backlash." *Journal of Feminist Studies in Religion* 10 (1994): 103-07.

CHAPTER **8**

Paula Gunn Allen

"Where I fit, I wasn't allowed to be. Where I was allowed to be, I was unacceptable. I fit nowhere."[1] This uneasy status with her place in life as a young girl never has left Paula Gunn Allen. As she matured into adulthood, she came to recognize that to fit in is to survive—a fundamental issue for Native Americans—as well as to be "safe" and "ordinary"—characteristics she rarely has felt.[2] Born Paula Marie Francis on October 24, 1939, in Cubero, New Mexico, Gunn Allen is a clan mother of the Laguna Oak clan, multilingual, lesbian/bisexual, and intensely psychic, dimensions of her identity that affect the rhetorical theory that emerges from her work.

NOTE: Excerpts from *The Sacred Hoop: Recovering the Feminine in American Indian Traditions,* by Paula Gunn Allen, © 1986, 1992 by Paula Gunn Allen, are reprinted by permission of Beacon Press, Boston. Excerpts from "Sipapu: A Cultural Perspective" (unpublished doctoral dissertation, University of New Mexico), by Paula Gunn Allen, are reprinted by permission of the author. Excerpts from "The Horse That I Ride: The Life Story of Paula Gunn Allen" (unpublished manuscript), by Jacqueline L. Collins, are reprinted by permission of the author.

Gunn Allen describes herself and her life as a "multicultural" experience. Her mother, Ethel Haines Gottlieb Francis, was Laguna Pueblo, Lakota, and Scottish. Her father, E. Lee Francis, who served as lieutenant governor of the state of New Mexico, was a full-blooded Lebanese born in the United States who spoke five languages. Her maternal grandmother was Scottish and Laguna; her maternal grandfather was Lakota, probably Metis; and her maternal step-grandfather was Jewish. The result of these different ethnicities and heritages, explains Gunn Allen, is that "I have lived in America all my life but I have never lived in America."[3] For many years, Gunn Allen tried to fit in by being just one thing; she thought she had to choose among her multiple identities, a dilemma that made her suicidal. Only recently has she come to acknowledge that all of these aspects are integral components of her self and that attempting to be only one is both futile and unhealthy.

Gunn Allen attended Catholic boarding school, an experience she describes as devastating to herself and to other Native Americans. Boarding schools were designed to "take Indians away from their homes so they wouldn't grow up to be Indians," Gunn Allen explains.[4] At these schools, Native children learned to raise their hands; to say, "Good morning sister"; to be maids or farm laborers; and to "be civilized."[5] The experience of boarding school for Native Americans over the generations, Gunn Allen asserts, is "psychic suicide, psychic homicide, psychic genocide."[6] Gunn Allen believes that the devastating effects of boarding schools on American Indians will last for generations, damaging their ability to parent and to function as Indians.

Throughout her years in boarding school, Gunn Allen spent much of her time reading, her way of protecting herself from the world around her. She decided as a young child to become "great with a capital G" and later an actress, an occupation her father detested.[7] Those plans changed when, in the middle of her first semester of classes at the University of New Mexico, Gunn Allen became pregnant and decided to marry: "In those days that's what you did. I couldn't become a single mother; therefore, I got married."[8] During her short and difficult marriage to a Lebanese man, Gunn Allen had two children, Gene and LauraLee. She also began to write poetry "out of desperation": "I think poetry worked for me because it's very visual; it's very confined. That helps when you have kids. . . . I had to work to raise the kids. It was good to have poetry as a form because I couldn't sustain my attention long enough to write fiction."[9]

During her marriage, Gunn Allen was "totally undisciplined" and "severely neurotic"—responses, in part, to her husband, whom she describes as "absolutely dreadful; he was a nut."[10] She explains that the family of four was "going down. Four of us were going to lose, at the very least, our minds. I could maybe salvage three of us. So, that's what I tried to do."[11] She left the marriage after three years but not before it had destroyed her self-esteem. Her husband, who eventually had the marriage annulled in the Catholic Church, was awarded all of the couple's property.

Over the next 14 years, Gunn Allen married two more times. Her second marriage, which she believes could have lasted, ended as a result of her husband's alcoholism. In 1970, Gunn Allen became a Bahá'í and met and married her third husband, also Baha'i, whom she describes as "Cherokee, Dutch . . . English. . . . twenty-three, and . . . beautiful." She explains, "I don't know how I wound up with him because I didn't even particularly like him," but the two "bonded in some sort of mystical way."[12] Soon after they were married, Gunn Allen became pregnant with twins, a pregnancy that made her extremely ill: "I was pregnant; I was bleeding all the time. I had to stay in bed flat on my back for weeks and weeks and weeks. The night the twins were conceived, our room was filled with blue light."[13]

While she was confined to bed, Gunn Allen's husband attended a Baha'i conference in Oklahoma. She communicated with her husband during his absence "just by thinking" and was having "weird" and "terrifying" visions about "ETs or something chasing me."[14] Since infancy, Gunn Allen has had experiences with extraterrestrial abductions, and she learned later that the visions she was having at the time of her pregnancy were either similar experiences or memories of those earlier abductions. She concluded, in fact, that "the ETs killed my son," Faud, one of the twins, who died a few months after he was born.[15] The other twin, Suleiman, survived.

A few months after the death of their child, Gunn Allen and her husband became disenchanted with some of the tenets of the Baha'i philosophy and left the faith. Gunn Allen's visions and psychic experiences continued: "Strange people kept showing up in my bedroom. All this stuff was going on night and day, all the time. They were always around; I was always seeing them."[16] Gunn Allen describes herself as very ill for most of these years because, in addition to the loss of her son and the continuing visions, she was responsible for the majority of the financial support of her family.

Not quite three years after the death of Faud, her oldest son, Gene, left to live with Gunn Allen's second husband—his adopted father. Twenty minutes after putting Gene on the plane, her husband told her he was leaving: "I'll never forgive him for that," Gunn Allen says.[17] She was "working far too hard" and commuting "all over the place," doing consulting, teaching, and multicultural education.[18] She also "was teaching four classes and was trying to deal with a couple of out of control teenagers": "I worked myself half to death."[19]

In 1977, Gunn Allen came out as a lesbian/bisexual. She chooses this term to describe herself because, although she often has fallen in love with men—particularly gay men—her primary attraction and affinity are for women.

Throughout her life, Gunn Allen has had experiences that made her realize she probably was a lesbian, but she acknowledges that it "was very hard to think of myself as gay in a heterosexual society. It's complicated."[20] She acknowledges that some of her suicide attempts prior to coming out were in response to her lesbianism, explaining that "it was a dreadful time and place to grow up. A place where everybody hates everything you are."[21] She not only had to come out as a lesbian but also "as an Indian," "a poet," "a teacher," "a strong woman," and "a leader." The response was negative: "[S]ociety didn't like it; society didn't like me."[22] Gunn Allen, however, attributes some of her professional success to her lesbianism. Before she came out, she says she "couldn't get anywhere. . . . I think what happened is that there weren't enough lesbian writers being published."[23]

Gunn Allen's two major relationships with women helped her to come to peace with her multiple identities and to stand up for herself. Her first relationship lasted more than four years, and during that time, Gunn Allen explains, "I came out as a full-blown dyke. I was really having fun. I was very, very happy. . . . In many ways, it was the first clear statement [I made] that I live my life, nobody else does."[24] During this time, Gunn Allen's partner began channeling for an entity named Wing, and over the years, Wing and Gunn Allen "talked a lot. I've got it on tape. He came through [her partner], but she did not remember the conversations."[25] In addition to the painful ending of her relationship, Gunn Allen acknowledges she really "hated losing Wing" when the two women broke up.[26]

Gunn Allen's second relationship with a woman began in 1981. This relationship was based on obsession, but, Gunn Allen explains, this was the last time she "did obsession. . . . I think now having gone through menopause, whatever that hormone storm was, it stopped. I simply have not done [obsession] since menopause, my very late forties."[27] Her relationship was unhealthy in other ways, too. As Gunn Allen explains, this partner

> went off with me and pretty much convinced me that she was in love with me. I don't think she ever was. She probably was turned on to me, this little Indian woman. It would help to give her some credentials that she had gone off with a colored girl. Find yourself a colored girl, and then you'll be a real feminist. By then lesbians had been using me for quite a while that way.[28]

When the relationship ended, Gunn Allen "went underground" in terms of relationships because she felt she could not trust herself or others. At this point, Gunn Allen recognized that she had made choices that were harmful to herself and her children. She had put love before her children and her own health, and she realized that such a focus is a "horrible thing. I really, really hated myself for that."[29] She began to see a therapist who helped her sort through her identities as an Indian, Lebanese, and white woman, and a second doctor helped her recover her UFO memories through hypnosis. As a result, Gunn Allen began to learn to trust herself and to rebuild her life.

Gunn Allen's writing focuses on her metaphysical, paranormal, and UFO-abduction experiences as well as her Native American, white, female, and lesbian identities. Her novel *The Woman Who Owned the Shadows* (1983), which took her 10 years to write, is semiautobiographical and is grounded in Native American and paranormal traditions and experiences. In it, she explores differences between the paranormal and normal worlds and suggests that the shadows, the place between the two worlds, is where she has lived most of her life.

In 1986, Gunn Allen published *The Sacred Hoop: Recovering the Feminine in American Indian Tradition*. In this book, she discusses the histories, writings, and spiritual recoveries of women in various Native American communities. She seeks in the book to present a "picture of American Indian life and literature unfiltered through the minds of western patriarchal colonizers."[30] The book is informed by a variety of disciplinary perspectives—folklore, psychology, anthropology, and women's studies, among others—but Gunn Allen explains that her method is grounded in her "own understanding of American Indian life and thought."[31] American Indian women's traditions, she notes, "have *never* been described or examined in terms of their proper, that is, woman-focused, context," and she offers *The Sacred Hoop* as a beginning remedy for this neglect.[32]

Gunn Allen's book *Grandmothers of the Light: A Medicine Woman's Sourcebook* (1991) is a collection of stories she gathered from various Native American communities. Each of the stories "contains information central to a woman's spiritual tradition" and is grounded in the goddesses. Gunn Allen sees the goddesses as the creative power that brings forth "through supernatural ritual a variety of beings that include the galaxy, the solar system, the planet with all of its resources and denizens, language, social systems, architecture, science, agriculture, hunting, and laws of action and interaction that secure harmony, balance, and propriety." Gunn Allen presents these stories in the hope that they may act as guides for individuals on "the perilous journey . . . that marks the boundary between the mundane world and the world of spirit."[33]

Gunn Allen has edited four anthologies: *Spider Woman's Granddaughters: Traditional Tales and Contemporary Writing by Native American Women* (1989), *Voice of the Turtle: American Indian Literature: 1900-1970* (1994), *As Long as the Rivers Flow: Nine Stories of Native Americans* (coedited with Patricia Clark Smith; 1996), and *Song of the Turtle: American Indian Literature: 1974-1994* (1996). All are compilations of stories written by other Native American writers. She traces the history of American Indian writing from the 1900s to the present and identifies key themes in the work of these writers. Gunn

Allen explains that her anthologies are about "re-membering": "I put the anthologies together as a way of putting the members of the body back together. You see, re-membering is to member again."[34]

Gunn Allen has also published numerous books of poetry. These include *The Blind Lion* (1974), *Coyote's Daylight Trip* (1978), *A Cannon between My Knees* (1981), *Star Child* (1981), *Shadow Country* (1982), *Wyrds* (1987), *Skins and Bones* (1988), *and Life Is a Fatal Disease* (1997). Her poetry reflects the various identities she shares with other Native American women and illustrates the struggles and joys that come from attempting to integrate these various selves. Yet another major theme in her poetry is the separation between the natural and the mystical worlds, a separation she sees as an illusion because the two "interpenetrate" one another.[35]

Although she enjoys writing, Gunn Allen believes that "anybody that made a good dinner has made a more important contribution, personally. Feeding people is more important than writing."[36] She says that she writes for two reasons—"to find out what I'm thinking and to protest."[37] For her, writing is a confrontational process; writers "are trying to find out what they really think. They hope that people will read what they write and tell them what they really think."[38] Protest is a second impetus for her writing. Gunn Allen's research led her to recognize the status of women in tribal communities, and when she compared it to the status of women in modern tribes, she became "angrier and angrier. . . . I just kept at it because I was furious. Either I had to write, or I would die from my anger and depression."[39]

Gunn Allen's involvement in the academic world is as varied as the other aspects of her life. Although she began her college career at the University of New Mexico, she received both her B.A. degree in English in 1966 and her M.F.A. degree in 1968 from the University of Oregon. She completed her Ph.D. in American studies at the University of New Mexico in 1975. She has taught classes in literature and Native American studies at the University of California at Berkeley; at San Francisco State University, where she also chaired the Native American Studies Department; at De Anza Junior College in California; at the University of New Mexico; and at Fort Lewis College in Colorado. She now teaches in the Department of English at the University of California at Los Angeles.

Gunn Allen has found that teaching Native American literature and studies can be depressing: "I think these subjects would make any Native American feel as suicidal as I felt when I began teaching these matters."[40] One way she copes with the painful content of her work is through her orientation to the world. She believes that to separate the spiritual from the material is to deny the nature of reality: "[A]long the way, I decided that there's no such thing as spiritual. It doesn't exist. That is to say, intangible and invisible are nonsense.

Washington, D.C., is invisible; I can't see it, can I? Does that mean it's not real? No, it doesn't mean that at all. It means I can't see that far."[41]

For Gunn Allen, reality is perceivable by degrees. Certain events, processes, and entities are perceived easily by most people, whereas others are not. She believes that most individuals are taught not to see many of the things she can see—they are discouraged in various ways from acknowledging them. Most individuals tailor their perceptions to what is appropriate for given situations. They do so because otherwise they may be labeled *nuts, delusional, visionary,* or *shamans.* The point is "that you're not doing the perceptual thing that's being done by everybody else."[42] Regarding her experiences and her orientation to life, Gunn Allen concludes: "I can't say that I can prove any of this. But as a therapist once pointed out, life is not a courtroom. . . . Nobody ever really will know what happened to anybody at any time for a fact."[43]

Gunn Allen offers the notion of a story line to explain her view of how and where individuals fit into society. The only way individuals can understand their experiences and places in the world is through stories: "I'm certain there isn't anything but the stories. I'm sure you're not here, and I'm not here . . . except as a story. Somewhere somebody's telling us, and we're characters. I really believe that's the truth."[44] Native Americans, animals, stars, planets, everything "is a character in the story. The whole galaxy is a part of the story."[45] There is no "real distinction between story and humanity or story and wolfanity or story and pine tree-anity. They all come together in a particular way. . . . That's why people are so into stories, especially Indians."[46]

Individuals must discover what their particular story lines are. All people are following story lines—central narratives that people actually live that are cyclical and repetitive. The fake story line is "the one you keep trying to live, but you can't. You drive yourself nuts trying to live the life you never made; it has nothing to do with you."[47] Despite the individual story lines that characterize all individuals' lives, what happens to a person is not personal. Events in individuals' lives simply represent the parts they have to play out in the larger stories that are the society and the universe. The individual's primary role in life is to help the story progress, to pass on information to those who might learn from that knowledge and those experiences.[48]

Gunn Allen sees her story line as chronicling her existence on the borders or living in the shadows, and she acknowledges this is not the story line for all people. For Gunn Allen, the challenge of life is to accept her story line on the boundaries, her own limits, and her place at the crossroads. She sees herself as a spiritual activist, as one among many who adds her thoughts to the hoop of life. She also recognizes that her role is to provide the "Native encyclopedia"—the background of the Native American culture that most white people do not have. The tasks she has set for herself do not make her life easy, but she revels in the challenges:

> I have always been compulsive; I'll always be a compulsive person. I wish I didn't have a tendency for depression. . . . I'm intense and passionate, and I'm exhausted all the time. That's me. I really wish I weren't all those things. I wish, I wish, I wish. I wish I were really rich. But actually I have an extraordinarily nice life. I'm a lucky girl. I worked very, very hard to get it this way. I love it.[49]

Nature of the World

Central to Gunn Allen's rhetorical theory is the idea that two worlds exist simultaneously. One world is a death culture that is brutal and frightening; the other is a spiritual and gynecentric—or woman-centered—world grounded in Thought Woman.

Death Culture

The death society is white, Western society—a society whose consciousness is plasticized, numbed, and so preoccupied with death that it will have to die. This is a culture that seems determined to destroy all that is Indian, all who are Indian, and Western culture itself.[50] Gunn Allen asserts that the death culture already has tried to destroy itself in two massive world wars; excessive nuclear buildup; television programming that promotes the "newest death craze, the newest death wave"; and literature and politics that are about death. White Western culture is "obsessed with dying," Gunn Allen explains, so "they're doing it. And I am taking that in a spiritual sense. You know, people in the tribal culture don't become full adults until they go through their death trips. It's required of them. And I think that that's what the Western world is doing. It's finally entering its puberty."[51]

One consequence of the death culture is genocide—in particular, the genocide of American Indians. Although the Indian wars are over, the death culture continues to "napalm Indians in Brazil" and forcibly sterilize Indian women in Bolivia.[52] It relocates, removes, and sterilizes American Indians in the United States to the extent that, in North America alone, the population of Indians is just over 1 million; estimates of the precontact Native population range from 20 million to 45 million.[53] "Consciously or unconsciously, deliberately, as a matter of national policy, or accidentally as a matter of 'fate,'" Gunn Allen explains, "*every single government,* right, left, or centrist in the western hemisphere is consciously or subconsciously dedicated to the extinction of those tribal people who live within its borders."[54] The impact of this genocide cannot be underestimated for Native writers and speakers. The pervasive question for Native Americans is how to survive "in the face of collective death"; awareness of probable extinction is present in "every thought, in every conversation."[55]

Anglo-Europeans' relentless and systematic attempts to exterminate Native Americans led to the creation of boarding schools in which Indian children received not only "education" but also abuse and the denial of tribal ways of living and knowing. Attempts at extermination also generated the development of reservations, with their accompanying high rates of unemployment, alcoholism, drug abuse, and even suicide. Generations of Native Americans have passed on these abuses and ways of coping to their children so that attempts at genocide not only dramatically reduced the American Indian population but also promoted a common loss of identity, a sense of despair, fragmentation, alienation, and isolation.

The genocide of Native Americans has occurred systematically in three primary ways: through displacement of the female creator, alteration of the Native American system of government, and replacement of the clan with the nuclear family. Many Native American tribes were egalitarian, gynecentric social systems with fluid boundaries between female and male. In most tribal systems in North America, the creator was seen as primarily female but also as an entity that possessed maleness, and the feminine was revered as deeply as the masculine. In contrast, the "Westerner tends to denigrate whatever he perceives as feminine, or, more properly, to ascribe those aspects that he values positively to masculinity and those which he negatively values to femininity."[56] As a result, a primary means of destroying Native American culture has been to displace the primacy of the female as creator with "male-gendered creators."[57]

A second mechanism of genocide of Native Americans was to alter their governing systems. This was accomplished through the replacement of truly democratic systems with male officials elected by individuals outside of the tribe. Gunn Allen labels this process *democracy coercion* and explains that early politicians "demanded that the tribes that wish[ed] federal recognition and protection institute 'democracy,' in which powerful officials [were] elected by majority vote."[58] The result was the disappearance of egalitarian and female-centered societies. Many Native Americans, Gunn Allen explains, preferred death, the punishment that resulted from refusing this "democracy," to "enslavement in their own land."[59]

The third mechanism of genocide was the replacement of the clan structure with the nuclear family. In this process, individuals were "pushed off their lands, deprived of their economic livelihood, and forced to curtail or end altogether pursuits on which their ritual system, philosophy, and subsistence depend."[60] The insertion of a nuclear family system alters the entire social framework common to many Native American tribes. Women's role is subsumed under that of the male, and the "psychic net that is formed and maintained by the nature of nonauthoritarian gynecentricity grounded in respect for diversity of gods and people is thoroughly rent."[61]

In addition, genocide occurred because of the proliferation of lies about how North America was "discovered"—its history and its treatment of American Indians and their practices and beliefs. Anglo-Europeans believe, for example, in "this business of Columbus,"[62] that there never have been structures other than patriarchal ones in the United States, that there are fierce distinctions among Native American tribes, and that Native women are barred from ceremonies and segregated from people during menstruation because they are "unclean."[63] These lies, Gunn Allen notes, are designed to perpetuate myths, to confuse Natives and non-Natives alike, to keep similar groups from uniting against common oppressions, and to destroy and denigrate cultures rooted in ritual and spirit.

Gunn Allen argues that the genocide practiced by the death culture grew out of "America's amazing loss of memory concerning its origins in the matrix and context of Native America."[64] American people, she explains, do not remember that many of their values, laws, food, agricultural techniques, medicine, wealth, "and a large part of [their] 'dream'" came from Native American practices, principles, and lands.[65] Many of the traditions that are passed off as "Western" or as "out-growths of European civilization" are grounded in Native American traditions and beliefs.[66] The world of the death culture is based on the "basic chauvinism in the American character": "[T]here is no law that is sacred to the white man, there is no truth that he honors more than power, and there is no end to his ability to take any means to justify his apparently insatiable lust for superiority."[67]

In summarizing the death culture, Gunn Allen writes: "The death society walks, hypnotized by its silent knowledge." It does not hear "the drum, quiet to the core." But the

> trees know.
> Look.
> They are dying.
> The small birds who walk heedless
> of the people swarming around them,
> know: they peck at sesame seeds trucked
> from factories far away and crumbs dropped from Rainbow
> buns. They
> do not fly at human approach. They
> act as if we are not there.[68]

Gunn Allen refers to the people living in the death culture as the "dying generation"—a generation that moves purposefully and whose members are well dressed in the latest trends and fashions but are ignorant of their fate.[69]

Thought Woman

Despite the efforts of those who inhabit the death culture, the tribal world has not been eradicated completely, and Gunn Allen's theory describes an alternative world based in Thought Woman. Thought Woman is the Grandmother spirit, the spirit "that pervades everything, that is capable of powerful song and radiant movement, and that moves in and out of the mind." This is the spirit of intelligence, thinking, and naming, the "spirit that informs right balance, right harmony, and these in turn order all relationships in conformity with her law."[70]

Thought Woman has many names and many emblems, including *Grandmother, Mother, Old Spider Woman, Thought Woman, Old Woman, Woman, Tse che nako,* and *Beautiful Corn Woman.*[71] Thought Woman has two sisters, whom She "sings . . . into life"—Uretsete and Naotsete (Uretsete sometimes is referred to as *he* and *father*).[72] A third entity, Iyetiko or Iyatiku (Beautiful Corn Woman or Corn Woman), also exists as a part of Thought Woman. Gunn Allen explains that "the most important function of this multiple divinity is creation, which in its earth phase becomes a continual process of relating humans to the matter and to the universe."[73] Thought Woman occupies the skies as well as the earth and seas; She is dynamic and powerful, bringing life, language, "corn and agriculture, potting, weaving, social systems, religion, ceremony, ritual, building, memory, intuition, and their expressions in language, creativity, dance," and "human-to-animal relations."[74]

Thought Woman's variety and multiplicity bear witness to her complexity; She is the true creator, for She generates thought, and thought always must precede phenomenal manifestation. Thought Woman "thinks," Gunn Allen explains, "so we are."[75] Central to understanding Thought Woman is to recognize Her as "She Who Thinks rather than She Who Bears"[76] or as "Creating-through-Thinking Woman."[77] "To her we owe our very breath," Gunn Allen explains, "and to her our prayers are sent."[78]

Thought Woman is not a passive entity, a symbol of the fertility goddess, or limited to a female role. To call her a fertility goddess is to "degrade her position and to reduce Indian religious thought to absurdity."[79] Gunn Allen explains that because Thought Woman "is the supreme Spirit," She "is both Mother and Father to all people and to all creatures."[80] Although She is "essentially or primarily female, She is not without her integral masculine components."[81] Masculinity in Thought Woman is manifest in the form of motion or movement, and the "most notable characteristic of masculine intelligence is its periodicity, especially when considered against a background of endurance which is feminine." Male energy may appear adversarial or polar, but it really is complementary, arising from female energy and returning to it, and it is as "divine and mysterious in nature as female energy."[82]

The terms *sacred, power,* and *politics* are closely linked in the world of Thought Woman and are intimately connected to the feminine. If something is "sacred" or "*wakan,*" it possesses power given to it by Thought Woman. Gunn Allen explains: "Sacred often means taboo; that is, what is empowered in a ritual sense is not to be touched or approached by any who are weaker than the power itself, lest they suffer negative consequences from contact." "Sacred" is similar to "*sacrifice,* which means 'to make sacred,'" and when something is made sacred, it is empowered. Blood, for example, has the "power to make something else powerful or, conversely, to weaken or kill it." Women's blood is infused with the power of Thought Woman, and women's bodies, Gunn Allen explains, are not unclean, as Westerners suggest, but can "bring vital beings into the world—a miraculous power unrivaled by mere shamanic displays." Menstrual blood and postpartum blood thus are "the water of life" and are considered sacred.[83]

Another term associated with Thought Woman, *power,* is not considered political or economic; rather, it is paranormal and supernatural and is linked to connections with spirits and matters of destiny. Gunn Allen describes the concept of power among tribal people as "related to their understanding of the relationships that occur between the human and nonhuman worlds." In American Indian traditions, "all are linked within one vast, living sphere"; this linkage is spiritual rather than material, and "its essence is the power that enables magical things to happen."[84]

Power involves listening to the spiritual and material worlds and seeing connections between them as well as engaging in the magical transformation of things. Magic is "an enduring sense of the fluidity and malleability, or creative flux, of things," and Gunn Allen argues that Westerners' rejection of "nonordinary states of consciousness is as unthinking as the Indian's belief in them is said to be."[85] Magical transformations take the form of the changing of

> objects from one form to another, the movement of objects from one place to another by teleportation, the curing of the sick (and conversely creating sickness in people, animals, or plants), communication with animals, plants, and nonphysical beings (spirits, katsinas, goddesses, and gods), the compelling of the will of another, and the stealing or storing of souls.[86]

Magical transformations also involve ritual, birth, menstruation, motherhood and mothering, maintaining the linkage between the material and nonmaterial worlds, death, growth, and various other aspects of tribal life. In maintaining a close relationship to the supernatural world and focusing on the balance and harmony present in all interactions, individuals honor a tradition that embraces supernatural as well as natural phenomena.

In the death culture, individuals tend to believe that humans are the only intelligent beings on this planet. In the world of Thought Woman, in contrast, the very nature of being is intelligence; thus, "those attributes possessed by human beings are natural attributes of *all* being."[87] Gunn Allen explains further:

> When one describes the universe in English, one is practically forced to divide it into two parts: one part is natural and one is supernatural. People have no real part in either, being neither wholly animal nor spirit. That is, the supernatural is discussed as though it were apart from people, and the natural as though people were apart from it. This necessarily forces English-speaking people into a position of alienation from the world that they live in. This isolation is entirely foreign to the Native American of whatever tribe. At base, every story, every song, every ceremony tells the Indian that each person is a part of a living whole, and that all parts of that whole are related to one another by virtue of their participation in the whole of being, just as all members of a family, clan or tribe are related by virtue of their participation in the "blood," the whole spirit of that grouping.[88]

The natural or normal state of existence in the world of Thought Woman, then, is an intelligence inherent in all beings and an interconnection between the spirit and material worlds.

A third term critical to an understanding of Thought Woman is *politics,* which cannot be considered without understanding the interconnection of the material and spiritual worlds. Politics and spirituality "are wings of the same bird," and "a politics bereft of spirit-centered awareness is an empty answer to oppression—one that would result in the destruction of the animals and the Indian people."[89] Before the "coming of the white man," Native American social systems were balanced and healthy. Institutions were seen to complement one another, and clear connections existed among all aspects of the Native American world. For the most part, the private or "inside" aspects of life were shared by all because they were intimately connected to the public or "outside" aspects. This view of politics has been described as the "inside being the outside,"[90] and it stems from the "sense of the connectedness of all things, of the spiritness of all things, of the intelligent consciousness of all things."[91]

Gunn Allen suggests that the inside as the outside is the "identifying characteristic of American Indian tribal" life.[92] Personal spiritual information, in the form of visions, dreams, and interactions with nonhuman beings, regularly becomes information for the entire community: "[T]raditional people insist that conversations with animals and supernaturals" are real, whereas "rationalists" argue that they are "clearly figments of overactive imaginations and 'mass hysteria.'"[93] Supernaturals, she explains, "live within the same environs that humans occupy, and interchanges with them are necessarily part of the fabric of human experience."[94] These interchanges supply vital information about every aspect of life, and individuals who inhabit the realm of Thought Woman attend to that information carefully. Black Elk, for example, made mental or spiritual phenomena "physical" in his sharing of visions;[95] Wovoka, the Paiute holy man and prophet, had a vision that became the Ghost Dance, which then led to visions by other participants in that ceremony; and Sweet Medicine's vision of the Sacred Arrows led to Black Elk's becoming a powerful healer. The vision, Gunn Allen explains, is experienced by only one person directly, but "it, like all aspects of Indian life, must be shared."[96]

Political decisions and actions, in sum, are interdependent with the survival of the natural and supernatural worlds—they cannot be seen as discrete or disconnected realms in the world of Thought Woman. Individuals do not choose between spiritual and political commitment in this world; rather, they remain grounded in both because both require and depend on the other. Political information, in addition, often comes in the form of visions and connections with the supernatural world and must be shared with all members of the community.

The culture of death and destruction may be the current hegemonic force, but, Gunn Allen notes, its power is waning. The belief in survival by Native Americans is a part of its weakening, although changes in the awareness of non-Native individuals also are a contributing factor. The survival of Natives and non-Natives depends on an awareness of the link between the political and the spiritual, and such awareness "gives rise to a deep confidence that we will survive because the kind of awareness possessed by tribal people is now spreading throughout the non-tribal, post-Christian, post-industrial populace by way of the women's movement and other activist groups."[97]

Voices are testifying to the destruction of colonization, the ways it "affects a people's understanding of their universe, their place within that universe, the kinds of values they must embrace and the actions they must [take] to remain safe and whole within that universe."[98] The world of death and extinction is one source of rhetorical activity, but the world of Thought Woman is a more powerful and enduring one.

Definition of Feminism

Gunn Allen's feminism is grounded in the ability to critique patriarchal thought and Western society. "It's very hard to question received wisdom that you've been [hearing] for twenty generations," she suggests, but numerous lies are told about Native American women in particular and all women in general as a result of a failure to question.[99] Popular notions of tribal women are intensely negative, and a feminist approach reveals not only the exploitation and oppression of Native American tribes by whites and white government but also areas of oppression within the tribes and the sources and nature of that oppression. Gunn Allen's focus on questioning assumptions is a path to understanding and healing the distortions commonly held by both Western and contemporary tribal peoples.

Feminism is crucial to understanding Native American thought and action because the field of Native American literature, until recently, has been "dominated by paternalistic, male-dominant modes of consciousness" that have "seriously skewed our understanding of tribal life and philosophy."[100] Feminist theory, when applied carefully, can call attention to errors embedded in dominant assumptions and correct them. The result is an understanding of Native American life that is at least "congruent with a tribal perceptual mode."[101]

From Gunn Allen's Native American perspective, feminism means recognizing that the stories told about tribal people from a Western perspective are inaccurate and that many of the stories told about tribal women from any perspective are distorted: "I am intensely conscious of popular notions of Indian women as beasts of burden, squaws, traitors, or, at best, vanished denizens of a long-lost wilderness."[102] A feminist will read contemporary stories with an eye for distortions and for the recognition that these stories, told as they are from a patriarchal frame, reveal more about "American consciousness" than they do "about the tribe."[103]

Gunn Allen's feminism also addresses national political issues. She advocates a council of elder women who would advise the president of the United States, the U.S. Senate and House of Representatives, and the Supreme Court, and she encourages feminists to turn their attention to issues in this country rather than focusing on issues of foreign affairs: "You know, I just get really annoyed. Everybody was out marching because of Desert Storm, but Rodney King gets beaten half to death, and I didn't hear a word."[104] If feminists in the United States would turn their energies toward conditions in this country, Gunn Allen asserts, "we could make a difference. . . . I often think the only real hope is feminism. That's on my good days."[105]

Gunn Allen recognizes that her definition of feminism is different from the definitions offered by individuals "steeped in either mainstream or radical versions of feminism's history."[106] Feminism, for Gunn Allen, is a return to the woman-centered, "gynarchical, egalitarian, and sacred traditions" of American Indian life.[107] It involves questioning Western assumptions about Native ways of life and replacing those assumptions with a view of tribal life that recognizes the "supreme deity" as "female, and social organization" as "matrilocal, matrifocal, and matrilineal." Her definition does not imply, however, the "domination

of men by women" but rather an egalitarian notion of femaleness and maleness.[108] Gynecratic tribes, in which women participate equally with men in
tribal governance at every level, provide the basic model for many of the visions
of liberation currently popular in the United States.

Grounded in the woman-centered Indian traditions, Gunn Allen's definition
of feminism also is rooted in the notion of appropriateness. She suggests that
regardless of where people are physically or spiritually, individuals "must be
appropriate"; this appropriateness leads to dignity. For the Lagunas, appropriateness means "to walk in balance. You have to be appropriate in any situation;
that's the law. That's the only law there is. Your behavior must be congruent
with the situation."[109] Feminism and appropriateness are about "hey, everybody's here. How are we going to interact to enhance everybody's, and I mean
everybody's, situation? The trees and the birds and the bees and the broccoli
and so on. That, to me, is the ideal that feminism represents. It can be that. Often
it is."[110]

Gunn Allen's feminism also incorporates notions of balance, particularly
with regard to the place of women and men in society. There is a balance
between femaleness and maleness in Native American life, and both the female
and the male play crucial—and different—roles in American Indian traditions.
One identity cannot be erased, nor can one be subsumed by the other. The male
and female are meant to be different and to perform different roles in Native
traditions. Uniting or blending the two so that they are indistinguishable "is one
of the things white people do. There is a male and there is a female. There is
not a 'unite' in there anywhere, and there never is in the tribes. And why should
they unite? They are different."[111]

The uniqueness and the separation of male and female constitute a form of
balance that Gunn Allen labels *mutual respect.* Women have a consciousness
different from men's just as they have different bodies: "We need each other,
but only if we recognize the validity of our own way, and therefore the validity
of the other person's way, are we ever going to be able to actually function
together."[112] Individuals should accept these differences and make use of them
because the traditions of women and men always have been separate and
interdependent. Rather than conceiving of differences as divisive, Gunn Allen
encourages a recognition of the complementarity of these separate structures.

One area that Gunn Allen acknowledges needs healing is the relationship
between white women and Native American women. She recognizes the considerable divisiveness that has occurred between these two groups and the need
for white women and Native women to cooperate on women's issues. White
women have considerable power—power they do not recognize and that Indian
women struggle to attain. Questioning Western assumptions and myths about
Native women—and women in general—will promote dialogue and healing

among women and shift the balance of power between Native and non-Native women currently in place.

Nature of the Rhetor

Gunn Allen describes two kinds of rhetors: Native Americans who live in the death culture, struggling to live within the Western structures of individualism and competition, and Native Americans who live in the world of Thought Woman, where the individual is necessarily part of a larger community. Native American rhetors in the death culture struggle with fragmentation, isolation, and the oppression of women. Native American rhetors in the world of Thought Woman, in contrast, live in a world of community and belonging sustained through interconnection, balance, and harmony.

Death Culture

In the death culture, as they try to assimilate into Western culture, tribal rhetors face a sense of alienation that rarely is experienced by non-Natives and is extremely difficult, if not impossible, for nontribal people to comprehend. In a culture where white individuals take belonging for granted, Native American rhetors must struggle with the issue daily. Gunn Allen explains that "estrangement is seen as so abnormal" in Native American culture that "narratives and rituals that restore the estranged to his or her place within the cultural matrix abound." Older tribal narratives are characterized by belonging, wholeness, and "an attractive absence of a sense of otherness,"[113] but these are less relevant for recent generations of American Indians who must cope with the effects of colonization. The result is a kind of fragmentation or ambiguity—an inability "*not* to be Indian" but also an inability "to be Indian."[114]

In the death culture, Native Americans continually face pressures to reject their Indianness. For those individuals who do, their perception of themselves as Westernized is "worked out in bouts of suicidal depression, alcoholism, abandonment of Indian ways, 'disappearance' into urban complexes, and verbalized distrust of and contempt for longhairs."[115] Others recognize that they cannot reject their Indianness as a way of coping with colonization, but even these individuals often live lives of frustration and anger at being caught between two or more cultures.

In the death culture, Native Americans often experience "isolation, powerlessness, meaninglessness, normlessness, lowered self-esteem, and self-estrangement, accompanied by anxiety, hopelessness, and victimization."[116] They also experience a sense of speechlessness or "tonguelessness," an inability to articulate experiences and knowledge in ways that will be heard and understood.[117] What Native Americans "bear witness to is not easily admissible into the consciousness of other Americans, and that inadmissibility" causes difficulty "in articulation and utterance."[118] In fact, Gunn Allen suggests, so different are the perspectives and experiences of Natives and non-Natives that Westerners regularly miss the complexity and real meaning of American Indian experiences.

Stereotypes of Native Americans do not help Natives overcome their alienation and speechlessness. Predominantly male, these stereotypes cast the American Indian as the warrior or cannibalistic savage; the persecuted noble red man; the powerless "innocent victim of fate"; or the passive, gentle pagan who worshipped the white man as a God. Damaging as they are in themselves, these stereotypes also reduce the Native American to single dimensions and to individuals who are separate from a larger community. Consequently, the stereotypes do not allow the Indian the "place of a human being."[119]

Because fundamental differences exist between the Western and Native treatments of the male and female, the experiences of fragmentation and alienation take on additional dimensions for Native women. Westerners tend to degrade all that is considered female, so Western chauvinism has led to images and stereotypes of the Native American woman as "beast, unclean object, household drudge or inconsequential but necessary appendage to tribal life"—identities that contradict the facts of Native life.[120] In addition, as female deities were replaced by masculine, Christianized ones, the role of women in tribal cultures in North America was altered drastically.[121] Once central to the existence of a community, women's unique positions of power and respect have been reduced considerably, and the loss of status for Native American women is so great that "Indian people themselves have lost all notion of what the status has been."[122]

As Native women become "deeply engaged in the struggle to redefine themselves," they must wrestle and cope with and harmonize the seemingly contradictory definitions of their identities.[123] In the death culture, Native American women vacillate between strength and self-destruction, between self-reliance and insecurity. Gunn Allen explains that Native women manage these opposing forces in various ways:

> [S]ome of us party all the time; some of us drink to excess; some of us travel and move around a lot; some of us land good jobs and quit them; some of us engage in violent exchanges; some of us blow our brains out. We act in these destructive ways because we suffer from the societal conflicts caused by having to identify with two hopelessly opposed cultural definitions of women.[124]

In the death culture, Gunn Allen concludes, Native American rhetors—both women and men—face "soul-theft, heart-theft, and mind-theft."[125] Asked to see themselves as individuals distinct from other individuals, their community, and the spirit world and asked to rank order individuals by sex, these rhetors face a crisis of identity unlike that faced by most Westerners. Dominated by estrangement and singularity, Native American rhetors are asked to reject the very heart of their being—Thought Woman.

Thought Woman

Both women and men can be rhetors in the world of Thought Woman, but Gunn Allen's rhetors are primarily women. This is the case because the female is "the source and generator of meaning"[126] and because women, particularly Native American women, are the keepers of wisdom. Gunn Allen privileges Native American women as rhetors, too, because they make the transition from death culture to the world of Thought Woman "over and over"; they "circle around the center of the fire where the darkest, hottest coals lie" and challenge the assumptions of the death culture.[127] The rhetor in the world of Thought Woman is the woman on the margins, the woman deemed invisible and unimportant by the death culture.

Gunn Allen's primary rhetor is not only female, but she may be lesbian as well. In the past, a lesbian in the Native American culture was a woman whose spiritual and physical connection was to other women. She was a "medicine woman in a special sense," functioning as a "participant in the Spirit (intelligence, force field) of an Entity or deity who was particularly close to earth."[128] She was believed to possess a power that could override the power of men, even powerful medicine men. Although the information available regarding lesbians and their power is scarce, Gunn Allen explains that lesbians were "required to follow the lead of Spirits and to carry out the tasks" assigned to them.[129] Lesbians were more than "an interesting tour through primitive exotica," according to Gunn Allen. Their link to supernatural forces gave them a necessary and unique role in American Indian life.[130] As tribes became more and more male centered, however, lesbians' position deteriorated and finally disappeared. Prior to patriarchy, however, both gay men and lesbians were seen as integral and positive components of the tribal system.

In her featuring of the lesbian as rhetor, Gunn Allen asks that Westerners reconfigure concepts of family, community, women, bonding, belonging, and power. In a tribal matrix, individuals are connected by both Spirit and blood, and the relationship to the Spirit world is the context in which lesbianism exists. The primary unit of family organization is not the household as Westerners understand it—mother, father, and children—but various individuals who may or may not be connected by blood. Families consist of various arrangements of "blood-kin, medicine-society 'kin,' adoptees, servants, and visitors who have a clan or supernatural claim on membership" to the household.[131] Families, then, are formed around spiritual connections as much as bloodlines; thus, lesbians are not separate from society but healthy and integral members of the tribe and family.

In the world of Thought Woman, the Native rhetor is guided by the recognition that to be separated from the community, from the land, and from Thought Woman is to be ill. Although Western attitudes and reasoning have encouraged a separation of self from community, rhetors in the world of Thought Woman recognize that healing occurs when individuals reconnect with these entities. The cure for separation and isolation is "a reorientation of perception" so that fragmented individuals can "know directly that the true nature of being is magical and the proper duty of the creatures, the land, and human beings is to live in harmony with what is."[132] Rhetors in the world of Thought Woman, then, are grounded in a spirit of belonging and interconnection. They recognize that life is organized by unity—by the Sacred Hoop or the medicine wheel—and assume "a place in creation" that allows all "animals, vegetables, and minerals (the entire biota, in short) the same or even greater privileges than humans."[133]

The rhetors in the world of Thought Woman, whether female or male, are able to work around the negative influences of the death culture. Gunn Allen explains that "American Indian people are remarkably resilient, and the old ways are remarkably durable." Although the government has worked for centuries to eliminate tribal people, values, and ways of living in the world, Native Americans have "clung tenaciously to life."[134] The survival of Native peoples over the centuries is a testament to their enduring strength; as Gunn Allen reminds her audiences, reports "of our demise have been greatly exaggerated."[135] She explains that there "is a permanent wilderness in the blood of an Indian, a wilderness that will endure as long as the grass grows, the wind blows, the rivers flow, and one Indian woman remains alive."[136]

Rhetorical Options

As a result of the two worlds Gunn Allen describes, two substantially different genres of rhetorical options exist. The rhetorical options in the death culture center on a rhetoric of misinterpretation and ways of coping with that misinterpretation. The rhetorical options in the world of Thought Woman—vision, myth, ritual, and ceremony—are grounded in the Sacred Hoop, the circular sacredness of all life.

Death Culture

Embedded in the realm of the death culture is one predominant form of rhetoric: misinterpretation. This rhetoric has perpetuated lies and enabled the death culture to continue its genocide and colonization of Native American peoples. To cope with the misinterpretation of the death culture, Gunn Allen recommends humor and metaphor as options for Native peoples as they come into contact with the death culture.

Misinterpretation

So perverted are "all attempts at understanding how the native peoples live, and how their systems worked" that virtually nothing Westerners have suggested about Native American practices or symbols is correct.[137] On a macroscopic level, misinterpretation occurred historically as Westerners ascribed patriarchal practices to a gynecentric culture and Western religious beliefs to Native American spirituality. Misinterpretation also occurred as judgments were made about the ineffectiveness of clan structures when assessed from a Western and patriarchal orientation and when individuality was emphasized over communal identities. In addition, the construction of Native Americans as childlike by Western individuals and institutions meant that Indianness was not recognized as a complex and mature state of existence, thus facilitating the misinterpretation of centuries-old practices.

Misinterpretation of Indian life also occurred in more microscopic ways. Gunn Allen suggests that "masculine" and "good" became synonymous, whereas "feminine" and "bad" or "inferior" were linked, denying autonomy and dignity to women.[138] The Native American connection to psychic and paranormal experiences was misinterpreted as a creation of the imagination rather than actual ways of life, and symbols revealed in visions and myths were mislabeled as *metaphor* rather than real. Repetition in ceremony and ritual was misinterpreted as an attempt to reduce fear and to ensure gratification when it actually operates to "unite people with the powers of the universe. . . . Repetition, magically speaking, increases spirit power."[139] American Indian literature was misinterpreted as underdeveloped and poorly crafted, and songs, dance, drumming, pottery, and ritual—all forms of literature in Native traditions—were not recognized as literature at all.

Misinterpretation has had devastating effects on tribal peoples. It facilitated the murder or relocation of millions of Indian people, the disruption of families and the placing of children in boarding schools, the trivialization of an entire culture, and the rejection of a healthy and viable orientation to the world. Misinterpretation continues to function to misrepresent Native American values, traditions, and practices, but Native American rhetors living in the death culture have two rhetorical options available to them to cope with misinterpretation and to maneuver around its painful effects: humor and metaphor.

Humor

Gunn Allen explains that the use of humor is widespread among American Indians and that it is used as a way of coping with the death culture's misinterpretation of Native ways and "the biting knowledge that living as an exile in one's own land necessitates."[140] Humor often is directed at the horrors of history and colonization and is one way to bring balance back into the life of an individual or a community.

Gunn Allen offers the coyote tales as one example of humor. Updated to reflect modern life, a portion of one of these tales goes as follows:

> Some white men came to Acoma and Laguna a hundred years ago
> and they fought over Acoma land and Laguna women and even now
> some of their descendents are howling
> in the hills southeast of Laguna.[141]

Gunn Allen explains the humor in this story, which is incomprehensible to those not familiar with the culture or the figure of the coyote. The tale identifies the importance of the land to the Acoma, the importance and great beauty of women to the Laguna, and the notion that "mixed-bloods are likely to be howling around in the hills because they are the offspring of the wily and salacious coyote. Indeed, 'coyote' to many Hispanic Americans refers to a half-breed, and that idea is also present in the poetic joke."[142]

The coyote, a complex and trickster figure in Native American traditions, is half creator, half fool, and known for greediness. Used humorously, the coyote functions as a metaphor for "all the foolishness and the anger that have characterized American Indian life in the centuries since invasion." The coyote possesses "an irreverence for everything—sex, family, bonding, sacred things, even life itself." Because of this irreverence, however, coyote survives. Underneath its shabby exterior lies considerable creative prowess, and the coyote stands as a symbol of "much that is shabby and tricky" in contemporary culture, "much that needs to be treated with laughter and ironic humor; it is this spirit of the trickster-creator that keeps Indians alive and vital in the face of horror."[143]

Metaphor

Metaphor, humorous or not, is also an important option in Native American rhetoric for dealing with the death culture. The most appealing metaphor, Gunn Allen explains, is one that combines "elements of tribal tradition with contemporary experience."[144] This use is exemplified in a poem, "3 AM," by Joy Harjo:

> 3 AM
> in the albuquerque airport
> trying to find a flight
> to old oraibi, third mesa
> TWA
> is the only desk open
> bright lights outline new york,
> chicago
> and the attendant doesn't know
> that third mesa
> is a part of the center
> of the world
> and who are we
> just two indians
> at three in the morning
> trying to find a way back.[145]
>
> (used by permission of Joy Harjo)

The poem and the metaphors in it, Gunn Allen explains, identify the common experiences of Native Americans—"a dual perception of the world: that which is particular to American Indian life, and that which exists ignorant of that life."[146] The two realms or perceptions are relevant to the American Indian only when they meet. When the two come together, sense must be made of the conflicting realities, and metaphors are used not only to recognize but to reconcile them. Gunn Allen explains that the "ideal metaphor will harmonize the contradictions and balance them so that internal equilibrium can be achieved, so that each perspective is meaningful and that in their joining, psychic unity rather than fragmentation occurs."[147]

The purpose of humor and metaphor is to reveal the harms done by the death culture and to honor the experiences of Native Americans. Although both also exist in the realm of Thought Woman, humor and metaphor are particularly powerful in the realm of the death culture because they speak to the pain of misinterpretation and recognize the disturbing effects of continuing to live in a foreign and unfriendly world.

Thought Woman

The interrelated forms of vision, myth, ritual, and ceremony are primary rhetorical options in the world of Thought Woman. Each is a complex, inseparable activity that blends the "greater self and all-that-is . . . into a balanced whole."[148] The concept of the Sacred Hoop clarifies this blending and the dynamic relationships among these rhetorical options. The Sacred Hoop suggests that there is a circle of being, a harmonious and balanced way of life, in which humans, animals, and natural and nonnatural entities exist and participate in "destiny at all levels, including that of creation."[149] The rhetorical options of vision, myth, ritual, and ceremony reflect this concept of the Sacred Hoop because they are interconnected and dynamic; because they rely on natural and supernatural phenomena; and because they bring individuals into harmony with themselves, the world around them, and the community in which they live. The Sacred Hoop reflects the orientation of Native American thought, which "is essentially mystical and psychic in nature," distinguished by "a kind of magicalness . . . an enduring sense of the fluidity and malleability, or creative flux, of things."[150] Primary manifestations of the Sacred Hoop, then, are vision, myth, ritual, and ceremony—interconnected aspects of this circle of life.

For the rhetorical options in the realm of Thought Woman to be seen as credible by Westerners, changes have to occur in the ways individuals think about rhetoric. The Native American rhetorical tradition is "non-linear, associative, synchronistic," and nonrational.[151] It reflects "a sense of events as occurring in an extended, circular, unified field of interaction," functioning without regard for chronology, predicting future events, and pulling from sources that most non-Natives see as spurious and unfamiliar.[152]

In addition, the rhetorical options in the world of Thought Woman are rooted in Native oral traditions. For Westerners, oral traditions often are most easily conceptualized as stories, and before Anglo-European influence and invasion, orality was central to the identity of tribal people because they taught individuals who they were, who they were supposed to be, where they came from, and who would follow. These oral traditions continue to celebrate the most meaningful elements of life and express the "deepest perceptions, relationships and attitudes of a culture."[153] They articulate the commonplace as well as the ceremonial and draw not only from commonly accepted forms of narrative but also from the song, ritual, drum, dance, blanket, pot, beadwork, painting, vision, ceremony, and dream, to name but a few.

American Indian literature is based on stories told in ritual ceremonies, and, as Gunn Allen explains, stories written on the page cannot be separated from the actual vision, ritual, or ceremony in which they originated. The idea of discrete genres of oral, written, danced, drummed, or beaded stories, for example, is not possible in Native traditions. Depending on the context, elements of diverse genres can occur simultaneously in one story, or a story in one genre may follow from or create a story in another. Ceremonies grow out of visions, and visions occur during ceremonies. Similarly, a story or ritual may have numerous additional stories and rituals embedded within it. Each informs the other and acts as a source of information or knowing; to divide these into separate categories and attempt to analyze them as distinct is to ignore the fundamental relationships among them.

Most sacred stories have been misinterpreted as "'primitive,' 'savage,' 'child-like,' and 'heathen'" by Westerners who do not possess the Native encyclope-dia—the framework necessary to understand Native traditions and symbols.[154] Oral forms of expression in Native American culture are seen to possess the "sacred power of utterance"; they are sacred power.[155] They emphasize relation-ship, egalitarianism, harmony, and the mythic and ceremonial cycles common and revered in tribal cultures.

Stories continue to shape and direct the forces that surround and determine humans and to prevent the Native "web of identity" from being destroyed completely.[156] Because Native stories are sacred and because they tend to be misunderstood by those outside a tribal culture, they rarely are shared with nontribal people. Gunn Allen explains the difficulty of sharing sacred stories:

> You don't talk about them. And also their world [that of tribal people] is so different, so—it's so completely different from the Western world that even if they would talk about it, you couldn't understand it. Even if you try very, very hard to get it exactly right, it's not going to translate. So the best you can do is translate intuitively and then readers have to read intuitively because there is no other way to do it. . . . [Y]ou have to develop a sensibility.[157]

The more familiar Westerners are with these traditions, Gunn Allen surmises, the "less startling" the rhetoric will be.[158]

Visions

Visions occur when individuals enter into altered states of being—when they receive information or participate in activities that Westerners would tend to label *nonrational.* A vision is a "gift of power and guidance" and a way of becoming whole, of affirming one's special place in the universe.[159] Because it is a "vehicle of transformation, of sharing, of renewal," vision "plays an integral part in the ongoing psychic life of a people." Gunn Allen suggests that "because of the centrality of vision" in Native American life, "the religious life of the tribe endures, even under the most adverse circumstances.[160]

Visions can last for days, as in the case of Black Elk, whose vision lasted 12 days, or they can last a much shorter period—days, hours, or moments. Indi-viduals often seek out visions, as in the Lakota tradition, when a woman or a man usually "goes after a vision after performing a particular ritual called hanblecheya or Lamenting for a Vision."[161] Individuals may be quite young, like Black Elk, when they have their first visions, or they may be more mature; the experience of vision is seen as a sign of maturity. Individuals also may have initial visions with subsequent visions occurring as they grow older.

Although a vision is experienced by a single individual, it always is brought back to the community to be shared. Every element of the vision is important and contains meaning for the community on the "deepest levels of human understanding," although that meaning may not be apparent for years or even centuries.[162] Each detail in a vision thus is shared and interpreted and then enacted as closely as possible in a ritual ceremony so that its power can "be revealed and renewed on earth."[163]

Many of the most sacred visions are not accessible to Westerners, and those that are should make no sense to them. In fact, Gunn Allen explains, because they lack the Native encyclopedia, if Westerners read a vision and say, "'Oh, I recognize this,'" they "are making a terrible mistake"—either there is something wrong with the text or the Westerner has misinterpreted the symbols.[164] The information in visions is so sacred and powerful that considerable danger exists for those who have access to a vision but not to the Native encyclopedia. So lacking in the necessary frame of reference are Westerners that Wallace Black Elk remarked that "giving this information to the whiteman is like giving matches to a small child, or a gun to a toddler. No wise adult would do so. No wise Indian will tell all they know, for the same kind of reasons."[165]

Myth and Ritual

When it is shared with the community, the vision is translated into myth. However, as Gunn Allen notes, the term *myth* has become so "polluted by popular misuse" that it is "difficult if not impossible at the present time to speak coherently" about it.[166] A myth is commonly understood to be a lie or an unfounded belief, something not based in reality; the term implies an intent to deceive or defraud. The real myth, Gunn Allen explains, is the "belief that there is such a thing as determinable fact" and that reality can be known through "fact-finding determinism."[167]

In Native American traditions, *myth* can be translated as a "'ritual,' that is, as a language construct that contains the power to transform something (or someone) from one state or condition to another." A myth is a "means of transmitting paranormal power" and, when put into written form, it becomes a prose record of a specialized relationship to the world.[168] It is a particular kind of story that allows people to see the universe as a holistic entity; themselves in relation to the universe, and "what we are, where we belong; and what we may be."[169] A myth articulates human thought and experience and allows individuals "to order and thus comprehend perception and knowledge."[170] Although the experiences and relationships present in a myth may be uncommon, the myth can help people become aware of the mysterious universe, to distinguish different orders of reality and experience, and to see the relationships among parts of themselves or the community from which they previously had been divided.

In tribal traditions, myth requires "a supernatural or non-ordinary kind of figure as its central character" and "relies on mystical symbols to convey" the significance of the myth.[171] Myth is enacted in a ritual, which occurs "when a person, a community, a region, a season, a wildlife cycle, or any other significant feature concerned with or impinging upon human life is in flux."[172] A ritual is a process of transformation that necessitates "liminality, literally a state of being on the threshold."[173] Ritual activities attempt to "manipulate or direct nonmaterial energies toward some larger goal," transforming a thing from one state to another.[174]

Among Native Americans of the Southwest, rituals are grounded in an understanding of Thought Woman and her sister goddesses.[175] Thought Woman is the "Dreamer, the ritual center," and the source of power in rituals.[176] Those who participate in rituals depend on and draw from her magic. As they recognize Her central power and force, they understand their contact with "supernatural and natural entities . . . accept their instruction, follow their directives, [and] generate and coordinate inter- and intra-species events."[177]

American Indian literature often is written in the form of ritual that leads to a circular, fragmented, and multilayered story not easily accessible to Westerners. Not only is the content unfamiliar, but the ritual or ceremonial structure of the story also adds to misunderstandings. For the Native American, however, ritual and myth are inseparable—they are "twin beings," functioning together to aid individuals in "entering and using the life-generating forces contained in and by the Great Mystery."[178]

Rituals differ according to the sex of the participants and are based on the experiences and roles individuals assume in a society. Women's rituals largely focus on continuity and men's on transitoriness or change. Women's rituals center on "birth, death, food, householding, and medicine (in the medical rather than the magical sense of the term)";[179] thus, women's rituals often are about continuance and regeneration. Although women do experience transformations accompanied by danger, blood, and even death, the focus of their rituals is on continuity within transformation because they "create life from their own flesh."[180] Men's rituals, in contrast, center on "risk, death, and transformation: that is, all that helps regulate and control change."[181]

Ceremony

The general purpose of a ceremony is integration—the fusing of individuals with other individuals, of the community with other "kingdoms," and of the "communal group with worlds beyond this one."[182] Ceremonies also have specific purposes, such as healing, harvesting, and journeying. Regardless of the specific purpose, ceremonies "create and support the sense of community that is the bedrock of tribal life."[183] In ceremonies, individuals lose their sense of isolation and individual personality and recognize and rediscover their place of harmony with the universe.

Ceremony is a ritual enactment of a myth, but Gunn Allen cautions individuals to remember that "ceremony, ritual, and myth are different ways of referring to the same spiritual event or metaphysical process."[184] Ceremony is composed of, among other elements, "songs, prayers, dances, drums, ritual movements, and dramatic address."[185] All ceremonies are chanted, drummed, and danced.

Native Americans, Gunn Allen explains, often will "refer to a piece of music as a 'dance' instead of a song, because song without dance is very rare, as is song without drum or other percussive instrument."[186] A drum, in addition, does not accompany a song; such a view would imply a separation between the music and voice where none exists. Drum and voice are fused and form an "integral whole," just as do those who are performing and those who are watching.[187] To describe a ceremony as containing prayer and songs, then, is misleading because the formal structure of the ceremony corresponds to the integrated, interconnected, and holistic view of the universe common in the world of Thought Woman. A ceremony, in addition, is layered—it contains other ceremonies, and to isolate ceremonies as single elements is inappropriate.

A ceremony includes participants who are physically present as well as those who are not, and all parties have roles to play in the ceremony. Ceremonial elements such as dancing by those physically present, for example, enhance communication between individuals at the ceremony and those who are not physically present. The repetition of "lengthy passages of 'meaningless' syllables" also is significant for both those who are present and those who are not; it alters states of consciousness, resulting in an "entrancing effect" that facilitates communication with those not physically present at the ceremony.[188] Repetition allows "thought and word to coalesce into one rhythmic whole" and is one of the best techniques available to produce the fusion and integration of the spiritual and material worlds that is central to ceremony.[189]

The psychic nature of structural devices in ceremony calls attention to the fact that Native Americans do not believe that reality exists somewhere outside the individual. For Native Americans, reality is "internal and communitarian,"[190] and ceremony brings individuals together in this understanding. The four mountains in the Mountain Chant ceremony of the Diné, for example, do not *stand for* mountains—they *are* the four "sacred mountains perceived in the state of *hozho* or beauty—a transcendent state."[191] Similarly, the color red, used by the Oglala in a ceremony, does not "'stand for' sacred or earth, but is the quality of being, the color of it, when perceived in a 'sacred manner' or from

the point of view of earth herself."[192] Ceremonial symbols have psychic qualities that reveal important internal worlds. The sun, the earth, or a tree, for
example, constitutes extraordinary truths, and the understanding it engenders
is key to appreciating the nature and meaning of ceremony.

Ceremonial literature—the expression of ceremony on the written page—includes all literature that is accompanied by ritual and music that produce
metaphysical states of consciousness. It is a sacred form of rhetoric in that it is
filled with force and power, but these two terms also require redefinition. Force
and power, in Native American ceremonial traditions, are not related to the
ability to control or dominate others. *Force* is the energy and information
gathered in a metaphysical state, and *power* is the ability to use that force
without being harmed by it. Certain individuals possess this ability to a greater
degree than others, and the term *medicine* is used to describe this ability. When
individuals are powerful, they have the ability to receive and use the energy or
force that comes to them metaphysically; they are not damaged, hurt, or
destroyed by this power, as some might be; and they are able to share this power
with others in the form of myths, rituals, and ceremonies.

In the world of Thought Woman, vision, myth, ritual, and ceremony facilitate
the integration of spirit and matter. They reflect a view of the world as
interrelated and a view of individuals as part of a community larger than the
earth itself. Although unusual in a Western framework and trivialized in the
death culture, vision, myth, ritual, and ceremony are fundamental and necessary
aspects of Thought Woman.

Through vision, myth, ritual, and ceremony, Native American rhetoric builds
a world of balance and integration. It resists the divisiveness of Western reason,
mentality, and epistemologies and embraces instead harmony and survival.
Gunn Allen explains that through these rhetorical options, the Sacred Hoop is
honored and discovered in preparation for the return of Thought Woman: "We
are recovering our heritage and uncovering the history of colonization. . . . And
we are busily stealing the thunder back, so it can empower the fires of life we
tend, have always tended, as it was ever meant to."[193]

Transformations of Rhetorical Theory

Rooted in Native American traditions, Gunn Allen's rhetorical theory provides
an alternative to the rhetorical theory conceived in Western Europe. Because of
her emphasis on the Sacred Hoop of life, the inherently interconnected nature
of individuals, and the importance of metaphysical states, Gunn Allen's theory
suggests transformations of the definition and goals of rhetoric, rationality,
power, and audience analysis and adaptation.

Definition of Rhetoric

The strict definition of rhetoric as persuasion is too limiting in Gunn Allen's theory. For Gunn Allen, rhetoric is appropriateness, or the use of symbols to ensure that each entity is respected and united in the circle of being. To be appropriate is to live a harmonious and balanced life, and rhetoric is the art of recognizing and affirming harmony and balance. In the world of Thought Woman, rhetoric as appropriateness means that whatever change might be advocated, it is measured according to its implications for the interconnections that characterize the Sacred Hoop. When considered from Gunn Allen's perspective, rhetoric is the art of recognizing interconnections and relationships and the ability to manifest those in discourse and symbol.

Purpose of Rhetoric

Altering the definition of rhetoric necessitates a reconsideration of its purpose. Unlike its traditional conceptualization as change or as winning an argument or debate, the purpose of rhetoric in Gunn Allen's theory is the facilitation of a return to Thought Woman and the perpetuation of the Sacred Hoop—two goals vastly different from change and winning. When individuals enter into the world of Thought Woman, they find themselves connected to others, the environment, and the spiritual world. The circle of life depends on these connections, and rhetoric, as a result, is an acknowledgment of the Sacred Hoop, its manifestation through community, and the sharing of reality through vision, myth, ritual, and ceremony.

Even when individuals do find themselves in the death culture, the purpose of rhetoric still is less clearly rooted in change efforts. In the death culture, the purpose of rhetoric is the translation of the misrepresentation of Native American life and identity—often through humor and metaphor—and is directed largely toward Native Americans experiencing alienation and isolation. Rhetoric also is used to escape the death culture and to return to the world of Thought Woman. In Gunn Allen's theory, desiring to change others or winning a discussion is replaced with goals consistent with Thought Woman and the Sacred Hoop—goals that are grounded in the articulation and manifestation of interconnection rather than persuasion.

Rationality

The notion of rationality as it is manifest in rhetoric is altered as well in Gunn Allen's theory. The rational discourse that is privileged in traditional rhetorical theory is rooted in an epistemology of logic that values systematic thinking, analysis, argument, support, and justification. Judgments about the effectiveness of acts rooted in this epistemology are made according to scientifically accepted knowledge—verifiable by reference to the external world. In Gunn Allen's theory, rationality is redefined to include and, in fact, to privilege altered states of being, connections to the spiritual world, and information from paranormal entities. In this "rationality of the shadows," knowledge is situated between the material and nonmaterial worlds. Such knowledge derives from personal experience, personal vision, and intuition; it cannot be verified outside of the individual rhetor. This kind of rationality, Gunn Allen asserts, is necessary for the continuation of the Sacred Hoop of life.

Rationality also is grounded in myth in Gunn Allen's theory but a framing of myth that is quite different from traditional theories. Myth is not only a way of knowing in Native American traditions but a way of being—an ontology. In American Indian traditions, myths are real experiences—they are events that actually happened and that are retold in order to pass on valuable information and clarify experiences. Myths, then, are not something told to help order a world or organize an experience; they are something actually lived that predict and educate as well as organize. Myths, too, are connected intimately to vision, ritual, and ceremony such that a separation of the three is impossible. Rationality, then, is both metaphysical and mystical and is shared and organized through the enactment of vision, myth, ritual, and ceremony.

Power

In traditional rhetorical theory, power is the ability to control others, to win, or to produce particular effects. In Gunn Allen's rhetorical theory, in contrast, power is the ability to use the force that comes during metaphysical states without causing any harm. To have power is to possess medicine—to have access to mystical knowledge—and to share that medicine or knowledge with others in myths, rituals, and ceremonies. Power operates mystically, uniting spirit and matter, and is expressed through rhetoric in order to promote connection and integration rather than hierarchy and domination. The symbols used to express power include the dance, song, drum, and bead, and they promote connection and integration among and within the community. In Gunn Allen's theory, power is a means of sharing information and explaining or enhancing relationships rather than dominating or controlling others.

Audience Adaptation

Gunn Allen's rhetorical theory also poses a challenge to traditional conceptions of audience analysis and adaptation. In her theory, tailoring messages so that their appeal is increased for particular audiences is inappropriate and, in fact, a violation of the information contained in messages. Rhetors do not alter aspects of the visions they recount or the myths they retell to make them more palatable to their audiences because all of the information that comes through a vision must be shared exactly as the individual received it. To omit crucial information, regardless of the audience's inability to understand, is to omit information that may be understood at some later date. Western notions of adapting messages to audiences so that they will understand, appreciate, and be persuaded by them are a violation of the integrity of the messages and of all of the individuals involved.

Gunn Allen's theory, in summary, challenges several of the foundations of traditional conceptualizations of rhetoric. From the definition of rhetoric to the manifestation of power to the assumptions or values inherent in rational epistemologies to notions of audience adaptation, Native American traditions and practices encourage rhetorical scholars to consider other ways of being, knowing, and communicating. The resulting rhetoric, Gunn Allen suggests, will have significant impact on Native Americans and non-Natives alike: Women will have more access to female traditions and resources; the effects of genocide and colonization will be understood more fully; and, perhaps most significantly, individuals will be prepared for the world of Thought Woman.

Bibliography

Books

Gunn Allen, Paula. *Grandmothers of the Light: A Medicine Woman's Sourcebook.* Boston: Beacon, 1991.

Gunn Allen, Paula. *The Sacred Hoop: Recovering the Feminine in American Indian Traditions.* 1986. Boston: Beacon, 1992.

Gunn Allen, Paula, ed. *Song of the Turtle: American Indian Literature: 1974-1994.* New York: One World/Ballantine, 1996.

Gunn Allen, Paula, ed. *Spider Woman's Granddaughters: Traditional Tales and Contemporary Writing by Native American Women.* Boston: Beacon, 1989.

Gunn Allen, Paula, ed. *Studies in American Indian Literature: Critical Essays and Course Designs.* New York: Modern Language Association, 1983.

Gunn Allen, Paula, ed. *Voice of the Turtle: American Indian Literature: 1900-1970.* New York: One World/Ballantine, 1994.

Gunn Allen, Paula. *The Woman Who Owned the Shadows.* San Francisco: Spinsters/Aunt Lute, 1983.

Gunn Allen, Paula, and Patricia Clark Smith, eds. *As Long as the Rivers Flow: Nine Stories of Native Americans.* New York: Scholastic, 1996.

Articles

Gunn Allen, Paula. "All the Good Indians." *The 60s without Apology.* Ed. Sohnya Sayers, Anders Stephanson, Stanley Aronowitz, and Fredric Jameson. Minneapolis: U of Minnesota P, 1984. 226-29.

Gunn Allen, Paula. "American Indian Fiction, 1968-1983." *A Literary History of the American West.* Ed. J. Golden Taylor. Fort Worth: Western Literature Association, Texas Christian UP, 1987. 1058-66.

Gunn Allen, Paula. "America's Founding Mothers: Our Native American Roots." *Utne Reader* 32 (1989): 108-09.

Gunn Allen, Paula. "Angry Women Are Building: Issues and Struggles Facing American Indian Women Today." *Race, Class, and Gender: An Anthology.* Ed. Margaret L. Andersen and Patricia Hill Collins. 2nd ed. Belmont, CA: Wadsworth, 1995. 32-36. Rpt. from *The Sacred Hoop: Recovering the Feminine in American Indian Traditions.* By Paula Gunn Allen. 1986. Boston: Beacon, 1992. 189-93.

Gunn Allen, Paula. "Answering the Deer: Genocide and Continuance in American Indian Women's Poetry." *Coming to Light: American Women Poets in the Twentieth Century.* Ed. Diane Wood Middlebrook and Marilyn Yalom. Ann Arbor: U of Michigan P, 1985. 223-32.

Gunn Allen, Paula. "The Autobiography of a Confluence." *I Tell You Now: Autobiographical Essays by Native American Writers.* Ed. Brian Swann and Arnold Krupat. Lincoln: U of Nebraska P, 1987. 141-54.

Gunn Allen, Paula. "'Border' Studies: The Intersection of Gender and Color." *Introduction to Scholarship in Modern Languages and Literatures.* Ed. Joseph Gibaldi. 2nd ed. New York: Modern Language Association, 1992. 303-19. Rpt. in *The Ethnic Canon: Histories, Institutions, and Interventions.* Ed. David Palumbo-Liu. Minneapolis: U of Minnesota P, 1995. 31-47.

Gunn Allen, Paula. "Ephanie." *Shantih* 4 (1979): 42-47.

Gunn Allen, Paula. "Essentially, It's Spring." *Studies in American Indian Literatures: Journal of the Association for Study of American Indian Literatures* 7 (1995): 87.

Gunn Allen, Paula. "Foreword." *Song of the Sky: Versions of Native American Songs and Poems.* Ed. Brian Swann. Ashuelot, NY: Four Zoas Night House, 1985. 15-19.

Gunn Allen, Paula. "Glastonbury Experience." *Religion and Literature* 26 (1994): 83-87.

Gunn Allen, Paula. "Going Home, December 1992." *Reinventing the Enemy's Language: Contemporary Native Women's Writings of North America.* Ed. Joy Harjo and Gloria Bird, with Patricia Blanco, Beth Cuthand, and Valerie Martínez. New York: W. W. Norton, 1997. 150-56.

Gunn Allen, Paula. "Grandmother of the Sun: The Power of Woman in Native America." *Weaving the Visions: New Patterns in Feminist Spirituality.* Ed. Judith Plaskow and Carol P. Christ. New York: HarperCollins, 1989. 22-28.

Gunn Allen, Paula. "How the West Was Really Won." *A Cultural Studies Reader: History, Theory, Practice.* Ed. Jessica Munns and Gita Rajan, with Roger Bromley. New York: Longman, 1995. 390-401.

Gunn Allen, Paula. "Interdependence." *Keys to the Open Gate: A Woman's Spirituality Sourcebook.* By Kimberley Snow. Berkeley, CA: Conari, 1994. 41-43.

Gunn Allen, Paula. "Judy Grahn: 'Gathering of the Tribe.'" *Contact II* 5 (1983): 7-9.

Gunn Allen, Paula. "Kochinnenako in Academe: Three Approaches to Interpreting a Keres Indian Tale." *North Dakota Quarterly* 53 (1985): 84-106.

Gunn Allen, Paula. "Lesbians in American Indian Cultures." *Conditions* 7 (1981): 67-87. Rpt. in *Conditions: Sixteen: A Retrospective* 16 (1989): 84-106; and *The Sacred Hoop: Recovering the Feminine in American Indian Traditions*. By Paula Gunn Allen. 1986. Boston: Beacon, 1992. 245-61.

Gunn Allen, Paula. "The Mythopoeic Vision in Native American Literature: The Problem of Myth." *American Indian Culture and Research Journal* 1 (1974): 3-13.

Gunn Allen, Paula. "The Psychological Landscape of *Ceremony*." *American Indian Quarterly: A Journal of Anthropology, History, and Literature* 5 (1970): 7-12.

Gunn Allen, Paula. "Powwow 79, Durango." *Braided Lives: An Anthology of Multicultural American Writing*. St. Paul: Minnesota Humanities Commission, 1991. 63-64.

Gunn Allen, Paula. "Quién es que anda?" *Chicago Review* 39 (1993): 24-26.

Gunn Allen, Paula. "The Sacred Hoop: A Contemporary Indian Perspective on American Indian Literature." *Literature of the American Indians: Views and Interpretations: A Gathering of Indian Memories, Symbolic Contexts, and Literary Criticism*. Ed. Abraham Chapman. New York: Meridian/New American, 1975. 111-35. Rpt. as "The Sacred Hoop: A Contemporary Perspective." *The Sacred Hoop: Recovering the Feminine in American Indian Traditions*. By Paula Gunn Allen. 1986. Boston: Beacon, 1992. 54-75; and in *Smoke Rising: The Native North American Literary Companion*. Ed. Joseph Bruchac and Janet Witalec, with Sharon Malinowski. Detroit: Visible Ink, 1995. 13-34.

Gunn Allen, Paula. "Selections from *Raven's Road*." *Living the Spirit: A Gay American Indian Anthology*. Ed. Will Roscoe. New York: St. Martin's, 1988. 134-52.

Gunn Allen, Paula. "Sky Woman and Her Sisters." *Ms.* Sept./Oct. 1992: 22-26. Rpt. (expanded version) as "When Women Throw Down Bundles: Strong Women Make Strong Nations." *The Sacred Hoop: Recovering the Feminine in American Indian Traditions*. By Paula Gunn Allen. 1986. Boston: Beacon, 1992. 31-42.

Gunn Allen, Paula. "Some Like Indians Endure." *Living the Spirit: A Gay American Indian Anthology*. Ed. Will Roscoe. New York: St. Martin's, 1988. 9-13. Rpt. in *Making Face, Making Soul/Haciendo Caras: Creative and Critical Perspectives by Feminists of Color.* Ed. Gloria Anzaldúa. San Francisco: Aunt Lute, 1990. 298-301.

Gunn Allen, Paula. "Special Problems in Teaching Leslie Marmon Silko's *Ceremony*." *American Indian Quarterly* 14 (1990): 379-86.

Gunn Allen, Paula. "Stealing the Thunder: Future Visions for American Indian Women, Tribes, and Literary Studies." *Redefining Sexual Ethics: A Sourcebook of Essays, Stories, and Poems*. Ed. Susan E. Davies and Eleanor H. Haney. Cleveland, OH: Pilgrim, 1991. 221-27. Rpt. in *The Sacred Hoop: Recovering the Feminine in American Indian Traditions*. By Paula Gunn Allen. 1986. Boston: Beacon, 1992. 262-68.

Gunn Allen, Paula. "A Stranger in My Own Life: Alienation in American Indian Poetry and Prose." *MELUS* [Society for the Study of the Multi-Ethnic Literature of the United States] 7 (1980): 3-19.

Gunn Allen, Paula. "Suicid/ing(ed) Indian Women." *The Woman That I Am: The Literature and Culture of Contemporary Women of Color.* Ed. D. Soyini Madison. New York: St. Martin's, 1994. 35-37.

Gunn Allen, Paula. "This Wilderness in My Blood: Spiritual Foundations of the Poetry of Five American Indian Women." *Coyote Was Here: Essays on Contemporary Native American Literary and Political Mobilization.* Ed. Bo Schöler. Aarhus, Denmark: SEKLOS/U of Aarhus, 1984. 95-115.

Gunn Allen, Paula. "When Women Throw Down Bundles: Strong Women Make Strong Nations." *Issues in Feminism: A First Course in Women's Studies.* Ed. Sheila Ruth. 3rd ed. Mountain View, CA: Mayfield, 1995. 187-94. Rpt. in *The Sacred Hoop: Recovering the Feminine in American Indian Traditions.* By Paula Gunn Allen. 1986. Boston: Beacon, 1992. 31-42.

Gunn Allen, Paula. "Who Is Your Mother? Red Roots of Feminism." *Graywolf Annual Five: Multicultural Literacy.* Ed. Rick Simonson and Scott Walker. St. Paul, MN: Graywolf, 1988. 13-27. Rpt. in "Who Is Your Mother? Red Roots of White Feminism." *The Sacred Hoop: Recovering the Feminine in American Indian Traditions.* By Paula Gunn Allen. 1986. Boston: Beacon, 1992. 209-21.

Gunn Allen, Paula. "'Whose Dream Is This Anyway?': Remythologizing and Self-Redefinition of Contemporary American Indian Fiction." *Literature and the Visual Arts in Contemporary Society.* Ed. Suzanne Ferguson and Barbara Groseclose. Columbus: Ohio State UP, 1985. 95-122.

Gunn Allen, Paula. "The Woman I Love Is a Planet; The Planet I Love Is a Tree." *Reweaving the World: The Emergence of Ecofeminism.* Ed. Irene Diamond and Gloria Feman Orenstein. San Francisco: Sierra Club, 1990. 52-57.

Gunn Allen, Paula, Lee Francis, and Mary Allen Francis. "This Business of Columbus." *Columbus and Beyond: Views from Native Americans.* Ed. Randolph Jorgen. Tucson, AZ: Southwest Parks and Monuments Association, 1992. 57-62.

Gunn Allen, Paula, and Kenneth Lincoln. "Contemporary Native American Poetry." *Jacaranda Review* 6 (1992) 53-55.

Gunn Allen, Paula, Janice Mirikitani, Cherríe Moraga, and Audre Lourde. "Against Apartheid." *Feminist Studies* 14 (1988): 417-52.

Gunn Allen, Paula, and Patricia Clark Smith. "Earthy Relations, Carnal Knowledge: Southwestern American Indian Women Writers and Landscape." *The Desert Is No Lady: Southwestern Landscapes in Women's Writing and Art.* Ed. Vera Norwood and Janice Monk. New Haven, CT: Yale UP, 1987. 174-96.

Poetry

Gunn Allen, Paula. *The Blind Lion.* Berkeley, CA: Throp Springs, 1974.

Gunn Allen, Paula. *A Cannon between My Knees.* New York: Strawberry, 1981.

Gunn Allen, Paula. *Coyote's Daylight Trip.* Albuquerque, NM: La Confluencia, 1978.

Gunn Allen, Paula. "Glastonbury Experience: For Peter." *Religion and Literature* 26 (1994): 81-82.

Gunn Allen, Paula. *Life Is a Fatal Disease: Collected Poems 1962-1995.* Albuquerque, NM: West End, 1997.

Gunn Allen, Paula. *Shadow Country.* Los Angeles: American Indian Studies Center, U of California, 1982.
Gunn Allen, Paula. *Skins and Bones: Poems 1979-87.* Albuquerque, NM: West End, 1988.
Gunn Allen, Paula. *Star Child.* Marvin, SD: Blue Cloud, 1981.
Gunn Allen, Paula. *Wyrds.* Santa Fe, NM: Taurean Horn, 1987.

Interviews

Coltelli, Laura. "Paula Gunn Allen." *Winged Words: American Indian Writers Speak.* Ed. Laura Coltelli. Lincoln: U of Nebraska P, 1990. 11-39.
Eysturoy, Annie O. "Paula Gunn Allen." *This Is about Vision: Interviews with Southwestern Writers.* Ed. William Balassi, John F. Crawford, and Annie O. Eysturoy. Albuquerque: U of New Mexico P, 1990. 95-107.
Sands, Kathleen M., and A. Lavonne Ruoff. "A Discussion of *Ceremony.*" *American Indian Quarterly: A Journal of Anthropology, History, and Literature* 5 (1979): 63-70.

Chapter 9

Trinh T. Minh-ha

"Since the self, like the work you produce, is not so much a core as a process, one finds oneself, in the context of cultural hybridity, always pushing one's questioning of oneself to the limit of what one is and what one is not."[1] This statement by filmmaker, composer, poet, and author Trinh T. Minh-ha suggests a primary feature of Trinh's work and life—a questioning and challenging of existing frameworks and boundaries of any kind.

Born in Hanoi, Vietnam, into a family of five sisters and one brother,[2] Trinh had a childhood marked by the poverty that many Vietnamese experienced during the Vietnam War: "I would join a number of Vietnamese women in saying that 'if equality consists of being poor together, then the Vietnamese society in its non-corrupted sectors [was] truly egalitarian!'"[3] Another dimension that characterized her life in Vietnam was "the feeling of being 'other,'" engendered

NOTE: Excerpts from *When the Moon Waxes Red: Representation, Gender and Cultural Politics,* by Trinh T. Minh-ha, copyright © 1991, and from *Framer Framed,* by Trinh T. Minh-ha, copyright © 1992, are reproduced by permission of Routledge, Inc.

by reading about the Vietnamese people—herself included—"as a cultural
entity offered up in writings by the European colonial community."[4]

The dominant feature of Trinh's childhood, however, was the Vietnam War
itself. In her family, "three different political factions existed"—factions largely
"bound to circumstances" rather than freely chosen.[5] One faction consisted of
the family members who remained in Hanoi; another of those who moved to
Saigon, where Trinh grew up; and a third of those involved with the National
Liberation Front. As a result, Trinh experienced the Vietnam War as a complex
reality that cannot be captured in the simple dualism of a conflict between pro-
and anticommunist forces that characterizes the perspective of many Americans
on the war. All three factions of her family "shared the insecurities of war,"[6] all
three "suffered under the regime to which they belong[ed], and all three had, at
one time or another, been the scapegoat of specific political moments." "As a
family however," Trinh explains, "we love each other dearly despite the absurd
situations in which we found ourselves divided."[7]

Trinh attended high school in Saigon and also studied music history and
theory, harmony, and piano at the National Conservatory of Music and Theater
of Saigon for a year. She completed her freshman year at the University of
Saigon and then chose to finish her college education in the United States,
leaving Vietnam in 1970 at the age of 17.[8] She preferred this option over study
in France (where her education would have been free) because she "wanted a
rupture . . . with the educational background in Vietnam that was based on a
Vietnamized model of the old, pre-1968 French system."[9]

Trinh regards as "a miracle" the path that enabled her to study in the United
States; it "was like throwing a bottle to the sea," she explains.[10] She blindly sent
out dozens of letters to universities in the United States, seeking admission into
work-study programs, a form of funding not usually available to international
students. Wilmington College in Wilmington, Ohio, accepted her, partly because the school's administrators wanted the college to have a student from
Vietnam. The work-study position with which she financed her education was
a clerical job in a local hospital.

As an international student, Trinh spent much of her time at Wilmington
College with other international students and with minority students, who often
were isolated from the mainstream European American students. Consequently,
she was introduced to a range of diverse cultures: "[T]he kind of education I
got in such an environment (more from outside than inside the classroom) would
not have been as rich if I had stayed in Vietnam or if I had been born in the
States. Some of my best friends there . . . were Haitians, Senegalese and Ken-
yans."[11] Trinh majored in music and French literature at Wilmington and
completed her B.A. degree in 1972.

Awarded a scholarship to study at the University of Illinois, Trinh completed
an M.A. degree in French literature, with a minor in ethnomusicology, in 1973.

An M.A. in music composition followed in 1976 and a Ph.D. in French and Francophone literatures in 1977, both completed at the University of Illinois. In 1974-75, while completing these degrees, Trinh spent a year in France as an exchange student, studying ethnomusicology and medieval and seventeenth-century French literature at the Université de Paris IV–Sorbonne and teaching English to French students in a lycée. A highlight of her year in Paris was the opportunity to study with noted Vietnamese ethnomusicologist and musician Tran van Khe.[12]

Following the completion of her doctorate, Trinh taught for three years at the National Conservatory of Music and Drama in Dakar, Senegal, in West Africa, teaching harmony and counterpoint, contemporary music analysis, non-Western music analysis, and music history. She also taught English at the American Cultural Center and at the Ministry of Higher Education of Senegal.

In 1983, Trinh became a research associate at the Center for the Study, Education and Advancement of Women at the University of California at Berkeley and spent three years doing research in Senegal under the auspices of the Center. In 1985, Trinh accepted a teaching position in the Department of Cinema at San Francisco State University, and in the fall of 1991, she taught as well at the University of California at Berkeley as a Chancellor Distinguished Professor. She joined the regular faculty at Berkeley as a professor in the Department of Women's Studies and the Film Studies Program in 1994.

Trinh also holds a position as a regular visiting faculty member at the London Consortium, which is composed of the Architectural Association School of Architecture, Birkbeck College, the University of London, the British Film Institute, and the Tate Gallery. She has held a number of other visiting appointments, including at the Society for the Humanities at Cornell University (1991); the Departments of Women's Studies and of Visual and Environmental Studies at Harvard University (1993); and the Women's Studies Program at Smith College in Northampton, Massachusetts (1994).

Trinh's writings cover a wide range of topics, including feminism, theories of contemporary art, postcolonial theories, filmmaking, and anthropology. Trinh's first book was *Un art sans oeuvre ou l'anonymat dans les arts contemporains (An Art without Masterpiece)* (1981), in which she describes the trend in Western art of the mid-twentieth century away from expressive modes to a depersonalized, Zen-influenced conception. Included in her discussion are the works of John Cage in music, Jacques Derrida in metaphysics, Marcel Duchamp and Andy Warhol in the visual arts, and Antonin Artaud in theater. Trinh explains that the application of Zen in the book is "not a 'return to my roots' but a grafting of several cultures onto a single body—an acknowledgment of the heterogeneity of my own cultural background."[13]

Trinh's second book was *African Spaces: Designs for Living in Upper Volta* (1985), coauthored with Jean-Paul Bourdier, a practicing architect and professor of architecture at the University of California at Berkeley. The subject of this book is the architecture of eight ethnic groups in Upper Volta, with a focus on the variety of design principles found in vernacular buildings. Trinh and Bourdier analyze architecture as a product and reflection of the "collective perception of space, attitudes, behaviors, and ritual practices of a society."[14] "The word 'dwelling', if one understands it as a verb and not a noun," they explain, "involves everything in life; it's a mode of living. The house in which and with which one lives for example, or the house that one has built, tells us a lot about the cultural practices of the individual inhabitants as well as of their society."[15]

Trinh's next book was a collection of poems, *En minuscules* (1987), written in French. Two themes dominate in these poems: writing and love. The poems explore the demands of writing and the joys, contradictions, failings, and memories associated with friendship and romantic relationships.

Woman, Native, Other: Writing Postcoloniality and Feminism (1989) has as its centerpiece the (de)construction of woman's identity, focusing particularly on Third World women and women of color in the diaspora, and it offers a criticism of the ethnographic envisioning of the other. Although the book was completed in 1983, Trinh was not able to find a publisher for it for many years; it was rejected by 33 presses before its publication. Trinh attributes the rejections to "marketable categories," "disciplinary regulations," and "conformist borders." She explains, "I was continuously sent back and forth from one publisher to another—commercial, academic, and small presses—each one equally convinced in its kind suggestions that the book would fit better in the other marketing context."[16]

Two of Trinh's books are collections of previous works and serve as overviews of her major ideas. *When the Moon Waxes Red: Representation, Gender and Cultural Politics* (1991), a collection of essays written by Trinh between 1980 and 1990, deals with the politics and practices of marginality, cinema, women's writing, the African novel, and art criticism. *Framer Framed* (1992) is a similar overview but with a focus on films and interviews. The first half of the book is devoted to the scripts of her films *Naked Spaces—Living is Round, Surname Viet Given Name Nam,* and *Reassemblage*; the second half consists of reprints of interviews with Trinh.

Trinh develops and expresses her ideas not only through theoretical writing but also through participation in the creative arts. She painted for many years and has performed in recitals and concerts on the piano, organ, percussion instruments, and the Vietnamese zither; she also has composed music. These artistic interests, rather than wide exposure to and love of movies, led her to filmmaking. She was "not at all a moviegoer" growing up in Vietnam; in fact, the number of films she saw before moving to the United States was limited. Nor was television an impetus for her filmmaking; she was "barely introduced to TV" in Vietnam, and then it was a collective experience, "since you had to line up in the streets with everyone else to look at one of the TVs made available to the neighborhood."[17]

Trinh's introduction to filmmaking was, in fact, a coincidence. She had friends who were filmmakers but never had thought of making a film herself until she was asked to speak in their classes about the musical dimension of film and the sound track. She then audited film classes conducted by Debra Meehan, a filmmaker and video artist, and began making films herself. Trinh now focuses more on filmmaking than on other activities: "I am still writing but for me composing music has become a little bit less urgent since film actually does allow me to pull together all my interests in the visual arts, poetry and music."[18] When she writes, shoots, and edits a film, the processes, for her, come "very close to those of composing music and of writing poetry."[19]

Although Trinh had made a number of super-8 films on diverse subjects, her first 16-mm film was *Reassemblage* (1982). Her experience in Senegal was the impetus for the film:

> In Senegal I found myself on this edge of being both an insider and an outsider. An insider because I shared with the African culture the historical experience of colonialism, but an outsider nonetheless because I certainly had everything to learn about the culture. . . . It was this experience that provoked a desire to make a film about Senegal that would not be based on an institutional body of knowledge or an institutional approach, but rather on the kind of things that happen during the process of experiencing without our being able to simply either show or talk *about*.[20]

A montage of visuals and sounds that focuses on the everyday activities of women in various villages, *Reassemblage* provides a critical response not only to the depiction of African societies in the commercial cinema but to the "anthropological I/eye" that characterizes ethnographic filmmaking.[21]

Trinh's second film, *Naked Spaces—Living Is Round* (1985), deals with relationships among women, houses, and the cosmos in West Africa, visually exploring the connections that exist between people and their living environments. *Naked Spaces* won the Blue Ribbon Award for best experimental feature at the American Film Festival in 1987 and the Golden Athena Award for best feature documentary in 1986. It also was part of the 1987 biennial of the Whitney Museum in New York City.

Trinh's film *Surname Viet Given Name Nam* (1989) revolves around questions of identity, popular memory, and culture and focuses on aspects of Vietnamese culture as manifest in the history and lives of Vietnamese women in both Vietnam and the United States. In this film, Trinh explains, she "was interested in exploring how we project ourselves through our own stories and analyses as well as how we are constituted through the image-repertoire that insiders and outsiders to the culture have historically fashioned and retained of us."[22] Trinh suggests that "Vietnam cannot be homogenized nor subsumed into an all-embracing identity" and invites viewers to consider "explanations and interpretations that differ according to gender, political affinity, and subject positioning."[23] *Surname Viet Given Name Nam* won the Blue Ribbon Award for best film-as-art feature at the American International Film Festival in 1990, the first prize for film as art at the San Francisco Museum of Art in 1990, and a Merit Award at the Bombay International Film Festival in India in 1990.

In *Shoot for the Contents* (1991), Trinh uses the allegorical figure of the dragon to explore questions of power and change as they relate to the contemporary shifts of culture and politics in China. In the film, these issues are explored through the prodemocracy demonstration in Tiananmen Square in Beijing. The film won the prize for best cinematography at the Sundance Film Festival in 1992 and the award for best experimental feature documentary at the Athens International Film Festival in 1992, and it was part of the 1993 biennial of the Whitney Museum in New York City.

A Tale of Love (1995) is a fictional narrative loosely inspired by a Vietnamese national poem, "The Tale of Kieu." In the original tale, the protagonist must prostitute herself to save her family; in Trinh's version, the main character is a freelance writer who researches the impact of the tale on the Vietnamese American community for a women's magazine. Trinh sees fiction film as like documentary film in that most "fiction films involve documentary elements, and most truthful documentaries include fictional elements." She discovered, however, in making *A Tale of Love,* that a film that is primarily fiction entails "a totally different process of working."[24] In her less fictional films, she usually does not start with a prepared script; rather, she makes choices according to what happens "during the process of materializing" the film.[25] In contrast, work on *A Tale of Love* involved "a derisive budget, a very tight schedule and a large crew. So the space for improvising and reflection during the process is reduced to the minimum."[26]

Trinh's films are difficult to categorize and to position in relation to a film tradition. She chooses to situate her films in relation to what she calls *third cinema*:

> The movement called third cinema is a movement that has rejected the stereotyped notion of what Third World cinema is, which is usually a film focused on a specific sociopolitical problem. . . . The third cinema distinguishes itself by raising questions at three stages: the stage of production (which concerns film language and how it is produced), the stage of distribution, and exhibition. In other words, films are made not as consumer goods, but made in order to provoke a situation where people would be discussing several issues and challenging each other in a specific subject or area.[27]

Trinh's films circulate largely in film festivals, museums, media arts centers, community organizations, and educational and university networks. They are distributed by nonprofit organizations such as Women Make Movies, Third World Newsreel, and the Museum of Modern Art in New York City; Lightcone in Paris; Cinenova in London; Image Forum in Tokyo; Idera Films in Vancouver; Freunde der Deutschen Kinemathek in Berlin; and the National Library of Australia Film and Video Lending Collection in Canberra.

Because she disavows filmmaking in a commercial context, funding her films is "a constant struggle" for Trinh: "Although I do enjoy teaching, the fact that I have to go on teaching, when I would rather just spend my time writing and making films, is because I prefer to continue working as a so-called independent filmmaker and not to have to count on any commercial profit from my films for survival."[28] Trinh's films have been funded, in part, through various fellowships, including Rockefeller Foundation Intercultural Film fellowships (1988-89, 1993-94), National Endowment for the Arts fellowships (1987-88, 1990-91, 1993-94), a Guggenheim fellowship (1990-91), an American Film Institute fellowship (1991), and the Maya Deren Award for independent film-making (1991).

Trinh's struggle to fund her various projects is a consequence of the nature of the work she chooses to do. In her films, theoretical writings, poetry, and music, Trinh is "always working at the borderlines of several shifting categories, stretching out to the limits of things, learning about [her] own limits and how to modify them."[29] For Trinh, however, such work constitutes a means of survival: "From one category, one label, to another, the only way to survive is to refuse. Refuse to become an integratable element. Refuse to allow names arrived at transitionally to become stabilized." As a result, her works and ideas remain "a surreptitious site of movement and passage whose open, communal character makes exclusive belonging and long-term residence undesirable, if not impossible."[30]

Nature of the World

The nature of the world Trinh identifies as the realm for rhetoric is a world of "rooted ideologies,"[31] a "dominant system of thought,"[32] or "established order in all its forms."[33] This is a world that has as its primary characteristic the "imperative to produce meaning according to established rationales."[34] Trinh's concern is not with the dominance of one particular system of thought or established order; any "single guiding schema" is problematic for her.[35] Hegemony itself—the authority or power of any particular perspective over others—is the condition she addresses.

A hegemonic system of thought is troublesome for Trinh because it often is unmarked; thus, it often is unnoticed and "confused with what is natural."[36] Such a system produces a sense of "'normalcy' or a state of validated 'common sense'" in which "familiar forms of analysis, interpretation, and communication" occur.[37] Consequently, hegemony constitutes a code that "excludes or invalidates all other ways of communicating"; it becomes, in effect, "the only way people can think about something."[38] Trinh finds a metaphor of veils to be useful in describing the limitations of the framework that constitutes a dominant ideology. She suggests that what individuals encounter as they face their own systems of representation is like *"veils that rise in front of us, framing the world in neat pieces. Until we have grown tall enough to look over the next veil, we believe the little we see is all there is to see."*[39]

The strength of a dominant ideology derives, in large part, from the consent of those who participate in it. As Trinh explains, the power and authority of hegemony often operate "via consent—hence its pernicious, long-lasting, and binding strength."[40] There are "no 'innocent people,' no subjects untouched" by an established order; as she explains, hegemony "does not really spare any of us."[41] Even those who might be expected to resist a hegemonic worldview— those who are oppressed by it—rarely are able to challenge the power involved because they, too, participate in the worldview and are co-opted by it: "Hegemony is established to the extent that the world view of the rulers is also the world view of the ruled."[42] The "colonizer and colonized have come to speak the same language."[43]

Most individuals are unable to resist a dominant ideology because of its subtle techniques of inducement. Although dominant ideologies once relied for their compulsion on explicit, overt forms of enforcement, they now are more indirect and subtle, relying on prevailing social codes. Trinh suggests that common techniques used to inscribe a dominant ideology include clichés, formulas, and stereotypes, all of which attempt to capture, solidify, and pin down the meanings of words and constructs. Much as butterflies in a collection are "pinned to a butterfly board,"[44] these techniques do not allow ways of thinking outside of narrow and prescribed confines. Classification also is used to maintain a dominant ideology, dividing the world into categories, creating a system of regularity and "frenzied 'disciplinarization.'"[45] Standardization serves a similar purpose, engendering sameness and prescribing one attitude, meaning, and truth for everyone's lives. This technique reduces "the world to the dominant's own image," promoting uniformity and "a monolithic view of the world."[46]

Trinh explicates various examples of dominant ideologies in her writings and films. One ideology that is a particular subject of focus for her is the one that infuses the system of documentary filmmaking. To suggest that the documentary form produces objectivity or the truth is to ignore its essence as a system constructed according to certain conventions. What is "put forward as *the* 'objective' way to document other cultures," Trinh asserts, "is a mere abidance by the conventions of documentary practice."[47]

Trinh cites as examples of documentary conventions "the sense of urgency, immediacy, and authenticity in the instability of the hand-held camera; the newsreel look of the grainy image"; and "the practice of translating and subtitling the words of the informants."[48] Similarly, real time "is thought to be more 'truthful' than filmic time" so that the long take and minimal or no editing "are declared to be more appropriate if one is to avoid distortions in structuring the material."[49] The "close-up is condemned for its partiality, while the wide angle is claimed to be more objective because it includes more in the frame, hence it can mirror more faithfully the event-in-context."[50] These conventions, Trinh explains, are just that—conventions—and are no more likely to produce truth than any other conventions.

Both makers of and audiences for documentary films have forgotten, Trinh asserts, that the "fathers of documentary . . . initially insisted that documentary is not News, but Art. . . . That its essence is not information . . . but something close to 'a creative treatment of actuality.'"[51] "Every representation of truth," Trinh explains, "involves elements of fiction, and the difference between so-called documentary and fiction in their depiction of reality is a question of degrees of fictitiousness."[52]

A world organized according to any single, dominant truth, then, is the world with which Trinh is concerned. She wants what is regarded as truth in any system to be seen simply as one of many possible meanings—"*a* meaning."[53] Her interest is not in "judging which truth is better than the other"[54] but in seeking to expose how any particular presentation of truth inevitably involves particular manipulations and constitutes "a question of ideology."[55]

Definition of Feminism

Trinh's perspective on feminism is incompatible with many traditional notions about feminism. Feminism is not the attempt to gain the power that men have or to extend the rights of men to women. "Imitating, copying, aping man," Trinh asserts, is not feminism's purpose.[56] Trinh rejects any kind of feminism that refers "to the 'male model'" for comparison because such comparison "unavoidably maintains the subject under tutelage"[57]—it continues to make the male the norm or the standard reference point. Feminism, she believes, should not be content with reforms that simply allow women to be more like men— "reforms that, at best, contribute to the improvement and/or enlargement of the identity enclosure."[58]

Trinh sees feminism as a movement that contributes to the questioning and challenging of established ideological systems. It is a "questioning of the dominant system"[59]—the "male-is-norm world" that is "taken for granted as the objective, comprehensive societal world."[60] Feminism challenges the "tradition carried on for the benefit of men and legally (not equitably) reinforced by laws invented, brought into operation, and distorted by men for men."[61] In its broadest sense, feminism is a way of thinking outside of established categories and boundaries: "[T]o assume responsibility as a feminist, is, necessarily, to be aware of the established limits and to remove the censure of 'non-categorical' thought";[62] it is a way "of thinking" that does "not *exclude*."[63] Trinh uses a metaphor of the moon to describe the kind of thinking that characterizes feminism: "The moon breeds like a rabbit. She causes the seeds to germinate and the plants to grow, but she exceeds all forms of regulated fecundity through which she is expected to ensure the system's functioning."[64]

Despite its capacity to open up new ways of thinking, feminism's potential as a liberating force has not been realized, in part because of its tendency toward monolithism. Feminism yearns for universality and a "generic *woman*," Trinh explains, which, "like its counterpart, the generic *man*, tends to efface difference within itself."[65] Although important differences exist among women, feminism often appears to be homogeneous because, as a result "of their more privileged status, white feminists have been taking up" the task of feminism "more extensively"; consequently, feminism "remains largely white in its visibility."[66] This tendency toward the construction of a unitary subject within feminism requires caution on the part of feminists of color and Third World feminists:

> [A]t the same time as you feel the necessity to call yourself a feminist while fighting for the situation of women, you also have to keep a certain latitude and to refuse that label when feminism tends to become an occupied territory. Here, you refuse, not because you don't want to side with other feminists, but simply because it is crucial to keep open the space of naming in feminism.[67]

Feminism's appearance of homogeneity, however, is not inherent or inevitable. Trinh sees feminism as quite "heterogeneous in its origins"; it results "from the works of both white women and women of color around the world," and the influence between the two groups "has always been mutual."[68] At times, women of color have "taken their cue from white women's sexual politics," thus contributing to the appearance of homogeneity in the movement, but, even then, the different perspectives they bring to feminism consistently have helped "to radicalize the feminist struggle." The multiplicity within feminism is likely to become more evident, Trinh believes, as "more women of color have access to education," resulting in "more and more rewriting work" of feminist theory by these women.[69]

Another reason for feminism's slow progress is the relationship that sometimes exists between white women and women of color in the movement. White women sometimes reinscribe and engage in the very practices of colonialization that they claim to oppose as feminists. They treat Third World women and women of color in much the same way they themselves are treated by men, thereby duplicating the "master-servant relationship."[70] For example, white women may treat women of color as inferior, invite them to participate in the movement only on white women's terms, and refuse to share power.[71] In other instances, they introduce "a Third World woman's voice in major feminist events . . . to validate what Western women have to say on certain issues and to give it a touch of universality."[72] Their behavior, in these cases, is not unlike "the anthropologist who invites the native to sit down at the table with him because he needs this native's presence to validate his arguments."[73] In such instances, the woman of color faces marginalization both from the ruling center and from within feminism, the "established margin."[74]

Examination of the relations between white feminists and feminists of color is a healthy sign of feminism's reflexivity, Trinh believes. If it is a way of thinking that involves a constant questioning of a dominant mode of thought, feminism itself must be subject to challenge and questioning: "If feminism is set forth as a demystifying force, then it will have to question thoroughly the belief in its own identity."[75] Feminists must avoid the construction of an official version of feminism, she warns, and resist the temptation "to turn feminism into a rigidly prescriptive practice, perpetuating thereby the same power relations as those established in the patriarchal system." Ideally, feminists' "questioning of the dominant system constantly pushes to the outer limits of what feminism is and what it is not."[76]

Trinh is not disturbed by the use of the term *postfeminist* to describe the current state of feminism. She sees postfeminism as "both a return to a nascent stage of feminism where the movement is at its most subversive, and a move forward to a stage in which we have learned from the many difficulties we've encountered that, in spite of all the refinements of sexist ideology, the fight is far from being over."[77] She asks:

Why see postfeminism mainly as a term that declares feminism outmoded or as a form of going beyond feminism? Why not understand it . . . as a different form of subjectivity that does not come "after" feminism so much as "with" feminism, remaining alert to the movement's political closures, and keeping it from reproducing the centered, unitary, masculine subject of representation?[78]

Nature of the Rhetor

In Trinh's theory, the rhetor has the potential to do the kind of challenging that Trinh sees as characteristic of feminism. But not all individuals are inclined to engage in such challenge. Trinh's conception of the rhetor is rooted in the distinction she makes between otherness and difference as standpoints from which to interact with and respond to others.

Individuals in privileged, dominant positions are inclined to use a lens of otherness to respond to others who are different from them. From this stance of otherness, rhetors assign identity to the other, reducing that identity "to a set of fixed values and practices."[79] The other becomes fixed, finite, and opposite of the self, reduced to "the simplicity of essences."[80] In this stance of otherness, the rhetor constantly must reconfirm "authority through the setting up of fences and of all kinds of disciplinary rules."[81]

A number of negative consequences result from relating to another through a frame of otherness. The "superficial understanding of the other" that characterizes otherness results in "a superficial understanding of oneself."[82] In such a relationship, the other is able to be consumed or treated as a commodity, and the identity of the other is turned into "a product that one can buy, arrange to one's liking, and/or preserve."[83] The other also is contained according to the rules of the Master. Trinh uses the term *authorized marginality* to explain the phenomenon whereby "the production of 'difference' can be supervised, hence recuperated, neutralized and depoliticized."[84] Authorized marginality is the practice of tolerating individuals' differences as long as they "conform with the established rules."[85] The purpose of keeping the other "within specific boundaries"[86] is to "spread the Master's values, comforting him in his godlike charity-giver role, protecting his lifestyle, and naturalizing it as the only, the best way."[87]

Marginalized or colonized individuals, in contrast, are less likely to respond to others out of a framework of otherness and are more likely to employ a framework of difference because of their marginalized position in the dominant culture. "Dominated and marginalized people have been socialized to see always more than their own point of view," explains Trinh.[88] These types of rhetors assume a dual position, looking "in from the outside while also looking out from the inside. Not quite the same, not quite the other,"[89] they stand "in that undetermined threshold place where" they constantly drift in and out.[90] The position of the Master, in contrast, is far more limited: "His vision is a one-way street; his privileged position hasn't allowed him to benefit from that double vision inherent in any dominated person—male or female."[91]

Trinh's ideal rhetor, then, is the individual who lives "fearlessly with and within difference(s)."[92] By *difference,* she does not mean difference as a "tool of segregation" or the "apartheid type of difference."[93] Rather, difference involves "effecting change on the prevailing state of things" by opening up to and creating a space for a new identity.[94] Relating to another out of difference involves interrogating one's identity or exploring one's sense of self through mediation of *"the image one has of the other."*[95] Difference is a means of constituting identity largely "through the process of othering"[96] because in "any encounter with the 'other', what you face is also yourself and your set of practices."[97]

The result of facing and working with difference is an undoing of the self and an undermining of *"the very idea of identity."* Such a stance dismantles "the very notion of core (be it static or not) and identity" because it defers "to infinity the layers whose totality forms 'I.'"[98] In relating to others as different rather than as other, the rhetor adopts a stance of movement, openness, metamorphosis, and "unsettlement."[99] In this space, "the self vacillates and loses its assurance," resulting in a "fundamental instability."[100] An orientation of difference creates a "realm in-between, where predetermined rules cannot fully apply"[101] and where "a new, fresh reality" is "created in the fearless crossing of the home-and-abroad or overhere-and-overthere boundaries."[102]

Adoption of the frame of difference that Trinh recommends enables the rhetor to recognize that the other is within the self: "As notions that serve an analytical purpose, otherness and sameness are more useful when they are viewed not in terms of dualities or conflicts but in terms of degrees and movements within the same concept, or better, in terms of differences both within and between entities."[103] As she explains, "The named 'other' is never to be found merely over there and outside oneself, for it is always over here, between Us, within Our discourse, that the 'other' becomes a nameable reality."[104]

Trinh's conception of the self, then, is not of an authentic, unified subject with a fixed identity. She challenges a view of identity as "the whole pattern of sameness within a being, the style of a continuing me that permeated all the changes undergone."[105] Identity is not "an essential, authentic core that remains hidden to one's consciousness and that requires the elimination of all that is considered foreign or not true to the self."[106] Trinh thus rejects the view that the "search for an identity is . . . a search for that lost, pure, true, real, genuine, original, authentic self."[107] She sees such a view of the self as problematic because the role it assigns to difference is a boundary that "distinguishes one identity from another."[108] Consequently, "the other is almost unavoidably either opposed to the self or submitted to the self's dominance. . . . Identity, thus understood, supposes that a clear dividing line can be made between I and not-I, he and she . . . between us here and them over there."[109]

In contrast to the conventional conception of the self, Trinh sees the rhetor's identity as a constant process of construction that results in a multiplicity of subjectivity or an infinity of "the layers of totality that forms I."[110] The self is a "place of hybridity,"[111] a "horizontal vertigo,"[112] or a "multiple presence."[113] It contains "a multiplicity of I's, none of which truly dominates."[114] The process of constructing and discovering the self "never leads to the True Self . . . but only to other layers, other selves."[115] In the "complex subjectivities"[116] that constitute the self, Trinh suggests, "there is no real me to return to, no whole self that synthesizes. . . . [T]here are instead, diverse recognitions of self through difference, and unfinished, contingent, arbitrary closures."[117]

The metaphor of the traveler captures for Trinh the nature of the self in interaction with the other from a stance of difference. Both the experience of traveling and the experience of interacting with someone who is different constitute processes "whereby the self loses its fixed boundaries—a disturbing yet potentially empowering practice of difference." "To travel," Trinh explains, "can consist in operating a profoundly unsettling inversion of one's identity: I become me via an other. Depending on who is looking, the exotic is the other, or it is me."[118] This same process operates in an interaction rooted in difference: "The voyage out of the (known) self and back into the (unknown) self sometimes takes the wanderer far away to a motley place where everything safe and sound seems to waver"—where the self is "profoundly destabilized."[119] The exiled, migrant, split self that characterizes the experience of travel, then, is the nature of the self interacting in difference with the other.

Rhetorical Options

Trinh offers a set of rhetorical options designed to enable the rhetor to disrupt the hegemonic nature of the world, including the stable self. Her options are ones that constitute "a constant questioning of the framing of consciousness"[120] and are designed to disturb "one's own thinking habits, dissipating what has become familiar and cliched."[121] They "set into relief the frame of thought within which operate the practices we accept." In "showing that what tends to be taken for granted can no longer be so," these options require that "change be effected on the frame itself."[122] Her rhetorical options, then, raise the question of "whether we are going to let ourselves be subjected to the dominant culture without challenging it."[123] Trinh's response is clear: "[O]ne need not consent or contribute to hegemony."[124]

In contrast to the options many rhetorical theorists advocate, Trinh's options are not ones that oppose, resist, or seek to change a particular ideology. She does not adopt an "anti-something" stance because this kind of opposition confines the rhetor to the framework established by the original ideology.[125] The "choice of a direction opposite to the one rejected," she asserts, "remains a reaction within the same frame of references."[126] "'*Breaking rules,*'" in other words, "*still refers to rules.*"[127] Trinh rejects opposition as a rhetorical stance because it "ultimately contributes to things remaining in place, because it tends more often than not to block critical thinking; it is unable to do much but repeat itself."[128]

Instead of rhetorical options that oppose a particular hegemony, Trinh suggests rhetorical options that offer a way of thinking that is different from that of the dominant hegemony—a way of thinking in which multiplicity and difference defy all attempts to unify and conform. Her rhetorical options "aim at producing a different hearing and a renewed viewing" in which the structures of the dominant way of thinking simply are not reproduced.[129] By presenting other ways of thinking, the options Trinh recommends inevitably render ineffective the dominant ideology: "The values that keep the dominant set of criteria in power are simply ineffective in a framework where one no longer abides by them."[130]

Trinh offers her rhetorical options not as prescriptions for others to follow but as heuristic devices: "I consider my work to be radically inefficient when it comes to prescriptions."[131] Instead, she seeks "to offer meaning in such a way that each reader [or viewer], going through the same statements and the same text, would find tools for herself (or himself) to carry on the fight in her (or his) own terms."[132] She engages in "critical work in such a way that there is room for people to reflect on their own struggle and to use the tools offered so as to further it on their own terms."[133]

In her effort to provide tools that individuals can use in their own processes of disrupting hegemonic systems of thought, Trinh offers and models two primary rhetorical options: violation of expectations and the honoring of multiplicity. With the option of violating expectations, she asks audiences to question and challenge current thought and practices. With the second option, honoring multiplicity, she asks them to participate in the creation of multiple meanings to replace the meaning advocated by the hegemonic system. Both of these options operate particularly effectively in the realm of the visual; although they can be adapted to discourse, Trinh's options derive from and model disruptions primarily in visual texts.

Violation of Expectations

One rhetorical option Trinh offers for rhetors to use in the disruption of hegemonic ideologies is the violation of expectations. With this option, rhetors violate the conventional expectations audiences are likely to bring with them to the experience of a text. This violation usually assumes the form of violating the rules of a particular form or genre. It is a marked characteristic, for example, of Trinh's films, in which she uses a variety of techniques to fracture the rules of documentary filmmaking, challenging "what people expect from a documentary" as well as the "rigidity of criteria" of documentary practice.[134] The practices she uses to violate expectations only begin to suggest how rhetors might violate expectations in the creation of their own messages, particularly visual ones.

Trinh's film *Surname Viet Given Name Nam* provides a good example of her violation of expectations in the genre of documentary film. In this case, she violates the expectations audiences are likely to have of the nature and function of interviews in documentary film. The film contains reenacted or restaged interviews with women, thus introducing fictional and staged forms deemed invalid by conventional documentary practice. For the film, Trinh translated into English transcripts of interviews that others had conducted with women in Vietnam and asked Vietnamese women in the United States to act out the interviews. The reenactment is deliberately ambiguous, but clues are provided in the film that the interviews are staged—clues that increasingly raise questions in viewers' minds as the film advances. The interviews look less and less "natural" until, finally, the women, in "real" interviews, discuss why they agreed to play the roles on-screen and the reactions of their friends and relatives to their involvement in the film.

With the juxtaposition of the staged and the real interviews in *Surname Viet Given Name Nam,* Trinh calls "attention to the politics of interviews" and sets "into relief the manipulations that tend to be taken for granted in documentary."[135] She exposes interviews as fictional devices and thus violates audiences' expectations of them as objective and truthful. Because interviews perform the functions of "authenticating information" and "validating the voices recruited for the sake of the argument the film advances," Trinh explains, they "are actually sophisticated devices of fiction."[136]

Trinh provides another example of the rhetorical option of violating expectations through her disruption of the rules of editing in the genre of documentary film. Trinh explains why she disavows the conventional editing techniques expected by audiences for documentary film:

> The illustrative relationship usually found in film between sound, image and text; the cosmetic role often attributed to music; and the exclusively informative function assigned to environmental sounds as well as to people's talking lull the viewers into a falsely secure world that is fabricated so as to give them the comforting illusion that they know where they go; they know what to expect, and can even foresee what the outcome will be.[137]

In contrast, viewers often use the term *fluid* to describe Trinh's editing style because it does not follow "*the ABCs of photography.*"[138] It "does not rely on slick visuals or on smooth transitions" and thus "does not bear the 'professional' seal."[139] Trinh's editing plays with viewers' expectations, disrupting them in various ways. Music is often cut off abruptly, jerking viewers out of the mood that has been created. The camera is not focused on the head and face of a woman being interviewed. The subtitles fade so quickly that they cannot be read. The visuals incorporate casual jump cuts, out-of-focus shots, jerky pans, and incongruous superimpositions.

Trinh also models how the rules of a genre can be violated in terms of sound, again to disrupt audiences' expectations. She explains standard procedure concerning sound in documentary films: "In many films the sound begins as soon as the titles appear on the screen and is typically used to get the audience into a certain mood."[140] In contrast, her film *Reassemblage,* for example, begins with silence over the titles, and only later is music introduced into the sound track. The silence is disquieting and disorienting and often makes audiences uncomfortable. But such use of silence by a rhetor suspends expectations. Music usually tells audiences what to expect, whereas moments of silence "are pauses that can make you become more aware of the sounds, or just leave you in peace, without any expectation."[141]

Rhetors also may violate expectations by crossing conventional genres and categories, refusing to stay confined within one genre in the creation of messages. In this kind of violation of expectations, boundaries are "ceaselessly called into question, undermined, modified"[142] in order to create the greatest possible variety of meanings: "To cut across boundaries and borderlines is to live aloud the malaise of categories and labels; it is to resist simplistic attempts at classifying, to resist the comfort of belonging to a classification, and of producing classifiable works."[143]

Trinh herself often crosses conventional genres and categories, mixing "[t]heater, dance, mime, art, architecture, music, film, video, *other.*"[144] Trinh's books violate expectations through the crossing of genres by combining different modes of writing—theory and poetry and discursive and nondiscursive languages. Trinh's films are characterized by a similar crossing of borders in that they cut across the boundaries of fiction, documentary, and experimental films. As she explains:

I never think of my films as specifically documentary or fictional, except when I send them off to festivals. Then I have to choose my jury. . . . For years, no matter which one I chose, it seemed as if I constantly made the "wrong" selection. When I chose "documentary," I knew the problem would have to do with what people expect from a documentary and the ensuing rigidity of criteria. Most of these specialized jurors not only had difficulty in accepting my films as documentaries but also hardly considered them befitting the social, educational, or ethnographic categories. The same problem occurred when I opted for "film art" or "experimental," because jurors of such a category tend to see "experimental" as a genre on its own rather than as a critical venture working upon "genre" itself.[145]

The result of the boundary crossing Trinh models in her films and books is an impurity that makes the fixing of one particular meaning difficult, if not impossible.

In the use of the rhetorical option of violation of expectations, rhetors violate genres by refusing to be confined by the rules and boundaries that define them or by combining a number of genres in one message or text. A variety of visual and aural techniques are available to disrupt audiences' expectations in the messages they create and disseminate.

Honoring of Multiplicity

A second rhetorical option that Trinh suggests rhetors can use to disrupt hegemonic thought is the honoring of multiplicity. With this option, rhetors maintain a deliberate openness to multiple meanings and acknowledge—and, in fact, feature—the complexity of perspectives inherent in representing and describing any phenomenon. In the honoring of multiplicity, rhetors do not seek to construct messages that are clear, transparent, and reductive; rather, they construct messages that are deliberately ambiguous and that encourage attention to and a valuing of multiple perspectives.

Trinh recognizes that an honoring of multiplicity violates conventional rules of rhetoric: "*Clear* expression, often equated with *correct* expression, has long been the criterion set forth in treatises on *rhetoric,* whose aim was to order discourse so as to *persuade.*"[146] Clarity is achieved, she notes, through normative, reductive formulas that provide "immediate accessibility. . . . The idea is clear and there's no need to strain the brain or the eye."[147] Clarity, however, has embedded within it a particular ideology, and "a demand for clear communication often proves to be nothing else but an intolerance for any language other than the one approved by the dominant ideology."[148] Clarity of meaning, according to Trinh, turns "an impoverishment of dominant thinking into a virtue."[149]

In contrast to engendering clarity, rhetors honor multiplicity by creating symbols and texts that have "no single message, no wrapped-up package to offer."[150] They provide "neither a personal nor a professional point of view," provide "no encased knowledge to the acquisitive mind," and have "no single story to tell nor any central message to spread."[151] Rhetors provide a message that does not settle "down with any single answer";[152] they refuse to "wrap it up or have the last word."[153] Consequently, readers or "viewers may not know what they are seeing, may not know how to see it,"[154] and the reading remains open, with audience members invited "to participate in the making of meaning."[155] When a pile of skulls is used in a film "to convey the horror of war and to signify death," for example, and the blurring of an image is used to signal "the passage of reality to dream,"[156] audiences typically have the confidence that they know what these images mean. Audiences lose this confidence when confronted with messages that honor multiplicity.

Although Trinh does not specify ways in which rhetors should practice the honoring of multiplicity in their own rhetoric, she models a number of techniques that suggest ways to prevent the construction of a single, reductive message from a text. Included among her techniques are the prevention of closure, the presentation of multiple views, and the use of varied repetition.

Prevention of Closure

One technique that rhetors can use to honor multiplicity is to prevent narrative closure. In this technique, no closure or ending point is provided to a message or text, thus disrupting the "commercial and ideological habits of our society" that "favor narrative with as definite a closure as possible."[157] The resulting message has "a sense of continuity," but it is "not the type of linearly closed continuity that leads . . . from a starting point to an ending point."[158] Instead, in such texts, "no emphasis is given to the finished product . . . . You don't follow an activity from a departure to an ending point."[159] Such texts are "headless and bottomless" so that readers and viewers can enter and exit at any point "without the feeling that they have missed 'the intrigue' or the 'main point.'"[160] In Trinh's film *Reassemblage,* for example, a shot is included of a man carving wood, but she never shows "the end product of his work."[161] A refusal to provide closure allows "things to build on one another," and the audience never loses "sight of the many possibilities generated or of the continuous weaving of the many threads initiated."[162]

Presentation of Multiple Views

Another means by which rhetors may choose to develop messages that honor multiplicity is by presenting multiple views of the same subject. This technique contrasts with the typical approach to the construction of messages to narrow, focus, and refine a perspective. Trinh provides an example of this refining process in visual rhetoric, where the "common practice among filmmakers and photographers [is] to shoot the same thing more than once and to select only one shot—the 'best' one—in the editing process."[163] Trinh's films, in contrast, model the presentation of multiple views in that they are marked by "the repeated inclusion of a plurality of shots of the same subject from very slightly different distances or angles."[164]

The technique of presenting multiple views is not limited to visual messages. Trinh illustrates the same technique of multiplicity with sound in her films when she presents multiple views through different voices. In her film *Naked*

Spaces—Living Is Round, for example, she uses three women's voices for the verbal text: "One voice, the bass voice, stays closest to the religious sayings and the African writings. Another voice, the higher voice, informs, according to the logic of Westerners. The third voice . . . is the voice that relates personal impressions and anecdotes."[165] For Trinh, "these voices constitute three ways of releasing information and of undermining the dominant documentary mode of informing."[166] The result is a multiplicity of readings of the film's message.

Repetition with Variation

A particular kind of repetition also may be used by rhetors to create messages that honor multiplicity. This repetition "is not just the automatic reproduction of the same, but rather the production of the same with and in differences."[167] It involves repetition of a sound or image, each time with slight variation. Again, Trinh models this technique in her films. She records a complete statement and then repeats different parts of it at different times, sometimes in its complete form and sometimes with various words missing. The meaning of the sentence is suspended, "alleviating it from the weight of correct syntax and definite affirmation or negation." The result is an offering to the audience of "a wider range of possible interpretations."[168]

Varied repetition also occurs when rhetors repeat a statement or image but vary the context so that the meaning changes with each new context. With this technique, a statement or an image is repeated exactly but "each time in juxtaposition with a different visual context. Thus, the meaning resulting from the first association keeps on being displaced." The first meaning is altered, extended, or supplemented so that "meanings interact with one another in the process."[169]

Trinh provides examples of this type of varied repetition in many of her films. In *Naked Spaces—Living Is Round,* for example, she takes "a Dogon (Mali) statement on adornment and desire or on the house as a woman" and juxtaposes "it with specific images of dwellings among the Kabye (Togo) and then again, among the Birifor (Burkina Faso)."[170] She often uses a similar technique with the music in her films. In both *Naked Spaces—Living Is Round* and *Reassemblage,* music from one African group first is heard with visual depictions of that group and then repeated, with variations, within other groups. Consequently, "reproduction is never quite the reproduction of the same, and viewers or readers are invited to return to a familiar ground only to find themselves drifting somewhere else."[171]

Trinh's use of rephotography in her films constitutes another example of varied repetition in which a statement or image is repeated but embedded in different contexts. In *Surname Viet Given Name Nam,* she shows a grainy, black-and-white image of three women moving in slow motion at the beginning of the film. The image appears three times throughout the film, each time slightly different in its framing and visual legibility. The third time they are seen, the women are presented as they were originally shot, with the original sound track of a male journalistic voice explaining that they are "captured prisoners, whose bodies were 'traditionally used by the enemy as ammunition bearers, village infiltrators and informers.'" This repetition in different contexts lifts "these news images out of their [original] contexts so as to make them serve a new context"; the result is that the images *"speak anew."*[172]

In choosing Trinh's rhetorical options of violating expectations and honoring multiplicity, rhetors come to "speak near by."[173] Trinh defines this mode of speaking as

> a speaking that does not objectify, does not point to an object as if it is distant from the speaking subject or absent from the speaking place. A speaking that reflects on itself and can come very close to a subject without, however, seizing or claiming it. A speaking in brief, whose closures are only moments of transition opening up to other possible moments of transition—these are forms of indirectness well understood by anyone in tune with poetic language. Every element constructed in [rhetoric] refers to the world around it, while having at the same time a life of its own. And this life is precisely what is lacking when one uses word, image, or sound just as an instrument of thought.[174]

Speaking near by is not simply a rhetorical technique but "an attitude in life, a way of positioning oneself in relation to the world."[175] "To save time and energy," Trinh suggests, "one is told to 'go at it' and devise short-cuts so as to take hold of the desired object as quickly as possible."[176] She disagrees with this orientation and recommends in its place speaking near by: "One can only approach things indirectly. Because, in doing so, one not only goes toward the subject of one's focus without killing it, but one allows oneself to get acquainted with the envelope, that is, all the elements which surround, situate or simply relate to it."[177]

The result of the speaking near by that is produced by the rhetorical options of violating expectations and honoring multiplicity is the creation, in messages, of "[h]ybridity, interstices, voids, intervals, in-betweenness"[178] or "an 'empty,' non-aligned, always-and-not-yet-occupied space."[179] This *"in-between-the-naming space"*[180] constitutes "a state of non-knowingness"[181] that corresponds to "'the colour of no colour' in which all colours are canceling each other out. The new hue is a distinct colour of its own, neither black nor white, but somewhere in between—*in the middle* where possibilities are boundless."[182] Trinh also describes this space as much like a "moment where suddenly everything stops; one's luggages are emptied out; and one fares in a state of non-knowingness, where the destabilizing encounters with the 'unfamiliar' or 'unknown' are multiplied and experienced anew."[183] The result of messages that create such a space for audiences is a "Void" in "which possibilities keep on renewing, hence nothing can be simply classified, arrested and reified."[184]

Transformations of Rhetorical Theory

Trinh's rhetorical theory is designed to facilitate the disruption of established systems. She seeks to challenge any dominant ideology through the use of options such as violating expectations and honoring multiplicity. Because rhetorical theory itself is a dominant, established system, Trinh's rhetorical theory is turned back on itself to question and disrupt its own ground and tradition. The result is a challenge to three fundamental rhetorical concepts: ideology, stability, and opposition.

Ideology

Many rhetorical theorists and critics analyze rhetorical texts to discover the particular ideologies they embody—the patterns or sets of ideas, assumptions, beliefs, values, and interpretations of the world reflected in the texts. They study the development, dissemination, and transformation of ideologies and the power relations embedded in them. At the end of this process of analysis, these critics usually evaluate the ideologies they discover, finding some to be better than others for various reasons. Some ideologies are found to be superior, for example, because they are more emancipatory in that they help to free individuals from particular thinking patterns, serve as better grounds for argument, or are more inclusive of multiple perspectives.

The criteria used to assess ideologies in Trinh's theory differ greatly, however, from those typically used by these theorists and critics. Trinh challenges the notion of ideology itself and sees any ideology or any single guiding schema as problematic. Some ideologies are not better than others because of the particular beliefs or values they embody; all ideologies are suspect simply because they are ideologies. Likewise, Trinh sees the rhetorical techniques used to keep ideologies in place—stereotypes, clichés, and other efforts to fix meanings—as much the same from one ideology to the next. "Good" ideologies do not involve rhetorical techniques that are somehow different from or better than those used by reputedly less noble ideologies. In Trinh's view, all ideologies and their strategies are tainted by the desire to rigidify, categorize, and stabilize, and thus ought to be challenged.

Stability

In many ways, traditional rhetorical theory is built on the notion of stability. Rhetors are encouraged to engage in critical thinking and careful research in order to adopt positions they can hold with confidence. They should hold these positions firmly and persistently, and they should develop and enhance the positions over time. From the base these stable positions provide, rhetors then can direct their efforts at defending and justifying them, further solidifying their commitment to the positions.

Rhetors' identities are presumed to have a similar kind of stability in traditional rhetorical theory. Although postmodern rhetorical theorists are challenging this stability, in classical rhetorical theory, the rhetor defines the self by the positions adopted on various issues and presents to the public a unified, coherent, definitive self created through the public articulation of positions. Waffling and contradiction in the rhetor's commitments and positions are indicative of weakness and are likely to detract substantially from the rhetor's credibility.

Rhetorical theory also manifests an ideology of stability in its privileging of clarity over ambiguity. Criteria for effective rhetoric often involve clarity, and rhetors are admonished to be precise, to define terms, and to provide sufficient context so that the meanings they evoke in audiences are relatively unambiguous and similar to the meanings they intend. The effort is again toward constancy and stability.

Trinh challenges the notion of stability in its various manifestations in rhetorical theory. She advocates disruption and ambiguity, calling for rhetoric to be open, complex, expansive, and uncertain. Trinh's rhetorical theory suggests that rhetoric should not be used as a tool for the definitive construction of positions, selves, and meanings but should instead "speak near by," approaching the object or individual to be known indirectly, from multiple perspectives, and with a refusal to settle. Similarly, rhetors should not seek to create stable identities through clear commitments and definitively held positions. Rather, they should adopt a stance of difference, opening up to others as a means of constantly questioning their own identities. Rather than a rhetoric rooted in the stability that reinforces ideologies, Trinh suggests the creation of messages that violate expectations and honor multiplicity.

Opposition

A third rhetorical construct that Trinh challenges is the oppositional or adversarial stance that characterizes much rhetorical activity. She does not believe that a rhetoric of opposition, as it is traditionally conceived, constitutes an effective means of change. Using oppositional strategies, rhetors engage a position, argue against it, and point out its flaws to attempt to create support for another position. Trinh rejects this "anti-something" stance because it keeps the rhetor confined to the ideological framework of the position that is the object of the challenge. Such a stance continues to support the original frame of reference because it refers to, engages, and accords power to that frame. Instead, Trinh suggests rhetorical options that facilitate thinking in ways that are different from what is opposed and thus do not reproduce dominant ideologies. Rhetors disrupt and transform rhetoric not by opposing a position but simply by refusing to abide by and to enact in their rhetoric the ideology inherent in that position.

Trinh's disruptions of traditional rhetorical notions create an entirely new framework for approaching rhetoric—a framework itself, of course, that she hopes will be subject to disruption and transformation in a continual process of challenging and questioning. "So where do you go from here?" Trinh asks. Her answer provides an excellent summary of the essence of her rhetorical theory and the transformation of traditional theory it requires:

> [T]ie/untie, read/unread, discard their forms; scrutinize the grammatical habits of your writing and decide for yourself whether they free or repress. Again, order(s). Shake syntax, smash the myths, and if you lose, slide on, *unearth* some new linguistic paths. Do you surprise? Do you shock? Do you have a choice?[185]

Bibliography

Books

Bourdier, Jean-Paul, and Trinh T. Minh-ha. *African Spaces: Designs for Living in Upper Volta*. New York: Africana/Holmes & Meier, 1985.

Bourdier, Jean-Paul, and Trinh T. Minh-ha. *Drawn from African Dwellings*. Bloomington: Indiana UP, 1996.

Ferguson, Russell, Martha Gever, Trinh T. Minh-ha, and Cornel West. *Out There: Marginalization and Contemporary Cultures*. New York: New Museum of Contemporary Art; Cambridge: MIT P, 1990.

Trinh T. Minh-ha. *Framer Framed*. New York: Routledge, 1992.

Trinh T. Minh-ha. *Un art sans oeuvre ou l'anonymat dans les arts contemporains*. Lathrup Village, MI: International, 1981.

Trinh T. Minh-ha. *When the Moon Waxes Red: Representation, Gender and Cultural Politics*. New York: Routledge, 1991.

Trinh T. Minh-ha. *Woman, Native, Other: Writing Postcoloniality and Feminism*. Bloomington: Indiana UP, 1989.

Articles

Bourdier, Jean-Paul, and Trinh T. Minh-ha. "The Architecture of a Lela Compound." *African Arts* 16 (1982): 68-72.

Bourdier, Jean-Paul, and Trinh T. Minh-ha. "Ko Architecture: A Case Study from Koena, Upper-Volta." *Tribus* 32 (1983): 113-25.

Bourdier, Jean-Paul, and Trinh T. Minh-ha. "Koumbili: Semi-Sunken Dwellings in Upper Volta." *African Arts* 16 (1983): 40-45, 88.

Bourdier, Jean-Paul, and Trinh T. Minh-ha. "Kusasi Dwellers and Dwellings." *Landscape* 27 (1983): 37-42.

Bourdier, Jean-Paul, and Trinh T. Minh-ha. "West African Vernacular Architecture." *Encyclopedia of Architecture, Design, Engineering and Construction.* Ed. Joseph A. Wilkes. Vol. 5. New York: John Wiley, 1988. 306-34.

Coppola, August, Carrol Blue, Joseph Camacho, and Trinh T. Minh-ha. "Film Panel." *The Arts in a Multicultural Society.* San Jose, CA: Distinguished Artists Forum, San Jose State U, 1986. 9-14.

Jayamanne, Laleen, Leslie Thornton, and Trinh T. Minh-ha. "If upon Leaving What We Have to Say We Speak: A Conversation Piece." *Discourses: Conversations in Postmodern Art and Culture.* Ed. Russell Ferguson, William Olander, Marcia Tucker, and Karen Fiss. New York: New Museum of Contemporary Art; Cambridge: MIT P, 1990. 44-66. Rpt. as "'Which Way to Political Cinema?'" *Framer Framed.* By Trinh T. Minh-ha. New York: Routledge, 1992. 243-65.

Trinh T. Minh-ha. "An Acoustic Journey." *Rethinking Borders.* Ed. John C. Welchman. Minneapolis: U of Minnesota P, 1996. 1-17.

Trinh T. Minh-ha. "All-Owning Spectatorship." *Quarterly Review of Film and Video* 13 (1991): 189-204. Rpt. in *When the Moon Waxes Red: Representation, Gender and Cultural Politics.* By Trinh T. Minh-ha. New York: Routledge, 1991. 81-105; and *Feminism and the Politics of Difference.* Ed. Sneja Gunew and Anna Yeatman. Boulder, CO: Westview, 1993. 157-76.

Trinh T. Minh-ha. "Aminata Sow Fall et l'espace du don." *Presence Africaine* 120 (1981): 70-80. Rpt. in *French Review* 55 (1982): 780-89; and (in English) as "Aminata Sow Fall and the Beggars' Gift." Trans. Elizabeth C. Wright. *When the Moon Waxes Red: Representation, Gender and Cultural Politics.* By Trinh T. Minh-ha. New York: Routledge, 1991. 169-83.

Trinh T. Minh-ha. "Black Bamboo." *CineAction!* 18 (1989): 56-60. Rpt. (expanded version) as "All-Owning Spectatorship." *Quarterly Review of Film and Video* 13 (1991): 189-204; in *When the Moon Waxes Red: Representation, Gender and Cultural Politics.* By Trinh T. Minh-ha. New York: Routledge, 1991. 81-105; and *Feminism and the Politics of Difference.* Ed. Sneja Gunew and Anna Yeatman. Boulder, CO: Westview, 1993. 157-76.

Trinh T. Minh-ha. "Bold Omissions and Minute Depictions." *Moving the Image: Independent Asian Pacific American Media Arts.* Ed. Russell Leong. Los Angeles: Asian American Studies Center and Visual Communications, U of California, 1991.

x

83-92. Rpt. in *When the Moon Waxes Red: Representation, Gender and Cultural Politics.* By Trinh T. Minh-ha. New York: Routledge, 1991. 155-66.

Trinh T. Minh-ha. "Commitment from the Mirror-Writing Box." *Making Face, Making Soul/Haciendo Caras: Creative and Critical Perspectives by Feminists of Color.* Ed. Gloria Anzaldúa. San Francisco: Aunt Lute, 1990. 245-55. Rpt. in *Women and Values: Readings in Recent Feminist Philosophy.* Ed. Marilyn Pearsall. 2nd ed. Belmont, CA: Wadsworth, 1993. 290-97; rpt. (expanded version) from *Women, Native, Other: Writing Postcoloniality and Feminism.* By Trinh T. Minh-ha. Bloomington: Indiana UP, 1989. 5-44.

Trinh T. Minh-ha. "Cotton and Iron." *Out There: Marginalization and Contemporary Cultures.* Ed. Russell Ferguson, Martha Gever, Trinh T. Minh-ha, and Cornel West. New York: New Museum of Contemporary Art; Cambridge: MIT P, 1990. 327-36. Rpt. in *When the Moon Waxes Red: Representation, Gender and Cultural Politics.* By Trinh T. Minh-ha. New York: Routledge, 1991. 11-26.

Trinh T. Minh-ha. "Critical Reflections." *Artforum* 28 (1990): 132-33.

Trinh T. Minh-ha. "Difference: A Special Third World Women Issue." *Discourse* 8 (1986-1987): 11-37. Rpt. in *Feminist Review* 25 (1987): 5-22; and (expanded version) *Woman, Native, Other: Writing Postcoloniality and Feminism.* By Trinh T. Minh-ha. Bloomington: Indiana UP, 1989. 79-116.

Trinh T. Minh-ha. "Documentary Is/Not a Name." *October* 52 (1990): 76-98. Rpt. (expanded version) as "The Totalizing Quest of Meaning." *Theorizing Documentary.* Ed. Michael Renov. New York: Routledge, 1993. 90-107; in *When the Moon Waxes Red: Representation, Gender and Cultural Politics.* By Trinh T. Minh-ha. New York: Routledge, 1991. 29-50; and *The Postmodern Arts: An Introductory Reader.* Ed. Nigel Wheale. New York: Routledge, 1995. 259-78.

Trinh T. Minh-ha. "Grandma's Story." *Blasted Allegories: An Anthology of Writings by Contemporary Artists.* Ed. Brian Wallis. New York: New Museum of Contemporary Art; Cambridge: MIT P, 1987. 2-30. Rpt. (expanded version) in *Women, Native, Other: Writing Postcoloniality and Feminism.* By Trinh T. Minh-ha. Bloomington: Indiana UP, 1989. 119-51.

Trinh T. Minh-ha. "Introduction." *Discourse* 8 (1986-87): 3-9.

Trinh T. Minh-ha. "Introduction." *Discourse* 11 (1989): 5-17.

Trinh T. Minh-ha. "The Language of Nativism: Anthropology as a Scientific Conversation of Man with Man." *American Feminist Thought at Century's End: A Reader.* Ed. Linda S. Kauffman. Oxford: Blackwell, 1993. 107-39. Rpt. from *Woman, Native, Other: Writing Postcoloniality and Feminism.* By Trinh T. Minh-ha. Bloomington: Indiana UP, 1989. 47-76.

Trinh T. Minh-ha. "L'Innecriture: Feminisme et litterature." *French Forum* 8 (1983): 45-63. Rpt. (in English) as "*L'Innecriture*: Un-Writing/Innermost Writing." Trans. Elizabeth C. Wright. *When the Moon Waxes Red: Representation, Gender and Cultural Politics.* By Trinh T. Minh-ha. New York: Routledge, 1991. 119-45.

Trinh T. Minh-ha. "Mechanical Eye, Electronic Ear and the Lure of Authenticity." *Wide Angle* 6 (1984): 58-63. Rpt. in *When the Moon Waxes Red: Representation, Gender and Cultural Politics.* By Trinh T. Minh-ha. New York: Routledge, 1991. 53-62.

Trinh T. Minh-ha. "Mother's Talk." *The Politics of (M)Othering: Womanhood, Identity, and Resistance in African Literature.* Ed. Obioma Nnaemeka. New York: Routledge, 1997. 26-32.

Trinh T. Minh-ha. "Nature's *r*: A Musical Swoon." *FutureNatural: Nature, Science, Culture.* Ed. George Robertson, Melinda Mash, Lisa Tickner, Jon Bird, Barry Curtis, and Tim Putnam. New York: Routledge, 1996. 86-104.

Trinh T. Minh-ha. "No Master Territories." *The Post-Colonial Studies Reader.* Ed. Bill Ashcroft, Gareth Griffiths, and Helen Tiffin. New York: Routledge, 1995. 215-68. Rpt. (excerpts) from "Cotton and Iron" and "Outside In Inside Out." *When the Moon Waxes Red: Representation, Gender and Cultural Politics.* By Trinh T. Minh-ha. New York: Routledge, 1991. 16-19, 73-76.

Trinh T. Minh-ha. "Not You/Like You: Post-Colonial Women and the Interlocking Questions of Identity and Difference." *Inscriptions* 3 (1988): 71-77. Rpt. in *Making Face, Making Soul/Haciendo Caras: Creative and Critical Perspectives by Feminists of Color.* Ed. Gloria Anzaldúa. San Francisco: Aunt Lute, 1990. 371-75.

Trinh T. Minh-ha. "Of Other Peoples: Beyond the 'Salvage' Paradigm." *Dia Art Foundation: Discussions in Contemporary Culture.* Ed. Hal Foster. Seattle, WA: Bay, 1987. 138-50.

Trinh T. Minh-ha. "Other Than Myself/My Other Self." *Travellers' Tales.* Ed. George Robertson, Melinda Mash, Lisa Tickner, Jon Bird, Barry Curtis, and Tim Putnam. New York: Routledge, 1994. 9-26.

Trinh T. Minh-ha. "Outside In Inside Out." *Questions of Third Cinema.* Ed. Jim Pines and Paul Willemen. London: British Film Institute, 1989. 133-49. Rpt. in *When the Moon Waxes Red: Representation, Gender and Cultural Politics.* By Trinh T. Minh-ha. New York: Routledge, 1991. 65-78.

Trinh T. Minh-ha. "Painting with Music: A Performance across Cultures." *Writings on Dance* [Australia] 13 (1995): 13-27. Rpt. in *Discourse* 18 (1996): 3-19.

Trinh T. Minh-ha. "The Plural Void: Barthes and Asia." Trans. Stanley Gray. *Sub-Stance* 36 (1982): 41-50. Rpt. in *When the Moon Waxes Red: Representation, Gender and Cultural Politics.* By Trinh T. Minh-ha. New York: Routledge, 1991. 209-22.

Trinh T. Minh-ha. "Questions of Images and Politics." *Independent* 10 (1987): 21-23. Rpt. in *When the Moon Waxes Red: Representation, Gender and Cultural Politics.* By Trinh T. Minh-ha. New York: Routledge, 1991. 147-52; and (excerpts and in Italian) as "Differenza e alterità." Trans. Liana Borghi. *Tuttestorie* 7 (1996): 39-41.

Trinh T. Minh-ha. "*Reassemblage*: Sketch of Sound Track." *Camera Obscura* 13-14 (1985): 104-11. Rpt. as "*Reassemblage*." *Framer Framed.* By Trinh T. Minh-ha. New York: Routledge, 1992. 95-105.

Trinh T. Minh-ha. "Script of *Reassemblage*" and "Script of *Naked Spaces—Living Is Round.*" *Screen Writings: Scripts and Texts by Independent Filmmakers.* Ed. Scott MacDonald. Berkeley: U of California P, 1995. 190-224.

Trinh T. Minh-ha. "*Shoot for the Contents*: A Film Script by Trinh T. Minh-ha." *Visual Anthropology Review* 8 (1992): 2-14.

Trinh T. Minh-ha. "*Surname Viet Given Name Nam.*" Resurgent: New Writing by Women. Ed. Lou Robinson and Camille Norton. Urbana: U of Illinois P, 1992.

198-208. Rpt. in *Framer Framed.* By Trinh T. Minh-ha. New York: Routledge, 1992. 49-91.

Trinh T. Minh-ha. "The Totalizing Quest of Meaning." *Theorizing Documentary.* Ed. Michael Renov. New York: Routledge, 1993. 90-107. Rpt. from *When the Moon Waxes Red: Representation, Gender and Cultural Politics.* By Trinh T. Minh-ha. New York: Routledge, 1991. 29-50; and in *The Postmodern Arts: An Introductory Reader.* Ed. Nigel Wheale. New York: Routledge, 1995. 259-78.

Trinh T. Minh-ha. "Two Statements on Film and Identity." *Inscriptions* 2 (1986): 52-53.

Trinh T. Minh-ha. "Wo/Man/Third/World." *Women and Language* 11 (1988): 6-7.

Trinh T. Minh-ha. "Writing Postcoloniality and Feminism." *The Post-Colonial Studies Reader.* Ed. Bill Ashcroft, Gareth Griffiths, and Helen Tiffin. New York: Routledge, 1995. 264-68. Rpt. (excerpts) from "Difference: 'A Third World Women Issue.'" *Woman, Native, Other: Writing Postcoloniality and Feminism.* By Trinh T. Minh-ha. Bloomington: Indiana UP, 1989. 82-90, 104.

Poetry

Trinh T. Minh-ha. "Le bain du photographe," "Nuit," "Par amour pour autrui," "Dia-monologue," "Rouge rayeé," and "Femme honnête." *Poésie 1* [Paris] 136 (1987): 71-76.

Trinh T. Minh-ha. *En minuscules.* Paris: Le Meridien Editeur, 1987.

Trinh T. Minh-ha. "For Love of Another" and "Silent Witness." *Aperture* 112 (1988): 62-63.

Trinh T. Minh-ha. "For Love of Another," "Refugee," and "Flying Blind." *City Light Review* 4 (1990): 142-44.

Trinh, Minh-ha. "A Rainy Day" and "Scent of Musk." *Premonitions: The Kaya Anthology of New Asian North American Poetry.* Ed. Walter K. Lew. New York: Kaya, 1995. 298-301.

Trinh T. Minh-ha. "With Curse, or Love," "Ecstasied," "A Rainy Day," "Looking at the Dream Screen," "Know by Heart," "Scent of Musk," "Casual Letter," "To Myself I Say," and "This Body." *Uncontrollable Bodies: Testimonies of Identity and Culture.* Ed. Rodney Sappington and Tyler Stallings. Seattle: Bay, 1994. 63-76.

Trinh T. Minh-ha. "Poems," "Wordwarring," "Little Death," "For a Show," and "That Voice." *Crash: Nostalgia for the Absence of Cyberspace.* Ed. Robert Reynolds and Thomas Zummer. New York: Thread Waxing Space, 1994. 119-20.

Films

Trinh T. Minh-ha. *Naked Spaces—Living Is Round.* Museum of Modern Art, Women Make Movies, Cinenova, Idera, National Library of Australia Film and Video Collection, 1985.

Trinh T. Minh-ha. *Reassemblage.* Women Make Movies, Third World Newsreel, Museum of Modern Art, Idera, Cinenova, Lightcone, Image Forum, 1982.

Trinh T. Minh-ha. *Shoot for the Contents.* Women Make Movies, Idera, Image Forum, Cinenova, 1991.
Trinh T. Minh-ha. *Surname Viet Given Name Nam.* Women Make Movies, Museum of Modern Art, Cinenova, Idera, Image Forum, National Library of Australia Film and Video Lending Collection, 1989.
Trinh T. Minh-ha. *A Tale of Love.* Women Make Movies, 1995.

Music

Trinh T. Minh-ha. *Four Pieces for Electronic Music.* 1975.
Trinh T. Minh-ha. *Poems.* 1976.

Interviews

Barringer, Tessa, Linda Tyler, Sarah Williams, and Toroa Pohatu. "Strategies of Displacement for Women, Natives and Their Others: Intra-views with Trinh T. Minh-ha." *Women's Studies Journal* [New Zealand] 10 (1994): 5-25.
Chen, Nancy N. "'Speaking Nearby': A Conversation with Trinh T. Minh-ha." *Visual Anthropology Review* 8 (1992): 82-91. Rpt. in *Visualizing Theory.* Ed. Lucien Taylor. New York: Routledge, 1994. 433-51.
Falkenberg, Pam. "Trinh T. Minh-ha: Interviewed by Pam Falkenberg: October 31, 1989." *Affirmative Actions: Recognizing a Cross-Cultural Practice in Contemporary Art.* Ed. Jeanne Dunning. Chicago: School of the Art Institute of Chicago, 1990. 13-19.
Hawkins, Kim. "Trinh T. Minh-ha's Fiction within a Fiction." *Film/Tape World* 8 (1995): 13-15.
Hirshorn, Harriet A. "Interview: Harriet A. Hirshorn and Trinh T. Minh-ha." *Heresies* 22 (1987): 14-17. Rpt. as "Questioning Truth and Fact." *Framer Framed.* By Trinh T. Minh-ha. New York: Routledge, 1992. 181-87.
Hulser, Kathleen. "Ways of Seeing Senegal: Interview with Trinh T. Minh-ha." *Independent* 6 (1983): 16-18.
Jamayane, Laleen, and Anne Rutherford. "Why a Fish Pond? An Interview with Trinh T. Minh-ha." *Independent* 14 (1991): 20-25. Rpt. as "'Why a Fish Pond?': Fiction at the Heart of Documentation." *Framer Framed.* By Trinh T. Minh-ha. New York: Routledge, 1992. 161-78.
Julien, Isaac, and Laura Mulvey. "'Who Is Speaking?': Of Nation, Community, and First-Person Interviews." *Feminism and Tradition in Aesthetics.* Ed. Peggy Zeglin Brand and Carolyn Korsmeyer. University Park: Pennsylvania State UP, 1995. 193-214. Rpt. from "'Who Is Speaking?': Of Nation, Community and First Person Interviews." *Framer Framed.* By Trinh T. Minh-ha. New York: Routledge, 1992. 191-210; and in *Feminisms in the Cinema.* Ed. Laura Pietropaolo and Ada Testaferri. Bloomington: Indiana UP, 1995. 41-59.
Liao, Hsien-hao et al. "Surname Viet, Given Name Nam, or/and Surname Nu, Given Name Ren: An Interview with the Vietnamese American Independent Film Maker

Trinh T. Minh-ha." *Chung-Wai Literary Monthly* [National Taiwan U] 22 (1994): 6-21.

MacDonald, Scott. "Trinh T. Minh-ha." *A Critical Cinema 2: Interviews with Independent Filmmakers.* Ed. Scott MacDonald. Berkeley: U of California P, 1992. 355-77. Rpt. as "Film as Translation: A Net with No Fisherman." *Framer Framed.* By Trinh T. Minh-ha. New York: Routledge, 1992. 111-33.

Mayne, Judith. "Feminism, Filmmaking and Postcolonialism: An Interview with Trinh T. Minh-ha." *Feminisms* [Women's Studies, Ohio State University] 3.5 (1990): 3-6 (Part 1) and 3.6 (1990): 3-6 (Part 2). Rpt. as "From a Hybrid Place: An Interview with Trinh T. Minh-ha." *Afterimage* 16 (1990): 6-9B; and as "From a Hybrid Place." *Framer Framed.* By Trinh T. Minh-ha. New York: Routledge, 1992. 137-48.

Morelli, Annamaria. "The Undone Interval: Trinh T. Minh-ha in Conversation with Annamaria Morelli." *The Post-Colonial Question: Common Skies, Divided Horizons.* Ed. Iain Chambers and Lidia Curti. New York: Routledge, 1996. 3-16.

Parmar, Pratibha. "Woman, Native, Other: Pratibha Parmar Interviews Trinh T. Minh-ha." *Feminist Review* [London] 36 (1990): 65-74. Rpt. as "Between Theory and Poetry." *Framer Framed.* By Trinh T. Minh-ha. New York: Routledge, 1992. 151-59.

Penley, Constance, and Andrew Ross. "Interview with Trinh T. Minh-ha." *Camera Obscura* 13/14 (1985): 87-103. Rpt. as "When I Project It Is Silent." *Framer Framed.* By Trinh T. Minh-ha. New York: Routledge, 1992. 225-40.

Reynaud, Berenice. "Trinh T. Minh-ha: At the Edge." *Cinemaya* [New Delhi, India] 25/26 (1994-95): 28-29.

Stephenson, Rob. "Interview with Trinh T. Minh-ha." *Millennium Film Journal* 19 (1987-88): 122-29. Rpt. (shortened version) as "Professional Censorship." *Framer Framed.* By Trinh T. Minh-ha. New York: Routledge, 1992. 213-21.

CHAPTER 10

Sally Miller Gearhart

Every now and again I get overwhelmed by the significance of the times I am living in. I have been waiting, it seems, all my life . . . for the movement that is now happening among women, for the birth of the womanpower that is presently on the rise. . . . [H]istory needs now the different energy that . . . conscious women can bring to it.[1]

With this statement, Sally Miller Gearhart captures the essence of her life and work. She seeks to ensure the survival of the planet, with its incredible diversity of life forms, through the communicative gifts and energy typically associated with feminist women.

Gearhart grew up in an environment that taught her that women "are the source of power, the heart of the action, the focal point of love."[2] She was born on April 15, 1931, in Pearisburg, Virginia, to Sarah Miller Gearhart and Kyle Montague Gearhart. Her parents' divorce when she was two years old intro-

NOTE: Excerpts from "Notes from a Recovering Activist," by Sally Miller Gearhart, are reprinted from *Sojourner: The Women's Forum,* vol. 21, no. 1, September 1995, with permission from the Sojourner Feminist Institute. Excerpts from "The Womanization of Rhetoric," by Sally Miller Gearhart, are reprinted from *Women's Studies International Quarterly,* vol. 2, pp. 195-201, 1979, with permission from Elsevier Science.

duced her to a world of women; she lived with her mother in a rooming house for women in Richmond, Virginia, where her mother was able to find work as a stenographer. When she reached school age, she returned to Pearisburg to live with her grandmother, another living situation that enabled her to witness and experience the friendship and support of women. "The text of my childhood," explains Gearhart, "was the patriarchal one":

> [M]en are the more important sex; they have the information, the skills, the tools, the opportunities, and the say-so; women participate in knowledge and power only through men. . . . Yet the unspoken message of my days, the subtext of my child-hood, was a different one: *Men do not matter.* No voice spoke those words, no headline announced it, no sermon suggested it. The women who surrounded me simply lived their lives as if men were, though occasionally nice or sometimes interesting, basically insignificant.[3]

Gearhart suggests that her "joy and pride in loving other women was at least in part a legacy" passed on to her by the women of her family and community.[4]

Gearhart attended Sweet Briar College, a women's college near Lynchburg, Virginia, where she earned a B.A. in drama and English in 1952. Her decision to be a college teacher led her to the completion of an M.A. degree in theater and public address at Bowling Green State University in Bowling Green, Ohio, in 1953. This was followed by a Ph.D. in theater, with minors in rhetoric and philosophy, at the University of Illinois in Urbana, completed in 1956. Gearhart spent the next 14 years teaching theater and speech at Stephen F. Austin State College in Nacogdoches, Texas (1956-59); MacMurray College in Jacksonville, Illinois (1959-60); and Texas Lutheran College in Seguin, Texas (1960-70).

Two equally influential forces characterized Gearhart's years in Texas and Illinois: her commitment to the Christian religion and her lesbianism. Gearhart considers the church (Methodist and Lutheran) to have been the greatest single institutional influence on her life, although looking back on the experience, she discovered her commitment was not total: "I was never able to make the leap, to give myself over to the Christian faith."[5] Because her lesbianism contradicted the tenets of her Christian faith, she led two lives—that of the popular and successful professor of speech, debate, and theater and that of the closeted lesbian, a life shared only with a few trusted friends. She hid the fact that she was a lesbian by dating gay men (also closeted) and by engaging in activities that perpetuated the stereotypes of femininity, such as sponsoring sororities, hosting teas for faculty women, directing homecoming pageants, and judging Miss Texas contests.

In the late 1960s, Gearhart began a series of dramatic changes that she later recognized as her conversion to feminism. In 1968, she immersed herself in sensitivity training and group-encounter techniques at the Western Behavioral

Sciences Institute in La Jolla, California, emerging "completely drained" of her "authoritarian ideas."[6] The following year, during her first sabbatical, she was studying philosophy at the University of Kansas in Lawrence when the killing of students on the Kent State University campus and antiwar sentiment began transforming the academy. She saw police officers beat students during protests and "realized that police weren't always the nice folks that help you across the street, that they can be an arm of an established fascist order."[7]

A summer spent doing consciousness-raising with friends completed the conversion: "I really had been trying to see the world in these patriarchal, Churchly terms and I realized that the whole bloody Church was built on women's oppression. *That* revelation bowled me over."[8] In addressing these issues, Gearhart found herself "smack in the middle of women's liberation and feeling very close to everybody who wanted to turn this system over."[9] Although she had failed to convert to Christianity, she *had* converted unquestionably to feminism: "I've been waiting for the women's movement all my life! I've known since I was a teenager, or even younger, that my primary emotional, intellectual, and erotic feelings were toward other women. But I never got to put it together until the women's movement came along."[10]

In the fall of 1970, Gearhart gave up her professional life in Texas and moved to San Francisco "in a lather of enthusiasm about liberation."[11] She supported herself during her first years in California by teaching part-time at six Bay Area colleges and universities and with the small fees she was paid for speaking on feminism and lesbianism in high school and college classes and at various conferences. In 1973, she was hired as a full-time lecturer in the Speech Communication Department at San Francisco State University; in 1975, she secured a tenure-track position there. She was awarded tenure in 1978 and taught at San Francisco State University until her retirement in 1992. During these years of teaching, Gearhart cofounded a B.A. program in women studies and helped to create and teach the first university course in the nation on sex roles and communication in 1972. At various times, she also served as chair of the Speech Communication Department, associate dean of the School of Humanities, and coordinator of the Women Studies Program.

Gearhart's work in academia was accompanied always by her efforts to transform society. As an activist, she worked on behalf of a number of causes: "In my time I've taken to the streets for feminism, lesbian/gay/bisexual pride, civil rights, sexual freedom, disability dignity, AIDS education, peace, jobs, justice, nonhuman animals, Central American solidarity, clean air, Jesse Jackson, the constitution, the redwoods, and the union."[12] Gearhart's activism has included, as well, participation in civic organizations such as the Council on Religion and the Homosexual, the San Francisco Women's Building, the San Francisco Mental Health Association, the Family Service Agency, and the Feminist Speaker's Network. "I am left with the profound sense that my life has been a gift," Gearhart explains, "and that I have been privileged to participate in a movement, in several movements, that are changing the very character of this society."[13]

One of Gearhart's best-known contributions as an activist was her statewide participation in the campaign to defeat Proposition 6, a ballot measure introduced by State Senator John Briggs in 1978 that would have given public schools in California the authority to fire any person who was a homosexual or who supported homosexuality. With Harvey Milk, the first openly gay supervisor in San Francisco, Gearhart stumped the state, speaking against the measure. Milk and Mayor George Moscone were assassinated later that year by former supervisor Dan White, an event recounted in the Academy Award-winning film *The Times of Harvey Milk* (1984), which chronicles Milk's life and features remembrances and commentary by Gearhart.

Gearhart's writings cross diverse genres and cover a range of topics. Her early works deal with religion and spirituality, particularly as they intersect with women, feminism, and lesbian/gay identities. Representative is her book *Loving Women/Loving Men: Gay Liberation and the Church* (1974), coedited with William R. Johnson. Other publications in which she assesses the Christian church from a lesbian/feminist perspective include "She Who Hath Ears" (1972) and "The Lesbian and God-the-Father" (1975). With her withdrawal from the institutional church, Gearhart turned to themes of spirituality in her writings, particularly as spirituality is defined and enacted by women. Representative is *A Feminist Tarot* (1976), coauthored with Susan Rennie, a recovery of the tarot from its traditional masculinist bias.

Gearhart often has contributed through her writing to the movements in which she has been involved, frequently bringing her knowledge of communication to bear on her subjects. By far the largest category of such work integrates her knowledge of communication with a feminist perspective. The best known of these is "The Womanization of Rhetoric" (1979), first prepared as a speech in 1975, in which Gearhart suggests that any attempt to persuade is an act of violence. "Syzygoty, Diasporady and Amoebeity" (1970) and "The Sword-and-the-Vessel versus the Lake-on-the-Lake: A Lesbian Model of Nonviolent Rhetoric" (1980), coauthored with Jane Gurko, are other examples of such work.

Gearhart's writing also includes fiction in the form of novels and short stories. She had not done any fiction writing until 1973, when she went into a mild trance and emerged with a short story, "Red Waters." About a year later, she explains, "something tripped inside me, and about five . . . stories all came out at once, just *chchcheww*. After that, it was almost as if I were pushed to sit down and write them."[14] The result was *The Wanderground: Stories of the Hill Women* (1978), a collection of stories about a group of women with psychic powers who have fled a violent, patriarchal, urban way of life to live in the hills in harmony with nature and with one another. Other fiction works followed, including short stories such as "Roxy Raccoon" (1988), "Flossie's Flashes" (1989), "Roja and Leopold" (1990), and "The Chipko" (1988), published in feminist and/or lesbian anthologies, journals, and magazines.

Gearhart believes that speculative or utopian fiction provides an opportunity for women to experiment with alternative conceptions of themselves and their place in the universe; thus, fantasy is "one of the first steps in political action."[15] But fantasy has acquired an even more important function for Gearhart:

> Fantasy fiction is in itself a part of the act of creating material reality. As the thoughts become words, they describe specific circumstances that do not presently exist. As more people believe in the fantasy—pay attention to it, give energy to it—it materializes or becomes reality. *Star Trek* is a good example of how this happens.[16]

At home in Willits, California, Gearhart writes feminist fiction, sings in a lesbian barbershop quartet, studies tai chi chuan and yoga, and spends time with the animals who share the forest around her. She continues to struggle to gain freedom for herself and to allow others the freedom to live their lives as they choose. She seeks to overturn a system rooted in values and characterized by practices that deny this freedom and self-determination: "I can't find the words for how important I think it is that all of us begin to come to some kind of consciousness of the way that we don't allow each other to *be,* in free ways. And it's that struggle that I spend my life engaged in."[17]

Nature of the World

The primary concern that motivates Gearhart's work is the survival of planet Earth. The women in *The Wanderground* participate in a ritual chant that summarizes the task Gearhart sees for herself and other rhetors: *"To work as if the earth, the mother, can be saved. To work as if our healing care were not too late."*[18] For Gearhart, the condition of the world that prompts her to action is clear: "The earth seems now to be giving us clear and unmistakable signals that she will not endure our rule over her much longer, that we are a renegade civilization, a dying civilization which may have passed up its opportunity for survival."[19] Gearhart elaborates on the idea that efforts to save the planet "may be too late." Human beings, she suggests, may have to "admit that we blew it and to take up our tents and silently steal away, completely out of the universe. . . . Then maybe with us gone from the earth, the earth can be restored to its life, to sustaining its natural cycles."[20]

The intensifying crisis of survival that affects the Earth is, in Gearhart's eyes, the result of a number of dangerous assumptions on which Western civilization has been built. Primary among them is the assumption that the "stronger always has the greater possibility of subduing the weaker."[21] Technology clearly manifests this assumption, for the bigger or more widespread the scientific or technological enterprise, the better it is believed to be. If, for example, "British and U.S. meat interests have the know-how and the political acumen to secure and clear-cut the Brazilian jungle for the raising of cattle, then surely the task must be theirs to do, a sort of manifest destiny." "At the heart of man's dominance of the earth and at the heart of all cultural invasion," asserts Gearhart, "lies the precept, 'might makes right.'"[22]

A second assumption that has contributed to the current global crisis is that if something is possible, it must be done. This axiom "can be alternatively stated, 'Any knowledge is virtuous and any step in its acquisition is thus wholly justified.'"[23] As a result of the worship of knowledge suggested in this assumption, technology takes on a life of its own, resulting in such consequences as nuclear waste, germ warfare, pesticides, pollution, and caged and tortured laboratory animals.

A third assumption that feeds the destruction of the planet is that anything done in the service of humankind is praiseworthy and even necessary. When climates change or food is short, other animals adapt or migrate. In contrast, human beings "change the landscape, the weather, and the planet itself to suit" their needs. As Gearhart explains, "*We* are not the adaptable species; we are the species that makes all else adapt to us."[24] Adherence to this axiom also enhances the conception of the human being as "the Crown of Creation, the top of the food chain, the species greater than which there [is] no other."[25] Consequently, Gearhart explains, we "see our needs, rights, and destinies as different from that of plants and other animals without understanding our dependence on them for our very lives and without the slightest acknowledgment that they might have worth equal to our own."[26]

A fourth assumption—that differences must be assigned some virtue or blame—is also a contributing factor to the destruction of the planet. Undergirding Western culture is the tenet that "simple differences between/among people are understood to have better-or-worse values."[27] Furthermore, evaluation is seen as natural and necessary: "It does not often occur to us that opposites might co-exist without an up/down relation."[28] The mind-set that accompanies this assumption is one of dominance and power-over that suggests "that all our lives there will be those above us and those below us, and that our task in life is to climb above more people than we allow to climb above us."[29]

A final axiom that is responsible for the current condition of the Earth is the notion that entities are separate from one another. A sense of connection with all other living beings would prevent exploitative ways of thinking and acting that now are seen as natural and normal:

> In my own experience, when I float down a river, I can feel myself to be a part of it and I relate to that river out of that feeling. But once I see myself apart from the

water . . . my relationship to the river becomes vastly changed. I find myself so much different from it that I can even consider damming it up, controlling it for my own purposes.[30]

The sense of separation fostered in this assumption also engenders violence because, as Gearhart explains, thinking "of myself as separate from another entity makes it possible for me to 'do to' that entity things I would not 'do to' myself."[31] A feeling of connection with other entities, in contrast, has clear consequences for her actions: "I will move around this world with lots less pushiness and lots more care; I might adopt a more respectful nurturing attitude toward the world, wishing all things health and longevity."[32]

Gearhart locates the origin of the axioms responsible for the current condition of the planet Earth and the disastrous consequences they have produced in patriarchy, or what she calls *malekind*. Gearhart asserts, "For me, the exercise of these assumptions on the part of male knowledge and male power is sufficient to indict the male of our species as the source of violence."[33] She suggests that malekind is characterized by competitiveness; authority-worship; an admiration for one person's power over another; an overemphasis on logic, objectivity, product, structure, and judgment; and a worship of the mind to the exclusion of the body.[34] What is missing from and what accounts for the dangerous consequences of patriarchy is, simply, "womanness and woman values"—the practices and values typically associated in Western culture with women.[35] Patriarchy simply does not allow for the expression of values such as nonviolence, cooperation, nurturance, compassion, and respect.

Gearhart's solution to the excesses of malekind is simply stated: If "the world is to move away from the escalating violence that shapes all of our lives, then the affairs of the world, and of the human species specifically, must be placed in the hands of women."[36] Gearhart sees "the rising up of women in this century to be the human race's response to the threat of its own self-annihilation and the destruction of the planet. In small ways, in big ways, it seems up to the world's women to take back their responsibilities as life-givers and sustainers."[37] "EITHER THE FUTURE IS FEMALE OR THE FUTURE IS NOT," asserts Gearhart.[38]

Definition of Feminism

For Gearhart, the values traditionally associated with women are needed to overturn the existing system and to ensure the survival of the planet. Not surprising, then, is that she sees feminism as the most fundamental of all liberation movements. Although she seeks liberation for all human beings, she begins with women:

Liberation is from domination, and the domination of women is the most fundamental of all domination. All other forms of exploitation spring from this pattern. This is not to say that a white middle-class woman has a rougher time of it than the male Chicano farm laborer. It is to say that the fundamental meaning of subjugation, of power over any person, has its clearest and earliest expression in the roles that women (and thus men) have been trapped in.[39]

Gearhart defines feminism as an ideology of change—"a revolt against the efforts of the dominant culture to alienate life from itself and to destroy life."[40] It is "a source, a wellspring, a matrix, an environment for the womanization . . . of Western civilization."[41] Gearhart's definition of feminism expands the movement beyond women: Feminism seeks to correct the oppression of all beings and involves a connection with the suffering of all others "so that together we can make it all stop." It is a joining of hands "to alter reality."[42]

Key to Gearhart's conception of feminism is a goal of liberation rather than an attainment of rights. Working for rights involves working to achieve justice within a system—securing a "slice of the pie." But the system is competitive and exploitative—it "is *poisonous*"—and "eating that pie will be just as disastrous in the future as going hungry for lack of it is today."[43] Simply to achieve equality within the system, for Gearhart, means participating "in a way of thinking and acting that's harmful to women, men, children and other living things."[44] In contrast, liberation involves destruction of the system; it constitutes "the effort to undermine and destroy the entire system of power-over other human beings."[45] Feminism, then, is the means to transform an unhealthy and dangerous system of domination into one that is life affirming and nurturing.

Nature of the Rhetor

For Gearhart, the ideal change agents—the ones who are most able to carry out the work of saving the planet—are women. Not all women are able to work as change agents in the way Gearhart envisions, however; the women who are Gearhart's agents are those who give their energy to women. For Gearhart, the more accurate term for the kind of woman who functions as a change agent is *lesbian,* a term with a specific definition for Gearhart.

The distinguishing characteristic of the lesbian for Gearhart is not the conventional one—a woman who has sexual relationships with women. Gearhart does not believe that expression of sexuality can or should be used to draw the line between lesbians and other women: "A number of women are 'trying sex' with other women these days; that's clearly not lesbianism. Contrarily, a number of women who have identified themselves as lesbians for years have never experienced a sexual relationship with another woman."[46] She also rejects the traditional definition of lesbianism because it describes lesbians in an interpersonal way—in terms of their relationships to others. "It's time," Gearhart asserts, that we defined ourselves "less in *inter*personal terms" and began thinking of ourselves "in ways that say who *we* are, not who our friends/lovers are."[47]

In an *intra*personal definition, lesbianism is characterized by two primary qualities. First, a lesbian is self-reliant. She *"is a woman who seeks her own self-nurturance."*[48] As Gearhart explains, "To be a lesbian is to be identified not by men or by a society made by men, but by me, by a woman . . . identified by/for me, by/for my own experience, by/for my own values."[49] Second, lesbianism is distinguished by self-love and a love for other women. In "a woman-hating society, one that teaches women to hate each other and to hate themselves," this dimension constitutes a miracle.[50] For Gearhart, then, any "woman who seriously moves toward" self-reliance, "toward self-love, toward woman-love," approaches "the lesbian lifestyle and political posture."[51] If she truly is woman identified, "she'll feel good about being called a lesbian, whether or not she's had any sexual relationship with another woman."[52]

The term *feminist* captures Gearhart's definition of the woman/lesbian who has the capacity to overturn the system and thus constitutes the rhetor she conceptualizes. The feminist rhetor is woman identified, offers her energy to women, loves herself and other women, and seeks self-reliance. With this mind-set, she possesses the requisite consciousness necessary to see the damaging effects of the current structure and to commit to its destruction. The world, asserts Gearhart, should be in the hands of just such feminist women.

Gearhart equivocates on the question of whether the qualities of the feminist women she sees as rhetors are essential qualities, socially constructed, or both. In some of her works, Gearhart notes that inherent qualities make women better suited than men to run the world:

> But if by believing that women are by nature less violent we reinforce the sex roles that have held women down for so long, then perhaps it is time to dare to admit that some of the sex-role mythology is in fact true and to insist that the qualities attributed to women (specifically empathy, nurturance and cooperativeness) be affirmed as human qualities capable of cultivation by men even if denied them by nature.[53]

Gearhart's view of essential qualities in women and men explains, in part, her reluctance to include gay men in her vision of the rhetor. Although she recognizes that the "gay man receives his share of society's misogyny"[54] and acknowledges that she has "gained a lot of deep friendships, affection, and respect for a lot of gay men,"[55] she believes that the sexual model that lies at the heart of much gay interaction reinforces and perpetuates—rather than challenges—the current system. The fixation of gay culture "upon the phallus—its size, its hardness, its performance"[56]—establishes a model of power-over, the model responsible for the destruction of humans and of the entire environment. As a result, gay liberation is largely unable to disrupt attitudes and activities of power-over, violence, domination, and oppression.

In some works, Gearhart sees feminist women's qualities as the result of sex-role socialization and chooses nurture over nature as the origin of their superior qualifications for leading the movement to save the planet. Sex-role socialization practices program "male people into patterns of creativity, rationality, independence, violence, objectivity, dominance, toughness, action, adventurousness and competition," whereas they program female people "into patterns of receptivity, irrationality, dependence, nurturance, subjectivity, submission, gentleness, passivity, domesticity and cooperation."[57] From this perspective, what is needed, as feminist women assume responsibility for the future, is that "women and men alike each find and affirm in themselves the non-male qualities, the neglected or devalued female body-ness that affirms [their] belonging to this planet."[58] Men "who have longed to touch the truly feminine parts of their psyches, who are not afraid to give up competing, profit, authority, possessing, power, and governing others, men who are not afraid to cry or yield or be silent" will be able, Gearhart believes, to participate as feminists in the redemption of the Earth.[59]

In yet other works, Gearhart's view of feminist women is somewhere between nature and nurture, with their qualities "both biological in [their] foundation and cultural in [their] enhancement."[60] She explains this position: "Even after decades of feminist research we do not know for sure about the nature of female and male people—whether or not the male is 'naturally' violent, the female 'naturally' nurturant—and we are not likely, while sex roles still exist, to ascertain anything in this regard."[61] Although unable to resolve the question of the origin of the feminist woman's characteristics, Gearhart concludes:

> [T]he last ten thousand years of global patriarchy have given us a vivid and grim idea of what happens when men are in charge. . . . [A]s a species and as a global village we have nothing to lose and everything to gain by reversing the present power circumstances and returning to women the fundamental responsibility for human affairs.[62]

Gearhart recognizes that she discusses the rhetor as a monolithic construct that assumes that all feminist women are very much alike. She acknowledges that major differences exist among feminist women that must be taken into account and addressed if feminism is to be successful in overturning the current system. These "divisions among women . . . that are really keeping us apart"[63] include not only the traditionally recognized ones of race, class, and age but also ones that often are overlooked, including our vast unconscious functions, our astrological differences, our differences in "cognitive style" (are we linear, wholistic, either, or both, in our learning, in our communication?), our differences in physical body (are we fat, tall, disabled, "butchy"), in psychological type (as in Jung's extrovert/introvert, thinking/feeling, sensation/intuitive combinations).[64]

Gearhart acknowledges that her own view of the feminist woman she names as the rhetor is affected by differences—including her privilege—that separate her from others:

As a lesbian feminist I commit myself to the hearing of the voices of women the world over, women who remind me that I am very lucky to have the time and the money to explore my psychological realities, women who remind me that I'd probably not have that privilege if they weren't picking bananas for twenty-five cents a day or scrubbing floors in my Aunt Helen's house for less than a subsistence wage. They remind me constantly that at the hands of U.S. imperialism *they* are paying a heavy price for *my* self-love.[65]

In response to this awareness, Gearhart resolves, "As a lesbian feminist the least I can do—the least, in fact, any of us can do—is to carry in our very bones the consciousness of the cost in blood and pain and death of our personal growth and freedom."[66]

Rhetorical Options

Gearhart's rhetorical theory is closely linked to her goal of overturning a system that is destroying the Earth and creating, in its place, a system that is life affirming and sustaining. Because transformation is the goal toward which Gearhart works, the central question underlying her rhetorical theory is, "How does it happen that people change their values, their attitudes, their behaviors?"[67] She elaborates:

Maybe the thing that's really important to me is that people do and can change. And the changes that I've gone through in my own life become an example of the way I think that it can happen. If I was who I was ten years ago, and now have changed to the point that I really feel like a rebel against so much of that, then it seems to me that there's hope for the rest of us.[68]

Gearhart initially suggested that four rhetorical options are available for transforming society: revolutionary action against the system, participation in alternative organizations, reform within the system, and re-sourcement. She later developed a fifth rhetorical option—enfoldment—designed primarily to create understanding and, in the process, possibly to transform society.

Revolutionary Action

One option available for feminists is political organizing aimed at revolution. This option involves the kinds of activities often associated with the New Left and antiwar movements of the late 1960s—acts such as bombings, kidnappings, sit-ins, and other disruptions of institutions. Feminist rhetors who are unable to commit the violence typically regarded as revolutionary action may engage in limited forms of this kind of action, such as spraying "some 3:00 A.M. graffiti on the ROTC's armory."[69] Revolutionary action is problematic in that it is antithetical to the values and principles of feminism and because many of the groups that engage in such activities are, themselves, sexist. As Gearhart explains, feminists who select this option often find themselves "struggling in vain" against their "brothers' (and sisters') rampant sexism" until their zeal winds "itself into a tight little ball of counterproductive rage."[70]

Alternative Organizations

A second rhetorical option Gearhart identifies is work with organizations that provide alternatives to the system, such as alternative health collectives and alternative schools. Many feminists do not have the money and time to devote to these organizations, however, because participation in them often does not provide the means for making a living. Such organizations also may be co-opted easily, especially if they become successful. Success often brings grants from mainstream foundations, and this encourages organizations to adhere to the dictates of their supporting foundations in order to preserve their funding. The organizations thus become institutions, losing sight of the needs of the people for whom they were created. Gearhart summarizes the fate of many alternative organizations with a representative anecdote: When feminists put their "energy into the alternative high school, it worked so well that the city paper wrote it up and Ford bought it with a grant."[71]

Reform within the System

A third option for social change is to work within an institution "for the sake of reforming the institution itself."[72] With this option, rhetors attempt to gain power within an institution in order to change it and make it work for them. This option is not technically a feminist action for Gearhart, however, because she defines as feminist efforts aimed at transforming a system or institution, not simply reforming it. Because reform is, in fact, the activity in which most feminist women find themselves involved and because it can serve functions that are congenial with feminism, Gearhart includes it as a rhetorical option.

Gearhart acknowledges that rhetors may opt to work for reform within a system or institution for a number of legitimate reasons. They may choose to try to reform an institution from within simply because they "have skills that the system will pay for" and "may find fulfillment in using those skills."[73] Work within an institution also allows feminist women rhetors to learn skills that will help them survive in a man's world—skills that they can put to use "for the protection and survival of other women" as well as themselves.[74] Still others may choose to try to reform organizations from within because they enjoy working with the other women employed there: "It is good to be working with women. Period."[75]

For rhetors who select the option of trying to reform an institution, the dangers are many. Work within an institution—such as a corporation or a university—may inspire unwarranted hope in the system; individuals may falsely believe, for example, that "if Goldenrod College hired a radical feminist, it must not be so bad."[76] Another difficulty is the "persistent energy drain" such work requires for rhetors, not only to themselves "but possibly to the women who love and support" them "outside the workplace."[77] The separation of feminist women rhetors from other women within and outside of the institution is another potential danger of reform from within. If they are working in a university, for example, feminists may discover that they are separated from other feminists in "privilege and prestige as well as in salary."[78] They are forced to separate themselves simply because of the nature of their positions: They separate from "the clerical staff whose lives, thought, and typing [they] will be called upon to judge" but also from their women colleagues who are supposed to sharpen their claws . . . in the time-honored tradition of competition and the 'adversary mentality.'"[79]

The greatest danger of reform for rhetors, however, lies in their inevitable co-optation by the institutions they seek to change. The more rhetors gain positions of power within institutions, the more inclined they are to forget that the very nature of the institutions is dedicated to their "self-hatred and submission."[80] As Gearhart asks, "If we are participating in the oppressive structure is there anything that can keep us—in our heads and in our behavior—from becoming a part of the enemy?"[81] Any resistance that reform rhetors offer to the system is channeled into and contained by a "subtle and insidious identification with the system."[82] Gearhart explains the process:

> If we are really making noises that cannot be ignored, and if the [institution] really senses that we are dangerous, our rebelliousness may become a matter of concern. . . . And so as individuals, we are separated out and awarded a crumb of power, for which we are expected to be undyingly grateful. . . . Whatever the crumb, our energy is now successfully channelled. We are adorned with garlands of red tape; we can be carefully watched. We can do less harm to the institution. We are . . . *conquered* (subdued, quieted, co-opted, tokenized, shut-up).[83]

Gearhart offers advice to rhetors who choose to work within institutions in an effort to reform the system. Such rhetors, she suggests, need to be willing to risk and to know when to risk: "We need to be prepared every minute to say or do whatever outrageous thing is necessary with the full knowledge that we may well lose money, position, or prestige. . . . More important, we have to know . . . that when we choose *not* to challenge the situation, then it is out of *wisdom* and not out of *fear* that we make that choice."[84]

Gearhart urges rhetors within institutions to "make clear that their own personal politics are not those" of the institution and to "support the institution as little as possible except where [they] feel it can be changed into a healthier place."[85] She suggests that feminists choose at least one small area where they consistently and relentlessly resist the institution's values. Such efforts might involve working for raises for secretaries, taking a stand against the experimental or educational use of animals in research, or working to establish and support a child-care center in the institution.

The work of reform also can be furthered through the creation of strong support systems with other feminist rhetors. Feminist rhetors seeking change within a system, Gearhart suggests, need other feminists to work with them, "all of them meeting regularly together, formulating strategies, making evaluations, praising and criticizing . . . holding and caring together."[86] Developing support systems also may take the form of establishing coalitions with other oppressed groups within the institution.

At the heart of Gearhart's recommendations is the maintenance of a feminist consciousness, which requires that rhetors be aware of what they are doing while they are doing it, "sustaining a constant state of reflection" upon their actions "even while those actions are going on."[87] Feminists who select the option of reform within the system must understand "that transformation of the system will come from another source . . . it will not come from the institution itself."[88] The important thing, then, is for rhetors working within a system to ask each day: "[D]o I understand how this system is using me? And can I commit myself every morning of the world to the ultimate destruction of that system?"[89] As a part of the daily assessment of the state of their commitment, rhetors must know that they "can and will at any given time disengage from the institution." They have "to be able to say: 'I can walk away from you, Goldenrod State College, and never come back. I give you my energy because I choose to and today may be our last day together.'"[90] "Every day," Gearhart asserts, "leaving must be seen as an option; and every day the price of our staying and the price of our leaving must be calculated."[91]

Re-Sourcement

Gearhart's fourth option for social change is re-sourcement, the transformation of the current system through a collective sharing of re-sourced or healing energy among feminist women. This option allows for the enactment of new values, new ways of understanding, and new ways of viewing reality because it constitutes a redemption of female values and life-generating forces. Gearhart calls this option *re-sourcement* because it involves rhetors' going to a new place for their energy: "To re-source is to find another source, an entirely different and prior one, a source deeper than the patriarchy and one that allows us to stand in the path of continuous and cosmic energy."[92]

Whereas Gearhart's first three rhetorical options are interpersonal in focus and deal with relations among individuals, re-sourcement begins with an intrapersonal process of "moving inward to the self"[93] to discover an inner "energy flow," a "cosmic energy," a "place of spiritual reality," or a reservoir of "womanenergy."[94] Accessing this internal source requires an affirmation of arational, extrarational, or unorthodox sources of knowing—"the 'occult,' the 'unconscious,' the 'intuitive'"; it requires "attention to dreams, visions, memories, creative modes, rituals, games, celebrations."[95] It involves, Gearhart explains, "writing stories, singing songs, playing parts, dreaming dreams, and dancing dances. And . . . listening to what animal friends tell me of deeds and essences, of how the stars brush our quiet minds."[96]

Despite its intrapersonal focus, re-sourcement cannot be realized in isolation. Although self-nurturance, self-love, and a sensed connection to the internal cosmic source are necessary, these activities cannot, by themselves, achieve re-sourcement. To approach the spirituality that inheres in re-sourcement, feminist women rhetors must become part of a matrix or a community. Gearhart explains: "My growing understanding of a female spirituality involves a *collective* quality. A spiritual experience in female terms . . . requires *that the experience be shared.*" In this sharing, the rhetor connects with other feminist women in a kind of "horizontal transcendence," resulting in "a discernible sense of a power 'beyond' each of us but not one 'above' or 'bigger.'"[97]

The process of re-sourcement, then, involves both individual nurturance and collective transcendence: "This 'presencing' . . . of women with each other, that joining together of our self-loving [selves], of our re-sourced channels of energy, is then at the same time both *internal* to each woman and *transcendent*—a transcendence created by energy from among equal participants."[98] Re-sourcement involves the connecting of rhetors with their internal energy sources and their intentionality to share that energy. The collective aspect of re-sourcement transforms the individual experience of cosmic energy into a political force; it politicizes the psychic or intrapersonal energy to which the rhetor connects: "What's significant to me is that we're doing it in twos and threes and fives and tens and groups rather than just individually."[99]

Gearhart finds no current word to be an adequate label for the process of "women-togethering or women-being-present-with-themselves-while-presenc-ing-with-others" that occurs in re-sourcement. She believes that the term *collective* is inadequate because it suggests a pooling or an aggregate, whereas the collectivity of re-sourcement is based on the uniqueness of each self participating, operating out of a commitment to self-nurturance. Gearhart suggests that the word *syzygy* (pronounced SIZZijee) be used to describe the experience of re-sourcement, meaning "conjunction of organisms without loss of identity." *Syzygious* would be the corresponding adjective, and the entity resulting from women being together in this state would be a *syzygium*.[100]

The experience of syzygium that results from re-sourcement is available to individual rhetors to draw upon at a later time. Following such an experience, they can touch or re-source that place of spiritual reality, re-creating that presencing and tapping into the "reservoirs of womanenergy."[101] Because the differences between psychic and physical energy are minimal, when rhetors access cosmic, psychic energy, it affects the nature and impact of the physical energy in their external worlds. By accessing this womanenergy, they are able to relate to their external environments in such "a way that it responds to them, out of their psychic energy."[102] They may use, for example, the energy to shield themselves from the hurtful activities that others direct at them, to protect themselves physically from potential attackers by depowering them psychically, or to send healing energy to a person who is in pain or sick.

For re-sourcement to have the best opportunity to transform the oppressive system, Gearhart once recommended separatism, believing that "there has to be a large enough separation of women from men to make a qualitative difference in history."[103] Gearhart defines *separatism* as "a drawing together of women with each other, not dependent on men (at least as independent of them as possible), and it means a drawing together of men with each other, independent of women."[104] It does not necessarily mean that feminist women rhetors would express themselves sexually with other women, but it does mean that they would separate themselves not only from men but also "from women whose energy goes to men."[105] As Gearhart explains, "In a world where every nook and cranny has been filled with superficialized and competitivized external energy, it is no wonder that any internally sourced power has had trouble being expressed—much less valued."[106]

Gearhart sees separatism as serving a number of functions that facilitate re-sourcement. It provides feminist women rhetors with the feeling of solidarity with others like themselves, facilitating self-identification and self-love. Without "the male presence" and the feelings of "excitement, competitiveness, exhibitionism, suspicion, embarrassment, inferiority, impotence, frustration, withdrawal, hostility, resentment, regret, fear, anger" that the presence of men tends to engender, separatism also provides a space where feminists may serve as visionaries of the future.[107] By isolating themselves from power-ridden dominant energy forms, they are able to discover and model alternatives to patriarchal structures and institutions.

Despite the important functions she sees for separatism, Gearhart acknowledges that complete "separatism is impossible at present, particularly if women want to continue to reproduce themselves."[108] Separatism thus can assume a variety of forms. For some feminist rhetors, it may mean actual physical separation from centers of culture, usually in rural areas; for others, separatism may mean only occasional separation—"a weekend or so out of linear time or a few moments each day in the athomeness of the self."[109] Separatism also may take the form of creating "matrices, atmospheres, closed environments, ghettos of re-sourcement, nourishing spaces, right in the midst of heavy competitive vibrations. While capitalism/patriarchy rages without, women gather in rituals of self-finding and home-coming."[110]

Yet another option Gearhart sees for separatism is the creation of buffer zones between separatist/re-sourcing and patriarchal communities. These areas are collective forces of health and solidarity that create the atmosphere for the further development of feminist consciousness on the part of women who are not yet feminists. These zones are likely to assume the form of organizations that are moving toward or already embody feminist practices and values and are places where many women work; women's studies programs at universities are examples of such organizations.

In Gearhart's conception of the buffer zone's function as a means of separatism, feminist women rhetors would rotate between these zones (usually in cities) and separatist/re-sourcing communities (usually in the country), a system that would allow city feminists time in rural areas in which to gather "strength and health, awareness and refreshment," after which they would rotate back into the city in the buffer areas until they needed re-sourcement again.[111] The rotation system would function, then, as a kind of dialectic both in rhetors' individual lives and in terms of the feminist movement as a whole. It would provide a means for rhetors to gather energy to be a force against the patriarchy as well as a way to take care of themselves when they are fighting the system from within.

Gearhart no longer wholeheartedly believes that separatism is necessary for the success of re-sourcement or any other rhetorical option. When she is in the world, talking and acting as an agent of change, operating within a female body, she still sometimes believes that separatism would be useful. But when she sees the rhetor as a spiritual self connected to the larger cosmic whole, separatism seems to her to be an irrelevant concept. From this perspective, she no longer wants to embrace separatism and sees the distinctions between female and male rhetors to be "quite blurred" when they are seen as spiritual, eternal beings.[112]

Gearhart's fourth rhetorical option of re-sourcement, in summary, "has very little to do with political parties, with money, or with revolution in the common sense of that term."[113] She points to the unique dimensions of re-sourcement as a rhetorical option:

I've called re-sourcement a political strategy but when I ask questions usually applicable to a political movement, I find unorthodox answers. Who is the enemy? There may be no "enemy" except a system. How do we deal with "the enemy"? As seldom as possible but when necessary by opening the way for his transformation into not-the-enemy. What weapons do we use? Our healing, our self-protection, our health, our fantasies, our collective care. How do we protect our ranks? By a buffer zone of women working in the patriarchy. How do we train for the battles? By practicing our arational skills.[114]

In her initial thinking about the four options, Gearhart believed that re-sourcement was superior to the others. The system is able to contain the other three options—revolutionary action, working within alternative organizations, and reform from within the system—and to neutralize their effects: "Daily the system anoints and assimilates more reforms into itself. . . . [B]ombings and kidnappings frighten us step-by-paranoid-step into the police state; alternative organizations seem less and less like alternatives or cease to exist altogether."[115] These options cannot succeed in overturning or transforming the system because the rules of the system "are devised and revised constantly by the dominant culture and enough of us can never become skilled enough fast enough to beat that system at its own game. Only something as powerful as that system itself can threaten it."[116] Gearhart initially saw re-sourcement as the only option "that can confront the patriarchy."[117]

Gearhart later acknowledged some important functions for the first three options and became less willing to dismiss them. These options, she came to see, give re-sourcement room and time to work, functioning to draw the enemy's fire, staving off the knowledge and reaction of the patriarchal system so that time and room can be bought for the "essential work of genuine transformation."[118] They also help prepare for transformation of the system, creating bubbles within patriarchal institutions that may be necessary for re-sourcement to work: "I can fantasize that when the psychic energy finally gets gathered . . . it may be that at that time we will *need* the room that those . . . college presidents and deans and so forth have made, in order for us to do what we need to do with this psychic energy."[119] All of the "approaches work together for change,"[120] she suggests, and she sees them as "having the possibility of working together with themselves and with the re-sourcement strategy, to make the whole picture."[121] Indeed, this is how Gearhart has chosen to live much of her life—developing her re-sourcement skills and, simultaneously, employing the other three options in her activist work.

Enfoldment

Gearhart characterizes her intellectual life as a dynamic between opposites. She often has taken a strong stand on an issue, insisting with great fervor that others accept her viewpoint, only to be struck suddenly by the truth of the opposite position. This is what happened in Gearhart's "conversion" to New Age metaphysics, which led to her development of the rhetorical option of enfoldment. For years, she had criticized the "psychobabble" of trance mediums and reincarnation enthusiasts as behaviors out of touch with the real world and devoid of social responsibility. She had criticized specifically the Seth books, a large body of material channeled by Jane Roberts and transcribed by Roberts's husband, Robert Butts. The Seth material—consistent with Buddhism, Hinduism, Christian Science, and quantum physics—suggests that material reality is created by individuals' thoughts, there is no evil in the universe, and all human beings are unique and often-incarnated expressions of the cosmic mind.

Gearhart believed none of these ideas until, as she reread the Seth book *The Nature of Personal Reality,* she found every sentence striking a chord of agreement within her. The book completely transformed her thinking about social change, and in 1995 she announced: "I'm not going to be an activist anymore. Don't mistake me: I feel more passionately than ever about issues of justice and peace and environmental health. And I still do backslide occasionally into speaking out or letter writing. . . . But I'm going about my life in a different way—a way, in fact, that I've scorned for 25 years."[122] She no longer seeks to change others; instead, she is developing a conception of activism and a theory of rhetoric that are consistent with her new beliefs.

Even as she was writing about and working to change people as a means of helping to ensure the survival of the planet, Gearhart was questioning the rhetorical theory in which those activities were rooted. Her questioning began with a challenge to the traditional definition of rhetoric as persuasion. She saw how rhetorical theory was designed with only one goal in mind:

> The patriarchs of rhetoric have never called into question the unspoken assumption that mankind (read "mankind") is here on the earth to alter his (read "his") environment and to influence the social affairs of other men (read "men"). Without batting an eye the ancient rhetors, the men of the church, and scholars of argumentation from Bacon, Blair and Whately to Toulmin, Perelman and McLuhan, have taken as given that it is a proper and even necessary human function to attempt to change others.[123]

Consequently, the theory that developed out of this tradition is dedicated to changing others to make the rhetor's own viewpoint prevail: "[W]e take a position, a stand, and we argue it out in debate fashion and reason will prevail. . . . If my reason is good and my evidence is accurate, you will ultimately believe as I do."[124] In this mode of interaction, audience members are seen as naive and less expert than the rhetor, and the primary mode of action in the world is attempting to persuade others to the rhetor's superior position.

Not only rhetorical tradition but virtually all of Western civilization has been built on the assumption that persuasion is appropriate and even desirable. This notion is so ingrained in Western culture that the conquest and conversion of others are seen as natural and normal:

> Our history is a combination of conquest and conversion. We conquered trees and converted them into a house, taking pride in having accomplished a difficult task. We conquered rivers and streams and converted them into lakes, marvelling in ourselves at the improvement we made on nature. We tramped with our conquering spaceboots on the fine ancient dust of the Moon and we sent our well-rehearsed statements of triumph back for a waiting world to hear.[125]

Not only do humans engage in the conquest and conversion of persuasion, but those acts generate a great deal of pleasure for them. In a world characterized by values of hierarchy and competition, to be able to conquer another, to convert another to one's own perspective, or "to penetrate the environment with the truth" brings satisfaction.[126] Gearhart acknowledges that virtually all individuals have "enjoyed the rush of power that has come with" the ability to persuade others—with the role of bearing "great messages" with persuasive appeal.[127] The reward gained from apparently successful efforts to make others change, then, is a feeling of self-worth that comes from controlling people and situations.

Breaking with thousands of years of rhetorical theory, Gearhart came to understand persuasion as violence: "This is what I didn't know I believed until I began writing, but it is absolutely fundamental to my beliefs about the ethics of communication—persuasion is a violent act. Any attempt to change anything else is a violent act."[128] The violence, she explains, lies "in the *intention* to change another." To attempt to persuade others violates their life worlds and devalues their lives and perspectives. Gearhart summarizes her view of persuasion: "[W]hen we began to seek to change any other entity," we violated "the integrity of that person or thing and our own integrity as well."[129]

Although rhetoricians often assert that rhetoric is an alternative to violence because it involves "talking it out instead of fighting it out," Gearhart rejects the idea that the persuasion that occurs through talk is substantially different from physical violence.[130] She sees "the difference between a persuasive metaphor and a violent artillery attack" to be "obscure and certainly one of degree rather than of kind."[131] The distinction that rhetoricians make between rhetoric and physical violence collapses because of the nature of energy:

> It is only in density that the energy fields surrounding each of us differ from the solid energy that is our physical bodies; it is only in density that the energy we

generate in our minds or our psyches differs from our auras. As Kurlian photography tracks down revolutionaries by the energy exuded from their very bodies and as Western medicine adopts techniques of visualization and fantasy in the curing of cancer, we realize that to thrust a sword into another person does not differ significantly from wishing them ill or from fantasizing a sword thrust into their heart.[132]

Gearhart is careful to explain that she has no problem with the concept of change itself: "To change other people or other entities is not in itself a violation. It is a fact of existence that we do so." In fact, human beings can and do change one another daily: "Our physical bodies respond to energy; even without our will they react in measurable ways to objects or people generating high energy. . . . Our physical being, our movement, our thoughts, our metaphors: all are forms of energy in constant and infinitely varied exchange."[133] Gearhart makes a distinction between "wanting things to change and wanting to change things."[134] To want things to change is not a problem; such a desire does not constitute violence. The violence lies in the intention to change other entities.

Gearhart's equation of persuasion with violence led her to question her own activism on behalf of various causes. She realized that she had spent her "life being violent" because she had been "attempting to change the world."[135] She recognized that she lived "a schizophrenic existence" in which her values were "at war" with her actions.[136] Her initial response to the contradiction was to rationalize her activism: "These are things I must resist, defend against, declare war upon, fight." But then she wondered, "Or must I?"[137]

Gearhart's efforts to reconcile her reconceptualization of rhetoric with her activism raised a number of questions for her: "There has to be a new way of communicating and what's it going to be? What's going to be a way of making a decision where we don't persuade?"[138] Furthermore, in such a form of rhetoric, how would social change occur? She asked:

If we are not to attempt to change our world, then is the alternative to sit forever in a quiet and desperate passivity? Must we choose between being an invader, a violent persuader, and a patient Griselda twiddling our thumbs and curbing our energy in the hope that some miraculous process will do it all for us? Surely it is of value to seek to alter injustices, to change oppressive societal institutions. Is there a way to relate to each other, to other entities, in acts that participate in the changing of our world but which do not themselves recapitulate our heritage of violence?[139]

Gearhart also wondered about the effects of her new beliefs about rhetoric on her own self-identity: "Even more horrifying, what if I keep playing this game (of friends/enemies, win/lose, perpetrator/victim, right/wrong) only because without the game I would have no identity? What would I do if I did not have my crusade? Who would I be?"[140]

The study of rhetoric, although historically exclusively concerned with persuasion, Gearhart felt, should be able to supply some of the answers: "The indictment of the profession is not an attack on the tools of rhetoric. . . . With our expertise in persuasion, rhetoricians and rhetorical theorists are in the best position to change our own use of our tools."[141] She set out to develop a new, nonviolent, nonpersuasive conception of rhetoric that constitutes a fifth rhetorical option she sees as available for rhetors.

Although Gearhart herself does not give her new rhetorical option a label, the term *enfoldment* captures its essence: "So when communication takes place between you and me, it's not a matter of my penetrating your mind, but of 'enfolding' you."[142] Gearhart explains the basic process of enfoldment as a rhetorical option: In enfoldment, rhetorical activity "takes the path of wrapping around the givee, of being available to her/him without insisting; our giving is a *presence,* an *offering,* an *opening,* a *surrounding,* a *listening,* a *vulnerability,* a *trust.*" At most, in enfoldment, the rhetor's action "takes the form of a push toward freedom for the givee, as in the act of *giving* birth."[143]

Enfoldment is based on a number of assumptions that are different from those that undergird traditional rhetorical theory. Whereas the four rhetorical options Gearhart had formulated previously—revolutionary action, working within alternative organizations, reform within organizations, and re-sourcement— have as their purpose changing individuals, enfoldment does not. Enfoldment is based on the assumption that the rhetor's goal is not to enlighten or persuade others; rather, it is to understand the perspectives of others—the nature of those perspectives, how they were developed, and why they make sense to those who hold them. More important than persuading others to change their views to those of the rhetor is "the connection of care and respect that is established between two people whom the system wants to characterize as enemies."[144]

A second assumption on which enfoldment is based is that change happens only when individuals choose to change. The effort "*to change other people doesn't work*";[145] "they must convert themselves."[146] This assumption is featured in a song sung by the women in Gearhart's book *The Wanderground*: "Never may I enter where the way is not open, never can I take her if she does not choose to go."[147] Communication, then, involves the implicit asking of the question, "[W]ill you communicate with me?" Rhetors then "have the will and choice of responding or ignoring" the question. As Gearhart explains: "If I knock on your door or enfold you forever and you don't answer, then you don't answer. There is no way I can force you to respond."[148]

Individuals choose to communicate with others and thus to open themselves up to the possibility of change if two conditions are present: the internal basis for change and an environment that enables change to happen. Gearhart explains these conditions:

> Mao Tse Tung in his essay "On Contradiction" gave us the metaphor of the egg and the stone. No one can change an egg into a chicken. If, however, there is the potential in the egg to be a chicken—what Mao called the "internal basis for change"—then there is the likelihood that in the right environment (moisture, temperature, the "external conditions for change") the egg will hatch. A stone, on the other hand, has no internal basis for hatching into a chicken and an eternity of sitting in the proper conditions of moisture and temperature will not make possible its transformation into a chicken.[149]

Gearhart illustrates with her own conversion to feminism the assumption that change happens only when people choose to change and the conditions under which such change occurs:

> First, it is true that with each step *I* changed my life. No one changed it for me. . . . Second, while it is true that *I* changed my life, it is also true that those external conditions were a climate, not a force. . . . It has been conversion, right enough, occurring only when I am internally ready and only in an atmosphere conducive to that change.[150]

A third assumption that undergirds the option of enfoldment is that changing oneself creates societal change. As Gearhart explains, "I'm assuming that *cleaning up my own act is the best contribution I can make to any cause.*"[151] Acting in the world according to the values and principles individuals would like to see in place in the world helps to create those values and principles on a larger scale. Instead of fighting an enemy using the enemy's tools, thus furthering the enemy's power and perpetuating the values and practices of violence, hierarchy, and competition, individuals can work to rid themselves of those tools and those values. Gearhart elaborates: "I've learned that my pain, anger, and/or hatred accomplish nothing except to render me ineffectual and to increase the problem by adding to the pain, anger, and hatred that already burden the world."[152] In contrast, actions that contribute respect, affirmation, support, understanding, and nurturing bring those qualities into the experiences of individuals and add them to the energy of the world. Gearhart trusts that such actions "can make a positive difference in the texture of all of our lives"[153] because they "gather energy to [themselves] and become a reality."[154]

A fourth assumption on which enfoldment is built is that there is no such thing as evil. "The universe is a safe place,"[155] Gearhart asserts, because it is a place of "'all right-ness' or well-being" characterized by "all-pervading" or unconditional love. Even in Gearhart's traditional activist days, when she "believed in Evil, in enemies, in the necessity to fight those Satanic forces that would deprive us all of peace, freedom, jobs, justice, and self-determination," dreams and hunches offered her different messages: "Sometimes they whispered, even as I was confronting him in my brightest feminist armor, 'This guy is not the enemy. He, too, is love.'"[156]

Gearhart describes the moment when she realized that a primary feature of the universe is love: "I stood for a moment in the big middle of an all-pervading love. In fact, I 'was' love, the great 'intransitive' love that has no specific object. I didn't 'love X,' or 'Y.' I just 'loved.'" In such a state, "neither party could ever do anything that would make the love 'stop.'"[157] Although Gearhart asserts that this "kind of love is still too incredible for [her] to contemplate receiving—or being,"[158] her brief experience of it suggests that the essential quality of the universe is goodness and that any "evil" is merely damage that has occurred in a falling away from good—it "is only a turning away from love."[159]

The assumptions that undergird enfoldment—its purpose is understanding, change happens only when individuals choose to change, changing oneself creates societal change, and the world is not evil—enable the rhetor "to operate differently in all communicative circumstances."[160] Rhetoric, as it is conceptualized in enfoldment, no longer has to do with the formulation of messages. Instead, rhetoric is "a deliberate creation or co-creation of an atmosphere in which people or things, if and only if they have the internal basis for change, may change themselves." It is the creation of an environment or matrix for connecting with and understanding the perspectives of others—"a mutual generation of energy for purposes of growth."[161] Rhetoric, then, is "an organic atmosphere that is the source of meanings" rather than a process in which rhetors, "like a god, give us the meanings."[162]

Gearhart suggests a number of communicative activities that engender enfoldment and embody her new definition of rhetoric. They are acknowledgment, search for common ground, mutual sharing of perspectives, willingness to yield, witnessing, and asking permission to share observations.

Acknowledgment

Acknowledgment is the rhetor's recognition of the presence of others and demonstration of respect for them and their perspectives. The essence of acknowledgment is that every being is a unique and necessary part of the pattern of the universe and thus has immanent value. Gearhart emphasizes the importance of acknowledgment as a basic communicative act, explaining that to deny the presence of another being denies "the communication that could take place between us."[163] Gearhart discusses how she implements the action of acknowledgment: "These days, I'm going the whole nine yards: I'm practicing acknowledging loggers as 'fellow travellers on Planet Earth,' . . . doing what they do just as I do what I do; I'm laying off any attempt to change or even judge them."[164] Instead, she simply is acknowledging them.

Search for Common Ground

Enfoldment also involves the rhetor's search for common ground with the audience. In this joining, the rhetor focuses on *"whatever interests or concerns [are held] in common."* Gearhart explains the process as one of looking for "the place where we are the same, where we can meet each other as beings who share the experience of living together on this planet." She introduces the shared belief or interest into the conversation, "and we talk about the thing that belongs to both of us."[165]

Gearhart provides examples of ways in which she has been able to establish common ground with those she once would have regarded as enemies. Talking with a Christian, anti-lesbian man who shined her boots in an airport, Gearhart discovered common ground in their favorite Bible verses.[166] With a cockfighter, Gearhart shared an appreciation of "the beauty of his fighting birds."[167] With a member of the National Rifle Association who was militantly against gun control, the common ground he and Gearhart discovered was an appreciation of "his Vietnam Commemorative M14."[168] Gearhart and a panhandler who was kicking his dog found they could share hints on flea control.[169] With an activist who pickets abortion clinics, Gearhart found common ground in the arrangements individuals need to make before joining a picket line:

"I never carry money, I wear comfortable shoes, and I pin my driver's license to my pocket," she said.
"Right," I replied, "And I have to get someone to feed my cats. Do you have children?"
"My sister takes care of them. I write phone numbers on my hand."
"And be careful not to wash your hands, right?"
"Right!" We laughed.[170]

The search for common ground, then, involves working to discover beliefs and values that the rhetor and the audience share and communicating on the basis of those beliefs and values.

Mutual Sharing of Perspectives

Mutual sharing of perspectives is the process of asking questions and listening on the part of both rhetor and audience so that both better understand the perspective of the other. The process is rooted in genuine curiosity and the effort to understand; the questions and answers are not used to establish the superiority of the rhetor's own perspective.

Gearhart offers several examples of situations of enfoldment in which she has participated in mutual sharing of perspectives. In communicating with a logger with whom she disagreed on timber practices, for example, she asked him to take her "into his world for a day or two" so she could "hear him and his buddies talk about what it means to be out of work in a poor [county] with a family to feed."[171] She did a logger's work, using a hook-crane to lift and load freshly cut redwoods onto a truck bed. She discovered much about the work that she had not understood before:

> It was an incredible rush! . . . I loved it. . . . They couldn't get me down from that machine for hours. . . . These guys can get that rush every day of their lives, many times a day, in their big machines, conquering the earth, exercising their hard-won skills, doing a difficult job well.[172]

Gearhart gives another example of an effort she made to understand by sharing perspectives with another, this time after initially employing traditional persuasive rhetoric. On a trip with a friend to upstate New York, Gearhart encountered a man "railing about all these women and abortion rights." Because of her own prochoice beliefs, Gearhart "took him on": "As a matter of fact, I took him on so loudly that we gathered a little crowd there in the Kennedy airport. I was screaming at him; I was trying to make him change. It was not successful, and it was pretty ugly, as a matter of fact. . . . They didn't have to actually physically separate us, but it was close to that."[173]

An hour later, as Gearhart was boarding the shuttle bus to take her to Plattsburg, her destination, she encountered the man again: "There was only one seat on that bus, and guess who it was next to? . . . He looked at me and I looked at him as if to say, 'Oh, my God, what are we going to do?'" Rather than continue to engage the man as she had in the airport, Gearhart decided to try something different and "began asking him about his life and about the things that he did," seeking to understand his perspective and the reasons it made sense to him. Gearhart explains that the conversation revealed that "it was even worse than I had originally thought. In fact, he was a chemist, and he had experimented on animals. He had grown up as a hunter and, of course, all that is absolutely counter to the things that I believe." Rather than attempting to convince him of the error of his ways, however, Gearhart continued to ask questions and to listen to the man, and he did the same as she shared her own perspectives and experiences with him. At the end of the interaction, neither of them had changed their original positions, but they had come to understand and to value one another's points of view.[174]

A mutual sharing of perspectives in enfoldment often requires emotional disengagement from a highly volatile situation. When a woman spoke of gay people as "damned Sodomites," instead of being angry and attacking the woman, as she would have done previously, Gearhart found herself "blessed with an amazing moment of equanimity." She asked, with genuine curiosity, "Cindy, what's a sodomite to you? I'm a lesbian, and I think that term includes me."[175] Such emotional disengagement fosters a psychological state in which the rhetor is more able to listen carefully to the perspective of the other and to share thoughts with a goal of understanding rather than persuasion.

Willingness to Yield

If the understanding that marks enfoldment is to occur, all individuals involved in the communication must be prepared to be changed in the mutually created setting. They must be "willing on the deepest level to yield" their positions "entirely to the other(s)."[176] The participants must be willing "to call into question things most inviolate" and "be willing to entertain other ideas."[177] Gearhart provides an example of this willingness to yield in her own opposition to hunting. When she is trying to communicate with a hunter, she explains, "that means that I've got to risk believing that hunting, say, may be in some cases a viable thing for human beings to do. And that's scary. But to make these kinds of liaisons, I've got to have that kind of attitude."[178]

Admission of a lack of complete information on the rhetor's part facilitates a willingness to yield. When rhetors acknowledge that they do not have—and never can have—full knowledge of a situation, they are less willing to judge the actions of others and are more willing to consider that their own perspectives may be in error. When Gearhart started to criticize a neighbor for allowing his cats to have kittens, for example, she realized that, from a cosmic perspective, she did not have all the information she needed: "Who was I to persuade him? How did I know what purpose those kittens might play in his life?"[179] Admission of insufficient information in a situation facilitates the rhetor's willingness to yield, a critical aspect of the practice of enfoldment.

Witnessing

Another communicative action that a rhetor may select in the practice of enfoldment is the process of witnessing. Witnessing is the observing and recording—without responding—of the words and actions of those the rhetor is seeking to understand. Witnessing is most often used with those who have been characterized as enemies in the past, and its purpose is not to collect evidence to be used against opponents in the future but to remind all those involved that they are part of the same substance and thus are interconnected. It is also a way for rhetors to communicate to others that they are holding them to high standards of behavior and are expecting them to act in ethical, humane,

and respectful ways. Witnessing signals acknowledgment that the participants
are acting out of their convictions, their integrity, and their best selves and that
"these 'best selves' are a part of the kinship" that the observer and the observed
"share on a deeper level." Witnessing is used sometimes, for example, when
human rights observers stand beside tribal people who are being harassed by
police: "[U]nsmiling, [they] write down everything that is said, that's all. They
just watch and listen and write." They thus acknowledge that there is a "Greater
Law" supporting the legal system and that both the police officer and the witness
honor it. As Gearhart explains, witnessing is "a kind of 'calling us home' to the
same family, the same mother."[180]

Asking Permission to Share Observations

Gearhart acknowledges that there may be times when rhetors have observations and insights they would like to share with others but want to do so in a
nondominating way that is respectful of others' integrity. She suggests a way to
engage in such sharing that does not take the form of a persuasive attempt or
an effort to establish the superiority of the rhetor's own perspective over that of
another. In these cases, Gearhart suggests that the rhetor ask the intended
recipients of the rhetor's observations if they are interested in hearing those
observations. For example, when an individual notices that the daughter of a
friend has extremely poor eating habits—so poor that they seem potentially
harmful to the child—she may say to the child's parents, "I have some serious
concerns about your daughter that I'd like to tell you about but only if you are
interested in hearing them. Are you?"[181] In this way, the rhetor respects the
parents' right to raise their child as they believe appropriate and does not impose
unwanted views on them.

The communication practices involved in enfoldment—acknowledgment,
search for common ground, mutual sharing of perspectives, willingness to yield,
witnessing, and asking permission to share observations—cannot be assessed
by the criterion typically used to assess the effectiveness of rhetoric. The
criterion for judgment of the success of enfoldment is not whether others
change—whether the rhetor's own perspective prevails in the world—because
winning and persuading are not the rhetor's goals in enfoldment. As Gearhart
acknowledges, the communicative practices involved in the enfoldment option
"win" nothing:

> The cockfighter is still trying to legalize the "sport"; the woman from Operation
> Rescue still tries to close down abortion clinics; the NRA man still proudly displays
> the bumper sticker on his pickup: "My wife? Yes. My dog? Maybe. My gun?
> Never!" And the loggers and road men still rev their chainsaws or bulldozers.[182]

Gearhart chooses to assess the effects of her new kind of rhetoric not by the changes that take place in the external world but by the changes that happen in her own life. She measures the effects of enfoldment by her feelings: "I *like* 'joining' better than fighting or running away, better even than marching for or rallying to a cause. I feel warm and light, sometimes even high, floating inches off the ground."[183] She also hopes that her "ministry of love to the 'enemy'" will contribute to his feeling "better about himself—more at peace, less angry, less under attack."[184]

The responses Gearhart generates from those she formerly saw as enemies suggest that they feel much as she does as a result of her use of enfoldment: "One man said to me, 'I still don't like your politics and I'm not sure I even like you, but you're sort of a family member that I'll always protect.'"[185] Gearhart's experience of talking to the antiabortion chemist and hunter on the bus to Plattsburg provides another example of the kinds of outcomes she has come to expect when she uses enfoldment. As Gearhart and the man met again, this time in the parking lot after the bus ride, they "came together in this terrific hug, both of us in tears, sobbing, crying like babies. I said, 'You know, I don't know what has happened here, but my life has been totally changed after today.' And he said, 'My life is totally changed, too, and I don't know what's happened.'"[186]

Gearhart's rethinking of rhetoric so that it engenders understanding and respect rather than persuasion has led her to reject the rhetorical options she once used in her activist work to change others. She calls herself a "recovering activist" and now attempts to practice enfoldment in her interactions with others.[187] She does not regret, however, her use of and commitment to the persuasive strategies she previously employed:

To tell the truth, I don't regret a single day of my past as an activist. I figure that the desire to stop injustices and heal the earth is an honest and an honorable one. It's a big part of who I have been as a being incarnated on this planet. . . . I wouldn't know what I know, and probably wouldn't be making the changes I'm making, without those experiences of activism.[188]

Although she is not always successful in her efforts to practice enfoldment, Gearhart now is committed to this new form of rhetoric:

But right now, I'm getting clear and unmistakable signals that it's time for another approach [other than persuasion]. If I can still hold strong to my standard of what is just and decent and appropriate behavior for human beings and yet go about my life with a new awareness, with joy in the process instead of my former debilitating pain, and if I can do all this without creating and maintaining "enemies," then I have to try it.[189]

Transformations of Rhetorical Theory

Gearhart's initial understanding of rhetorical theory was consistent with the practices and values of the rhetorical tradition—she saw rhetoric as a means to change others through persuasion. Her later conception of rhetorical theory, however, embodied in the rhetorical options of re-sourcement and enfoldment, challenges traditional conceptions of several mainstays of rhetorical theory. The assumptions and practices of re-sourcement and enfoldment transform the definition of rhetoric, the appropriate realm for rhetoric, the audience, and the nature of the change process. In addition, Gearhart offers new rhetorical options and new criteria for judging the effectiveness of rhetoric, thus expanding the rhetorical repertoire available for individuals who want to use rhetoric to facilitate greater understanding and connection in the world.

Definition of Rhetoric

Gearhart's challenge to rhetorical theory begins at a fundamental level with a challenge to the definition of rhetoric. In her theory, rhetoric is not the attempt to persuade others through the use of symbols; she rejects persuasion because it violates the integrity of the audience. Instead, she sees rhetoric as the creation or cocreation of an atmosphere, environment, or matrix in which change may occur. This conception challenges not only the nature of the essence of the rhetorical act—creating atmospheres rather than formulating messages to change the perspectives or behaviors of others—but also the goal of rhetoric. The goal, in Gearhart's theory, is to understand another individual and to connect with that person in a relationship of care and respect; it is not to influence, persuade, or change another.

Realm for Rhetoric

Rhetoric traditionally has been seen as operating primarily or having the most impact in the public realm, affecting decisions and policies concerning individuals' public lives. Gearhart challenges the public as the appropriate realm for rhetoric with her rhetorical options of re-sourcement and enfoldment, both of which involve rhetorical actions that take place largely in the intrapersonal and interpersonal realms. Re-sourcement involves accessing a cosmic energy through intrapersonal means such as intuition, dreams, and rituals, whereas enfoldment involves interpersonal activities such as acknowledging another, listening to another, communicating a willingness to change, searching for common ground, and asking permission to share observations. These place the realm of rhetorical activity squarely in the realm of the private and, although this rhetorical activity eventually may affect public events and policies, its focus is on creating environments interpersonally. In Gearhart's theory, then, rhetoric initially has the most impact in the private—not the public—realm.

Audience

Gearhart's rhetorical theory involves a different conception of the audience from the one that characterizes traditional rhetorical theory. Her conception of the audience challenges the traditional construct in three ways. In contrast to traditional views, the audience is not seen as separate from the rhetor, uninformed or naive, and passive in comparison to the rhetor.

In Gearhart's view, no separation or division exists between the rhetor and the audience. As a result, the rhetor cannot exploit, objectify, or seek to change audience members. To do so would be disrespectful of the integrity of both the rhetor and the audience. Because of the connection between rhetor and audience, the processes of audience analysis and adaptation also are not the same kinds of processes they are in traditional rhetorical theory. The rhetor does not analyze the audience in order to make an appeal to the audience more effective. Instead, the rhetor seeks to reinforce an already existing connection to develop a deeper understanding of the audience.

Gearhart does not see the audience as naive or uninformed, in contrast to a rhetor who is expected and assumed to be enlightened and in possession of some truth that the audience lacks. Audience members are seen as having legitimate perspectives and ways of approaching the world, and the rhetor's task is to understand and acknowledge them. The rhetor seeks to discover how audience members came to hold the positions they do and how those positions make sense to them; audience members are viewed as the experts on their own lives.

Gearhart reconceptualizes the rhetor and the audience in yet another way: Both engage in the same kind of rhetorical activity. The rhetor does not create messages, speak, or write while the audience somewhat passively interprets, listens to, or reads the message formulated by the rhetor. Instead, audience and rhetor are cocreators of rhetoric, with both involved in the creation of the environment that constitutes rhetoric. Both thus are simultaneously rhetor and audience, affecting one another and the environment mutually and reciprocally.

Change

The nature of the change process is transformed in two primary ways in Gearhart's rhetorical theory. Traditional rhetoric is built on the assumption that if a rhetor does her or his job properly—if a message is organized well enough, has sufficient forms of support, has an effective introduction and conclusion, and is created by a rhetor with high ethos—audience members are likely to be persuaded. They will be unable to resist, in short, the rhetor's appeal. Gearhart suggests, in contrast, that rhetorical messages will have no effect unless and until audience members decide to change; individuals must convert themselves. The creation of an atmosphere in which people feel free to change, if they so desire, is the best possible way to create a stimulus for change—not the formation of persuasive messages intended and designed to change others.

Gearhart introduces another radical notion into the traditional assumptions about change in rhetoric. External or societal conditions are most likely to change when rhetors change themselves. The focus for rhetors is no longer on persuading others to change as a means to transform a situation; rather, it is on enacting the change desired in their own lives. Change happens, if it is going to, through rhetors' modeling of new ways of being that others may choose to adopt in their own lives. The best contribution rhetors can make to changing something in the world, then, is to act in ways that manifest the changes they desire.

Rhetorical Options

Gearhart's theory alters conventional rhetorical theories in yet another way: It expands the rhetorical options available to rhetors beyond those provided in traditional rhetorical theory. Gearhart's options are not forms of support that a rhetor can use to bolster an argument; rather, they are options that facilitate the creation of an atmosphere of connection and understanding. Rhetors create an environment in which individuals (including the rhetor) change if they choose to by making use of, for example, the occult, the unconscious, the intuitive, dreams, vision, memories, and rituals. These options involve efforts to understand others, adoption of a stance of willingness to yield, and discovery of connections with others. Not only does Gearhart incorporate as options rhetorical forms not commonly accepted as rhetoric, but her options work largely on the rhetor's self as they contribute to the creation of a particular environment.

Assessment of Rhetoric

Dramatically different criteria from those that characterize traditional rhetorical theory mark Gearhart's approach to assessing the effectiveness of rhetoric. The primary criteria by which traditional messages are judged are whether they are persuasive or not and whether the persuasion is accomplished in an ethical manner. For Gearhart, whether others change their viewpoints on an issue is irrelevant in terms of the effectiveness of rhetoric. Rhetoric's effectiveness is measured by the changes that happen in rhetors' own lives, particularly in terms of how they feel. If rhetors feel love, care, connection, and warmth as a result of their interactions with others, Gearhart sees their rhetoric as effective;

if, on the other hand, they feel disconnected, angry, and frustrated, their rhetoric is not effective.

Gearhart's transformations of rhetorical theory suggest numerous ways in which rhetorical constructs might be reconfigured and expanded. With her reconceptualization of some of the most fundamental dimensions of traditional rhetorical theory, she creates a rhetoric rooted in a commitment to enacting values of respect, love, and understanding. This new rhetoric, she hopes, will be the impetus for the creation of environments in which individuals will choose to change in ways that contribute to more humane lives for all:

> We are perhaps on the brink of understanding that we do not have to be persuaders, that we no longer need to intend to change others. We are not the speaker, the-one-with-the-truth, the-one-who-with-his-power-will-change-lives. We are the matrix, we are she-who-is-the-home-of-this-particular-human-interaction, we are a co-creator and co-sustainer of the atmosphere in whose infinity of possible trans-formations we will all change.[190]

Bibliography

Books

Gearhart, Sally Miller. *The Wanderground: Stories of the Hill Women.* 1978. Boston: Alyson, 1984.

Gearhart, Sally, and Susan Rennie. *A Feminist Tarot.* 1976. Boston: Alyson, 1981.

Gearhart, Sally, and William R. Johnson, eds. *Loving Women/Loving Men: Gay Liberation and the Church.* San Francisco: Glide, 1974.

Articles

Bangberg, Oranda P. [Sally Miller Gearhart]. "'Charlie's Angel' Visits Headwaters, 1999." *Willits News* [CA] 25 Sept. 1996: 2.

Gearhart, Sally. "Another View of the Same Moon from Another City's Streets." *Womanspirit: A Feminist Quarterly* 3 (1976): 41-44.

Gearhart, Sally M. "The Bride." *Response in Worship—Music—the Arts* [Lutheran Society for Worship, Music, and the Arts] 10 (1968): 13-17.

Gearhart, Sally Miller. "The California Coalition for Traditional Values: View from a Dyke." *San Francisco Bay Times* Nov. 1989: 8, 9, 51.

Gearhart, Sally Miller. "The Coming Chill." *Inviting Transformation: Presentational Speaking for a Changing World.* By Sonja K. Foss and Karen A. Foss. Prospect Heights, IL: Waveland, 1994. 122-26.

Gearhart, Sally M. "District 5 Elections: Gearhart Debates 'Gay Seat.'" *Plexus* Nov. 1979: 3, 19.

Gearhart, Sally M. "An End to Technology: A Modest Proposal." *Machina ex Dea: Feminist Perspectives on Technology.* Ed. Joan Rothschild. New York: Pergamon, 1984. 171-82.

Gearhart, Sally M. "Eulogy for Harvey." *Glen Park Perspective* [CA] 28 Nov. 1978: 3.

Gearhart, Sally Miller. "First Love at Sweet Briar." *The New Our Right to Love: A Lesbian Resource Book.* Ed. Ginny Vida. New York: Simon & Schuster, 1996. 36-40. Rpt. in *Love Shook My Heart.* Ed. Irene Zahava. Los Angeles: Alyson, 1998. 33-48.

Gearhart, Sally Miller. "The First Time Ever." *Virgin Territory 2.* Ed. Shar Rednour. New York: Richard Kasak, 1997. 17-30.

Gearhart, Sally Miller. "The Future—If There Is One—Is Female." *Reweaving the Web of Life: Feminism and Nonviolence.* Ed. Pam McAllister. Philadelphia: New Society, 1982. 266-84.

Gearhart, Sally Miller. "Future Visions: Today's Politics: Feminist Utopias in Review." *Women in Search of Utopia: Mavericks and Mythmakers.* Ed. Ruby Rohrlich and Elaine Hoffman Baruch. New York: Schocken, 1984. 296-309.

Gearhart, Sally Miller. "Gay Civil Rights and the Roots of Oppression." *Gayspeak: Gay Male and Lesbian Communication.* Ed. James W. Chesebro. New York: Pilgrim, 1981. 275-85.

Gearhart, Sally Miller. "If the Mortarboard Fits: Radical Feminism in Academia." *Learning Our Way: Essays in Feminist Education.* Ed. Charlotte Bunch and Sandra Pollack. Trumansburg, NY: Crossing, 1983. 2-18.

Gearhart, Sally Miller. "I Left my Boots Behind." *Willits News* [CA] 26 Oct. 1988: 2.

Gearhart, Sally. "The Lesbian and God-the-Father." *Persuasion: Understanding, Practice and Analysis.* By Herbert W. Simons. Menlo Park, CA: Addison-Wesley, 1975. 338-42.

Gearhart, Sally. "The Miracle of Lesbianism." *Loving Women/Loving Men: Gay Liberation and the Church.* Ed. Sally Gearhart and William R. Johnson. San Francisco: Glide, 1974. 119-52.

Gearhart, Sally M. "The Neglect of the Upper Ten." *Response in Worship—Music—the Arts* [Lutheran Society for Worship, Music, and the Arts] 4 (1962): 83-89.

Gearhart, Sally Miller. "A New Diet for a Small Planet." *Lesbian Contradiction* 22 (1988): 14-16.

Gearhart, Sally Miller. "Notes from a Recovering Activist." *Sojourner: The Women's Forum* 21 (1995): 8-11.

Gearhart, Sally Miller. "Opinion." *PAWS [Performing Animals Welfare Society] News* Sept. 1988: 15.

Gearhart, Sally M. "Our Feast of Fools." *Response in Worship—Music—the Arts* [Lutheran Society for Worship, Music, and the Arts] 7 (1965): 79-82.

Gearhart, Sally Miller. "The Pit Bull Opportunity." *Reality Change* [Seth Network International] Summer 1994: 28-31. Rpt. in *Storming Heaven's Gate: An Anthology of Spiritual Writings by Women.* Ed. Amber Coverdale Vecchione. New York: Penguin, 1997. 103-12.

Gearhart, Sally. "She Who Hath Ears." *Women and the Word: Toward a Whole Theology.* Ed. Jean Crosby and Jude Michaels. Berkeley, CA: Office of Women's Affairs of the Graduate Theological Union, 1972. 76-83.

Gearhart, Sally Miller. "Small-Town Girl Makes Dyke." *Testimonies: Lesbian Coming-Out Stories.* Ed. Karen Barber and Sarah Holmes. Boston: Alyson, 1994. 11-21.

Gearhart, Sally Miller. "The Spiritual Dimension: Death and Resurrection of a Hallelujah Dyke." *Our Right to Love: A Lesbian Resource Book.* Ed. Ginny Vida. Englewood Cliffs, NJ: Prentice Hall, 1978. 187-93.

Gearhart, Sally Miller. "Use of Laboratory Animals Unnecessary for AIDS Research." *ROAR News* [Rural Women's Resources, Inc., Ukiah, CA] 1 (1988): 1, 3, 5.

Gearhart, Sally Miller. "The Womanization of Rhetoric." *Women's Studies International Quarterly* 2 (1979): 195-201.

Gearhart, Sally. "Womanpower: Energy Re-Sourcement." *The Politics of Women's Spirituality: Essays on the Rise of Spiritual Power within the Feminist Movement.* Ed. Charlene Spretnak. Garden City, NY: Doubleday, 1982. 194-206.

Gearhart, Sally, and Bill Johnson. "The Gay Movement in the Church." *Loving Women/Loving Men: Gay Liberation and the Church.* Ed. Sally Gearhart and William R. Johnson. San Francisco: Glide, 1974. 61-88.

Gearhart, Sally, and Peggy Cleveland. "On the Prevalence of Stilps." *Quest: A Feminist Quarterly* 1 (1975): 53, 55-64.

Glockenspiel, Esmeralda P. [Sally Miller Gearhart]. "Syzygoty, Diasporady and Amoebeity." *San Francisco Gay Free Press* Nov. 1970: 12-13.

Gurko, Jane, and Sally Gearhart. "The Sword-and-the-Vessel versus the Lake-on-the-Lake: A Lesbian Model of Nonviolent Rhetoric." *Bread and Roses: Midwestern Journal of Issues and the Arts* 2 (1980): 26-30.

Martin, Del, and Sally Gearhart. "Afterthought: Lesbians as Gays and as Women." *We'll Do It Ourselves: Combatting Sexism in Education.* Ed. David Rosen, Steve Werner, and Barbara Yates. Lincoln: Student Committee, Study Commission on Undergraduate Education and the Education of Teachers, U of Nebraska Curriculum Development Center, 1974. 271-87.

Short Stories

Gearhart, Sally Miller. "The Chipko." *Love, Struggle and Change: Stories by Women.* Ed. Irene Zahava. Freedom, CA: Crossing, 1988. 169-83. Rpt. in *Ms.* Sept./Oct. 1991: 64, 66-69; and *Finding Courage: Writings by Women.* Ed. Irene Zahava. Freedom, CA: Crossing, 1989. 99-110.

Gearhart, Sally Miller. "Down in the Valley." *Word of Mouth: 150 Short-Short Stories by 90 Women Writers.* Ed. Irene Zahava. Freedom, CA: Crossing, 1990. 51-52.

Gearhart, Sally Miller. "The Dying Breed." *The Fourth Womansleuth Anthology: Contemporary Mystery Stories by Women.* Ed. Irene Zahava. Freedom, CA: Crossing, 1991. 56-65.

Gearhart, Sally Miller. "Flossie's Flashes." *Lesbian Love Stories.* Ed. Irene Zahava. Freedom, CA: Crossing, 1989. 89-94. Rpt. in *An Intimate Wilderness: Lesbian Writers on Sexuality.* Ed. Judith Barrington. Portland, OR: Eighth Mountain, 1991. 188-92; and *Women of the 14th Moon: Writings on Menopause.* Ed. Dena Taylor and Amber Cloverdale Sumrall. Freedom, CA: Crossing, 1991. 240-44.

Gearhart, Sally. "A Letter from the Future." *Between the Species* 2 (1984): 37-38.

Gearhart, Sally Miller. "Roja and Leopold." *And a Deer's Ear, Eagle's Song and Bear's Grace: Animals and Women.* Ed. Theresa Corrigan and Stephanie Hoppe. San Francisco: Cleis, 1990. 136-47.

Gearhart, Sally Miller. "Roxy Raccoon." *Through Other Eyes: Animal Stories by Women.* Ed. Irene Zahava. Freedom, CA: Crossing, 1988. 81-89.

Gearhart, Sally Miller. "Whose Woods These Are." *Inviting Transformation: Presentational Speaking for a Changing World.* By Sonja K. Foss and Karen A. Foss. Prospect Heights, IL: Waveland, 1994. 127-31.

Gearhart, Sally Miller. "Wondercrone: Her Humble Origins." *Sinister Wisdom #53—Old Lesbians/Dykes* 53 (1994): 108-13.

Sotomayor, Sally [Vivian Sotomayor and Sally Miller Gearhart]. "Marta's Magic." *Tomboys: Tales of Dyke Derring-do.* Ed. Lynne Yamaguchi and Karen Barber. Los Angeles: Alyson, 1995. 200-11.

Interviews

Clark, Jil. "Sally Gearhart: Spirituality vs. Politics." *Gay Community News* [Boston] 15 Dec. 1979: 8-9.

Gearhart, Sally Miller. Videotaped interview, Jan. 1993.

Gearhart, Sally, Lani Silver, Sue Talbot, Rita Mae Brown, Jeanne Cordova, and Barbara McLean. "A Kiss Does Not a Revolution Make." *The Tide* 3 (1974): 3, 25, 29, 30.

Gearhart, Sally, Sarah Schulman, Joan Nestle, Barbara Hammer, and Jennifer Lorvick. "Lesbian Roundtable." Ed. Arlene Stein and Jackie Urla. *On Our Backs* 3 (1988): 16-19.

Karr, M. A. "Sally Gearhart: Wandering—and Wondering—on Future Ground." *The Advocate* 21 Feb. 1980: 21-22.

Mills, Eric. "Enriching and Expanding the Animal Movement: Dr. Sally Gearhart Talks about Sexism, Racism and Coalition-Building." *Agenda* 111 (1983): 4-7, 33.

Phenix, Lucy Massie, and Nancy Adair. "Sally." *Word Is Out: Stories of Some of Our Lives.* Ed. Nancy Adair and Casey Adair. San Francisco: New Glide; New York: Delacorte, 1978. 248-63.

Sturgis, Susanna J. "Discovering the Wanderground: An Interview with Sally Gearhart." *Off Our Backs* 10 (1980): 24-25, 27.

CHAPTER **11**

Sonia Johnson

"I will live to see women's spirit sweep over the earth like wildfire: out of men's control, untamable, cleansing, renewing, awakening. I will live to see women walking hand in hand the world over. I will live to see us *free*!"[1] As this statement suggests, Sonia Johnson's work and life are directed to creating and living women's world—to realizing the full possibilities of women's freedom.

Sonia Johnson's vision of the possibilities of a world centered on women and women's values stands in sharp contrast to her upbringing in the Church of Jesus Christ of Latter-day Saints and her life as a Mormon housewife and mother. She was born in Malad, Idaho, the middle child of five. Her parents, Ida Howell Harris and Alvin Harris, were schoolteachers in Washakie, a Shoshone Indian reservation nearby. Shortly after her birth, the family moved to Ferron, Utah, then to Preston, Idaho, and finally to Logan, Utah.[2]

NOTE: Excerpts from *From Housewife to Heretic, Going Out of Our Minds: The Metaphysics of Liberation, Wildfire: Igniting the She/Volution,* and *The Ship That Sailed into the Living Room: Sex and Intimacy Reconsidered,* by Sonia Johnson, and from *Out of This World: A Fictionalized True-Life Adventure,* by Sonia Johnson and Jade DeForest, are reprinted by permission of the authors.

The church was the center of the family's activities; family prayer both mornings and evenings was standard, and the family attended church for about four hours every Sunday. During the week, there were auxiliary classes for women, teenagers, and children. As Johnson explains: "The church *was* our lives. Life without the church was unthinkable. At every meeting, every social function, the concepts of the religion were in some way clarified, the purpose being to strengthen the resolve of the Saints to follow them."[3]

Johnson completed high school and attended Utah State University in Logan, earning a B.A. degree in English. There she met Richard Johnson, whom she married a year after her graduation. They had four children, born in different locations as she followed her husband to various teaching positions and pursued her own education. Eric was born while she was working on her M.A. degree at Rutgers University; Kari was born hours after she finished writing her dissertation for her Ed.D. degree, also from Rutgers; Marc was born in California, where Johnson and her husband were both teaching; and Noel was born in Malaysia, where her husband brought the family to live a simple existence on the beach, away from the madness of contemporary society.[4]

When the Johnsons finally settled in Sterling, Virginia, both Johnson and her husband began to read feminist literature at the urging of a friend. But Johnson felt no inclination to translate what she was reading into action:

> But I didn't really understand the revolutionary implications of what I was reading and of what was beginning to happen to me. Ideas and insights were crashing about in my head, but their yeasty meaning hadn't penetrated my bones, weren't yet swimming in my blood, beating with my heart. I was intellectually engaged, but the business of re-creating myself had barely begun.[5]

Not until the Mormon Church became active in opposing the Equal Rights Amendment (ERA) did Johnson's intellectual involvement with feminism turn to activism.

Johnson began hearing about the ERA shortly after her move to Virginia. The more the church raised the issue, the more miserable she became about its anti-ERA stance. Although she had not actually heard the text of the ERA, she disliked the church's involvement with a political issue because hearing politics discussed in church interfered with her "feelings of reverence and worship."[6] Thus, she was pleased when, in the spring of 1977, the president of her stake scheduled a visit to her ward to talk about the ERA.[7] "*Finally,*" she thought, "we're going to hear something intelligent on the other side of this issue!"[8] The stake president, however, began by saying he had not prepared any formal remarks for the evening but realized, on his way to the meeting, that he ought to have something concrete to say about the proposed amendment to the

Constitution. He had heard there was an article about the ERA in *Pageant* magazine, so he stopped on the way to the meeting to pick up a copy and read the article during the opening song and prayer.

Johnson's reaction was one of despair: "We had brought him our pain and our longing to believe, and he had given us *Pageant*."[9] When the president read the text of the ERA—"Equality of rights under the law shall not be denied or abridged by the United States or by any State on account of sex"[10]—Johnson became an immediate convert to feminism:

> I knew instantly what the women's movement was all about; I knew it in my very bones. It hit me like a ten-ton truck. I knew where women were in this society and where they had been for thousands of years, despite the rhetoric to the contrary, and I thought I would die of knowing.[11]

Johnson's epiphany was the impetus to feminist action, and one of her first acts was to join the march in Washington, D.C., in July 1978 for ratification of the ERA. Johnson marched with other Mormon women under a banner of "Mormons for ERA." When Senator Birch Bayh decided to hold hearings on the ERA in the Senate Subcommittee on Constitutional Rights, he wanted women from various religious traditions who favored the amendment to testify. His staff members recalled the banner and contacted Johnson to ask her to participate. Her testimony on August 4, 1978, was her first public statement for the ERA—and the beginning of an intense period of activism on behalf of the amendment that included speechmaking, demonstrations, media appearances, and meetings with church members on both sides of the issue.

The leaders in Johnson's church became increasingly agitated about Johnson's activities on behalf of the ERA and were pressured by their superiors to do something about them. Despite her constant reminder to church leaders that her support of the ERA was a purely political matter and that she was not in opposition to the church as a religion, on November 14, 1979, she received a summons to a bishops' court charged with considering her excommunication. Johnson was charged with "evil speaking of the Lord's anointed," violating "the law of consecration," and not maintaining the proper "general attitude and expression."[12]

At the trial, held on December 1, 1979, additional, previously unstated charges were added to the list, including "hampering the church's worldwide missionary effort" and "damaging other church programs, including temple work, the welfare program, family home evening, genealogy, and family preparedness."[13] Johnson knew from the moment she walked into the hearing that she had lost—that she was, in fact, being excommunicated for what she later would call her "uppityness": "It was no use struggling—I had lost long ago. I had lost when I decided to be a human being and not a role. I knew . . . that nothing anyone could say or do would stop the patriarchal wheels from grinding me to dust."[14] Johnson received the letter of excommunication on December 5, 1979.

Johnson's initial feminist activism on behalf of the ERA and eventual excommunication took place against the background of a divorce from her husband. He had returned from a six-month teaching position in Liberia to suggest that they get a secret divorce in order to free their relationship from society's stereotypical expectations, "which leave couples with so little emotional room to maneuver that relationships strangle in their own web of role restrictions."[15] Johnson agreed, in part because she appreciated the fact that her husband finally was taking some initiative in working on their relationship. Two days after they signed the "fake" divorce papers, however, he announced that he wanted the divorce to be real. He stayed with her through her excommunication for the sake of appearances but moved out a week after the trial.[16]

Johnson's conversion to feminism, her subsequent excommunication, and her divorce are detailed in her first book, *From Housewife to Heretic* (1981). Although the year in which these events transpired was difficult, Johnson wholeheartedly embraced the possibilities of a new and different life:

> While on one level I was devastated, going about the wretched business of burying my dead—a marriage, a faith, a large portion of a past—on another I was moving eagerly and confidently ahead about the business of living more fully than I had ever done, using all my senses, all my powers. Never for one second would I have chosen to return to life as it had been before. Because however much I hurt . . . I was aware the whole time that I was involved in some personally momentous, infinitely desirable, even miraculous process of growing up—and up.[17]

The next phase of Johnson's feminist evolution was characterized by civil disobedience. Her first act of civil disobedience occurred when the Republican Party dropped the ERA from its platform in 1980.[18] Johnson and 11 other women chained themselves to the entrance to the Republican National Headquarters in Washington, D.C., on August 26, 1980, in what was probably the first civilly disobedient action on behalf of the ERA.[19] She engaged in many more such actions—chaining herself to the gates of a new Mormon temple opening in Bellevue, Washington; burning Ronald Reagan in effigy; and going over the White House gate on Susan B. Anthony's birthday to "take a message to our otherwise totally inaccessible president."[20]

Perhaps the best known of her acts of civil disobedience was Johnson's participation in a fast for the ERA in Illinois, one of the states that had not ratified the amendment. Johnson was one of eight fasters who, beginning on

May 9, 1981, sat for three hours each day in the Illinois legislature, dressed in white with purple sashes, in an effort to dramatize the need for passage of the ERA. Although the fasters' general goal was to "soften the adamantine heart of the Illinois legislature" and thus to secure passage of the amendment, Johnson intended the action to serve several other goals as well: to begin "the third phase of the women's movement," in which women would "begin to be active rather than reactive"; to communicate to women "how worthy we are—how worthy of sacrifice, how worthy of risk"; and to "provide women with a model for courage."[21]

The fast invoked a variety of responses, none of which resulted in ratification of the amendment in Illinois. A major legislative response was to eat—the legislators ate constantly. Aides told the fasters "they'd never seen so much food consumed on the floor in their entire experience with the legislature."[22] In addition, on the 14th day of the fast—in the last month of the legislative session, when legislators frequently work around the clock—the speaker of the house dismissed the House for 10 days, obviously intending to provoke an end to the fast. But the fasters were still there when the session resumed.

The responses from the press and spectators were equally varied. Some members of the press ridiculed and trivialized the fast with headlines such as "They needed to lose weight anyway."[23] Others championed the fasters' courage and cause. Letters poured in from advocates on both sides of the ERA and both supporting and condemning the fasting strategy. The fasters also received hundreds of visits, many from women who stood before them speechless, unable to do anything but weep.[24]

The ERA was defeated by five votes in the Illinois legislature on June 22, 1982, despite the considerable attention paid to the fasters. At that point, there was little reason to continue, so the women broke their fast after 45 days, toasting one another and the press with grape juice.[25]

Although increasingly cognizant, during the fast, that the political system in the United States is designed deliberately to work against women, Johnson decided to run for president of the United States. The idea first was suggested to her when, flying to a speaking engagement, a woman recognized her and said, "I've just come from an executive committee meeting of the Citizens Party and your name keeps coming up as a possible candidate for president on our ticket."[26] Johnson did not take the request seriously until she was asked to speak at the national convention of the Citizens Party in the summer of 1983. She finally agreed to run as the party's candidate, primarily because of the opportunity for millions of people to hear some radical feminist philosophy. She also believed, however, that political campaigns could be "genuine instruments of change" if the candidates had "no desire for victory" and concentrated on "the victory of ideas."[27] Further, she believed a "shift of consciousness" could occur when people walked into the voting booth and saw "for the first time in living memory and in a national election, a woman's name on the ballot, a woman they could actually vote for for President of the United States."[28]

Johnson knew, however, that if she could not take herself seriously as a presidential candidate, no one else would, either. Thus, the first challenge in her campaign was to imagine herself as president:

> If I didn't believe I could perform adequately as President, I would convey this to the people in my audiences, the reporters, everyone. We wear our perceptions of ourselves on our skins. How could I go around this country talking about women's taking ourselves seriously, about everyone taking women seriously, if I couldn't do it myself?[29]

As soon as she asked herself what she would do as president, she realized that not only did she know what to do, but "most women I knew also understood what to do better than any man we've seen try to be President in our lifetimes."[30] Taught to believe that the job is so difficult, complex, and perilous that only an individual with "a special kind of genius" can handle it, Johnson came to the opposite conclusion: "The truth is that if Ronald Reagan—and most of his predecessors—can even go through the *motions* of being President, it has to be a simple job."[31]

As she spoke around the country during her campaign, Johnson asked those in her audiences to call out what they would do if they were president. Their responses, which included dismantling nuclear weapons, eliminating pornography, giving farmers a chance, scrapping plans for Star Wars, and stopping arms sales to everyone, demonstrated to Johnson how much more simple politics actually is than it is believed to be: "Even doing dishes can look awkward and can turn into a mess if one doesn't understand certain basic principles."[32]

Although Johnson did not win the presidency, she was the first alternative candidate in the United States to receive federal primary matching funds.[33] The experience further confirmed her assumptions about women's power and capabilities: "[W]omen can do not only infinitely more than we think we can, we can do anything we need to do. And since right now what we need to do is to save the earth, watching myself and the women working in my campaign all over the country gave me daily draughts of faith that we can and will do it."[34]

The campaign for president also convinced Johnson that working within patriarchy to create change was not the way to transformation. The title of her second book, *Going Out of Our Minds: The Metaphysics of Liberation* (1987), captures her break with patriarchy: "Going out of our minds means making a genuine, permanent disengagement announcement and from that moment not taking men or patriarchy seriously ever again; not denying them, simply forgetting them. Patriarchy and men are both profoundly irrelevant."[35]

The period surrounding Johnson's bid for the presidency included another major change in her life: She fell in love with Susan Horwitz, a counselor she had gone to see after the fast for the ERA. Johnson had believed that she was "hopelessly heterosexual,"[36] although she recognized that her primary commitment was to women and that she loved women and preferred their company. "I don't find women sexually interesting," she explained. "Though I don't want a male in my life, I still feel a zing when I'm around an attractive one. And I've never in my whole life felt a zing or anything approximating one around a woman, not *any* woman, no matter how lovely."[37]

But one day, while sitting and talking to Horwitz, Johnson realized she felt like kissing her—that she had come to love her: "I simply recognized that I had learned to love Susan, as I loved my mother, as I loved myself, as I loved my children. . . . But in addition—and this was the victory—I felt the inclination to express it by making adult, sexual love with her."[38] Johnson realized that although lesbianism and feminism do not necessarily go hand in hand, for her, lesbianism represented the ultimate breaking of the patriarchal taboo:

> Because it is the way of being in the world that is most destructive of male supremacy, Lesbianism is highest treason. For women to take our energy and attention, our sexuality, our primary loyalty, our deepest affinity out of the service of men and to bestow it all, all this richness, all our treasure, upon women, is the most powerful subversion of patriarchy possible on earth.[39]

The ongoing process of Johnson's feminist evolution continued, and she traced her thoughts, feelings, and practices of this evolution in her next three books. In *Wildfire: Igniting the She/Volution* (1989), she challenges women's efforts to resist patriarchy and to secure change within existing systems. Johnson came to understand that if virtually every institution functions to preserve patriarchy—thus ensuring that women's needs are not met—attempting to change those institutions only perpetuates patriarchy. In *Wildfire*, she analyzes a variety of institutions—including universities, politics, and 12-step programs—to demonstrate the ways in which they function counter to women's interests. In order to maintain her own personal integrity in regard to these issues, she stopped reading newspapers, listening to the news, and voting—acts she believes only continue to support patriarchy's version of reality. By continuing to interact with this reality, Johnson believes, "we proceed to . . . make it concrete," to "real-ize it."[40]

The next step in Johnson's feminist evolution dealt specifically with the issue of relationships. In *The Ship That Sailed into the Living Room: Sex and Intimacy*

Reconsidered (1991), she shares her increasing discontent with the process of relationships as they are constructed in patriarchy. Her opening image is of a ship that appeared on the doorstep the day she and Horwitz decided to have a relationship:

> [O]ur Ship had known it would have the upper hand in our home. It was well aware that from birth both Susan and I had been profoundly socialized to believe that a relation Ship was the one acquisition absolutely essential to our happiness. . . . We would so passionately believe that we *must* have it that a Ship could do with us just about as it pleased.[41]

The Ship dominated their lives, dictating that they meet the expectations for a relationship in contemporary U.S. culture: to live together, sleep together, spend most of their time together, and compromise and negotiate for the sake of the relationship.[42] Johnson came to see that falling in love in patriarchy and choosing to relate to another under the commands of "relationShipness" constitute, in fact, a fall into "prefabricated mindtracks that prevent us from seeing and knowing our loved one as she is and therefore from having an authentic experience."[43]

Johnson realized that all efforts at relationships are "pitifully superficial and futile attempts to deal with the real issue . . . that every human contact is tainted with hierarchy." Under patriarchy, "women's most positive values, such as genuine affection and intimacy, can hardly be born, let alone survive."[44] She understood that all relationships transform "something basically lovely, free, and life-enhancing into doomed relationShipness." Such relationships involve objectifying the other, viewing the other as "something that exists for [one's] delight or safety or other use," and submerging the self instead of finding one's own way.[45]

Instead of continuing to do relationships in the manner prescribed by patriarchy, Johnson chose to question and experiment with every facet of relationships in order to understand, create, and experience genuine intimacy outside of patriarchy. Although she later realized how much her experiments still were grounded in patriarchal conditioning rather than coming from her authentic "Wild Self," she was committed to examining her "feelings and insights" as she practiced being sexual and intimate "outside the purview of a Ship."[46] She knew she wanted to discover the "depth of feeling" of which her body was capable and "to listen for the voice" of her conditioning so that she "could continue to eradicate it." She also wanted to "learn what intimacy really was" and to "practice taking responsibility" only for herself, "behaviors that were impossible under the despotic eye of the officer on the bridge of a relation Ship."[47]

Johnson realized that she could not truly begin to experiment with relationships and continue in a relationship with Horwitz, no matter how painful living apart from her would be: "I knew absolutely that I couldn't drag the corpse of society's deadly dream of intimacy around with me any more, that I wanted out of relationShipness as designed by the fathers forever."[48] Thus, Horwitz moved out of their home, and Johnson continued to explore the nature of relationships and how to create them outside the bounds of patriarchy.

Johnson has been joined in her experiments by Jade DeForest, who is equally interested in the practice of nonpatriarchal forms of intimacy. Johnson and DeForest are not lesbians, not a couple, not interested in doing relationships, and not interested in being sexual as traditionally defined.[49] Neither woman does anything in relation to the other that she does not want to do; to do otherwise would violate her integrity as well as suggest that the other is not capable of doing her own life. Johnson and DeForest approach their interaction, then, from a stance of absolute authenticity and integrity:

> Since the truth is that this moment is all we ever have of life, we can honestly say to one another only such things as, "This is how I feel right now. I can't promise you how I'll feel or what I'll want in the next moment because I have no way of knowing. But you *can* count on me to be as true to myself every moment as I can be, and in this way also true to you. You can know for sure that when I am being and doing exactly what I want every minute, not sacrificing, being in my power as much as I can, I cannot deceive you or endanger you. Because there will be no subterranean motives, no manipulation, no murk, you will also always know who you are dealing with."[50]

Intimacy, as defined by patriarchy, is only one vestige of patriarchal brainwashing that Johnson and DeForest are attempting to exorcise from their lives; they have experimented with all kinds of activities in order to live free of patriarchal trappings. In what they call a "fictionalized true-life adventure" titled *Out of This World* (1993), Johnson and DeForest describe dealing with fear of the dark, weight gain, allergies, and chronic physical limitations—DeForest's bad back and Johnson's varicose veins—in accordance with women's reality. Johnson and DeForest describe the women's world in which they now live as one of "love, joy, contentment, peace, and abundance. . . . A world where all living things exist harmoniously and in balance because there is no maleness to cause turmoil and suffering. A world elegantly and exquisitely simple and pure."[51]

Nature of the World

Johnson's conceptualization of the world as oppressive to women has remained constant throughout her feminist evolution. The significance of women's oppression for her, however, has changed dramatically. Initially, oppression was something to which she felt compelled to respond in the hopes of changing patriarchy. Now, attuned to women's world, she chooses not to give further attention to the oppressive conditions of patriarchy and devotes herself instead to living women's world. Johnson's rhetorical theory, then, contains two worlds—the world of patriarchy and women's world—but only the latter is of interest to her at this time in her feminist evolution.

Patriarchy

Johnson's early efforts as a feminist were directed at ending patriarchy's oppression of women. She characterized the oppression of women as "archetypal" and considered the oppression of women to be fundamental—the oppression upon which all other oppressions are modeled. According to Johnson, patriarchy is deadly and pervasive; it is "a brilliantly organized and endlessly funded all-out war against women"[52] that men learned "in their kitchens and bedrooms, their caves and huts" and "subsequently applied . . . in all areas of their lives."[53] Johnson elaborates: "This is the truth of women's lives: that we live in a world where invisible institutions with inaudible voices command men to do everything possible to stop us from being fully human, fully ourselves; to hunt us down, and, if necessary, to slaughter us, emotionally and physically."[54]

Johnson is careful to note that although patriarchy affords all men automatic privilege in a world of hierarchical ordering based on sex, such privilege does not automatically make all men monsters. All men, however, "participate in and collude with a monstrous culture," and "almost no man, no matter how gentle, no matter how liberal, could bear to reject the innumerable privileges . . . of being male."[55] This explains women's failure to raise their sons to be feminists; they are unable to "change the basic formative fact of men's lives—which is that every man born automatically has violence-based-and-perpetuated-privilege."[56]

In the hierarchy that constitutes patriarchy, the primary value is "face"—"the imperative always to be in the strong, on-top male position." Saving face gives rise, in turn, to other masculine values: "competition, linear dichotomization (us/them, good guys/bad guys), domination by force, violence as the prime problem solver, materialism, efficiency, objectivity."[57] The formula for success in patriarchy, then, is an endless chant of "bigness, control, winning, money, status, fear, hatred, scarcity, violence."[58]

That men have privilege in patriarchy does not mean, however, that they have real power. Johnson describes how men, because they "own the language and can name their hanky-panky whatever they wish . . . have always tried to name it something highly politic, something with terrific propaganda force."[59] Thus, when men name patriarchy *powerful,* women believe themselves to be powerless because they do not behave as men behave. In reality, according to Johnson, men's power is "wishful thinking" because patriarchy is a philosophy of weakness. It is a weak and nongenerative power because it "sprang from profoundly negative impulses, from motives of hatred and revenge, from a lust to destroy all that was womanly and creative of life, all, that is, that was powerful."[60]

The manner in which patriarchy has reversed the powerful and the powerless is a characteristic of how it functions. "[N]othing men have said is true—at least in the way they said it was," Johnson asserts.[61] Patriarchy "always lies," and "its lies are exact reversals of the truth." Whatever "it says is the healthiest way to do things is always the most destructive; and . . . whenever it insists that there is only one right way, there are always hundreds of other, better, ways."[62] Patriarchy reverses and dichotomizes everything to create a world that is exactly the opposite of what truly is: "Total reversal holds sway in the world: pain is pleasure, hate is love, war is peace, authoritarianism is democracy, insanity is lucidity, cowardice is courage."[63] For Johnson, then, the overriding characteristic of patriarchy is that it "is a sham"—a complete denial and reversal of the true nature of the world.[64] Its assertion of the values of hierarchy and domination are just that—assertions that have no basis in universal fact.

Women's World

The privileged position patriarchy has constructed for men, which is a reality internalized by women and men alike unless the reality of feminism intercedes, no longer holds any interest for Johnson. Rather than resisting patriarchy, she devotes herself to exploring the nature of women's world and manifesting it in every aspect of her life. The world Johnson envisions when women let go of patriarchy is not simply a world in which women are taken into account; it is different in every way: "I look out upon the world men have made . . . and I don't see anything I would have done as they have done it. *Not one single thing.* Their system does not reflect me at all, neither my mode of being in the world nor my world view."[65]

The first step toward realizing women's world, according to Johnson, is to stop attending to men and start attending only to women. Even when still involved in efforts to change patriarchy, Johnson glimpsed the need to stop paying attention to men. During the fast for the ERA, she realized that she should have organized an action around laughter because anything else suggested that women were taking men seriously:

If I hadn't been so weak . . . I would have organized a very different sort of action. My ardent fantasy was to plant dozens of women equipped with laugh boxes throughout the audience in the gallery, women who would, at a prearranged signal, periodically drown with laughter the pompous circus down on the floor of the

legislature. . . . How could we be taking it and them so seriously? Laughter was the
only appropriate response.[66]

Johnson asks women to turn their attention from men and to concentrate on
what women have to offer: "I want women . . . to stop bowing at men's feet. . . .
I want women to recognize our own magnificent female powers of mind and
spirit and to trust them without verification from the men.[67] Johnson herself has
decided never to listen to a man again, a policy that includes refusing to answer
questions from men in the audiences at her lectures: "I'll never listen to any
man again, dead or alive, Indian chief or prime minister. Maleness is maleness,
totally antagonistic to my well-being as a woman."[68] She summarizes: "WE
MUST TAKE OUR EYES OFF THE GUYS!"[69]

As soon as women shift their attention from men, new possibilities begin to
appear: "As soon as we change our feeling that the men and what they are doing
is what is important in the world—that it is important *at all*"—we will "see a
new reality opening before us. Until then, we will be stuck fast in the patriarchal
mind, wasting our energies, trapped and despairing."[70] As an indication of what
can happen when attention shifts from men to women, Johnson recalls the
slogan "'What if somebody gave a war and nobody came.' Well, there *is* a war
against women," she asserts, "and if we don't come, this war can't go on."[71]
She elaborates:

> I imagine that the next Sunday or Holy Day . . . the men in charge . . . look out upon
> their congregations and see . . . *no women!* No women at all! . . . No women, ever
> again.
>   And I imagine that during the next election year, no women organize, raise
> money, stump, stamp, campaign, or come to the polls. . . .
>   I see the men crying in terror: Where are the slaves? Their whole ugly edifice in
> danger of collapse. *Because they can't do patriarchy without us!*
>   And us, where are we? . . . We're where our feelings of wholeness, strength, and
> joy are guiding us, doing our own work, taking responsibility in the new world we're
> building, letting the old one disintegrate, as it most surely would without our energy,
> our attention, and our faith.[72]

Giving women full attention, then, is the first step in manifesting women's
world. It is a world governed by an orientation to the present, a focus on living,
self-change, and a powerful kind of interconnected intimacy.

Present Orientation

A focus on the present rather than the past or future is a primary principle
that characterizes women's world. Johnson's realization that there is no linear
time is the basis for this principle:

Atomic science tells us that, contrary to how we have been conditioned to perceive it, time does not move from here to there, it is *not* like a river, it is not "passing," not going anywhere. Instead, it simply *is,* like the ocean, and we are in it as fish are in the sea. Time is our medium. We are at any moment in all the time there ever was or ever will be, surrounded by time in the form, paradoxically, of, at once, only an instant and also eternity.[73]

Johnson's orientation to time means that only in the present can anything be created or changed. Johnson suggests that one "of the cruelest crimes of patriarchy has been to teach us to project our thoughts into a future that will never come . . . or focusing us back into a past that is only memories of a present, keeping us unaware of the locus of our power in the present moment."[74] The notion that the means are the ends thus becomes not just a moral precept but a basic principle of reality; what happens in the present always and automatically is creating the future "because the means are the ends, *how* we behave is *what* we get."[75]

The notion of present time as the only time there is also has implications for the notion of process. Johnson came to realize that the idea of process not only contradicted an orientation to present time—and thus actually was not a necessary part of reality—but, in all likelihood, actually perpetuated process. Perhaps, she speculated, "we go through process because we think process is necessary, the 'way things are.' Perhaps belief in process *produces* process, and that if we believed in instantaneous change instead, we would get *that.*"[76]

Johnson later realized that perhaps there was even more involved in the persistent belief in process. Humans actually may choose process over instantaneous change because it is more manageable: "Instantaneous change is overwhelming, very frightening," so humans devise a process that allows them to acclimatize to change. In other words, humans may opt for the process of "*getting* there instead of just *being there*" because, otherwise, they would have to deal with how powerful they really are.[77] Johnson believes, then, that a present orientation means "we can change reality with incredible rapidity—instantaneously," but she acknowledges that humans are likely to continue to choose process until they "become braver," until they "dare experiment with the frightening possibilities a little at a time."[78] For Johnson, a present orientation is fundamental to creating a different world; it means that world can be created at any moment: "[W]e *do now* what we want to be doing in the future, we *be now, feel now* how we thought we could be and feel only in some future time."[79]

Self-Change

Another principle of women's world is that the only change available is self-change: "We must simply give up forever the idea that we can change

anything *through* someone else. . . . We can only change ourselves."[80] For
Johnson, this realization came after years of feminist activism, in which she
lobbied men and tried to get them to change, and from her years as a mother.
She realized she had not succeeded in getting her own four children to change
in the directions she wanted, so expecting "these guys [she] didn't even know"
to change was unreasonable:

> I began to remember how I had these four human beings on this planet who had
> come right out of my womb—I had created them. . . . They were partly me, and we
> adored each other, we loved each other, we respected each other. . . . And I
> remember how I had never ever been able to make them do what I wanted from the
> moment they were born. They really wanted to . . . because they loved me. They
> tried very hard but they really couldn't do their lives the way I wanted them to.[81]

The expectation, then, that men she did not even know would change to please
her seemed unrealistic and unworkable.

Johnson began to explore the possibilities for women when they sought to
access and live their own power rather than give their power away to others.
She describes women's power as coming from within, "from how we feel about
ourselves, from believing that we are powerful and that anyone who has to
control others by violence is weak and fearful and simply no match for us."[82]
When women feel and act out of this power, they break free of "the patriarchal
imperative that we must change men, getting them to do for us what must be
done, free of the lie that we cannot do it ourselves."[83] As a result, other changes
happen: "[T]he change in ourselves not only *can* but always *does* change
something or somebody else, and it is the only thing that can."[84] In other words,
once change happens within, a simultaneous change is manifest in the world at
large.

The realization that no one can make another change also led Johnson to an
awareness of how harmful and disrespectful efforts to change others are. She
came to realize that, in fact, she was being manipulative and even abusive when
she sought to get those around her to change—Horwitz, her children, friends,
bishops, pornographers, legislators, rapists, judges, or presidents. Such efforts
set up power-over relationships that are antithetical to the values of women's
world.

Furthermore, the effort to make others change communicates that they are
not capable of making their own life choices and constructs them as victims—
and Johnson is unable to accept victimhood as part of women's world: "I knew
that pressure or coercion of any kind for any purpose—even purposes I might
perceive as crucial—was always part of mensgame, always oppressive, always
sadomasochistic, and could change nothing, except for the worse."[85] She
explains that there "are no victims among us, only women . . . who were once

victims and are no more. So we must never think of any woman in that way. . . . [E]very woman is capable of taking responsibility for herself and . . . only she, never we, must do it."[86] Victims, in other words, are the natural consequence of efforts to change others.

Recognizing how victims are created, Johnson and DeForest now practice and manifest the "no-victim" mode in all aspects of their lives: "Neither of us can tolerate victimhood anymore, in anyone or anything. We told Tamale, that brown dog there, that what was keeping us from respecting and loving her fully was her victim behavior. . . . She changed overnight."[87] Similarly, Johnson told a ficus tree that she wasn't going to spray her for scale anymore:

> She didn't have to be a victim, I told her, but if she wanted to be, if she got so much satisfaction from it that she didn't want to change, she couldn't live in this house. . . . I told her this wasn't meant as a threat, simply a reality. There are no victims in women's world, only peers. . . . The day after I reviewed the truth with her, she began to free herself of parasites.[88]

The creation of an entirely new world—women's world—is not a monumental task, as many believe, because it is created internally: "Right here in the midst of the wreckage of the old order, we must build the new one. . . . [T]he new world is within us; it is not a geographical space."[89] For Johnson, the new world has a much better chance of succeeding than earlier feminist visions of physical community because each individual has the capacity to create the new world: "[E]ach of us has got to own this dream. Each of us must long for its realization, touch it, smell it, breathe it, live at least half our lives in it. Refuse that old nonsense, that old nightmare called patriarchy, *by thinking and behaving as if it had already disappeared from the earth.*"[90] The world envisioned becomes a reality as soon as each individual makes the internal shift in awareness:

> This means that if we want a future world in which women are not afraid—of rape and poverty and humiliation and other male violence—there is only one way to create it and that is by being unafraid now. We can't first try to change the men so women don't have to be afraid of them. If we do this now, we make the future one in which women, in fear, continue to try to change men. We can't get to fearlessness from being afraid. . . . We make a fear-free world by being unafraid in this moment, the only moment we live.[91]

The rejection of any kind of change other than self-change is basic to Johnson's view of women's world. Women's world is created, is creating itself, in the moment as women simply change themselves—by feeling, imagining, and enacting the new world.

Focus on Living

The actualization of women's world in the present leads to a focus on living in women's world; individuals do not need to work toward something because that something already is. The need to work does not exist in Johnson's vision of women's world; in fact, Johnson sees the work ethic and all of its manifestations as simply additional evidence of patriarchy's reversal. Working implies doing something for the sake of future time—to make a living, earn a paycheck, or save for a rainy day. All of these future-oriented tasks suggest that needs are not being met. When all needs are met, as they are in women's world, there is no "need to toil to be allowed to live."[92]

If the world as it was meant to be is allowed to flourish, working is not the only activity to be discarded. Learning is another tenet of patriarchy Johnson no longer accepts; like working, learning suggests a progression of tasks done for the benefit of future time. Johnson rejects the notion that humans are put on this earth to learn certain lessons necessary for their improvement and progress as beings. Instead, she believes that "our spirits are perfect, already knowing everything," and that the learning that takes place in life is a by-product of living and not the reason for it.[93] Johnson uses an analogy from the natural world to express the attitude with which she believes humans should approach life: "Someone has said that humans are the otters of the universe. That feels right to me. I like the feeling that we have come here to this beautiful planet lightly, playfully, joyfully to experiment with the amazing possibilities of ourselves."[94]

In contrast to patriarchy, the focus in women's world is on living rather than on working and learning: "'The meaning of life is to be alive.' . . . [T]o live right now, to perceive, to feel, to sense, to experience, to enjoy this moment—this, I believe, is the reason we choose to come back into a body and live in a physical world."[95] Living in "vibrant aliveness" is our only "task": "Is there anything more important to do than to be aware of and enjoy being alive every moment?"[96]

Intimacy

Women's world also is founded on the principle of intimacy, although not the kind of intimacy found in patriarchy, which is characterized by "the feeling of being most possessed" or owned by another.[97] Johnson realized that such a definition of intimacy is, in fact, nothing more than another example of patriarchal reversal, "making us believe slavery is freedom, making us believe it feels wonderful."[98]

Johnson's starting point in her search for intimacy was the realization that she could not make commitments to others but only to herself. She realized that unless she could be true to herself at all times, she could not relate intimately to others, which she knew meant interacting with her authenticity and integrity intact. She recognized, in other words, that any commitments she made on behalf of intimacy could be commitments only to herself. She thus approaches commitment in this way:

> So I make no promises, no commitments to you, dear lover, except that you can count on me never to do anything I don't want to do. Though I truly am as you see and know me now, a large part of who I am is my determination not to remain emotionally or intellectually anywhere long enough to fall sleep again and doze my life away. I am committed to deepening and expanding and flourishing as my Self dictates for the duration of my life.[99]

Efforts to remain true to herself, to do only what she desires in relation to others, and to divorce herself from patriarchy's reversals culminated in an experience that Johnson recognized as the intimacy she had been seeking. Making love one afternoon, she decided to see what would happen if she did only what she wanted to do the entire time—not worrying about her partner's pleasure unless she felt like it at the moment. Rather than assuming orgasm was her goal, she decided to see how long she could stay in "the exquisite pre-orgasm state of excitement and what would happen as the time lengthened." Throughout her experiment, she heard patriarchal voices in her head telling her to focus on her partner, to get up and do something important, and the like—but Johnson continued in this state for several hours, suspecting that "what I was doing *was* the important thing to be doing right then and . . . that there was potential in sexuality that frightened the socks off them, a potential they didn't want me to discover."[100]

As she began to think about ways to bring her experiment to a close, she realized that she had not yet succeeded in ridding herself of either/or, linear thought in terms of sex; she still assumed "there were only two possibilities" for closure: "Orgasm or no-orgasm." Instead of choosing either, she "stepped off the dichotomous road onto a path" that she had not known was there—one of thousands of paths "off the plateau of sexual excitement" and found herself "in the night sky."[101]

In this new space, she experienced an "ecstasy" she never had felt before, seeing and feeling herself, the moon, and the stars from inside, "knowing one another completely and adoring what we learned." Overwhelmed with bliss and happiness, she knew she "had experienced genuine intimacy in the sky that night, and it bore no resemblance" to what she previously had called intimacy, in degree or in kind.[102] It was the most powerful kind of connection imaginable. Further, Johnson realized from this experience that there are many paths to genuine intimacy in addition to sex—"meditation, music, dance, conversation"—and that it is a "state of nearly complete creativity" that certainly is "something worth sticking around for."[103]

Several features characterize women's world and make it substantially different from—in fact, the complete opposite of—patriarchy. Whereas patriarchy is built on saving face and other superficial expressions of power, women's world is grounded in a present orientation, a focus on living and self-change, and an intimacy of interconnection. These characteristics or principles combine to create a "universe that wishes all life well."[104]

Definition of Feminism

Johnson's work and life are characterized by an absolute commitment to women and all aspects of their lives—cognitive, emotional, and physical. Johnson's account of her conversion to feminism, when she first heard the text of the ERA, provides a sense of the depth and totality of her feminist commitment:

> "I am a feminist. In fact, I am a *radical* feminist!" I didn't even know what that meant, but I knew that radical meant "at the root" and I knew that at the very roots of my soul I had been changed, that I would never be the same, nor would I wish to be. I knew what women have to know, I felt what women have to feel, to become fully human.[105]

Although she no longer uses the word *feminism* because of its implications of "the women's auxiliary, women hanging about on the fringes of the men's club begging to be let in,"[106] Johnson has constructed feminism as a total life engagement that "is not about 'issues' at all." Rather, feminism is "a perspective, a way of looking at all the issues," a "totally different human possibility, a non-patriarchal way of being in the world. It is about a new universal habit, a new mind."[107] Johnson describes feminism as "the most inclusive and descriptive analysis of the human situation on earth."[108] It is also the most dangerous because the act of giving one's "full, first, and total loyalty" to women is the most taboo-defying—and the most transformative—philosophy in existence.[109]

Nature of the Rhetor

The rhetor as conceptualized by Johnson is suggested by her own answer to the question, "Who are you?" "I am Sonia—woman, human being, glad to be alive, loving every second of it. I was dead and am alive. I had wandered far from home and have at last found my way home again."[110] The authority and sense of self implicit in this stance are the starting points for Johnson's conception of the rhetor.

The rhetor is an ordinary woman, not significantly different from other women. Unlike the criterion of expertness valued by patriarchy, this ordinariness is the source of women's strength and power:

> Any female who has lived a day on the earth is already an expert on what it means to be female. She already knows more about who she is, how she feels, what she wants and needs than all the men who ever lived put together could ever know about her. No man on earth, no matter how good or well-meaning, has the answer for any woman, let alone for *all* women.[111]

Johnson attributes her discovery of the truth of women's authority to an incident when she had prayed to know what she had been "trying to avoid knowing for a very long time—probably all my life—because I've been too afraid to face it." She immediately heard her own voice say, "Patriarchy is a sham."[112] She realized she heard her own voice—not God's—because of her own expertness as a woman: "*I* was the authority about my life, about what being female meant to my existence. *I* was the one who could speak with understanding and truth about myself."[113]

The authority of ordinary women also signals that every woman is worthy of being taken seriously. At the time of the fast for the ERA, Johnson believed that one of her main goals in taking part in the fast was to "tell the women in this country how important they are. It would say, there are eight women in Springfield who think your dignity and your human rights are worth giving their lives for."[114] That women rarely are taken seriously made the fast itself even more important: "It's stunning to be taken seriously as a woman. It hardly ever happens."[115] Johnson's rhetor not only takes herself and her own authority seriously, but she trusts the competence of other women. Johnson explains:

> Knowing that I am an ordinary woman, and having discovered what I am capable of, I feel a degree of optimism about women in general that I have never felt before. Since I have not only survived but triumphed, I have learned that triumph, not just survival, is possible for women like me, ordinary women, everywhere. We are all more than we dream. All stronger and more courageous, all better and wiser.[116]

Johnson illustrates her basic trust in the capabilities of women rhetors by describing a time when her mother accompanied her to a women's peace camp. Johnson had just come out as a lesbian, a revelation with which her mother was struggling. Her mother spent much of her time at the camp talking to lesbians and trying to understand lesbian relationships. When some of Johnson's friends worried about how "alien and bizarre" lesbianism probably would seem to Johnson's mother, Johnson's response embodied her belief that each person can take care of herself: "My mother is a wonderful, strong woman. Don't matronize her. Tell her what she wants to know."[117] This stance captures the basic approach to interactions in women's world: Competence is assumed and expected.

The competence that characterizes Johnson's rhetor requires an additional quality as well—self-responsibility. It is a notion that, like many others, has evolved over time for Johnson. At first, Johnson assumed the responsibility for telling other women what to do. For example, when the process of her excommunication from the Mormon Church began, she told other supporters of the ERA to remain church members: "I thought I knew what was best for all Mormons for ERA. I told all those hundreds of sufferers, 'Don't leave the church; that's not the solution. The church has been good for us, it has made us what we are, and I don't think that's a minor accomplishment.'"[118] Johnson now believes, however, that rhetors must not take responsibility for anyone or anything else because to do so diminishes the competence and freedom of the other:

> When we take responsibility for other people in any way, we encourage them to doubt their own competence. So instead of helping them, we insult, limit, and disable them. If it were clear to us all that no one's purpose on the planet is to be responsible for anyone's feelings but her own or for meeting anyone else's needs, and that any attempt to usurp another's accountability is unethical and coercive, we could begin to think in earnest about freedom.[119]

For Johnson's rhetor, then, self-responsibility translates into regarding all other individuals as capable of managing their own lives. Johnson explains this stance: "I . . . trusted that other women were doing the best they could at the moment, as I was, and that, like me, all they needed from others in order to get on with their personal work was to be unconditionally accepted as the experts on their own lives."[120] She asks others to act on this philosophy in this way: "Unasked, don't propose plans to me, don't think up ideas for me. . . . If I want suggestions or help, I'll ask for them. . . . I want to decide what advice and help I need, and I want the choice of getting it or not."[121]

Johnson's notions of competence and self-responsibility are rooted in the assumption that rhetors have choices about how to live their lives. When they are given the responsibility for making their own choices about how to be, they will make the choices that are right for them: "No matter how badly a woman's been damaged by mensmachine, she always has choices, and every single second of her life she can choose among an infinite number of them."[122] Some women may be more fearful of change than others, but the possibility for change is always present, regardless of circumstances or conditions. Johnson's basic optimism that women are competent and can take care of themselves is strong:

> Women are extraordinary beings, every one of us. . . . far more powerful, far more everything than we can begin to believe or give ourselves credit for. Given this, and

that we're constantly making choices—we can't help it, that's what it is to live—any of us could opt to change *if we wanted to badly enough.*[123]

Johnson's recognition that every woman, every rhetor, is responsible for her own life has provoked fundamental changes in two areas critical to her own life—her writing and speaking and her role as a mother. She realized that articulating her beliefs in books and in lectures essentially took the responsibility for learning away from others; others tried to follow in her footsteps rather than live their own lives. Thus, Johnson has no plans to write further or to attempt to teach others what she has learned as a female human being on this planet: "That stance is blatantly sadomasochistic. I want women who are doing this on their own . . . who are figuring it out for themselves."[124] Johnson is now simply living her life and figuring out what she needs to figure out, and she trusts that other women can and will do likewise.

Johnson's realization that self-responsibility is fundamental led her to a dramatic rethinking of motherhood as well. She realized that, under patriarchy, mothers are not allowed to fulfill the self-responsibility that is a basic tenet of agency because they are required always to put the needs of their children first: That "we have been coerced into putting their needs first *whether we felt like it or not, wanted to or not* at the moment, is evidence of the gross, and I think deliberate, mis-organization of society into nuclear family units based on ownership."[125] She realized that making her own happiness dependent upon how her children behaved or whether they were happy, safe, and secure was a direct violation of her conceptualization of the rhetor as someone in charge of her own life—and only her own life.

Self-responsibility and motherhood, as practiced in patriarchy, could no longer coexist if women's world were to be realized: "I was getting hold of a basic principle of power, that when we make our feelings of well-being or security or safety dependent upon someone else's behavior, we hand them the opportunity, even the invitation, to destroy us."[126] Mothering was an especially clear case of giving someone the responsibility to do just that. Johnson realized that even though her children were grown,

once we've done a relationship with someone, there's no way to stop doing it. Even though they don't need it, I'm still in "taking care" mode with those four people, and if I stick in there, the albatross of motherhood will be hanging around my neck when I'm a tottering old woman and my kids are gray and paunchy.[127]

Johnson's personal resolution to this dilemma was to "divorce" her children in order to rid herself of her patriarchal ownership of them—an ownership that negated the self-responsibility on the part of all involved that she sought to foster. She told each of her children that she no longer would own them, be

responsible for their happiness or well-being, or remain interested in them in
any way. In fact, she would not contact them again, and they should not contact
her. The artificial ties of motherhood were broken, allowing Johnson's children
to develop their own support systems and to assume full responsibility for their
lives.[128]

At the same time, Johnson recognized that children could be reared in a way
that honors the sense of self-responsibility that is critical to her conception of
the rhetor. In her vision, children would belong to no one; rather, they would
be "absolutely free from birth"—free from the child-parent relationship and its
demands.[129] Furthermore, children would be cared for only "by women who
wanted to do it, and not exclusively by those women who had given birth to
them."[130] Johnson imagines the possible impact of this kind of mothering on the
well-being of children:

> That means that every woman who holds you, feeds you, plays with you, sings to
> you, tells you stories, bathes you, dresses you, rocks you to sleep, does it because
> she really loves doing it, really wants to, and freely chooses you over everything
> else she might have been doing. She is with you out of totally free choice!
> Imagine how easy it will be for you to love yourself in such circumstances. All
> you ever see in anyone's face is total approval, total joy in your existence and in
> your ways, total acceptance and genuine love.[131]

The rhetor Johnson envisions, then, takes care of herself. Although she may
not have special expertise, intelligence, or training—important qualifying considerations under patriarchy—she is an expert nonetheless because she is an
authority on her own life. She has the skills she needs to make her own decisions
and to take charge of her life. She not only recognizes but puts into practice the
principle that individuals cannot be responsible for anyone or anything but
themselves.

Rhetorical Options

The manner in which Johnson's rhetor enacts women's world is grounded in the
notion of experimentation. For Johnson, experimentation is the only way to sort
through belief systems, come to understand the extent to which they have been
constructed by patriarchy, and develop new ways of being in the world: "Feminism to me had always meant experimentation. . . . So because I wanted a new
world, I had no choice but to at least try to do something else—*anything* else.
I knew from experience that taking such risks could jettison my mind out of its
ruts and expose it to a vast range of new possibilities."[132] Questioning every
aspect of her beliefs provides the rhetor with other perspectives, broadens the
possibilities for action, and encourages "wildness and creativity."[133]

Johnson's rhetorical options, then, are experiments about new ways to do the world. These options have evolved through two stages—those designed to address patriarchy and those that function to realize women's world. Her initial experiments with and efforts on behalf of feminism were designed to change patriarchy through strategies of resistance and representation. But as her activism continued into civil disobedience, Johnson came to see that all of these efforts were reactions that only assured the continuation of patriarchy. Thus, she moved into rhetorical modes focused on being as the way to manifest women's world.

Patriarchy

Johnson's first feminist actions were designed to produce changes in the present system and included demonstrating, protesting, signing petitions, and voting. She found herself increasingly dissatisfied with these approaches, however, because she felt as if she were "living constantly in reaction." She realized that "when we identify ourselves in *opposition* to something we become its unwitting accomplices. By bestowing the energy of our belief upon it, by acquiescing to it, we reinforce it as reality. The very difficult truth is that WHAT WE RESIST PERSISTS."[134]

Resistance is incapable of bringing about change; in fact, it has the opposite effect from what is intended. Rather than producing change in the existing system, it strengthens it. Johnson recognized that women have resisted patriarchy in every way imaginable for at least 5,000 years, but such resistance has not worked. The image of patriarchy as a fortress on a hill clarified for her how resistance simply makes patriarchy stronger:

> Looking down the hill a short distance, I saw the women, thousands of them, a huge battering ram in their arms, crying, "We've got to get through to the men! We've got to make them stop! We've got to get them to understand that they're destroying everything!" They run at the gate with the ram. . . . Over and over again, for five long millennia. . . . Some women are pole-vaulting over the walls, shouting as they leap: "If we can just get in there, we can change everything!"[135]

Behind the gate, however, all action is directed at reinforcing patriarchy, and unwittingly the women end up perpetuating what they intended to break down:

> [T]he men, drunk with adrenalin, are being spurred by the assault to incredible heights of creativity. They have invented bionic metals to reinforce the gate and walls wherever the ram reveals a weak spot, gradually making the fortress impregnable, impenetrable. . . . The assault, by forcing them to strengthen, refine, and embellish the original edifice, serves to entrench patriarchy further with every Whoom![136]

Women cannot depend on men to represent their interests or help them in their efforts to transform the system because men inevitably support patriarchy. Johnson gives as an example *Roe v. Wade,* which many activists cite as an example of change accomplished within the system with the assistance of men. Johnson, however, argues just the opposite—that the legalization of abortion kept women from learning how to be independent of men's control of their bodies:

> The women's health movement has taught us . . . that almost any one of us can learn to perform a simple abortion. Trusting ourselves, trusting other women, feeling sure of ourselves and understanding how critical it is to be independent of men's medical control, we must all learn to do it. . . .
> Then no matter what laws men make to try to control our bodies, those laws will be, quite simply, unenforceable.[137]

Johnson rejects, then, all forms of resistance, which do nothing more than sustain the basic structures of patriarchy. She chooses to focus instead on rhetorical options that bring into being women's world.

Women's World

The rhetorical options in women's world are centered in the notion of being, the primary means of manifesting women's world. Johnson offers four additional options that help rhetors actualize being: attention to feelings, acting out of desire, gift giving, and unconditional touch. All of these options demonstrate how different in every way women's world is from patriarchy.

Being

Johnson's rhetorical option of being is a natural extension of the principles that constitute women's world. Rather than resisting or attempting to change the existing system, Johnson believes that living the life that is desired in the present moment is all that is necessary to bring about women's world. Women do not need to work toward, envision, or affirm a new future in order to realize it, as Johnson once believed; all that is necessary is to begin living the desired life fully in the present: "Live today as you want the world to be."[138]

In enacting this rhetorical option, rhetors in Johnson's rhetorical theory do not ask what they need to do to change the world, a question Johnson was asked repeatedly by women at her lectures. For Johnson, the question is not "What should we do?" but "How should we be?" Being—experiencing, living, fully appreciating—is what creates women's world: "There is simply being there, being now the way we want to be and the way we want women to be in a new world, not doing other 'interim' things in some futile effort to *get* there."[139]

Being—not doing—is what produces change in the universe: The "surest route to transformation is not what we *do* but how we *are* . . . it's not doing but being that rearranges the stars of destiny. . . . [O]ut of who I *am,* out of who we *are* —not out of acts of desperation or resistance—is coming the new world."[140]

The rhetor who concentrates on being is, in fact, doing precisely what needs to be done for a new world to come into existence:

> Patriarchy cannot exist in the presence of life and joy and fearlessness and love of self, so all the while any of us are experiencing these feelings, we make and hold a space in the cosmos where there is no oppression of women. When enough of us create such a space inside and around ourselves, when enough of us feel free of the imperatives of this system, moment by moment, freedom will become reality for all women in the world.[141]

Johnson summarizes: "[I]f we want a world in which women have integrity and are independent, self-governing and untamed—and patriarchy cannot survive women's being any of these—we have to have integrity, be independent, self-governing, and wild *right now.* . . . That world is either right now or it is never."[142]

Johnson discusses four particular options—attending to feelings, acting out of desire, gift giving, and unconditional touch—as examples of how to enact being in women's world. These are forms of expression that enabled her to think in new ways about women's world; thus, they are ways of manifesting being that may make the concept more understandable to others as well.

Attention to Feelings

Feelings are a means by which to remain cognizant of and centered in the present moment and thus constitute a way to enact being. Although devalued in patriarchy, Johnson realized that when she truly began to experience her feelings, without trying to share them or talk about them, she was especially awake and conscious—"a seething mass of unexpelled energy."[143] She surmised that perhaps "'expressing our feelings' is a way of avoiding feeling. . . . Perhaps we are trained to respond because response gives our power away."[144] Paying attention to feelings—but not necessarily expressing them—is a way to stay fully alive and engaged in the present.

Most important, however, feeling a particular way creates the reality embodied by that feeling. Thus, feelings are not only a manifestation of being—a way to connect with women's world in the moment—but they also actualize women's world. When women act out of feelings of self-worth, for example, they create a world characterized by worthiness:

[W]e immediately create a world in which we are worthy. We can tell when we truly love and respect and honor ourselves because we are no longer able to behave like slaves. We do not have to plan how not to; we simply find that when we respect ourselves we cannot, for instance, beg men, cannot lobby them. Appropriate new behavior comes out of appropriate new feelings.[145]

Johnson believes that when sufficient numbers of women understand the principle of feeling as a means to create a particular kind of world, that world will exist: "As soon as enough of us—and it doesn't need the majority, just the critical mass of us—feel right now how we thought we were going to feel down the road sometime when the men had changed . . . that is the moment when that mind will become the general mind of the planet."[146]

Acting Out of Desire

Johnson's focus on living rather than working leads to another mode of enactment that helps realize being: Individuals should do exactly what they want at every moment. For individuals to violate personal integrity by acting against their desires means the breaking of their connections with all parts of the universe. In order to have a new world, Johnson asserts, "we must figure out how everyone's needs can be completely filled without any of us doing a single thing we don't really want to do, *without even the smallest sacrifice.*"[147] Everything necessary for freedom "depends on our learning to let everyone and everything do only what they want to do, to go their own ways and be free."[148]

In a world in which all needs are met, all creatures make their own contributions without having to spend time and effort at tasks they do not care about or that meet the needs of others but not themselves. Johnson turns to an example from nature to emphasize this point:

Though the birds and flowers, the fauna and flora, contribute a great deal and are indispensable members of the world community, they do not "toil." With them as our model . . . perhaps we can begin to trust that if each of us does what gives us pleasure and what we do well, if each of us follows our natural bent and honors it, we too will enhance the flow of life, facilitate its cycles, meet all human needs, and have all that we ourselves require.[149]

Individuals doing only what they desire is not selfish, as this principle would be labeled in patriarchy. Rather, it means truly operationalizing the notion that the means are the ends—that working toward something never will accomplish that end. Instead, living in the present in ways that meet individual needs preserves a connection with every other being on the planet. Meeting their own needs is the most natural way for individuals to sustain the world and its rhythms, a truth forgotten in the distortions of patriarchy.

Gift Giving

Gift giving constitutes a third practice that facilitates the realization of women's world. As a prototype for interaction, gift giving occurred to Johnson as she was struggling to answer the question of how to earn a living in women's world. Unable to answer the question, she finally realized that if she could not answer it no matter how much time she devoted to it, then it probably was the wrong question.[150] Thus, she began to consider the place of money in patriarchy and to imagine a world without it. Her thinking led her to gift giving—already in existence and practiced by many women—as the answer to how needs are met in women's world.

Gift giving is based not on a system of exchange but on a value that does not even exist in patriarchy—"that the needs of living beings and our life systems be met."[151] In giving a gift, the giver concentrates on satisfying needs without expectation of return. Gifts are given on the basis of filling needs or truly giving pleasure, and those who give "arrive at a common understanding of human needs and how to satisfy them in all their variety, an understanding that links them to all other human beings."[152] In the process of gift giving, no one's needs or desires are compromised, and no one is "working" or striving to meet those needs. Gift giving fosters abundance and connection, and the gift "flows on and out, the circle of givers and receivers expanding exponentially and overlapping in all directions."[153]

In order to describe the nature of a world in which gift giving is the mode of operation, Johnson imagines a small town "where the foremost desire of the citizenry is that everyone have everything necessary for health and joy." To achieve this, "everyone in town *does what they want to do all the time,* loyal first to their own welfare while remaining fully aware of their critical interconnection with everyone else's."[154] What is required is simply "maintaining the flow."[155] Johnson elaborates:

> What it does require is a deep love for life and all living things, for their individual and interconnected, interdependent rhythms, cycles, and energies. It requires a profound respect for oneself and faith that the springs of one's inner power loop through and among those of every other part of the universe, from the Milky Way's innumerable systems to the newborn kittens under the porch. It requires the fearless delight in ambiguity that comes from immersion in the present and that renders regulation and its requisite hierarchy not only irrelevant but odious.[156]

Gift giving, then, allows members of women's world simply to be, without having to engage in forms of work or exchange that contradict the nature of women's world.

Unconditional Touch

Like gift giving, which solves the dilemma of how needs are met in a world in which all individuals do as they please, unconditional touch solves the difficulty of how to interact intimately with others without setting up expectations of return and exchange. Johnson suggests that touch, like gift giving, is an option particularly suited to women's world: "I think that touch is how women communicated with one another before men came, and is still the only way we can really know other women."[157] Johnson recognizes that touch always has been important to women, but because touch is almost always conceptualized sexually by men, when women touch men, it usually leads to sex. She suggests that perhaps "a lot of women have babies just so they can touch as much as they want without having to do sex. Animals and children are the only place in mensworld where we can do that."[158]

Touching unconditionally is not done with the expectation of reciprocal touch nor is it used to communicate anything other than simply the desire to touch another. Johnson uses as an example her touching of DeForest's leg:

> I'm touching your leg, right? I'm touching it *only* because at this moment I really want to, because it feels good to my hand, because right now it satisfies *me*. I have no ulterior motive, nothing that I'm trying surreptitiously to convey. It's not a way to communicate that I find you attractive and therefore hope you'll start thinking of going to bed with me. I'm not using it to say that I'd like you to touch me, too. I'm not trying to make you feel better. It isn't a means to some end. It's exactly, openly, genuinely only what it seems to be—me wanting to enjoy the touch at this moment.[159]

In women's world, touch is not used to meet personal needs beyond simply the pleasure of the touch itself. The use of touch for other ends—sex or sexual harassment, for example—disappears when each party in the interaction holds no expectations for touch beyond the present moment.

Johnson suggests that women's world is possible and present in the moment; it is available as soon as women begin to realize it through the option of being. It does not require that women work hard enough, find the right strategies, wait for the right time, or in any way do something they do not want to do in order to have future happiness. In women's world, each woman is, from the moment of her birth, fully functioning, aware, and courageous—someone who assumes complete responsibility only for herself and lives in the world in which she wants to exist. Johnson now spends her time living in just such a world: "Women's world: a world with no separation, no loneliness, where everything is connected to everything else—the women and the trees and the animals and the birds, all one. A world of arousal and power and infinite possibility."[160]

Two metaphors that Johnson uses capture the passionate and liberatory possibilities of her rhetorical options: the metaphors of fire and flying. Both images are interspersed throughout her writings from her earliest days as a feminist. During her activism on behalf of the ERA, she participated in an action held on July 4, 1981, that was labeled "Relighting Feminist Fires." At a demonstration later the same year at the White House, the theme resurfaced on a banner: "On Fire for the ERA."[161] Johnson also has noted, on several occasions, a strong connection with her suffragist foremothers and their burning passion for justice and freedom: "Come back and ignite us again. . . . Dear sisters, help us be all on fire!"[162]

The image of fire became more metaphorical as Johnson's thinking evolved, until it became a symbol for each woman's contribution to the new world: "We have now an unfailing fire, we women with our torches and our blazing looms. Like flame-winged doves escaped from our cages, all over the world we are mutinously, bravely burning."[163] The flame ultimately stands for women's creative spirit, overtaking the world like wildfire as individual women "become one more flame in the wildfire of femaleness that is blazing through the universe, reshaping the proud and passionate order of things and reforging the human soul."[164]

The liberatory imagery of flying functions similarly to that of the metaphor of fire for Johnson. Just as the fire imagery had its origins in her early days as a feminist activist, so did the metaphor of flight. Beginning in October of 1979, Mormons for ERA flew a banner behind a plane over the international assembly of Mormon leaders; it read, "Mormons for ERA are everywhere!"[165] This was followed by banners at dozens of other conferences and demonstrations across the country, making flying a specialty of Mormons for ERA.[166] What began literally as a way to make a point became a symbol for the individual and collective liberation of women.

Johnson tells of a recurring dream she had of soaring above the earth like an astronaut. Taking this as a sign that "I'm finally free, and anything is possible," she now believes in the metaphoric as well as the literal promise of that dream. She insists that "one of these days soon, I'm going to fly."[167] A second dream added yet another dimension to the metaphor of flying. In this dream, she was in New York City and was able to fly just high enough to get past the fourth floors of the buildings. She realized that she could not make progress because a woman was hanging on to her legs. Although delighted that she "could fly *at all*," she also recognized the woman who was keeping her from flying higher: "Her name was Sonia Johnson."[168] She suggests that "we keep ourselves from soaring,"[169] and in her new life in women's world, she continues to disengage from patriarchal ways of thinking and to choose instead options that make flying—in every definition of that word—possible.

Transformations of Rhetorical Theory

Johnson's rhetorical theory transforms five basic components central to traditional rhetoric: exigence, the nature of change, the audience, ethos, and strategy. As a result, her theory fundamentally alters the nature of rhetoric, a shift demonstrated in the rhetorical option that is central to her theory—being. Her rhetoric is grounded in being and not in doing, in the realization of "how to be fully and freely Sonia, how to feel the power of my woman's life all through my body and all through my consciousness, every moment of every day. From this, I am incredibly certain, everything necessary will follow."[170]

Exigence

In traditional rhetorical theory, rhetoric responds to an exigence—something that is not as it should be and that needs to be changed. This system, condition, structure, or defect becomes the target of the responsible rhetor, who seeks to address and correct it. At times, this exigence is social—a perceived lack in matters that affects group concerns. At other times, the exigence is material—a structure or institution that is the target of change. In still other instances, the exigence is psychological or emotional—a felt lack or defect for which rhetors seek correction.

Johnson's theory dramatically reconceptualizes the exigence and how it functions in a rhetorical situation. In particular, she addresses the exigence of oppression, conceived by most social movement theorists as a major condition that must be confronted and overturned. More likely than not, this targeted exigence is difficult to change because of the power, strength, and intractability of the structures and practices that establish and reinforce it; nevertheless, with skill, the rhetor can effect the desired change. Johnson, however, disagrees. Not only does she not see oppression as a powerful exigence, but she no longer sees it as an exigence at all. Patriarchy or oppression is only a sham in her theory—weak and vulnerable because of the inaccurate, unhealthy foundations on which it is based. It is extremely vulnerable to collapse and will do so as soon as individuals—and women in particular—stop giving it attention and energy and withdraw their support from it. Considering oppression an exigence that women must address only maintains it as a source of power. Johnson, then, dismisses the need to address oppression; she thus calls into question the need to address any exigence at all. This attitude bears directly on her approach to change.

Change

When there is no exigence to address—when the world is allowed to be in its state of harmony and interconnection—there is no need to focus on change.

Rhetorical efforts designed to produce change in a person or system inevitably fail and, in fact, function to shore that system up. Johnson's rhetorical theory suggests an alternative to this cycle of response and resistance—creating and living in another reality rather than spending time and energy on an existing one that not only does not meet but, in fact, subverts those needs at every turn.

Johnson's approach to change is based on internal rather than external change. The transformation of conditions and people outside of the rhetor does not produce change or have an impact beyond simply reproducing that system. Changes made within the internal self, on the other hand, produce lasting effects. Once rhetors decide to change themselves, they set in motion processes that manifest change in the external world as well. They create spaces and alternatives in which individuals can experiment with and experience living new lives.

When Johnson's notions of time are taken into account—when time is not seen as linear but is viewed as the simultaneous experience of past, present, and future—rhetorical efforts undertaken in the present to create change in the future are even more irrelevant and unworkable. Only in the present can something be created or changed, and what is done in the present is the future. Any change that happens occurs in the immediate moment, when women go out of their minds, "knowing that women are now the only relevant people on earth as far as change is concerned, women and the way we view the world, the way we live in it at our best."[171]

Audience

Johnson's notions of change also have implications for the nature of the audience in Johnson's rhetorical theory. Unlike traditional theories, in which audience members often are seen as not very knowledgeable, perhaps incompetent, and at least inexperienced, in Johnson's theory they are seen as the foremost experts on their own lives. The only thing that anyone can control or change is the self. Thus, the auditors in Johnson's theory are considered extraordinary beings—powerful, competent, wonderful, and strong—and Johnson is confident that they will make the choices that are right for them. They do not need to be patronized by an "expert" rhetor who gives them the truth about some state or condition because they are peers with the rhetor— equally competent, wise, capable, and responsible.

Ethos

Ethos, or credibility, is conceptualized in traditional rhetorical theory as intelligence, moral character, and goodwill. Although Johnson's belief in self-authority challenges the concept generally—the rhetor does not need to be an expert in some external body of knowledge in order to be credible—her rhetorical theory challenges, in particular, the dimension of goodwill. Rhetors traditionally are expected to exhibit concern for their audiences by demonstrating that they are interested in audience members' welfare, unselfish in their own motivations, and uninterested in personal gain. Johnson's rhetorical approach, however, challenges this perspective, advocating instead that rhetors do only what they desire at any moment.

Johnson's revised view of goodwill does not mean that rhetors do not care about others. They care deeply, but they recognize that only in caring for the self can true compassion be expressed: "I want compassion and generosity, first from myself. If I can understand and love myself, I will be merciful and loving to others."[172] What is required in interactions with others, according to Johnson, is simply self-love, which results in "love of others out of which springs behavior in the best interests of everyone."[173] In taking as their primary task the deepening, expanding, and flourishing of their own selves, rhetors contribute to the ongoing harmony and rhythms of the universe. They contribute to the effortless meeting of everyone's needs in true connection with all other beings on the planet.

Strategy

Johnson's conceptions of exigence, change, and time drastically alter the construct of rhetorical strategy, the basic unit of data for traditional rhetoricians when they theorize about rhetoric, analyze texts, or construct messages. A *strategy* is an action a rhetor takes that is designed to accomplish a goal or to produce an effect in the future. Inherent in this conception of strategy are a separation of means and ends and a dichotomy of cause and effect, both at odds with Johnson's nonlinear conception of time. Johnson rejects this notion of strategy because, in her theory, rhetors no longer engage in rhetorical activities designed to meet exigences, change conditions, or achieve goals in the future. Instead, they employ what she refers to as *present-ing* or what might be seen as *enactments,* in which they enact in the present the world they wish to experience in the future. This world is available immediately once this principle itself is recognized: "We don't need to wait for someone to show us the ropes. We are the ones we've been waiting for. Deep inside us we know the feelings we need to guide us. Our task is to learn to honor our own inner knowing."[174]

Rhetorical Option of Being

All of the rhetorical transformations that Johnson suggests serve as the basis for a rhetorical option not theorized within traditional rhetoric—being. Being is living the life that is desired in the present moment. Rhetors do not need to work toward or envision a new future in order to manifest it; they simply live the way they want the world to be. For Johnson, the question "How should we be?" replaces the traditional question "What should we do?", completely overturning the goal-oriented, strategic function for traditional rhetoric. The most radical option for action, then, is to live in the present: "I 'am' in the present the way I hoped to be sometime in the new feminist world. I practice seeing and feeling the vibrant colors around me, feel the breeze on my skin, breathe deeply and often, touch everything, wake up, come alive, be unafraid, forgive myself, love myself madly, be joyful."[175]

Because Johnson's rhetorical theory so thoroughly challenges many standard constructs within the rhetorical tradition, it disrupts that tradition dramatically. She has created a theory characterized by a commitment to an entirely new set of values and ways of being. She invites rhetors to experience this alternative possibility—what she calls *women's world*—the world as it was before patriarchy's imposition of itself upon the planet. Leaving behind patriarchal thinking, structures, and strategies, she creates a world in which rhetoric as it traditionally is defined is unnecessary. There is no need to attempt to move people from one idea to another when all beings participate in the same natural cycles that characterize the universe, share the same values about the nature of the world, and joyfully experience life in all its abundance. Johnson summarizes this rhetorical orientation:

> What I am doing now is walking by the side of any woman who is traveling in my direction, listening to her ideas about how we can practice being free, sharing with her the fullness of my heart at having her company in this greatest of all human journeys . . . widening and clearing the path as we walk; clearing resting places.[176]

Bibliography

Books

Johnson, Sonia. *From Housewife to Heretic.* 1981. Garden City, NY: Anchor/Doubleday, 1983.

Johnson, Sonia. *Going Out of Our Minds: The Metaphysics of Liberation.* Freedom, CA: Crossing, 1987.

Johnson, Sonia. *The Ship That Sailed into the Living Room: Sex and Intimacy Reconsidered.* Estancia, NM: Wildfire, 1991.

Johnson, Sonia. *Wildfire: Igniting the She/Volution.* Estancia, NM: Wildfire, 1989.

Johnson, Sonia, and Jade DeForest. *Out of This World: A Fictionalized True-Life Adventure.* Estancia, NM: Wildfire, 1993.

Articles

Johnson, Sonia. "Ship of Fools?" *Ms.* Sept./Oct. 1991: 94-95.

Johnson, Sonia. "Sonia Johnson Speaks of Creating a 'Women's World.'" *Hot Wire* Sept. 1990: 37-39.

Johnson, Sonia. "The Woman Who Talked Back to God and Didn't Get Zapped!" *Feminist Frontiers: Rethinking Sex, Gender, and Society.* Ed. Laurel Richardson and Verta Taylor. New York: Random, 1983. 97-103. Rpt. (shortened version) from *From Housewife to Heretic.* Garden City, NY: Anchor/Doubleday, 1983. 101-62.

Notes

1. Introduction

1. Adrienne Rich, *On Lies, Secrets, and Silence: Selected Prose 1966-1978* (New York: W. W. Norton, 1979) 35.

2. Rebecca West, *The Young Rebecca,* ed. Jane Marcus (London: Macmillan, 1982).

3. Cheris Kramarae, "Feminist Theories of Communication," *International Encyclopedia of Communications,* ed. Erik Barnouw, vol. 2 (New York: Oxford UP, 1989) 157.

4. Gloria Anzaldúa, "Haciendo caras, una entrada," *Making Face, Making Soul/Haciendo Caras: Creative and Critical Perspectives by Feminists of Color,* ed. Gloria Anzaldúa (San Francisco: Aunt Lute, 1990) xxv.

5. Anzaldúa xxvi.

6. bell hooks, *Teaching to Transgress: Education as the Practice of Freedom* (New York: Routledge, 1994) 65.

2. Feminist Perspectives in Rhetorical Studies: A History

1. Karlyn Kohrs Campbell, "The Rhetoric of Women's Liberation: An Oxymoron," *Quarterly Journal of Speech* 59 (1973): 74-86.

2. Campbell, "Women's Liberation" 84.

3. Cheris Kramer, "Women's Speech: Separate but Unequal?" *Quarterly Journal of Speech* 60 (1974): 14.

4. Kramer, "Women's Speech" 24.

5. Kramer, "Women's Speech" 24.

6. Robin Lakoff, *Language and Woman's Place* (New York: Harper Colophon, 1975) 7.

7. Sally Miller Gearhart, "The Womanization of Rhetoric," *Women's Studies International Quarterly* 2 (1979): 195-201.

8. Gearhart 195.

9. Gearhart 198.

10. Kathleen Edgerton Kendall and Jeanne Y. Fisher, "Frances Wright on Women's Rights: Eloquence versus Ethos," *Quarterly Journal of Speech* 60 (1974): 58-68.

11. Ronald Fischli, "Anita Bryant's Stand against 'Militant Homosexuality': Religious Fundamentalism and the Democratic Process," *Central States Speech Journal* 30 (1979): 262-71.

12. Dorothy M. Mansfield, "Abigail S. Duniway: Suffragette with Not-So-Common Sense," *Western Speech* 35 (1971): 24-29.

13. Ardyce C. Whalen, "The Presentation of Image in Ella T. Grasso's Campaign," *Central States Speech Journal* 27 (1976): 207-11.

14. Mary Pinola and Nancy E. Briggs, "Martha Wright Griffiths: Champion of Women's Rights Legislation," *Central States Speech Journal* 30 (1979): 228-40.

15. Stephen H. Browne, "Encountering Angelina Grimké: Violence, Identity, and the Creation of Radical Community," *Quarterly Journal of Speech* 82 (1996): 55-73; Phyllis M. Japp, "Esther or Isaiah? The Abolitionist-Feminist Rhetoric of Angelina Grimké," *Quarterly Journal of Speech* 71 (1985): 335-48; and Ellen Reid Gold, "The Grimké Sisters and the Emergence of the Women's Rights Movement," *Southern Speech Communication Journal* 46 (1981): 341-60.

16. Wayne N. Thompson, "Barbara Jordan's Keynote Address: The Juxtaposition of Contradictory Values," *Southern Speech Communication Journal* 44 (1979): 223-32.

17. Ellen M. Ritter, "Elizabeth Morgan: Pioneer Female Labor Agitator," *Central States Speech Journal* 22 (1971): 242-51.

18. A. Cheree Carlson, "Defining Womanhood: Lucretia Coffin Mott and the Transformation of Femininity," *Western Journal of Communication* 58 (1994): 85-97.

19. Frederick Trautmann, "Harriet Beecher Stowe: Public Readings in the Central States," *Central States Speech Journal* 24 (1973): 22-28.

20. Diane Dees, "Bernadette Devlin's Maiden Speech: A Rhetoric of Sacrifice," *Southern Speech Communication Journal* 38 (1973): 326-39.

21. John C. Zacharis, "Emmeline Pankhurst: An English Suffragette Influences America," *Speech Monographs* 38 (1971): 196-206.

22. J. Jeffery Auer, "The Image of the Right Honourable Margaret Thatcher," *Central States Speech Journal* 30 (1979): 289-310.

23. Charlotte L. Stuart, "Mary Wollstonecraft's *A Vindication of the Rights of Man*: A Rhetoric Reassessment," *Western Journal of Speech Communication* 42 (1978): 83-92.

24. We will not offer a complete account of all of the studies about women and the women's movement published during this period. A comprehensive survey of such studies appears in Karen A. Foss and Sonja K. Foss, "The Status of Research on Women and Communication," *Communication Quarterly* 31 (1983): 195-204. Karlyn Kohrs Campbell also has sought to preserve and compile a history of women speakers in the United States in several volumes: *Man Cannot Speak for Her: A Critical Study of Early Feminist Rhetoric,* vol. 1 (Westport, CT: Greenwood, 1989); Karlyn Kohrs Campbell, comp., *Man Cannot Speak for Her: Key Texts of the Early Feminists,* vol. 2 (Westport,

CT: Greenwood, 1989); Karlyn Kohrs Campbell, ed., *Women Public Speakers in the United States, 1800-1925: A Bio-Critical Sourcebook* (Westport, CT: Greenwood, 1993); and Karlyn Kohrs Campbell, ed., *Women Public Speakers in the United States, 1925-1993: A Bio-Critical Sourcebook* (Westport, CT: Greenwood, 1994).

25. For an extended discussion of this issue, see Karen A. Foss and Sonja K. Foss, *Women Speak: The Eloquence of Women's Lives* (Prospect Heights, IL: Waveland, 1991) 3-6.

26. The expansion of categories even within traditional rhetorical contexts, such as public address, is evidence of the ongoing nature of this process. See, for example, Kristin S. Vonnegut, "Listening for Women's Voices: Revisioning Courses in American Public Address," *Communication Education* 41 (1992): 26-39. Vonnegut incorporates into her public address course diverse rhetorical documents such as pamphlets by Mercy Otis Warren, the letters of Abigail Adams, and Mary Rowlandson's account of her kidnapping by Indians.

27. Brenda Robinson Hancock, "Affirmation by Negation in the Women's Liberation Movement," *Quarterly Journal of Speech* 58 (1972): 264-71.

28. Martha Solomon, "The 'Positive Woman's' Journey: A Mythic Analysis of the Rhetoric of STOP ERA," *Quarterly Journal of Speech* 65 (1979): 262-74.

29. Sonja K. Foss, "The Equal Rights Amendment Controversy: Two Worlds in Conflict," *Quarterly Journal of Speech* 65 (1979): 275-88.

30. Susan Zaeske, "The 'Promiscuous Audience' Controversy and the Emergence of the Early Woman's Rights Movement," *Quarterly Journal of Speech* 81 (1995): 191-207.

31. Karlyn Kohrs Campbell, "Gender and Genre: Loci of Invention and Contradiction in the Earliest Speeches by U.S. Women," *Quarterly Journal of Speech* 81 (1995): 479-95.

32. Cheryl R. Jorgensen-Earp, "The Lady, the Whore, and the Spinster: The Rhetorical Use of Victorian Images of Women," *Western Journal of Communication* 54 (1990): 82-98.

33. Susan Schultz Huxman, "Mary Wollstonecraft, Margaret Fuller, and Angelina Grimké: Symbolic Convergence and a Nascent Rhetorical Vision," *Communication Quarterly* 44 (1996): 16-28.

34. Hamida Bosmajian and Haig Bosmajian, eds., *This Great Argument: The Rights of Women* (Reading, MA: Addison-Wesley, 1972).

35. Patricia Scileppi Kennedy and Gloria Hartmann O'Shields, *We Shall Be Heard: Women Speakers in America, 1828-Present* (Dubuque, IA: Kendall Hunt, 1982) xiii.

36. Judith Anderson, *Outspoken Women: Speeches by American Women Reformers, 1635-1936* (Dubuque, IA: Kendall Hunt, 1984).

37. Victoria L. DeFrancisco and Marvin D. Jensen, eds., *Women's Voices in Our Time: Statements by American Leaders* (Prospect Heights, IL: Waveland, 1994) ix-x.

38. Campbell, *Man Cannot Speak,* vol. 1.

39. Campbell, *Man Cannot Speak,* vol. 2, ix.

40. Campbell, *Women Public Speakers in the United States, 1800-1925*; and Campbell, *Women Public Speakers in the United States, 1925-1993.*

41. Barbara Bate and Anita Taylor, "Introduction: Women's Realities and Women's Talk," *Women Communicating: Studies of Women's Talk,* ed. Barbara Bate and Anita Taylor (Norwood, NJ: Ablex, 1988) 1.

42. Foss and Foss, *Women Speak.*

43. Randall A. Lake, "Order and Disorder in Anti-Abortion Rhetoric: A Logological View," *Quarterly Journal of Speech* 70 (1984): 425-43.

44. Celeste Condit Railsback, "The Contemporary American Abortion Controversy: Stages in the Argument," *Quarterly Journal of Speech* 70 (1984): 410-24; and Celeste Michelle Condit, *Decoding Abortion Rhetoric: Communicating Social Change* (Urbana: U of Illinois P, 1990).

45. Mari Boor Tonn, "Donning Sackcloth and Ashes: *Webster v. Reproductive Health Services* and Moral Agony in Abortion Rights Rhetoric," *Communication Quarterly* 44 (1996): 265.

46. Nathan Stormer, "Embodying Normal Miracles," *Quarterly Journal of Speech* 83 (1997): 172-91.

47. Mari Boor Tonn, "Militant Motherhood: Labor's Mary Harris 'Mother' Jones," *Quarterly Journal of Speech* 82 (1996): 1-21.

48. Mary M. Lay, Billie J. Wahlstrom, and Carol Brown, "The Rhetoric of Midwifery: Conflicts and Conversations in the Minnesota Home Birth Community in the 1990s," *Quarterly Journal of Speech* 82 (1996): 383-401.

49. Julia T. Wood, ed., "Special Section: 'Telling Our Stories': Sexual Harassment in the Communication Discipline," *Applied Communication Research* 20 (1992): 349-418.

50. Shereen G. Bingham, ed., *Conceptualizing Sexual Harassment as Discursive Practice* (Westport, CT: Praeger, 1994).

51. Campbell, *Man Cannot Speak,* vol. 1, 12.

52. Campbell, *Man Cannot Speak,* vol. 1, 13.

53. Bonnie J. Dow and Mari Boor Tonn, " 'Feminine Style' and Political Judgment in the Rhetoric of Ann Richards," *Quarterly Journal of Speech* 79 (1993): 287.

54. Bonnie J. Dow, "Feminism, Difference(s), and Rhetorical Studies," *Communication Studies* 46 (1995): 106-17.

55. Jane Blankenship and Deborah C. Robson, "A 'Feminine Style' in Women's Political Discourse: An Exploratory Essay," *Communication Quarterly* 43 (1995): 353.

56. Shawn J. Parry-Giles and Trevor Parry-Giles, "Gendered Politics and Presidential Image Construction: A Reassessment of the 'Feminine Style,' " *Communication Monographs* 63 (1996): 346.

57. Elizabeth Bell, "Listen Up. You Have To: Voices from 'Women and Communication,' " *Western Journal of Communication* 61 (1997): 89-100.

58. Karen A. Foss and Sonja K. Foss, "Personal Experience as Evidence in Feminist Scholarship," *Western Journal of Communication* 58 (1994): 39-43.

59. Bonnie J. Dow, "Politicizing Voice," *Western Journal of Communication* 61 (1997): 243-51.

60. Carole Spitzack and Kathryn Carter, "Research on Women's Communication: The Politics of Theory and Method," *Doing Research on Women's Communication:*

Perspectives on Theory and Method, ed. Kathryn Carter and Carole Spitzack (Norwood, NJ: Ablex, 1989) 11-39.

61. Katherine Hawkins, "Exposing Masculine Science: An Alternative Feminist Approach to the Study of Women's Communication," *Doing Research on Women's Communication: Perspectives on Theory and Method,* ed. Kathryn Carter and Carole Spitzack (Norwood, NJ: Ablex, 1989) 40.

62. Hawkins 54-55.

63. Karen A. Foss and Sonja K. Foss, "Incorporating the Feminist Perspective in Communication Scholarship: A Research Commentary," *Doing Research on Women's Communication: Perspectives on Theory and Method,* ed. Kathryn Carter and Carole Spitzack (Norwood, NJ: Ablex, 1989) 73.

64. Foss and Foss, "Incorporating the Feminist Perspective" 74-81.

65. Sheryl Perlmutter Bowen and Nancy Wyatt, eds., *Transforming Visions: Feminist Critiques in Communication Studies* (Cresskill, NJ: Hampton, 1993).

66. Mark Hickson III, Don W. Stacks, and Jonathan H. Amsbary, "Active Prolific Female Scholars in Communication: An Analysis of Active Research Productivity, II," *Communication Quarterly* 40 (1992): 350-56.

67. Carole Blair, Julie R. Brown, and Leslie A. Baxter, "Disciplining the Feminine," *Quarterly Journal of Speech* 80 (1994): 384.

68. Blair, Brown, and Baxter 399.

69. Blair, Brown, and Baxter 400.

70. This presentation later was published: Karen A. Foss, "Feminist Scholarship in Speech Communication: Contributions and Obstacles," *Women's Studies in Communication* 12 (1989): 1-10.

71. Cheris Kramer, "Language/Sex Research in Great Britain," *Women and Language News* 2 (1977): 4-5.

72. Julia T. Wood and Gerald M. Phillips, "Report on the 1984 Conference on Gender and Communication Research," *Women's Studies in Communication* 7 (1984): 63.

73. Lois Self, "What Distinguishes/Ought to Distinguish Feminist Scholarship in Communication Studies? Progress toward Engendering a Feminist Academic Practice," *Women's Studies in Communication* 11 (1988): 1.

74. Self 2.

75. Julia T. Wood, "Feminist Scholarship in Communication: Consensus, Diversity, and Conversation among Researchers," *Women's Studies in Communication* 11 (1988): 27.

76. Cheris Kramarae, *Women and Men Speaking: Frameworks for Analysis* (Rowley, MA: Newbury, 1981) xvi.

77. A revised version of this presentation later was published: Brenda Dervin, "The Potential Contribution of Feminist Scholarship to the Field of Communication," *Journal of Communication* 37 (1987): 107-21.

78. Dervin 113.

79. Lana F. Rakow, "Looking to the Future: Five Questions for Gender Research," *Women's Studies in Communication* 10 (1987): 79-86.

80. Rakow, "Looking" 79.

81. Rakow, "Looking" 79.

82. Rakow, "Looking" 79.

83. Lana F. Rakow, "Preface," *Women Making Meaning: New Feminist Directions in Communication,* ed. Lana F. Rakow (New York: Routledge, 1992) viii.

84. Julia T. Wood, "Gender and Moral Voice: Moving from Woman's Nature to Standpoint Epistemology," *Women's Studies in Communication* 15 (1992): 1-24.

85. Maureen A. Mathison, "Complicity as Epistemology: Reinscribing the Historical Categories of 'Woman' through Standpoint Feminism," *Communication Theory* 7 (1997): 157.

86. Mark P. Orbe, "From the Standpoint(s) of Traditionally Muted Groups: Explicating a Co-cultural Communication Theoretical Model," *Communication Theory* 8 (1998): 1.

87. See, for example, bell hooks, "Feminism: A Transformational Politic," *Theoretical Perspectives on Sexual Difference,* ed. Deborah L. Rhode (New Haven, CT: Yale UP, 1990) 185-93.

88. Marsha Houston, "Language and Black Woman's Place: Evidence from the Black Middle Class," *For Alma Mater: Theory and Practice in Feminist Scholarship,* ed. Paula Treichler, Cheris Kramarae, and Beth Stafford (Urbana: U of Illinois P, 1985) 177-93; Marsha Houston, "What Makes Scholarship about Black Women and Communication Feminist Communication Scholarship?" *Women's Studies in Communication* 11 (1988): 28-31; Marsha Houston, "Feminist Theory and Black Women's Talk," *Howard Journal of Communications* 1 (1989): 187-94; Marsha Houston, "The Politics of Difference: Race, Class, and Women's Communication," *Women Making Meaning: New Feminist Directions in Communication,* ed. Lana F. Rakow (New York: Routledge, 1992) 45-59; and Marsha Houston, "When Black Women Talk with White Women: Why Dialogues Are Difficult," *Our Voices: Essays in Culture, Ethnicity, and Communication,* ed. Alberto Gonzalez, Marsha Houston, and Victoria Chen, 2nd ed. (Los Angeles: Roxbury, 1994) 187-94.

89. Lisa A. Flores, "Creating Discursive Space through a Rhetoric of Difference: Chicana Feminists Craft a Homeland," *Quarterly Journal of Speech* 82 (1996): 152.

90. Dana L. Cloud, "Hegemony or Concordance? The Rhetoric of Tokenism in 'Oprah' Winfrey's Rags-to-Riches Biography," *Critical Studies in Mass Communication* 13 (1996): 115-37.

91. Barbara Biesecker, "Coming to Terms with Recent Attempts to Write Women into the History of Rhetoric," *Philosophy and Rhetoric* 25 (1992): 140-61; and Karlyn Kohrs Campbell, "Biesecker Cannot Speak for Her Either," *Philosophy and Rhetoric* 26 (1993): 153-59.

92. Biesecker 144.

93. Dow, "Feminism, Differences(s)."

94. Celeste Michelle Condit, "In Praise of Eloquent Diversity: Gender and Rhetoric as Public Persuasion," *Women's Studies in Communication* 20 (1997): 91-116.

95. Sonja K. Foss, Cindy L. Griffin, and Karen A. Foss, "Transforming Rhetoric through Feminist Reconstruction: A Response to the Gender Diversity Perspective," *Women's Studies in Communication* 20 (1997): 117-35.

96. Sharon D. Downey, "Rhetoric as Balance: A Dialectical Feminist Perspective," *Women's Studies in Communication* 20 (1997): 137-50.

97. Wood, " 'Telling Our Stories' "; and Janice Hocker Rushing, "Feminist Criticism," *Southern Communication Journal* 57 (1992): 83-155.

98. Foss and Foss, "The Status of Research" 202.

99. Carole Spitzack and Kathryn Carter, "Women in Communication Studies: A Typology for Revision," *Quarterly Journal of Speech* 73 (1987): 419.

100. Katherine Kurs and Robert S. Cathcart, "The Feminist Movement: Lesbian-Feminism as Confrontation," *Women's Studies in Communication* 6 (1983): 21, 13.

101. Belle A. Edson, "Bias in Social Movement Theory: A View from a Female-Systems Perspective," *Women's Studies in Communication* 8 (1985): 34-45.

102. Mary Rose Williams, "A Reconceptualization of Protest Rhetoric: Women's Quilts as Rhetorical Forms," *Women's Studies in Communication* 17 (1994): 20-44.

103. Williams 40.

104. Cheris Kramarae and Paula A. Treichler, with Ann Russo, eds., *A Feminist Dictionary* (Boston: Pandora, 1985) 1.

105. Kramarae and Treichler, with Russo 194.

106. Sonja K. Foss and Cindy L. Griffin, "A Feminist Perspective on Rhetorical Theory: Toward a Clarification of Boundaries," *Western Journal of Communication* 56 (1992): 330-49.

107. Sonja K. Foss and Cindy L. Griffin, "Beyond Persuasion: A Proposal for an Invitational Rhetoric," *Communication Monographs* 62 (1995): 2-18.

108. Cindy L. Griffin, "Women as Communicators: Mary Daly's Hagography as Rhetoric," *Communication Monographs* 60 (1993): 158-77.

109. Cindy L. Griffin, "Rhetoricizing Alienation: Mary Wollstonecraft and the Rhetorical Construction of Women's Oppression," *Quarterly Journal of Speech* 80 (1994): 293-312.

110. Cindy L. Griffin, "A Web of Reasons: Mary Wollstonecraft's *A Vindication of the Rights of Woman* and the Re-Weaving of Form," *Communication Studies* 47 (1996): 272-88.

111. Cindy L. Griffin, "The Essentialist Roots of the Public Sphere: A Feminist Critique," *Western Journal of Communication* 60 (1996): 21-39.

112. Foss and Foss, *Women Speak* 1-22.

113. Douglas Thomas, "Rethinking Pedagogy in Public Speaking and American Public Address: A Feminist Alternative," *Women's Studies in Communication* 14 (1991): 43.

114. Thomas 52.

115. Sonja K. Foss and Karen A. Foss, *Inviting Transformation: Presentational Speaking for a Changing World* (Prospect Heights, IL: Waveland, 1994).

116. "The Women's University: A Symposium," *Communication Education* 45 (1996): 315-66.

117. Cheris Kramarae, "Centers of Change: An Introduction to Women's Own Communication Programs," *Communication Education* 45 (1996): 318.

118. Kramarae, "Centers of Change" 319.

3. Cheris Kramarae

1. Cheris Kramarae, "Feminist Theories of Communication," *International Encyclopedia of Communications,* ed. Erik Barnouw, vol. 2 (New York: Oxford UP, 1989) 157.

2. Cheris Kramarae, e-mail to Sonja K. Foss, 29 Nov. 1997.

3. Cheris Kramarae, letter to Sonja K. Foss, 14 June 1997.

4. Cheris Kramarae, "The Language of Cyberspace: Searching the Social Messages," U of Illinois, Urbana, 23 Mar. 1994.

5. Kramarae, "Language of Cyberspace."

6. Kramarae, letter to Sonja K. Foss, 14 June 1997.

7. Kramarae, "Language of Cyberspace."

8. Kramarae, e-mail to Sonja K. Foss, 29 Nov. 1997.

9. Kramarae, letter to Sonja K. Foss, 14 June 1997.

10. Cheris Kramarae, e-mail to Sonja K. Foss, 31 Dec. 1997.

11. Brinlee Kramer, "Brinlee Kramer," *Women Who Do and Women Who Don't Join the Women's Movement,* ed. Robyn Rowland (Boston: Routledge & Kegan Paul, 1994) 169.

12. Cheris Kramarae, "A Visiting Scholar," *CSWS [Center for the Study of Women in Society] Review* [U of Oregon] 1988: 15.

13. Kramarae, "Visiting Scholar" 15.

14. Kramarae, "Visiting Scholar" 15.

15. Cheris Kramarae, *Women and Men Speaking: Frameworks for Analysis* (Rowley, MA: Newbury, 1981) viii.

16. Kramarae, e-mail to Sonja K. Foss, 29 Nov. 1997.

17. H. Jeanie Taylor, Cheris Kramarae, and Maureen Ebben, "WITS: An Introduction," *Women, Information Technology, and Scholarship,* ed. H. Jeanie Taylor, Cheris Kramarae, and Maureen Ebben (Urbana: Board of Trustees, U of Illinois, 1993) 7.

18. Cheris Kramarae, letter to Sonja K. Foss, 26 Jan. 1998.

19. Paula A. Treichler, Cheris Kramarae, and Beth Stafford, "Introduction," *For Alma Mater: Theory and Practice in Feminist Scholarship,* ed. Paula A. Treichler, Cheris Kramarae, and Beth Stafford (Urbana: U of Illinois P, 1985) xiii.

20. Lana Rakow and Cheris Kramarae, introduction to "Man/dated Language," *The Revolution in Words: Righting Women 1868-1871,* ed. Lana Rakow and Cheris Kramarae (New York: Routledge, 1990) 161.

21. Cheris Kramarae and Paula A. Treichler, with Ann Russo, eds., *A Feminist Dictionary* (Boston: Pandora, 1985) 1.

22. Kramarae and Treichler, with Russo 15.

23. Kramarae and Treichler, with Russo 372, 222.

24. Marsha Houston and Cheris Kramarae, "Speaking from Silence: Methods of Silencing and of Resistance," *Discourse and Society* 2 (1991): 398.

25. Kramarae, "Visiting Scholar" 14-15.

26. Cheris Kramarae, "A Feminist Critique of Sociolinguistics," *Journal of the Atlantic Provinces Linguistic Association* 8 (1986): 8.

27. Cheris Kramarae, "Redefining Gender, Class and Race," *Beyond Boundaries: Sex and Gender Diversity in Communication,* ed. Cynthia M. Lont and Sheryl A. Friedley (Fairfax, VA: George Mason UP, 1989) 318.

28. Kramarae, *Women and Men Speaking* 72.

29. Kramarae, *Women and Men Speaking* 119.

30. Cheris Kramarae, "The Condition of Patriarchy," *The Knowledge Explosion: Generations of Feminist Scholarship,* ed. Cheris Kramarae and Dale Spender (New York: Teachers College P, 1992) 400.

31. Cheris Kramarae, "Gender and Dominance," *Communication Yearbook 15,* ed. Stanley A. Deetz (Newbury Park, CA: Sage, 1992) 470.

32. Cheris Kramarae, Muriel Schulz, and William M. O'Barr, "Introduction: Toward an Understanding of Language and Power," *Language and Power,* ed. Cheris Kramarae, Muriel Schulz, and William M. O'Barr (Beverly Hills, CA: Sage, 1984) 16.

33. Nancy M. Henley and Cheris Kramarae, "Gender, Power, and Miscommunication," *"Miscommunication" and Problematic Talk,* ed. Nikolas Coupland, Howard Giles, and John M. Wiemann (Newbury Park, CA: Sage, 1991) 19-20.

34. Kramarae and Treichler, with Russo 10.

35. Cheris Kramarae, "Telling Tales about Women and Communication: What Do We Dare to Say?" Speech Communication Association Convention, San Antonio, TX, 21 Nov. 1995.

36. Kramarae, "Feminist Critique" 8.

37. Cheris Kramarae and Dale Spender, "Exploding Knowledge," *The Knowledge Explosion: Generations of Feminist Scholarship,* ed. Cheris Kramarae and Dale Spender (New York: Teachers College P, 1992) 8.

38. Cheris Kramarae and Mercilee Jenkins, "Women Changing Words Changing Women," *Sprachwandel und feministische Sprachpolitik: Internationale Perspektiven,* ed. Marlis Hellinger (Wiesbaden, Germany: Westdeutscher Verlag, 1985) 13.

39. Cheris Kramarae, "Technology Policy, Gender, and Cyberspace," *Duke Journal of Gender Law and Policy* 4 (1997): 152.

40. Cheris Kramarae, "Irregular Women's Periodicals," WHIM Conference on Linguistic Humor, Arizona State U, Tempe, Apr. 1982.

41. Kramarae, "Condition of Patriarchy" 397.

42. Kramarae, "Condition of Patriarchy" 403.

43. Cheris Kramarae, e-mail to Sonja K. Foss, 28 Feb. 1998.

44. Kramarae, "Condition of Patriarchy" 402.

45. Kramarae, e-mail to Sonja K. Foss, 28 Feb. 1998.

46. Cheris Kramarae, e-mail to Sonja K. Foss, 1 Mar. 1998.

47. Kramarae, e-mail to Sonja K. Foss, 28 Feb. 1998.

48. Mercilee M. Jenkins and Cheris Kramarae, "A Thief in the House: Women and Language," *Men's Studies Modified: The Impact of Feminism on the Academic Disciplines,* ed. Dale Spender (New York: Pergamon, 1981) 12.

49. Kramarae, *Women and Men Speaking* 1.

50. Kramarae and Jenkins, "Women Changing Words" 10.

51. Candace West, Michelle M. Lazar, and Cheris Kramarae, "Gender in Discourse," *Discourse as Social Interaction,* ed. Teun A. van Dijk (Thousand Oaks, CA: Sage, 1997) 121.

52. Kramarae and Treichler, with Russo 8.

53. Kramarae and Treichler, with Russo 2.

54. Kramarae and Treichler, with Russo 8.

55. Cheris Kramarae, "Punctuating the Dictionary," *International Journal of the Sociology of Language* 94 (1992): 137-38.

56. Cheris Kramarae, "A Teaching Module on Informal Communication Networks: Who Is Listening to Women," International Workshop, "Women, Households, and Development: Building a Database," Indo-U.S. Project between M.S. University of Baroda, Gujarat, India, and U of Illinois, Urbana, 1988.

57. Cheris Kramarae and Paula A. Treichler, "Power Relationships in the Classroom," *Gender in the Classroom: Power and Pedagogy,* ed. Susan L. Gabriel and Isaiah Smithson (Urbana: U of Illinois P, 1990) 41.

58. Cheris Kramarae, "Response to Perry: 'Sex Stereotypes, Social Rules and Education: Changing Teaching and Teaching Change,' " *Theoretical and Critical Perspectives on Teacher Change,* ed. Phyllis Kahaney, Linda A. M. Perry, and Joseph Janangelo (Norwood, NJ: Ablex, 1993) 42.

59. Kramarae and Spender, "Exploding Knowledge" 12.

60. Kramarae and Treichler 55.

61. Kramarae and Treichler 54.

62. Kramarae and Treichler 56.

63. Kramarae and Treichler 54.

64. Cheris Kramarae, "Gotta Go Myrtle, Technology's at the Door," *Technology and Women's Voices: Keeping in Touch,* ed. Cheris Kramarae (New York: Routledge & Kegan Paul, 1988) 4.

65. Kramarae, "Gotta Go" 3.

66. Barrie Thorne, Cheris Kramarae, and Nancy Henley, "Language, Gender and Society: Opening a Second Decade of Research," *Language, Gender and Society,* ed. Barrie Thorne, Cheris Kramarae, and Nancy Henley (Rowley, MA: Newbury, 1983) 17.

67. Barrie Thorne, Cheris Kramarae, and Nancy Henley, "Imagining a Different World of Talk," *Women in Search of Utopia: Mavericks and Mythmakers,* ed. Ruby Rohrlich and Elaine Hoffman Baruch (New York: Schocken, 1984) 180.

68. Thorne, Kramarae, and Henley, "Imagining" 181.

69. Henley and Kramarae 29.

70. Kramarae, e-mail to Sonja K. Foss, 1 Mar. 1998.

71. H. Jeanie Taylor and Cheris Kramarae, "Creating Cybertrust from the Margins," *Renaissance in Social Science Computing,* ed. Orville Vernon Burton (Urbana: U of Illinois P, in press).

72. Cheris Kramarae and Jana Kramer, "Legal Snarls for Women in Cyberspace," *Internet Research: Electronic Networking Applications and Policy* 5 (1995): 19.

73. Maureen Ebben and Cheris Kramarae, "Women and Information Technologies: Creating a Cyberspace of Our Own," *Women, Information Technology, and Scholarship,* ed. H. Jeanie Taylor, Cheris Kramarae, and Maureen Ebben (Urbana: Board of Trustees, U of Illinois, 1993) 17.

74. Kramarae, "Feminist Theories" 158.

75. Elizabeth Arveda Kissling and Cheris Kramarae, "Stranger Compliments: The Interpretation of Street Remarks," *Women's Studies in Communication* 14 (1991): 76.

76. Cheris Kramarae, "Harassment and Everyday Life," *Women Making Meaning: New Feminist Directions in Communication,* ed. Lana F. Rakow (New York: Routledge, 1992) 111.

77. Kramarae, "Harassment" 111.

78. Kissling and Kramarae 76.

79. Kissling and Kramarae 88.

80. Kramarae, "Harassment" 109.

81. Kramarae, "Harassment" 117, 101.

82. Kissling and Kramarae 76.

83. Kramarae and Jenkins, "Women Changing Words" 10.

84. Kramarae, e-mail to Sonja K. Foss, 1 Mar. 1998.

85. Kramer 170.

86. Kramarae, e-mail to Sonja K. Foss, 28 Feb. 1998.

87. Kramarae, e-mail to Sonja K. Foss, 28 Feb. 1998.

88. Kramarae, "Response to Perry" 44.

89. Kramarae, "Telling Tales."

90. Kramarae, "Telling Tales."

91. Taylor and Kramarae.

92. Kramarae and Spender, "Exploding Knowledge" 3.

93. Kramarae, "Feminist Critique" 9.

94. Cheris Kramarae, "Centers of Change: An Introduction to Women's Own Communication Programs," *Communication Education* 45 (1996): 318.

95. Kramarae, "Centers of Change" 319.

96. Kramarae, "Centers of Change" 319.

97. Kramarae, e-mail to Sonja K. Foss, 28 Feb. 1998.

98. Cheris Kramarae, "Feminist Uses of the New Information Technologies: A Mind Stretch?" Speech Communication Association Convention, Miami Beach, FL, Nov. 1993.

99. Cheris Kramarae, "Shaking the Conventions of Higher Education or Appropriate and Appropriated Technology," Women, Information and Technology in Industry and Education Conference, Queensland U of Technology, Brisbane, Austral., 5 Dec. 1997.

100. Kramarae, e-mail to Sonja K. Foss, 28 Feb. 1998.

101. Quoted in Kramarae, e-mail to Sonja K. Foss, 1 Mar. 1998.

102. Kramarae, e-mail to Sonja K. Foss, 28 Feb. 1998.

103. Kramarae, "Telling Tales."

104. Kramarae, "Punctuating" 149.

105. Kramarae, "Shaking the Conventions."

106. Kramarae, "Shaking the Conventions."

107. Taylor and Kramarae.

108. Taylor and Kramarae.

109. Jana Kramer and Cheris Kramarae, "Gendered Ethics on the Internet," *Communication Ethics in an Age of Diversity*, ed. Josina M. Makau and Ronald C. Arnett (Urbana: U of Illinois P, 1997) 236.

110. Kramarae, "Shaking the Conventions."

111. Kramarae and Spender, "Exploding Knowledge" 10.

112. Kramarae and Spender, "Exploding Knowledge" 10.

113. Kramarae, "Punctuating" 150.

114. Kramarae and Spender, "Exploding Knowledge" 10.

115. Kramarae, "Feminist Theories" 157.

116. Kramarae, "Condition of Patriarchy" 400.

117. Kramarae, "Gotta Go" 11.

118. Cheris Kramarae, "Feminists as Dancers and Equilibrium Busters," Speech Communication Association Convention, New Orleans, Nov. 1994.

119. Kramarae and Spender, "Exploding Knowledge" 6.

120. Kramarae, e-mail to Sonja K. Foss, 28 Feb. 1998.

121. Cheris Kramarae, "Chronic Power Problems," *Toward the Twenty-First Century: The Future of Speech Communication*, ed. Julia T. Wood and Richard B. Gregg (Cresskill, NJ: Hampton, 1995) 214-15.

122. Kramarae and Treichler, with Russo 1.

123. Kramarae and Treichler, with Russo 62.

124. Cheris Kramarae and Mercilee M. Jenkins, "Women Take Back the Talk," *Women and Language in Transition*, ed. Joyce Penfield (Albany: State U of New York P, 1987) 150.

125. Kramarae and Spender, "Exploding Knowledge" 9.

126. Kramarae and Jenkins, "Women Take Back" 150.

127. Cheris Kramarae, "Changing the Complexion of Gender in Language Research," *Handbook of Language and Social Psychology*, ed. Howard Giles and W. Peter Robinson (New York: John Wiley, 1990) 347.

128. Kramarae, "Redefining Gender" 319.

129. Kramarae and Spender, "Exploding Knowledge" 10.

130. Kramarae and Spender, "Exploding Knowledge" 3.

131. Kramarae and Spender, "Exploding Knowledge" 3.

132. Kramarae and Jenkins, "Women Take Back" 148.

133. West, Lazar, and Kramarae 121.

134. Kramarae and Jenkins, "Women Take Back" 137.

135. Kramarae and Treichler, with Russo 16.

136. Kramarae and Jenkins, "Women Take Back" 149.

137. Taylor and Kramarae.

138. Kramarae, e-mail to Sonja K. Foss, 28 Feb. 1998.

139. Cheris Kramarae, "Do We Really Want More Control of Technology?" Tokyo Symposium on Women, Tokyo, 1988.

140. Kramarae, "Shaking the Conventions."

141. Cheris Kramarae, "Talk of Sewing Circles and Sweatshops," *Technology and Women's Voices: Keeping in Touch,* ed. Cheris Kramarae (New York: Routledge & Kegan Paul, 1988) 148.

142. Thorne, Kramarae, and Henley, "Language, Gender and Society" 8.

143. Kramarae, "Irregular Women's Periodicals."

144. Kramarae and Jenkins, "Women Take Back" 147.

145. Kramarae and Spender, "Exploding Knowledge" 6.

146. Kramarae, "Gotta Go" 7.

147. Jenkins and Kramarae, "Thief" 19.

148. Kramarae, "Teaching Module."

149. Kramarae and Treichler, with Russo 17.

150. Houston and Kramarae 394.

151. Kramarae and Treichler, with Russo 17.

152. Houston and Kramarae 395.

153. Kramarae, "Condition of Patriarchy" 403.

154. Cheris Kramarae, "The Language of Multicultural Feminism," *CSWS [Center for the Study of Women in Society] Review* [U of Oregon] 1989: 3.

155. Kramarae, "Multicultural Feminism" 3.

156. Jenkins and Kramarae, "Thief" 17.

157. Taylor and Kramarae.

158. Jenkins and Kramarae, "Thief" 13.

159. Thorne, Kramarae, and Henley, "Imagining" 186.

160. Kramarae, e-mail to Sonja K. Foss, 28 Feb. 1998.

161. Kramarae, "Feminist Theories" 158.

162. Kramarae and Spender, "Exploding Knowledge" 14.

163. Cheris Kramarae, "Proprietors of Language," *Women and Language in Literature and Society,* ed. Sally McConnell-Ginet, Ruth Borker, and Nelly Furman (New York: Praeger, 1980) 62.

164. Kramarae and Jenkins, "Women Take Back" 140.

165. Kramarae and Jenkins, "Women Changing Words" 15.

166. Kramarae and Jenkins, "Women Changing Words" 14.

167. Kramarae and Jenkins, "Women Take Back" 139-40.

168. Kramarae, "Multicultural Feminism" 5.

169. Kramarae, "Multicultural Feminism" 5.

170. Kramarae and Treichler, with Russo 11.

171. Kramarae and Jenkins, "Women Changing Words" 13.

172. Kramarae and Jenkins, "Women Take Back" 140.

173. Kramarae and Jenkins, "Women Take Back" 140.

174. Kramarae and Treichler, with Russo 11.

175. Kramarae, "Telling Tales."

176. Houston and Kramarae 398.

177. Jenkins and Kramarae, "Thief" 19.

4. bell hooks

1. bell hooks, *Outlaw Culture: Resisting Representations* (New York: Routledge, 1994) 2-3.

2. Hooks does not capitalize the initial letters of her name. We capitalize her name here only in situations in which any word not usually capitalized would be capitalized—at the start of a sentence, for example.

3. "Hooks, bell." *Current Biography* 56 (1995): 28; and bell hooks and Cornel West, *Breaking Bread: Insurgent Black Intellectual Life* (Boston: South End, 1991) 67.

4. bell hooks, *Talking Back: Thinking Feminist, Thinking Black* (Boston: South End, 1989) 10.

5. bell hooks, "Girls Together: Sustained Sisterhood," *Sister to Sister: Women Write about the Unbreakable Bond*, ed. Patricia Foster (New York: Anchor-Doubleday, 1995) 166.

6. hooks, "Girls Together" 166.

7. hooks, "Girls Together" 167.

8. bell hooks, *Teaching to Transgress: Education as the Practice of Freedom* (New York: Routledge, 1994) 119.

9. hooks, *Talking Back* 128.

10. bell hooks, "Black Is a Woman's Color," *Bearing Witness*, ed. Henry Louis Gates Jr. (New York: Pantheon, 1991) 345.

11. hooks, "Black" 347.

12. hooks and West 69.

13. bell hooks, "Challenging Men," *Sparerib* 217 (1990): 13.

14. bell hooks, *Bone Black: Memories of Girlhood* (New York: Henry Holt, 1996) 98.

15. hooks, *Talking Back* 5.

16. hooks, *Talking Back* 7.

17. hooks, *Talking Back* 5-6.

18. hooks, "Black" 342.

19. hooks, *Teaching* 60.

20. bell hooks, "Writing from the Darkness," *Tri-Quarterly* 75 (1989): 74.

21. hooks, *Outlaw Culture* 9-10.

22. hooks and West 149.

23. hooks and West 66.

24. hooks and West 149.

25. hooks, "Writing" 72.

26. hooks, "Writing" 75.

27. hooks and West 149-50.

28. bell hooks, *A Woman's Mourning Song* (New York: Harlem River, 1993) 8.

29. hooks, *Woman's Mourning Song* 5.

30. hooks, *Talking Back* 100.

31. bell hooks, "Marginality as Site of Resistance," *Out There: Marginalization and Contemporary Cultures,* ed. Russell Ferguson, Martha Gever, Trinh T. Minh-ha, and Cornel West (New York: New Museum of Contemporary Art; Cambridge: MIT P, 1990) 342.

32. hooks, *Talking Back* 58, 59.

33. bell hooks, *Killing Rage: Ending Racism* (New York: Henry Holt, 1995) 229.

34. hooks, *Killing Rage* 228.

35. hooks and West 148.

36. Quoted in Ingrid Sischy, "Bell Hooks," *Interview* 25 (1995): 126.

37. Quoted in Helma Lutz, "Feminist Theory in Practice: An Interview with Bell Hooks: Encounter with an Impressive Female Academic Fighter against Multiple Forms of Oppression," *Women's Studies International Forum* 16 (1993): 422.

38. hooks, *Talking Back* 29.

39. hooks, *Teaching* 16.

40. bell hooks, "Power to the Pussy: We Don't Wannabe Dicks in Drag," *Madonnarama: Essays on Sex and Popular Culture,* ed. Lisa Frank and Paul Smith (San Francisco: Cleis, 1993) 66.

41. hooks, *Outlaw Culture* 232.

42. hooks, "Power to the Pussy" 66.

43. hooks, *Outlaw Culture* 231.

44. bell hooks, "Feminism and Black Women's Studies," *Sage* 6 (1989): 54.

45. bell hooks, *Ain't I a Woman: Black Women and Feminism* (Boston: South End, 1981) 13.

46. hooks, *Outlaw Culture* 6.

47. bell hooks, *Reel to Real: Race, Sex, and Class at the Movies* (New York: Routledge, 1996) 1.

48. hooks, *Teaching* 207.

49. hooks, *Killing Rage* 7.

50. bell hooks, *Wounds of Passion: A Writing Life* (New York: Henry Holt, 1997) xxii.

51. bell hooks, "Critical Reflections," *Artforum* 33 (1994): 65.

52. hooks, "Critical Reflections" 100.

53. hooks and West 72.

54. hooks, *Talking Back* 81.

55. hooks, *Talking Back* 9.

56. hooks, *Talking Back* 162.

57. hooks, *Outlaw Culture* 91-92.

58. hooks, *Talking Back* 163.

59. hooks, *Talking Back* 9.

60. Quoted in "Hooks, bell," *Current Biography* 28.

61. hooks, *Outlaw Culture* 202.

62. hooks, *Talking Back* 19.

63. hooks, *Outlaw Culture* 200.

64. hooks, *Talking Back* 19.

65. hooks, *Talking Back* 175.

66. bell hooks, *Feminist Theory: From Margin to Center* (Boston: South End, 1984) 29.

67. Quoted in Lutz 425.

68. hooks, *Killing Rage* 194.

69. bell hooks, *Art on My Mind: Visual Politics* (New York: New, 1995) xii.

70. hooks, *Teaching* 173.

71. bell hooks, *Yearning: Race, Gender, and Cultural Politics* (Boston: South End, 1990) 155.

72. hooks, *Talking Back* 20-21.

73. hooks, *Talking Back* 21.

74. hooks, *Feminist Theory* 35.

75. hooks, *Feminist Theory* 36.

76. hooks, *Talking Back* 21.

77. hooks, *Killing Rage* 271.

78. hooks, *Talking Back* 176.

79. hooks, *Talking Back* 176.

80. hooks, *Killing Rage* 7.

81. hooks, *Feminist Theory* 17-18.

82. hooks, *Feminist Theory* 18.

83. hooks, *Feminist Theory* 26.

84. hooks, *Ain't I a Woman* 195.

85. hooks, *Feminist Theory* 31.

86. hooks, *Feminist Theory* 24.

87. hooks, *Talking Back* 25.

88. hooks, *Feminist Theory* 34.

89. hooks, *Talking Back* 22.

90. hooks, *Feminist Theory* 29.

91. hooks, *Killing Rage* 99.

92. hooks, *Feminist Theory* 158.

93. hooks, *Ain't I a Woman* 192.

94. hooks, *Feminist Theory* 163, 159.

95. hooks, *Talking Back* 54.

96. hooks, *Feminist Theory* 163.

97. hooks, *Ain't I a Woman* 190.

98. hooks, *Ain't I a Woman* 190.
99. hooks, *Teaching* 71.
100. hooks, *Feminist Theory* 1, 3.
101. hooks, *Feminist Theory* 1.
102. hooks, *Feminist Theory* 2.
103. hooks, *Feminist Theory* 97.
104. hooks, *Feminist Theory* 134.
105. hooks, *Feminist Theory* 98.
106. hooks, *Feminist Theory* 98-99.
107. hooks, *Feminist Theory* 98.
108. hooks, *Feminist Theory* 133.
109. hooks, *Feminist Theory* 135.
110. hooks, *Ain't I a Woman* 1.
111. hooks, *Feminist Theory* preface.
112. hooks, *Teaching* 72.
113. hooks, *Killing Rage* 151.
114. hooks, *Feminist Theory* 161.
115. hooks, *Feminist Theory* 15.
116. hooks and West 152.
117. hooks, *Teaching* 202.
118. hooks, *Yearning* 149.
119. hooks, "Marginality" 342.
120. hooks, *Feminist Theory* preface.
121. hooks, *Feminist Theory* preface.
122. hooks, *Yearning* 149-50.
123. hooks, *Talking Back* 16.
124. hooks, *Feminist Theory* 15.
125. hooks, *Feminist Theory* 14.
126. hooks, *Ain't I a Woman* 7.
127. hooks, *Ain't I a Woman* 7.
128. hooks, *Talking Back* 47.
129. hooks, *Talking Back* 46.
130. hooks, *Art* 10.
131. hooks, *Yearning* 29.
132. hooks, *Teaching* 90, 91.
133. hooks, *Art* 12.
134. hooks, *Teaching* 91-92.
135. hooks, *Teaching* 91.
136. hooks, *Outlaw Culture* 217.
137. hooks, *Outlaw Culture* 5.
138. hooks, *Killing Rage* 110.

139. bell hooks, *Sisters of the Yam: Black Women and Self-Recovery* (Boston: South End, 1993) 1-2.

140. hooks, *Outlaw Culture* 5.

141. hooks, *Yearning* 8.

142. hooks, *Killing Rage* 193.

143. hooks, *Yearning* 218.

144. hooks, *Yearning* 63.

145. hooks, *Teaching* 70.

146. bell hooks, "Future Feminist Movements," *Off Our Backs* 20 (1990): 9.

147. hooks, *Yearning* 63-64.

148. hooks, *Outlaw Culture* 78-79.

149. hooks, *Feminist Theory* 111.

150. hooks, *Talking Back* 40.

151. hooks, *Teaching* 65.

152. hooks, *Feminist Theory* 111.

153. hooks, *Outlaw Culture* 241.

154. hooks, *Teaching* 48.

155. Quoted in Sischy 125.

156. hooks, *Outlaw Culture* 6.

157. hooks, *Outlaw Culture* 242.

158. hooks, *Sisters* 40.

159. hooks, *Teaching* 108-09.

160. hooks, *Yearning* 94.

161. Quoted in Lutz 420.

162. hooks, *Sisters* 25.

163. hooks, *Talking Back* 129.

164. hooks, *Talking Back* 3.

165. hooks, *Outlaw Culture* 210.

166. hooks, *Talking Back* 108.

167. hooks, *Talking Back* 111.

168. hooks, *Talking Back* 14.

169. hooks, *Talking Back* 106.

170. bell hooks, "The Hill-Thomas Hearing," *Artforum* 31 (1992): 13.

171. hooks, *Teaching* 130.

172. hooks, *Talking Back* 16.

173. hooks, *Art* 113.

174. hooks, *Outlaw Culture* 66.

175. hooks, *Outlaw Culture* 70.

176. hooks, *Outlaw Culture* 66.

177. hooks, *Outlaw Culture* 72.

178. hooks, *Talking Back* 129.

179. hooks, *Killing Rage* 193.

180. hooks, *Killing Rage* 193.

181. hooks, *Yearning* 22.

182. hooks, *Outlaw Culture* 219.

183. hooks, *Killing Rage* 194.

184. hooks, *Talking Back* 26.

185. John Perry Barlow and bell hooks, "An Intimate Conversation," *Shambhala Sun* 4 (1995): 63.

186. hooks, *Outlaw Culture* 241, 54.

187. hooks, *Outlaw Culture* 90.

188. bell hooks, *Black Looks: Race and Representation* (Boston: South End, 1992) 5.

189. hooks, *Art* 3.

190. hooks, *Black Looks* 5.

191. hooks, *Killing Rage* 110.

192. hooks, *Sisters* 97.

193. hooks, *Outlaw Culture* 90.

194. hooks, *Outlaw Culture* 156.

195. hooks, *Yearning* 7.

196. hooks and West 104.

197. hooks, *Yearning* 156.

198. Quoted in Lisa Jones, "Rebel without a Pause," *Village Voice,* 13 Oct. 1992: 10.

199. hooks, *Yearning* 184.

200. bell hooks, "Sorrowful Black Death Is Not a Hot Ticket," *Sight and Sound* 4 (1994): 12.

201. hooks, *Outlaw Culture* 220.

202. hooks, *Outlaw Culture* 217.

203. hooks, *Black Looks* 4.

204. hooks, *Art* 7, 108.

205. hooks, *Art* 138.

206. hooks, *Yearning* 111.

207. hooks, *Yearning* 112.

208. Quoted in Jones, "Rebel" 10.

209. hooks, *Sisters* 83.

210. hooks, *Outlaw Culture* 237.

211. hooks, *Art* xv.

212. hooks, *Art* 120.

213. hooks, *Art* 120.

214. hooks, *Art* 14.

215. hooks, *Teaching* 12.

216. hooks, *Talking Back* 102.

217. hooks, *Yearning* 15.

218. Quoted in David Trend, "Representation and Resistance: An Interview with Bell Hooks," *Socialist Review* 24 (1994): 126.

219. hooks, *Teaching* 207.

220. hooks, *Talking Back* 101.

221. hooks, *Teaching* 140-41.

222. hooks, *Talking Back* 52.

223. hooks, *Teaching* 7.

224. hooks, *Talking Back* 52.

225. hooks, *Talking Back* 54.

226. hooks, *Teaching* 8.

227. hooks, *Killing Rage* 255.

228. hooks, *Feminist Theory* 110.

229. hooks, *Feminist Theory* 109.

230. Quoted in Lisa Jones, "Sister Knowledge," *Essence* May 1995: 258.

231. hooks, *Killing Rage* 261-62.

232. hooks, *Feminist Theory* 108.

233. hooks, *Killing Rage* 257.

234. hooks, *Killing Rage* 262.

235. Kenneth Burke, *A Rhetoric of Motives* (1950; Berkeley: U of California P, 1969) 118, 138-41, 265.

236. hooks, *Killing Rage* 262.

5. Gloria Anzaldúa

1. Gloria Anzaldúa, "La prieta," *This Bridge Called My Back: Writings by Radical Women of Color,* ed. Cherríe Moraga and Gloria Anzaldúa, 2nd ed. (New York: Kitchen Table: Women of Color, 1983) 205.

2. Gloria Anzaldúa, *Borderlands/La Frontera: The New Mestiza* (San Francisco, CA: Aunt Lute, 1987) 9.

3. Anzaldúa, *Borderlands* 9.

4. Anzaldúa, "La prieta" 200.

5. Anzaldúa, "La prieta" 199.

6. Anzaldúa, "La prieta" 199.

7. Anzaldúa, "La prieta" 198.

8. Quoted in AnnLouise Keating, "Writing, Politics, and *las Lesberadas: Platicando con* Gloria Anzaldúa," *Frontiers: A Journal of Women Studies* 14 (1993): 123.

9. Anzaldúa, "La prieta" 199.

10. Anzaldúa, *Borderlands* 16.

11. Quoted in Keating 118-19.

12. Anzaldúa, "La prieta" 200.

13. Anzaldúa, *Borderlands* 65.

14. Anzaldúa, *Borderlands* 16.

15. Anzaldúa, *Borderlands* 73.

16. Anzaldúa, *Borderlands* 67, 66.

17. Cherríe Moraga and Gloria Anzaldúa, "Introduction," *This Bridge Called My Back: Writings by Radical Women of Color,* ed. Cherríe Moraga and Gloria Anzaldúa, 2nd ed. (New York: Kitchen Table: Women of Color, 1983) xxiv, xxiii.

18. Anzaldúa, *Borderlands* preface.

19. Gloria Anzaldúa, *Making Face, Making Soul/Haciendo Caras: Creative and Critical Perspectives by Feminists of Color* (San Francisco: Aunt Lute, 1990) xvi.

20. Anzaldúa, *Making Face* xvi.

21. Anzaldúa, *Making Face* xvi.

22. Anzaldúa, *Borderlands* 59.

23. Anzaldúa, *Borderlands* 3.

24. Quoted in Keating 129. We have chosen to capitalize the word throughout to capture the fullest range of meanings for the term *Borderlands.*

25. Anzaldúa, *Borderlands* 3.

26. Gloria Anzaldúa, "Artist Statement," curriculum vita, n.d., 1.

27. Anzaldúa, *Making Face* 377.

28. Anzaldúa, *Borderlands* preface.

29. Anzaldúa, *Borderlands* 2-3.

30. Anzaldúa, *Borderlands* 63.

31. Anzaldúa, *Making Face* xxii.

32. Anzaldúa, *Making Face* xxiii.

33. Anzaldúa, "La prieta" 205.

34. Anzaldúa, *Making Face* xv.

35. Anzaldúa, *Making Face* xv.

36. Quoted in Anzaldúa, *Making Face* xv.

37. Anzaldúa, *Making Face* xv.

38. Anzaldúa, *Borderlands* preface.

39. Gloria Anzaldúa, *Making Face* 377.

40. Quoted in Keating 129.

41. Gloria Anzaldúa, "Curator's Statement," curriculum vita, n.d., 1.

42. "Entre Américas: El Taller Nepantla," exhibition catalog, San Jose Center for Latino Arts, 1 Oct.–2 Dec. 1995.

43. Anzaldúa, *Borderlands* 77.

44. Anzaldúa, *Making Face* 379.

45. Anzaldúa, *Making Face* 379.

46. Anzaldúa, *Making Face* 379.

47. Anzaldúa, *Making Face* 379.

48. Anzaldúa, *Borderlands* 77.

49. Anzaldúa, *Borderlands* 82-83.

50. Anzaldúa, *Making Face* xv.

51. Anzaldúa, *Making Face* xvi.

52. Anzaldúa, *Borderlands* 22.

53. Anzaldúa, *Borderlands* preface.

54. Anzaldúa, *Borderlands* 23.

55. Rafael Perez-Torres, *Movements in Chicano Poetry* (Cambridge: Cambridge UP, 1995) 206.

56. Anzaldúa, *Borderlands* 84.

57. Anzaldúa, *Making Face* xxvii.

58. Gloria Anzaldúa, "Afterword: A Movement of Women," *This Way Daybreak Comes: Women's Values and the Future,* ed. Annie Cheatham and Mary Clare Powell (Philadelphia: New Society, 1986) 224-25.

59. Anzaldúa, "Afterword" 225.

60. Anzaldúa, "Afterword" 224.

61. Anzaldúa, "Afterword" 226.

62. Anzaldúa, *Borderlands* preface.

63. Anzaldúa, *Borderlands* 3.

64. Anzaldúa, *Making Face* 383.

65. Anzaldúa, *Making Face* 383.

66. Anzaldúa, *Making Face* 383.

67. Anzaldúa, *Making Face* 378.

68. Anzaldúa, *Making Face* 380.

69. Anzaldúa, *Borderlands* 49.

70. Gloria Anzaldúa, "Nos/Otras: What Divides and Unites Us," U of New Mexico, Albuquerque, 15 Apr. 1995.

71. Anzaldúa, *Borderlands* 49.

72. Anzaldúa, *Making Face* 379.

73. Anzaldúa, *Making Face* 378-79.

74. Anzaldúa, *Making Face* 146.

75. Anzaldúa, *Borderlands* 173.

76. Anzaldúa, *Making Face* 380.

77. Perez-Torres 235.

78. Anzaldúa, *Borderlands* 38.

79. Anzaldúa, *Borderlands* 69.

80. Gloria Anzaldúa, "Metaphors in the Tradition of the Shaman," *Conversant Essays: Contemporary Poets on Poetry,* ed. James McCorkle (Detroit: Wayne State UP, 1990) 99-100.

81. Anzaldúa, "Metaphors" 100.

82. Anzaldúa, *Borderlands* 70.

83. Anzaldúa, "Metaphors" 100.

84. Gloria Anzaldúa, "Foreword to the Second Edition," *This Bridge Called My Back: Writings by Radical Women of Color,* ed. Cherríe Moraga and Gloria Anzaldúa, 2nd ed. (New York: Kitchen Table: Women of Color, 1983).

85. Anzaldúa, *Making Face* 380.

86. Perez-Torres 96.

87. Anzaldúa, *Borderlands* 11.

88. Anzaldúa, *Borderlands* 11.

89. Perez-Torres 93.

90. Anzaldúa, "La prieta" 208.

91. Anzaldúa, *Borderlands* 70-71.

92. Gloria Anzaldúa, "Bridge, Drawbridge, Sandbar or Island: Lesbians-of-Color Hacienda Alianzas," *Bridges of Power: Women's Multicultural Alliances,* ed. Lisa Albrecht and Rose M. Brewer (Philadelphia: New Society, 1990) 216-31.

93. Anzaldúa, "Bridge, Drawbridge" 223.

94. Anzaldúa, *Borderlands* 48.

95. Anzaldúa, "Bridge, Drawbridge" 223.

96. Anzaldúa, "Bridge, Drawbridge" 223.

97. Anzaldúa, *Borderlands* 21. Anzaldúa invokes the figure of La Llorona, whose name translates as "the one who weeps or wails." Malinche, an Aztec woman who became the interpreter and wife of Hernando Cortes, is memorialized as La Llorona because she killed her two sons to keep her husband from taking them back to Spain. She continues to grieve for eternity, waiting for her sons' return. Anzaldúa sees weeping and wailing as one of the few forms of protest available to Aztec women, and its tradition continues in the kind of resistance Anzaldúa describes with the island metaphor.

98. Anzaldúa, *Making Face* 378.

99. Anzaldúa, *Borderlands* 73.

100. Anzaldúa, *Making Face* 378.

101. Anzaldúa, *Making Face* 386.

102. Anzaldúa, "Afterword" 225.

103. Anzaldúa, *Borderlands* 21.

104. Anzaldúa, "Foreword."

105. Anzaldúa, "Foreword."

106. Anzaldúa, "Bridge, Drawbridge" 219.

107. Anzaldúa, "Bridge, Drawbridge" 223.

108. Anzaldúa, "Bridge, Drawbridge" 223.

109. Anzaldúa, "Bridge, Drawbridge" 224.

110. Anzaldúa, "Bridge, Drawbridge" 223-24.

111. Anzaldúa, "Bridge, Drawbridge" 224.

112. Anzaldúa, "Bridge, Drawbridge" 224.

113. Anzaldúa, "Bridge, Drawbridge" 224.

114. Anzaldúa, "Bridge, Drawbridge" 224.

115. Anzaldúa, "Bridge, Drawbridge" 224.

116. Anzaldúa, *Making Face* xxiv.

117. Anzaldúa, *Borderlands* 66.

118. Anzaldúa, *Borderlands* 67.

119. Anzaldúa, *Borderlands* 67.

120. Anzaldúa, *Making Face* xxiv.

121. Anzaldúa, *Making Face* xxiv.

122. Anzaldúa, *Making Face* xxiv-xxv.

123. Anzaldúa, "Foreword."

124. Anzaldúa, *Borderlands* 195.

125. Kenneth Burke, *A Rhetoric of Motives* (Berkeley: U of California P, 1969) xiv, 21, 24, 46, 55.

126. Anzaldúa, *Making Face* xxvi.

6. Mary Daly

1. Mary Daly, *Outercourse: The Be-Dazzling Voyage* (New York: HarperCollins, 1992 [available in the United States through Trafalger Square Publishing]) 1.

2. Daly, *Outercourse* 19.

3. Daly, *Outercourse* 19, 20.

4. Daly, *Outercourse* 20.

5. Daly, *Outercourse* 20.

6. Daly, *Outercourse* 21.

7. Daly, *Outercourse* 28.

8. Daly, *Outercourse* 27.

9. Daly, *Outercourse* 42.

10. Daly, *Outercourse* 43.

11. Daly, *Outercourse* 47.

12. Daly, *Outercourse* 47.

13. Daly, *Outercourse* 48.

14. Daly, *Outercourse* 48.

15. Daly, *Outercourse* 54-55.

16. Daly, *Outercourse* 55.

17. Mary Daly, personal interview, 1 May 1998.

18. Daly, *Outercourse* 95. See also Janice Raymond, "A Decade of Academic Harassment," *Handbook for Women Scholars,* ed. Monika Kehoe (San Francisco: Americas Behavioral Research Corporation, 1982) 82.

19. Daly, *Outercourse* 96.

20. Raymond 83; and Daly, *Outercourse* 206.

21. Daly, *Outercourse* 229.

22. Mary Daly, in Cahoots with Jane Caputi, *Websters' First New Intergalactic Wickedary of the English Language* (Boston: Beacon, 1987 [available in the United States through Trafalger Square Publishing]) 100. The concept of the Wickedary first appears in Mary Daly, *Pure Lust: Elemental Feminist Philosophy* (Boston: Beacon, 1984 [available in the United States through Trafalger Square Publishing]).

23. Quoted in Karen A. Brophy, "An In-Depth Look at the Daly Controversy," *The Heights* [student newspaper, Boston College] 3 Apr. 1989: 16.

24. Daly, *Outercourse* 335.

25. Daly, *Outercourse* 335.

26. Daly, in Cahoots with Caputi 76.

27. Daly, *Pure Lust* 1.

28. Daly, *Pure Lust* 2-3.

29. Mary Daly, *Beyond God the Father: Toward a Philosophy of Women's Liberation* (Boston: Beacon, 1985) 7.

30. Daly, *Pure Lust* 50.

31. Daly, *Pure Lust* 55.

32. Daly, *Pure Lust* 55.

33. Mary Daly, "The Women's Movement: An Exodus Community," *Religious Education* 67 (1972): 330, 328.

34. Daly, "The Women's Movement" 328.

35. Daly, "The Women's Movement" 328.

36. Mary Daly, "The Forgotten Sex: A Built-in Bias," *Commonweal* 81 (15 Jan. 1965): 509-10.

37. Mary Daly, *Gyn/Ecology: The Metaethics of Radical Feminism* (Boston: Beacon, 1978) 109.

38. Daly, *Gyn/Ecology* 111.

39. Daly, *Pure Lust* 2.

40. Daly, in Cahoots with Caputi 63. The concept of the Background first appears in *Gyn/Ecology*.

41. Daly, *Gyn/Ecology* 3.

42. Daly, in Cahoots with Caputi 268.

43. Daly, *Beyond God* 36, 189.

44. Daly, *Beyond God* 198.

45. Daly, in Cahoots with Caputi 67. The concept of Biophilia first appears in *Gyn/Ecology*.

46. Daly, in Cahoots with Caputi 89. The concept of Pure Lust first appears in *Pure Lust*.

47. Daly, *Gyn/Ecology* 31.

48. Daly, *Gyn/Ecology* 33.

49. Daly, *Pure Lust* 388.

50. Daly, *Beyond God* xvii.

51. Daly, *Beyond God* xvii.

52. Daly, *Gyn/Ecology* 6-7.

53. Daly, *Gyn/Ecology* 340.

54. Daly, *Gyn/Ecology* 341.

55. Daly, in Cahoots with Caputi 75. The concept of Radical Feminism first appears in *Beyond God*.

56. Daly, *Gyn/Ecology* 12.

57. Daly, *Pure Lust* 112.

58. Daly, *Pure Lust* 165.

59. Daly, *Pure Lust* 21.

60. Daly, *Pure Lust* 20-21.

61. Daly, *Pure Lust* 22.

62. Daly, *Pure Lust* 23.

63. Daly, in Cahoots with Caputi 234.

64. Daly, *Gyn/Ecology* 8, 17.

65. Daly, in Cahoots with Caputi 232. The concept of Totaled Women first appears in *Gyn/Ecology*.

66. Daly, in Cahoots with Caputi 224. The concept of sadofeminism first appears in *Pure Lust*.

67. Daly, *Gyn/Ecology* 17.

68. Daly, *Pure Lust* 11-12.

69. Daly, *Pure Lust* 11, 12.

70. Daly, *Pure Lust* 12.

71. Daly, *Pure Lust* 12, 13.

72. Daly, in Cahoots with Caputi 167. The concept of the Spinster first appears in *Gyn/Ecology*.

73. Daly, *Pure Lust* 13.

74. Daly, *Pure Lust* 13-14.

75. Daly, *Pure Lust* 14-15.

76. Daly, *Pure Lust* 15.

77. Daly, *Pure Lust* 16.

78. Daly, *Gyn/Ecology* 14-16.

79. Daly, *Gyn/Ecology* 113-77.

80. Daly, *Gyn/Ecology* 115.

81. Daly, *Gyn/Ecology* 136-37.

82. Daly, *Gyn/Ecology* 157.

83. Daly, *Gyn/Ecology* 180.

84. Daly, *Gyn/Ecology* 187.

85. Daly, *Gyn/Ecology* 186.

86. Daly, *Gyn/Ecology* 224.

87. Daly, *Gyn/Ecology* 225.

88. Daly, *Gyn/Ecology* 233-50.

89. Daly, *Gyn/Ecology* 19.

90. Daly, *Gyn/Ecology* 19-20.

91. Daly, *Gyn/Ecology* 18.

92. Daly, *Gyn/Ecology* 3.

93. Daly, *Gyn/Ecology* 7.

94. Daly, "The Forgotten Sex" 510.

95. Daly, "The Women's Movement" 327.

96. Daly, "The Women's Movement" 327.

97. Daly, "The Women's Movement" 330.

98. Daly, *Gyn/Ecology* 15.

99. Daly, *Gyn/Ecology* 53.

100. Daly, *Gyn/Ecology* 55.

101. Daly, *Beyond God* 5. Daly originally used the label *trivialization* but then changed to *depreciation* because *Trivia* is one of the names for the Triple Goddess. Trivia is "commonly encountered at crossroads" and also indicates the "commonplace character of meeting with the Goddess." Daly, in Cahoots with Caputi 174.

102. Daly, *Beyond God* 5.

103. Daly, *Beyond God* 5.

104. Daly, *Beyond God* 5.

105. Daly, *Beyond God* 95.

106. Daly, *Beyond God* 95.

107. Cited in Daly, *Gyn/Ecology* 144.

108. Daly, *Gyn/Ecology* 145.

109. Mary Daly, *The Church and the Second Sex* (Boston: Beacon, 1968; New York: Harper Colophon, 1975) xxix.

110. Daly, in Cahoots with Caputi 240.

111. Daly, in Cahoots with Caputi 242.

112. Daly, in Cahoots with Caputi 244.

113. Daly, in Cahoots with Caputi 245.

114. Daly, in Cahoots with Caputi 245.

115. Daly, in Cahoots with Caputi 246.

116. Daly, in Cahoots with Caputi 247.

117. Daly, *Pure Lust* 25.

118. Daly, *Pure Lust* 25.

119. Daly, *Pure Lust* 24, 25.

120. Daly, *Pure Lust* 25.

121. Daly, *Pure Lust* 27.

122. Daly, *Pure Lust* 27.

123. Daly, *Gyn/Ecology* 3.

124. Daly, *Beyond God* 8.

125. Daly, *Beyond God* 8-9.

126. Daly, *Gyn/Ecology* 3.

127. Daly, in Cahoots with Caputi xxi.

128. Daly, in Cahoots with Caputi xxii.

129. Daly, in Cahoots with Caputi xxii.

130. Daly, in Cahoots with Caputi 14.

131. Daly, in Cahoots with Caputi 16.

132. Daly, in Cahoots with Caputi 16.

133. Daly, in Cahoots with Caputi 16.

134. Daly, in Cahoots with Caputi 17.

135. Daly, in Cahoots with Caputi 18.

136. Daly, in Cahoots with Caputi 18.

137. Daly, in Cahoots with Caputi 20.

138. Daly, in Cahoots with Caputi 27.

139. Daly, in Cahoots with Caputi 31, 30.

140. Daly, in Cahoots with Caputi 34.

141. Daly, in Cahoots with Caputi 39.

142. Quoted in Daly, in Cahoots with Caputi 40.

143. Daly, *Gyn/Ecology* 333.

144. Daly, *Gyn/Ecology* 339-40.

145. Daly, *Gyn/Ecology* 341.

146. Daly, *Gyn/Ecology* 345.

147. Daly, *Gyn/Ecology* 319.

148. Daly, in Cahoots with Caputi 165.

149. Daly, "The Women's Movement" 331; and Mary Daly, "The Spiritual Dimension of Women's Liberation," *Radical Feminism,* ed. Ann Koedt, Ellen Levine, and Anita Rapone (New York: Quadrangle, 1973) 266.

150. Daly, "The Women's Movement" 331.

151. Daly, in Cahoots with Caputi 77. The concept of Gynergy first appears in *Beyond God.*

152. Daly, *Gyn/Ecology* 377.

153. Daly, in Cahoots with Caputi 96. The concept of Spinning first appears in *Gyn/Ecology.*

154. Daly, *Gyn/Ecology* 394.

155. Daly, *Gyn/Ecology* 396-400.

156. Daly, *Gyn/Ecology* 401.

157. Daly, in Cahoots with Caputi 261.

158. Daly, in Cahoots with Caputi 263.

159. Daly, in Cahoots with Caputi 264.

160. Daly, in Cahoots with Caputi 264.

161. Daly, in Cahoots with Caputi 265.

162. Daly, in Cahoots with Caputi 267.

163. Daly, in Cahoots with Caputi 268.

164. Daly, in Cahoots with Caputi 275.

165. Daly, in Cahoots with Caputi 275.

166. Daly, in Cahoots with Caputi 284.

167. Daly, *Beyond God* 6.

168. Daly, *Beyond God* 11.

169. Mary Daly, "The Courage to See: Religious Implications of the New Sisterhood," *Christian Century* 22 Sept. 1972: 1108.

170. Lloyd F. Bitzer, "The Rhetorical Situation," *Philosophy and Rhetoric* 1 (1969): 1-14.

7. Starhawk

1. Starhawk, *The Fifth Sacred Thing* (New York: Bantam, 1993) 300.

2. Starhawk, personal interview, 23 June 1997.

3. Starhawk, *The Spiral Dance: A Rebirth of the Ancient Religion of the Great Goddess* (San Francisco: HarperCollins, 1989) 2.

4. Starhawk, M. Macha NightMare, and the Reclaiming Collective, *The Pagan Book of Living and Dying: Practical Rituals, Prayers, Blessings, and Meditations on Crossing Over* (New York: HarperCollins, 1997) 6-9.

5. Starhawk, *Truth or Dare: Encounters with Power, Authority, and Mystery* (San Francisco: Harper & Row, 1990) 7.

6. Starhawk, *Truth* 7.

7. Starhawk, *Truth* 8.

8. Starhawk, *Truth* 7.

9. Starhawk, *Truth* 8.

10. Starhawk, personal interview.

11. Starhawk, personal interview.

12. Starhawk, *Truth* 121.

13. Starhawk, personal interview.

14. Starhawk, *Truth* 152.

15. Starhawk, personal interview.

16. Starhawk, personal interview.

17. Starhawk, personal interview.

18. Starhawk, personal interview.

19. Starhawk, personal interview.

20. Starhawk, *Truth* 151.

21. Starhawk, personal interview.

22. Starhawk, *Spiral Dance* 3.

23. Quoted in Starhawk, *Spiral Dance* 5.

24. Starhawk, *Spiral Dance* 2.

25. Starhawk, *Dreaming the Dark: Magic, Sex and Politics* (Boston: Beacon, 1988) xxv.

26. Starhawk, *Dreaming* xxx.

27. Starhawk, *Truth* [ix].

28. Starhawk, personal interview.

29. Starhawk, NightMare, and the Reclaiming Collective xxi.

30. Starhawk, NightMare, and the Reclaiming Collective xxiv.

31. Starhawk, *Fifth Sacred Thing* n. pag.

32. Starhawk, *Dreaming* x.

33. Starhawk, *Truth* 84.

34. Starhawk, *Truth* 9.

35. Starhawk, *Truth* 66.

36. Starhawk, *Truth* 81.

37. Starhawk, *Truth* 53

38. Starhawk, *Truth* 63.

39. Starhawk, *Dreaming* 34.

40. Starhawk, *Truth* 32.
41. Starhawk, *Truth* 9.
42. Starhawk, *Truth* 14.
43. Starhawk, *Truth* 9.
44. Starhawk, *Truth* 14.
45. Starhawk, *Dreaming* 48.
46. Starhawk, *Truth* 314.
47. Starhawk, *Dreaming* 9.
48. Starhawk, *Dreaming* 10.
49. Starhawk, *Spiral Dance* 23.
50. Starhawk, *Truth* 21.
51. Starhawk, *Dreaming* 80.
52. Starhawk, *Truth* 116.
53. Starhawk, *Truth* 198.
54. Starhawk, *Dreaming* 73.
55. Starhawk, *Truth* 15.
56. Starhawk, *Spiral Dance* 10.
57. Starhawk, *Dreaming* 4-5.
58. Starhawk, *Dreaming* 5.
59. Starhawk, *Truth* 22.
60. Starhawk, *Truth* 314.
61. Starhawk, *Spiral Dance* 8.
62. Starhawk, *Spiral Dance* 199.
63. Starhawk, personal interview.
64. Starhawk, personal interview.
65. Starhawk, *Spiral Dance* 207.
66. Starhawk, personal interview.
67. Starhawk, personal interview.
68. Starhawk, personal interview.
69. Starhawk, *Spiral Dance* 41.
70. Starhawk, *Dreaming* 63.
71. Starhawk, *Dreaming* 63.
72. Starhawk, *Truth* 66.
73. Starhawk, *Dreaming* 63.
74. Starhawk, *Dreaming* 35.
75. Starhawk, *Dreaming* 3.
76. Starhawk, *Dreaming* 35.
77. Starhawk, *Dreaming* 36.
78. Starhawk, *Dreaming* 35.
79. Starhawk, *Dreaming* 35.
80. Starhawk, *Truth* 118.
81. Starhawk, *Truth* 119.

82. Starhawk, *Truth* 119.
83. Starhawk, *Truth* 120.
84. Starhawk, *Truth* 119.
85. Starhawk, *Truth* 118.
86. Starhawk, *Truth* 176.
87. Starhawk, *Truth* 177.
88. Starhawk, *Truth* 177.
89. Starhawk, *Truth* 177.
90. Starhawk, *Truth* 178.
91. Starhawk, *Truth* 193-94.
92. Starhawk, *Truth* 196.
93. Starhawk, *Truth* 196.
94. Starhawk, *Truth* 139.
95. Starhawk, *Truth* 140.
96. Starhawk, *Truth* 141.
97. Starhawk, *Truth* 140.
98. Starhawk, *Truth* 141.
99. Starhawk, *Truth* 161.
100. Starhawk, *Truth* 160.
101. Starhawk, *Truth* 163.
102. Starhawk, *Spiral Dance* 238.
103. Starhawk, *Truth* 206.
104. Starhawk, *Truth* 205.
105. Starhawk, *Truth* 203.
106. Starhawk, *Truth* 231.
107. Starhawk, *Truth* 232.
108. Starhawk, *Truth* 239.
109. Starhawk, *Truth* 232.
110. Starhawk, *Truth* 233.
111. Starhawk, *Truth* 237.
112. Starhawk, *Truth* 244.
113. Starhawk, *Truth* 244.
114. Starhawk, *Truth* 117.
115. Starhawk, *Truth* 231.
116. Starhawk, *Truth* 241.
117. Starhawk, *Truth* 4.
118. Starhawk, *Truth* 20.
119. Starhawk, *Truth* 340.
120. Starhawk, *Truth* 340.
121. Starhawk, *Truth* 340.
122. Starhawk, *Truth* 247.
123. Starhawk, *Truth* 241.

124. Starhawk, *Dreaming* 41.

125. Starhawk, *Dreaming* 41.

126. Starhawk, *Dreaming* 155.

127. Starhawk, *Truth* 98; and Starhawk, "Ritual as Bonding: Action as Ritual," *Weaving the Visions: New Patterns in Feminist Spirituality,* ed. Judith Plaskow and Carol P. Christ (San Francisco: HarperCollins, 1989) 326. Starhawk's *The Spiral Dance* is a work of rituals, invocations, exercises, and magic. We do not cite specific rituals here; instead, we refer the interested reader to *The Spiral Dance* for rituals and exercises that are designed for specific situations and needs.

128. Starhawk, *Truth* 98.

129. Starhawk, *Truth* 98.

130. Starhawk, *Truth* 100.

131. Starhawk, *Dreaming* 47.

132. Starhawk, *Truth* 99.

133. Starhawk, *Truth* 100-12.

134. Starhawk, *Spiral Dance* 64.

135. Starhawk, *Spiral Dance* 64.

136. Starhawk, *Truth* 103-04.

137. Starhawk, *Truth* 104-05.

138. Starhawk, *Truth* 6.

139. Starhawk, *Dreaming* 13.

140. Starhawk, *Truth* 107.

141. Starhawk, *Truth* 111.

142. Starhawk, *Truth* 112.

143. Starhawk, *Truth* 256.

144. Starhawk, *Truth* 10.

145. Starhawk, *Truth* 11.

146. Starhawk, *Truth* 257.

147. Starhawk, *Truth* 257.

148. Starhawk, *Truth* 257.

149. Starhawk, *Truth* 258.

150. Starhawk, *Truth* 258.

151. Starhawk, *Truth* 258.

152. Starhawk, *Truth* 258.

153. Starhawk, *Truth* 260.

154. Starhawk, *Truth* 259.

155. Starhawk, *Truth* 265.

156. Starhawk, *Truth* 265.

157. Starhawk, *Truth* 265.

158. Starhawk, *Truth* 265.

159. Starhawk, *Truth* 265.

160. Starhawk, *Truth* 265-66.

161. Starhawk, *Truth* 266.
162. Starhawk, *Dreaming* 129.
163. Starhawk, *Dreaming* 129.
164. Starhawk, *Truth* 267.
165. Starhawk, *Truth* 267.
166. Starhawk, *Truth* 269.
167. Starhawk uses these same concepts in her novel *The Fifth Sacred Thing* but renames each of the roles as the voices of White Deer, Hawk, Coyote, and Salmon. *Fifth Sacred Thing* 45.
168. Starhawk, *Dreaming* 115.
169. Starhawk, *Truth* 277.
170. Starhawk, *Truth* 278.
171. Starhawk, *Truth* 279.
172. Starhawk, *Truth* 280.
173. Starhawk, *Truth* 281.
174. Starhawk, *Truth* 282.
175. Starhawk, *Truth* 282.
176. Starhawk, *Dreaming* 116.
177. Starhawk, *Dreaming* 118.
178. Starhawk, *Dreaming* 116.
179. Starhawk, *Dreaming* 117.
180. Starhawk, *Dreaming* 117.
181. Starhawk, *Dreaming* 118.
182. Starhawk, *Spiral Dance* 13.

8. Paula Gunn Allen

1. Paula Gunn Allen, quoted in Jacqueline L. Collins, "The Horse That I Ride: The Life Story of Paula Gunn Allen," unpublished ms., 11.
2. Quoted in Collins 28.
3. Paula Gunn Allen, personal interview, 6 Feb. 1998.
4. Quoted in Collins 16.
5. Quoted in Collins 13, 19.
6. Quoted in Collins 16.
7. Quoted in Collins 7.
8. Quoted in Collins 30.
9. Quoted in Collins 33.
10. Quoted in Collins 37, 31.
11. Quoted in Collins 32.
12. Quoted in Collins 69.
13. Quoted in Collins 69.
14. Quoted in Collins 70.

15. Quoted in Collins 70.

16. Quoted in Collins 74.

17. Quoted in Collins 73.

18. Quoted in Collins 72.

19. Quoted in Collins 74.

20. Quoted in Collins 98.

21. Quoted in Collins 270.

22. Quoted in Collins 270.

23. Quoted in Collins 166-67.

24. Quoted in Collins 165.

25. Gunn Allen, personal interview.

26. Quoted in Collins 169.

27. Quoted in Collins 274.

28. Quoted in Collins 275.

29. Quoted in Collins 298.

30. Paula Gunn Allen, *The Sacred Hoop: Recovering the Feminine in American Indian Traditions* (Boston: Beacon, 1992) 6.

31. Gunn Allen, *Sacred Hoop* 6.

32. Gunn Allen, *Sacred Hoop* 268.

33. Paula Gunn Allen, *Grandmothers of the Light: A Medicine Woman's Sourcebook* (Boston: Beacon, 1991) xiii.

34. Quoted in Collins 80.

35. Quoted in Collins 308.

36. Quoted in Collins 347-48.

37. Gunn Allen, personal interview.

38. Quoted in Collins 115.

39. Quoted in Collins 95.

40. Gunn Allen, personal interview.

41. Gunn Allen, personal interview.

42. Quoted in Collins 129.

43. Quoted in Collins 152.

44. Quoted in Collins 80.

45. Quoted in Collins 307.

46. Quoted in Collins 216.

47. Quoted in Collins 246.

48. Gunn Allen, personal interview.

49. Quoted in Collins 246-47.

50. Laura Coltelli, "Paula Gunn Allen," *Winged Words: American Indian Writers Speak,* ed. Laura Coltelli (Lincoln: U of Nebraska P, 1990) 30.

51. Quoted in Coltelli 30.

52. Paula Gunn Allen, *Shadow Country* (Los Angeles: American Indian Studies Center, U of California, 1982) 34-35.

53. Gunn Allen, *Sacred Hoop* 189.

54. Gunn Allen, *Sacred Hoop* 190.

55. Gunn Allen, *Sacred Hoop* 156.

56. Paula Gunn Allen, "Sipapu: A Cultural Perspective," diss., U of New Mexico, 1975, 16.

57. Gunn Allen, *Sacred Hoop* 41.

58. Gunn Allen, *Sacred Hoop* 41.

59. Gunn Allen, *Sacred Hoop* 41.

60. Gunn Allen, *Sacred Hoop* 41-42.

61. Gunn Allen, *Sacred Hoop* 41-42.

62. Paula Gunn Allen, Lee Francis, and Mary Allen Francis, "This Business of Columbus," *Columbus and Beyond: Views from Native Americans,* ed. Randolph Jorgen (Tucson, AZ: Southwest Parks and Monuments Association, 1992) 57.

63. Gunn Allen, *Sacred Hoop* 46.

64. Gunn Allen, *Sacred Hoop* 211.

65. Gunn Allen, *Sacred Hoop* 211.

66. Gunn Allen, "Sipapu" 3.

67. Gunn Allen, "Sipapu" 16, 9-10.

68. Gunn Allen, *Shadow Country* 39.

69. Gunn Allen, *Shadow Country* 40.

70. Paula Gunn Allen, "Grandmother of the Sun: The Power of Woman in Native America," *Weaving the Visions: New Patterns in Feminist Spirituality,* ed. Judith Plaskow and Carol P. Christ (New York: HarperCollins, 1989) 22.

71. Gunn Allen, "Sipapu" 28.

72. Gunn Allen, *Sacred Hoop* 16.

73. Gunn Allen, "Sipapu" 31.

74. Gunn Allen, *Sacred Hoop* 15.

75. Gunn Allen, *Grandmothers* 28.

76. Gunn Allen, *Sacred Hoop* 15.

77. Paula Gunn Allen, " 'Whose Dream Is This Anyway?': Remythologizing and Self-Redefinition of Contemporary American Indian Fiction," *Literature and the Visual Arts in Contemporary Society,* ed. Suzanne Ferguson and Barbara Groseclose (Columbus: Ohio State UP, 1985) 118.

78. Gunn Allen, "Grandmother of the Sun" 22.

79. Gunn Allen, "Sipapu" 29.

80. Gunn Allen, *Sacred Hoop* 15.

81. Gunn Allen, "Sipapu" 40.

82. Gunn Allen, *Grandmothers* 108.

83. Gunn Allen, *Sacred Hoop* 28.

84. Gunn Allen, *Sacred Hoop* 22.

85. Gunn Allen, *Sacred Hoop* 68.

86. Gunn Allen, *Sacred Hoop* 22.

87. Paula Gunn Allen, *Studies in American Indian Literature: Critical Essays and Course Designs* (New York: Modern Language Association, 1983) 8.

88. Gunn Allen, "Sipapu" 92.

89. Paula Gunn Allen, "This Wilderness in My Blood: Spiritual Foundations of the Poetry of Five American Indian Women," *Coyote Was Here: Essays on Contemporary Native American Literary and Political Mobilization,* ed. Bo Schöler (Aarhus, Denmark: SEKLOS/U of Aarhus, 1984) 99.

90. Gunn Allen, "This Wilderness" 97.

91. Gunn Allen, *Sacred Hoop* 167.

92. Gunn Allen, *Sacred Hoop* 167.

93. Gunn Allen, *Grandmothers* 5-6.

94. Gunn Allen, *Grandmothers* 7.

95. Gunn Allen, "Sipapu" 73.

96. Gunn Allen, "Sipapu" 74.

97. Gunn Allen, "This Wilderness" 99.

98. Gunn Allen, *Sacred Hoop* 90.

99. Quoted in Collins 354.

100. Paula Gunn Allen, "Kochinnenako in Academe: Three Approaches to Interpreting a Keres Indian Tale," *North Dakota Quarterly* 53 (1985): 84.

101. Gunn Allen, "Kochinnenako" 85.

102. Gunn Allen, *Sacred Hoop* 214.

103. Gunn Allen, "Kochinnenako" 99.

104. Quoted in Collins 352.

105. Quoted in Collins 353.

106. Gunn Allen, *Sacred Hoop* 214.

107. Gunn Allen, *Sacred Hoop* 223.

108. Gunn Allen, *Sacred Hoop* 223.

109. Quoted in Collins 132.

110. Quoted in Collins 355.

111. Quoted in Annie O. Eysturoy, "Paula Gunn Allen," *This Is about Vision: Interviews with Southwestern Writers,* ed. William Balassi, John F. Crawford, and Annie O. Eysturoy (Albuquerque: U of New Mexico P, 1990) 102. Allen explains that vision quests were different for women and men because of their different bodies: "As far as I understand, it *was* different for women. A person with the female anatomy might go on a mountain top vision quest; but by and large she stayed very near the village. There are reasons for that. For one thing, how far do you have to go when you have so much happening in your own body?" Quoted in Eysturoy 99.

112. Quoted in Eysturoy 102-03.

113. Gunn Allen, *Sacred Hoop* 127.

114. Gunn Allen, *Sacred Hoop* 134.

115. Gunn Allen, *Sacred Hoop* 134-35.

116. Gunn Allen, *Sacred Hoop* 129.

117. Gunn Allen, *Sacred Hoop* 138.

118. Gunn Allen, *Sacred Hoop* 157.

119. Gunn Allen, *Sacred Hoop* 132.

120. Gunn Allen, "Sipapu" 18.

121. Quoted in Eysturoy 102.

122. Quoted in Coltelli 13.

123. Gunn Allen, *Sacred Hoop* 43.

124. Gunn Allen, *Sacred Hoop* 48-49.

125. Paula Gunn Allen, "Deep Purple," *Spider Woman's Granddaughters: Traditional Tales and Contemporary Writing by Native American Women,* ed. Paula Gunn Allen (Boston: Beacon, 1989) 198.

126. Gunn Allen, *Sacred Hoop* 268.

127. Paula Gunn Allen, " 'Border' Studies: The Intersection of Gender and Color," *Introduction to Scholarship in Modern Languages and Literatures,* ed. Joseph Gibaldi, 2nd ed. (New York: Modern Language Association, 1992) 306.

128. Gunn Allen, *Sacred Hoop* 257.

129. Gunn Allen, *Sacred Hoop* 257.

130. Gunn Allen, *Sacred Hoop* 260.

131. Gunn Allen, *Sacred Hoop* 248.

132. Gunn Allen, *Studies* 132.

133. Gunn Allen, *Sacred Hoop* 56-57.

134. Gunn Allen, "This Wilderness" 113.

135. Paula Gunn Allen, "Introduction," *Song of the Turtle: American Indian Literature: 1974-1994,* ed. Paula Gunn Allen (New York: One World/Ballantine, 1996) 6.

136. Gunn Allen, "This Wilderness" 114.

137. Gunn Allen, "Sipapu" 17.

138. Gunn Allen, "Sipapu" 17-18.

139. Gunn Allen, "Sipapu" 103.

140. Gunn Allen, *Sacred Hoop* 158.

141. Gunn Allen, *Sacred Hoop* 158.

142. Gunn Allen, *Sacred Hoop* 158.

143. Gunn Allen, *Sacred Hoop* 158.

144. Gunn Allen, *Sacred Hoop* 160.

145. Quoted in Gunn Allen, *Sacred Hoop* 161.

146. Gunn Allen, *Sacred Hoop* 161.

147. Gunn Allen, *Sacred Hoop* 161.

148. Gunn Allen, *Sacred Hoop* 55.

149. Gunn Allen, *Sacred Hoop* 57.

150. Gunn Allen, *Sacred Hoop* 68.

151. Paula Gunn Allen, "American Indian Fiction, 1968-1983," *A Literary History of the American West,* ed. J. Golden Taylor (Fort Worth: Western Literature Association, Texas Christian UP, 1987) 1058.

152. Gunn Allen, "American Indian Fiction" 1059.

153. Gunn Allen, "Sipapu" 111.

154. Gunn Allen, "Sipapu" 84.

155. Gunn Allen, *Sacred Hoop* 56.

156. Gunn Allen, *Sacred Hoop* 45.

157. Quoted in Coltelli 24.

158. Paula Gunn Allen, "Introduction," *Voice of the Turtle: American Indian Literature: 1900-1970,* ed. Paula Gunn Allen (New York: One World/Ballantine, 1994) 8.

159. Gunn Allen, *Sacred Hoop* 107.

160. Gunn Allen, *Sacred Hoop* 116.

161. Gunn Allen, *Sacred Hoop* 108.

162. Gunn Allen, *Sacred Hoop* 108.

163. Gunn Allen, *Sacred Hoop* 114.

164. Quoted in Coltelli 25.

165. Quoted in Gunn Allen, "Sipapu" 25-26.

166. Gunn Allen, *Sacred Hoop* 102.

167. Gunn Allen, personal interview.

168. Gunn Allen, *Sacred Hoop* 103.

169. Gunn Allen, "Sipapu" 56.

170. Gunn Allen, *Sacred Hoop* 104.

171. Gunn Allen, "Sipapu" 59-60.

172. Gunn Allen, "Introduction," *Song of the Turtle* 11-12

173. Gunn Allen, "Introduction," *Song of the Turtle* 11.

174. Gunn Allen, *Sacred Hoop* 80.

175. Among the Navajo, these include Changing Woman and White Shell Woman. Gunn Allen, personal interview.

176. Gunn Allen, "Whose Dream" 118.

177. Gunn Allen, *Grandmothers* 15.

178. Gunn Allen, *Grandmothers* 8.

179. Gunn Allen, "Whose Dream" 102-03.

180. Gunn Allen, "Whose Dream" 118.

181. Gunn Allen, "Whose Dream" 103.

182. Gunn Allen, *Sacred Hoop* 62.

183. Gunn Allen, *Sacred Hoop* 63.

184. Gunn Allen, personal interview.

185. Gunn Allen, *Sacred Hoop* 62.

186. Gunn Allen, "Sipapu" 98.

187. Gunn Allen, "Sipapu" 98.

188. Gunn Allen, *Sacred Hoop* 63.

189. Gunn Allen, "Sipapu" 97.

190. Gunn Allen, personal interview.

191. Gunn Allen, personal interview.

192. Gunn Allen, "Sipapu" 104.

193. Gunn Allen, *Sacred Hoop* 188.

9. Trinh T. Minh-ha

1. Trinh T. Minh-ha, quoted in Pratibha Parmar, "Between Theory and Poetry," *Framer Framed,* by Trinh T. Minh-ha (New York: Routledge, 1992) 156-57.

2. Trinh's date of birth and parents' names are not included in this chapter because she finds questions about such information to be "ideologically questionable." Trinh T. Minh-ha, letter to Sonja K. Foss, 5 June 1997. She explains that "the ideology of 'starting from the source' has always proved to be very limiting." Quoted in Nancy N. Chen, " 'Speaking Nearby': A Conversation with Trinh T. Minh-ha," *Visual Anthropology Review* 8 (1992): 82.

3. Quoted in Harriet A. Hirshorn, "Questioning Truth and Fact," *Framer Framed,* by Trinh T. Minh-ha (New York: Routledge, 1992) 182. We cite the most accessible sources for all works that appear in more than one source. In some instances, wording differs among the various sources; the quotations we use are from the cited sources.

4. Quoted in Hirshorn 181.

5. Quoted in Chen 83.

6. Quoted in Hirshorn 182.

7. Quoted in Chen 83.

8. Hirshorn 181.

9. Quoted in Chen 84.

10. Quoted in Chen 83.

11. Quoted in Chen 84.

12. Chen 84.

13. Quoted in Judith Mayne, "From a Hybrid Space," *Framer Framed,* by Trinh T. Minh-ha (New York: Routledge, 1992) 141.

14. Jean-Paul Bourdier and Trinh T. Minh-ha, *African Spaces: Designs for Living in Upper Volta* (New York: Africana/Holmes & Meier, 1985) 2.

15. Quoted in Tessa Barringer, Linda Tyler, Sarah Williams, and Toroa Pohatu, "Strategies of Displacement for Women, Natives and Their Others: Intra-views with Trinh T. Minh-ha," *Women's Studies Journal* [New Zealand] 10 (1994): 7.

16. Quoted in Mayne 138.

17. Quoted in Scott MacDonald, "Film as Translation: A Net with No Fisherman," *Framer Framed,* by Trinh T. Minh-ha (New York: Routledge, 1992) 111.

18. Quoted in Barringer, Tyler, Williams, and Pohatu 6.

19. Quoted in Chen 85.

20. Quoted in Pam Falkenberg, "Trinh T. Minh-ha: Interviewed by Pam Falkenberg: October 31, 1989," *Affirmative Actions: Recognizing a Cross-Cultural Practice in Contemporary Art,* ed. Jeanne Dunning (Chicago: School of the Art Institute of Chicago, 1990) 15.

21. Trinh T. Minh-ha, curriculum vita, 1995.

22. Quoted in Parmar 158.

23. Quoted in Isaac Julien and Laura Mulvey, " 'Who Is Speaking?': Of Nation, Community and First Person Interviews," *Framer Framed,* by Trinh T. Minh-ha (New York: Routledge, 1992) 192.

24. Quoted in Berenice Reynaud, "Trinh T. Minh-ha: At the Edge," *Cinemaya* [New Delhi, India] 25/26 (1994-95): 29.

25. Quoted in Laleen Jayamane and Anne Rutherford, " 'Why a Fish Pond?': Fiction at the Heart of Documentation," *Framer Framed,* by Trinh T. Minh-ha (New York: Routledge, 1992) 174.

26. Quoted in Reynaud 29.

27. Trinh T. Minh-ha, in August Coppola, Carrol Blue, Joseph Camacho, and Trinh T. Minh-ha, "Film Panel," *The Arts in a Multicultural Society* (San Jose, CA: Distinguished Artists Forum, San Jose State U, 1986) 13.

28. Quoted in Jayamane and Rutherford 174.

29. Quoted in Mayne 137.

30. Trinh T. Minh-ha, "An Acoustic Journey," *Rethinking Borders,* ed. John C. Welchman (Minneapolis: U of Minnesota P, 1996) 6.

31. Trinh T. Minh-ha, "Critical Reflections," *Artforum* 28 (1990): 132.

32. Quoted in Constance Penley and Andrew Ross, "When I Project It Is Silent," *Framer Framed,* by Trinh T. Minh-ha (New York: Routledge, 1992) 237.

33. Trinh T. Minh-ha, *When the Moon Waxes Red: Representation, Gender and Cultural Politics* (New York: Routledge, 1991) 114.

34. Trinh, *Moon* 88.

35. Trinh, "Critical Reflections" 133.

36. Trinh, *Moon* 149.

37. Trinh, "Critical Reflections" 132.

38. Quoted in Barringer, Tyler, Williams, and Pohatu 12, 11.

39. Trinh, *Moon* 155.

40. Trinh T. Minh-ha, *Woman, Native, Other: Writing Postcoloniality and Feminism* (Bloomington: Indiana UP, 1989) 49.

41. Trinh, *Moon* 93, 148.

42. Trinh, *Moon* 148.

43. Trinh, *Woman, Native, Other* 58.

44. Trinh, *Woman, Native, Other* 48.

45. Trinh, *Moon* 8.

46. Trinh, *Moon* 164, 49.

47. Quoted in MacDonald 119.

48. Trinh, *Moon* 40, 59.

49. Trinh, *Moon* 34.

50. Trinh, *Moon* 34.

51. Trinh, *Moon* 38.

52. Quoted in Mayne 145.

53. Trinh, *Moon* 30.

54. Quoted in Mayne 146.

55. Quoted in Hirshorn 186.

56. Trinh, *Moon* 120.

57. Trinh, *Woman, Native, Other* 96.
58. Trinh, *Woman, Native, Other* 96.
59. Quoted in Parmar 152.
60. Trinh, *Moon* 103.
61. Trinh, *Woman, Native, Other* 114.
62. Trinh, *Moon* 120.
63. Quoted in Penley and Ross 233.
64. Trinh, *Moon* 6.
65. Trinh T. Minh-ha, "Wo/Man/Third/World," *Women and Language* 11 (1988): 6.
66. Quoted in Parmar 153, 151.
67. Quoted in Parmar 151-52.
68. Quoted in Parmar 153.
69. Quoted in Parmar 153.
70. Trinh, *Woman, Native, Other* 86.
71. Trinh, *Woman, Native, Other* 85-86.
72. Quoted in Penley and Ross 238.
73. Quoted in Penley and Ross 238.
74. Trinh, *Moon* 18.
75. Trinh, *Woman, Native, Other* 96.
76. Quoted in Parmar 152.
77. Quoted in Parmar 152.
78. Laleen Jayamanne, Leslie Thornton, and Trinh T. Minh-ha, " 'Which Way to Political Cinema?': A Conversation Piece," *Framer Framed*, by Trinh T. Minh-ha (New York: Routledge, 1992) 257.
79. Trinh T. Minh-ha, "Of Other Peoples: Beyond the 'Salvage' Paradigm," *Dia Art Foundation: Discussions in Contemporary Culture*, ed. Hal Foster (Seattle: Bay, 1987) 139.
80. Trinh, *Moon* 149.
81. Quoted in Barringer, Tyler, Williams, and Pohatu 22.
82. Trinh, "Of Other Peoples" 148.
83. Trinh, *Woman, Native, Other* 88.
84. Trinh, "Acoustic Journey" 8.
85. Trinh, *Woman, Native, Other* 87.
86. Trinh T. Minh-ha, "Other Than Myself/My Other Self," *Travellers' Tales,* ed. George Robertson, Melinda Mash, Lisa Tickner, Jon Bird, Barry Curtis, and Tim Putnam (New York: Routledge, 1994) 13.
87. Trinh, *Moon* 22.
88. Quoted in Mayne 140.
89. Trinh T. Minh-ha, "Not You/Like You: Post-Colonial Women and the Interlocking Questions of Identity and Difference," *Inscriptions* 3 (1988): 76.
90. Trinh, *Moon* 74.
91. Trinh, *Moon* 123.

92. Trinh, *Woman, Native, Other* 84.

93. Trinh, "Not You" 73.

94. Quoted in Barringer, Tyler, Williams, and Pohatu 13.

95. Trinh, *Moon* 73.

96. Trinh, "Other Than Myself" 18.

97. Quoted in Barringer, Tyler, Williams, and Pohatu 22.

98. Trinh, *Woman, Native, Other* 96.

99. Trinh, "Acoustic Journey" 7.

100. Trinh, *Moon* 48.

101. Trinh, *Moon* 157.

102. Quoted in Barringer, Tyler, Williams, and Pohatu 12.

103. Trinh, "Of Other Peoples" 140.

104. Trinh, "Acoustic Journey" 1.

105. Trinh, "Not You" 71-72.

106. Trinh, "Not You" 71.

107. Trinh, "Not You" 71.

108. Trinh, "Not You" 72.

109. Trinh, "Not You" 71.

110. Trinh, "Not You" 72.

111. Quoted in MacDonald 129.

112. Trinh T. Minh-ha, "Introduction," *Discourse* 8 (1986-87): 3.

113. Trinh, *Woman, Native, Other* 94.

114. Quoted in Penley and Ross 237.

115. Trinh, "Introduction" 3.

116. Quoted in MacDonald 121.

117. Quoted in Parmar 157.

118. Trinh, "Other Than Myself" 23.

119. Trinh, "Other Than Myself" 23.

120. Quoted in MacDonald 123.

121. Trinh, *Moon* 21.

122. Trinh, "Critical Reflections" 132.

123. Quoted in Barringer, Tyler, Williams, and Pohatu 22.

124. Quoted in Rob Stephenson, "Professional Censorship," *Framer Framed,* by Trinh T. Minh-ha (New York: Rutherford, 1992) 219.

125. Quoted in Stephenson 216.

126. Trinh, *Moon* 120.

127. Trinh, *Moon* 59.

128. Quoted in Mayne 138.

129. Trinh, *Moon* 84.

130. Trinh, *Moon* 71.

131. Quoted in Barringer, Tyler, Williams, and Pohatu 18.

132. Quoted in Parmar 154.

133. Quoted in Chen 84-85.

134. Quoted in Mayne 139.

135. Quoted in Jayamane and Rutherford 165.

136. Quoted in Julien and Mulvey 193.

137. Quoted in Hirshorn 187.

138. Quoted in Penley and Ross 225.

139. Quoted in Hirshorn 187.

140. Quoted in Penley and Ross 227.

141. Quoted in Penley and Ross 228.

142. Trinh, "Critical Reflections" 133.

143. Trinh, *Moon* 107-08.

144. Trinh T. Minh-ha, "Painting with Music: A Performance across Cultures," *Writings on Dance* [Australia] 13 (1995): 14.

145. Quoted in Mayne 139.

146. Trinh, *Woman, Native, Other* 16.

147. Trinh, *Moon* 111-12.

148. Trinh, *Moon* 84.

149. Trinh, *Moon* 84.

150. Quoted in Hirshorn 186.

151. Trinh, *Moon* 84.

152. Quoted in MacDonald 116.

153. Quoted in Jayamane and Rutherford 163.

154. Patricia Ticineto Clough, *Feminist Thought: Desire, Power, and Academic Discourse* (Cambridge, MA: Blackwell, 1994) 126.

155. Trinh, in Coppola, Blue, Camacho, and Trinh 13.

156. Trinh, *Moon* 111.

157. Trinh, *Moon* 147.

158. Quoted in Stephenson 214.

159. Quoted in Penley and Ross 230.

160. Quoted in Annamaria Morelli, "The Undone Interval: Trinh T. Minh-ha in Conversation with Annamaria Morelli," *The Post-Colonial Question: Common Skies, Divided Horizons,* ed. Iain Chambers and Lidia Curti (New York: Routledge, 1996) 6.

161. Quoted in Penley and Ross 230.

162. Quoted in Morelli 7.

163. Quoted in MacDonald 115.

164. Quoted in MacDonald 115.

165. Trinh, in Coppola, Blue, Camacho, and Trinh 12.

166. Quoted in Stephenson 215.

167. Quoted in MacDonald 114.

168. Quoted in Morelli 12.

169. Quoted in Stephenson 215.

170. Quoted in MacDonald 124.

171. Quoted in Morelli 12.

172. Quoted in Julien and Mulvey 210.

173. Quoted in Hirshorn 182.

174. Quoted in Chen 87.

175. Quoted in Chen 87.

176. Quoted in Morelli 3.

177. Quoted in Morelli 4.

178. Quoted in Morelli 9.

179. Quoted in Julien and Mulvey 205.

180. Trinh, *Moon* 112.

181. Quoted in Stephenson 215.

182. Trinh T. Minh-ha, "Nature's *r*: A Musical Swoon," *FutureNatural: Nature, Science, Culture,* ed. George Robertson, Melinda Mash, Lisa Tickner, Jon Bird, Barry Curtis, and Tim Putnam (New York: Routledge, 1996) 99.

183. Quoted in MacDonald 119.

184. Quoted in Chen 89.

185. Trinh, *Woman, Native, Other* 20.

10. Sally Miller Gearhart

1. Sally Gearhart, "Womanpower: Energy Re-Sourcement," *The Politics of Women's Spirituality: Essays on the Rise of Spiritual Power within the Feminist Movement,* ed. Charlene Spretnak (Garden City, NY: Doubleday, 1982) 206.

2. Sally Miller Gearhart, "Small-Town Girl Makes Dyke," *Testimonies: Lesbian Coming-Out Stories,* ed. Karen Barber and Sarah Holmes (Boston: Alyson, 1994) 18.

3. Gearhart, "Small-Town Girl" 18.

4. Gearhart, "Small-Town Girl" 21.

5. Quoted in Arthur Lazere, "Sally Gearhart: Building a Professional Life," *New York Native* 20 Apr. 1987: 22.

6. Quoted in Lucy Massie Phenix and Nancy Adair, "Sally," *Word Is Out: Stories of Some of Our Lives,* ed. Nancy Adair and Casey Adair (San Francisco: New Glide; New York: Delacorte, 1978) 256.

7. Quoted in Jil Clark, "Sally Gearhart: Spirituality vs. Politics," *Gay Community News* [Boston] 15 Dec. 1979: 8.

8. Quoted in Clark 8.

9. Quoted in Clark 8.

10. Quoted in Phenix and Adair 249.

11. Sally Miller Gearhart, letter to Sonja K. Foss, 26 Apr. 1993.

12. Sally Miller Gearhart, "Notes from a Recovering Activist," *Sojourner: The Women's Forum* 21 (1995): 8.

13. Gearhart, letter to Sonja K. Foss, 26 Apr. 1993.

14. Quoted in Susanna J. Sturgis, "Discovering the Wanderground: An Interview with Sally Gearhart," *Off Our Backs* 10 (1980): 24.

15. Sally Miller Gearhart, "The Scholar as Activist," Plenary Session, Western Regional Fulbright Conference, San Francisco State U, 12 June 1980.

16. Sally Miller Gearhart, personal interview, 14 May 1996.

17. Quoted in Phenix and Adair 257.

18. Sally Miller Gearhart, *The Wanderground: Stories of the Hill Women* (Boston: Alyson, 1984) 195.

19. Sally Miller Gearhart, "The Womanization of Rhetoric," *Women's Studies International Quarterly* 2 (1979): 197-98.

20. Sally Gearhart, Lani Silver, Sue Talbot, Rita Mae Brown, Jeanne Cordova, and Barbara McLean, "A Kiss Does Not a Revolution Make," *The Tide* 3 (1974): 30.

21. Sally Miller Gearhart, "The Future—If There Is One—Is Female," *Reweaving the Web of Life: Feminism and Nonviolence,* ed. Pam McAllister (Philadelphia: New Society, 1982) 269.

22. Sally M. Gearhart, "An End to Technology: A Modest Proposal," *Machina ex Dea: Feminist Perspectives on Technology,* ed. Joan Rothschild (New York: Pergamon, 1984) 179.

23. Gearhart, "End to Technology" 177.

24. Gearhart, "End to Technology" 171.

25. Gearhart, "End to Technology" 178.

26. Gearhart, "End to Technology" 178.

27. Sally Gearhart and Peggy Cleveland, "On the Prevalence of Stilps," *Quest: A Feminist Quarterly* 1 (1975): 56.

28. Sally Gearhart, "The Women's Movement: One Vision," Annual Meeting, Council on Religion and the Homosexual, Glide Memorial United Methodist Church, San Francisco, 16 Mar. 1971.

29. Gearhart and Cleveland 56.

30. Gearhart, "Women's Movement."

31. Gearhart, "The Future" 268.

32. Gearhart, "The Future" 268.

33. Gearhart, "The Future" 270.

34. Gearhart, "Women's Movement."

35. Gearhart, Silver, Talbot, Brown, Cordova, and McLean 30.

36. Gearhart, "The Future" 270.

37. Gearhart, "The Future" 270.

38. Gearhart, "The Future" 284.

39. Gearhart, "Women's Movement."

40. Sally Gearhart, "The Miracle of Lesbianism," *Loving Women/Loving Men: Gay Liberation and the Church,* ed. Sally Gearhart and William R. Johnson (San Francisco: Glide, 1974) 130.

41. Gearhart, "Womanization" 201.

42. Gearhart, "Miracle" 131.

43. Sally Gearhart, "What Are We Doing?" Golden Gate Chapter, National Organization for Women, San Francisco, 8 Mar. 1975.

44. Gearhart, "What Are We Doing?"

45. Sally Gearhart, "She Who Hath Ears," *Women and the Word: Toward a Whole Theology,* ed. Jean Crosby and Jude Michaels (Berkeley, CA: Office of Women's Affairs of the Graduate Theological Union, 1972) 77.

46. Sally Miller Gearhart, "Gay Civil Rights and the Roots of Oppression," *Gayspeak: Gay Male and Lesbian Communication,* ed. James W. Chesebro (New York: Pilgrim, 1981) 282.

47. Sally Miller Gearhart, "The Spiritual Dimension: Death and Resurrection of a Hallelujah Dyke," *Our Right to Love: A Lesbian Resource Book,* ed. Ginny Vida (Englewood Cliffs, NJ: Prentice Hall, 1978) 187.

48. Sally Gearhart, "The Lesbian and God-the-Father," *Persuasion: Understanding, Practice and Analysis,* by Herbert W. Simons (Menlo Park, CA: Addison-Wesley, 1975) 339.

49. Gearhart, "Lesbian and God-the-Father" 339.

50. Gearhart, "What Are We Doing?"

51. Sally Gearhart, "Psychological Empowerment: Woman-Love," International Women's Year Conference, San Francisco, 24 Oct. 1975.

52. Gearhart, "Lesbian and God-the-Father" 339.

53. Gearhart, "The Future" 271.

54. Gearhart, "Gay Civil Rights" 281.

55. Quoted in Sturgis 25.

56. Jane Gurko and Sally Gearhart, "The Sword-and-the-Vessel versus the Lake-on-the-Lake: A Lesbian Model of Nonviolent Rhetoric," *Bread and Roses: Midwestern Journal of Issues and the Arts* 2 (1980): 30.

57. Gearhart, "Miracle" 123.

58. Gearhart, "Women's Movement."

59. Gearhart, "Women's Movement."

60. Gearhart, "She Who Hath Ears" 80.

61. Gearhart, "The Future" 270.

62. Gearhart, "The Future" 270.

63. Gearhart, Silver, Talbot, Brown, Cordova, and McLean 25.

64. Sally Gearhart, "Another View of the Same Moon from Another City's Streets," *Womanspirit: A Feminist Quarterly* 3 (1976): 44.

65. Gearhart, "Psychological Empowerment."

66. Gearhart, "Psychological Empowerment."

67. Gearhart, letter to Sonja K. Foss, 26 Apr. 1993.

68. Quoted in Phenix and Adair 257.

69. Sally Miller Gearhart, "If the Mortarboard Fits: Radical Feminism in Academia," *Learning Our Way: Essays in Feminist Education,* ed. Charlotte Bunch and Sandra Pollack (Trumansburg, NY: Crossing, 1983) 7.

70. Gearhart, "Mortarboard" 7.

71. Gearhart, "Mortarboard" 8.
72. Gearhart, "Mortarboard" 7.
73. Gearhart, "Mortarboard" 7.
74. Gearhart, "Miracle" 147.
75. Gearhart, "Mortarboard" 18.
76. Gearhart, "Mortarboard" 8.
77. Gearhart, "Mortarboard" 8.
78. Gearhart, "Mortarboard" 8.
79. Gearhart, "Mortarboard" 8.
80. Gearhart, "Miracle" 146.
81. Gearhart, "Miracle" 146-47.
82. Gearhart, "Mortarboard" 9.
83. Gearhart, "Miracle" 145.
84. Gearhart, "Miracle" 149.
85. Gearhart, "Scholar as Activist."
86. Gearhart, "Mortarboard" 9.
87. Gearhart, "Mortarboard" 10.
88. Gearhart, "Mortarboard" 9.
89. Gearhart, "What Are We Doing?"
90. Gearhart, "Mortarboard" 10.
91. Gearhart, "Miracle" 149.
92. Gearhart, "Womanpower" 195.
93. Gearhart, "Womanpower" 195.
94. Gearhart, "Spiritual Dimension" 191.
95. Gearhart, "Spiritual Dimension" 190.
96. Quoted in Nancy Jesser, "Gearhart, Sally Miller," *Feminist Writers,* ed. Pamela Kester-Shelton (Detroit: St. James, 1996) 193.
97. Gearhart, "Spiritual Dimension" 191.
98. Gearhart, "Spiritual Dimension" 191.
99. Quoted in Sturgis 24.
100. Gearhart, "Womanpower" 198-99.
101. Gearhart, "Spiritual Dimension" 191.
102. Quoted in Sturgis 24.
103. Quoted in Phenix and Adair 258.
104. Sally Miller Gearhart, "What Is a Homosexual?" San Francisco State U, 22 May 1971.
105. Del Martin and Sally Gearhart, "Afterthought: Lesbians as Gays and as Women," *We'll Do It Ourselves: Combatting Sexism in Education,* ed. David Rosen, Steve Werner, and Barbara Yates (Lincoln: Student Committee, Study Commission on Undergraduate Education and the Education of Teachers, U of Nebraska Curriculum Development Center, 1974) 279.
106. Gearhart, "Womanpower" 196-97.

107. Sally Miller Gearhart, letter to Sweet Briar College, 16 Jan. 1972.

108. Sally Miller Gearhart, "Future Visions: Today's Politics: Feminist Utopias in Review," *Women in Search of Utopia: Mavericks and Mythmakers,* ed. Ruby Rohrlich and Elaine Hoffman Baruch (New York: Schocken, 1984) 301.

109. Gearhart, "Womanpower" 200.

110. Gearhart, "Another View" 42.

111. Gearhart, "Another View" 43.

112. Gearhart, letter to Sonja K. Foss, 26 Apr. 1993.

113. Gearhart, "Womanpower" 199.

114. Gearhart, "Womanpower" 203.

115. Gearhart, "Womanpower" 195.

116. Gearhart, "Womanpower" 195.

117. Gearhart, "Another View" 43.

118. Gearhart, "Womanpower" 200.

119. Quoted in Sturgis 24.

120. Gearhart, "Mortarboard" 8.

121. Quoted in Sturgis 24.

122. Gearhart, "Recovering Activist" 8.

123. Gearhart, "Womanization" 195.

124. Quoted in M. A. Karr, "Sally Gearhart: Wandering—and Wondering—on Future Ground," *The Advocate* 21 Feb. 1980: 22.

125. Gearhart, "Womanization" 196.

126. Gearhart, "Womanization" 201.

127. Gearhart, "Womanization" 201.

128. Quoted in Karr 22.

129. Gearhart, "Womanization" 197.

130. Quoted in Karr 22.

131. Gearhart, "Womanization" 197.

132. Gearhart, "Womanization" 196.

133. Gearhart, "Womanization" 196.

134. Sally Miller Gearhart, "Whose Woods These Are," *Inviting Transformation: Presentational Speaking for a Changing World,* by Sonja K. Foss and Karen A. Foss (Prospect Heights, IL: Waveland, 1994) 130.

135. Quoted in Karr 22.

136. Gearhart, "The Future" 268.

137. Gearhart, "Recovering Activist" 8.

138. Quoted in Karr 22.

139. Gearhart, "Womanization" 198.

140. Gearhart, "Recovering Activist" 8.

141. Gearhart, "Womanization" 196.

142. Quoted in Karr 22.

143. Gearhart, "Womanpower" 198.

144. Gearhart, personal interview.

145. Gearhart, "Recovering Activist" 8.

146. Gearhart, "Womanpower" 205.

147. Gearhart, *Wanderground* 75.

148. Quoted in Karr 22.

149. Gearhart, "Womanization" 198.

150. Gearhart, "Womanpower" 204-05.

151. Gearhart, "Recovering Activist" 8.

152. Gearhart, "Recovering Activist" 10.

153. Gearhart, "Recovering Activist" 8.

154. Quoted in Jesser 193.

155. Sally Miller Gearhart, videotaped interview, Jan. 1993.

156. Quoted in Jesser 192.

157. Sally Miller Gearhart, "The Pit Bull Opportunity," *Reality Change* [Seth Network International] Summer 1994: 31.

158. Gearhart, "Pit Bull" 31.

159. Quoted in Jesser 193.

160. Gearhart, "Womanization" 198.

161. Gearhart, "Womanization" 198.

162. Gearhart, "Womanization" 200.

163. Gearhart, videotaped interview.

164. Gearhart, "Recovering Activist" 8.

165. Gearhart, "Recovering Activist" 9.

166. Gearhart, "Recovering Activist" 10.

167. Gearhart, "Recovering Activist" 9.

168. Gearhart, "Recovering Activist" 9.

169. Gearhart, "Recovering Activist" 10.

170. Sally Miller Gearhart, "The California Coalition for Traditional Values: View from a Dyke," *San Francisco Bay Times,* Nov. 1989: 8.

171. Gearhart, "Recovering Activist" 9.

172. Gearhart, "Recovering Activist" 9.

173. Gearhart, videotaped interview.

174. Gearhart, videotaped interview.

175. Sally Miller Gearhart, "Retreating into the Thick of It," Conference on Gender and Communication, Denison University, Granville, OH, 12 Apr. 1996.

176. Gearhart, "Womanization" 199.

177. Gearhart, videotaped interview.

178. Quoted in Eric Mills, "Enriching and Expanding the Animal Movement: Dr. Sally Gearhart Talks about Sexism, Racism and Coalition-Building," *Agenda* 111 (1983): 5.

179. Gearhart, "Retreating."

180. Gearhart, letter to Sonja K. Foss, 26 Aug. 1997.

181. Gearhart, letter to Sonja K. Foss, 26 Aug. 1997.

182. Gearhart, "Recovering Activist" 9.
183. Gearhart, "Recovering Activist" 9.
184. Gearhart, "Recovering Activist" 10.
185. Gearhart, "Recovering Activist" 9.
186. Gearhart, videotaped interview.
187. Gearhart, "Recovering Activist" 8.
188. Gearhart, "Recovering Activist" 11.
189. Gearhart, "Recovering Activist" 11.
190. Gearhart, "Womanization" 200.

11. Sonia Johnson

1. Sonia Johnson, *Wildfire: Igniting the She/Volution* (Albuquerque, NM: Wildfire, 1989) 272.

2. Sonia Johnson, *From Housewife to Heretic* (Garden City, NY: Anchor-Doubleday, 1983) 66-70.

3. Johnson, *Housewife* 84.

4. Johnson, *Housewife* 54.

5. Johnson, *Housewife* 92.

6. Johnson, *Housewife* 101.

7. A *stake* is a territorial unit in the Church of Jesus Christ of Latter-day Saints that comprises a group of smaller units called *wards*.

8. Johnson, *Housewife* 103.

9. Johnson, *Housewife* 104.

10. For information about the history and defeat of the Equal Rights Amendment, see Jean Hoff-Wilson, ed., *Rights of Passage: The Past and Future of the ERA* (Bloomington: Indiana UP, 1986).

11. Johnson, *Housewife* 107.

12. Johnson, *Housewife* 279.

13. Johnson, *Housewife* 326.

14. Johnson, *Housewife* 324-25.

15. Johnson, *Housewife* 17.

16. Johnson, *Housewife* 230-31.

17. Johnson, *Housewife* 388.

18. Sonia Johnson, *Going Out of Our Minds: The Metaphysics of Liberation* (Freedom, CA: Crossing, 1987) 11.

19. Johnson, *Going* 12.

20. Johnson, *Going* 23.

21. Johnson, *Going* 68-69.

22. Johnson, *Going* 71.

23. Quoted in Johnson, *Going* 62.

24. Johnson, *Going* 74-76.

25. Johnson, *Going* 94.

26. Johnson, *Going* 187.

27. Johnson, *Going* 192.

28. Johnson, *Going* 194.

29. Johnson, *Going* 206-07.

30. Johnson, *Going* 207.

31. Johnson, *Going* 208.

32. Johnson, *Going* 208.

33. Johnson, *Going* 224.

34. Johnson, *Going* 229-30.

35. Johnson, *Going* 347.

36. Johnson, *Going* 123.

37. Johnson, *Going* 96-97.

38. Johnson, *Going* 107.

39. Johnson, *Going* 124.

40. Johnson, *Wildfire* 11.

41. Sonia Johnson, *The Ship That Sailed into the Living Room: Sex and Intimacy Reconsidered* (Estancia, NM: Wildfire, 1991) 2. When Johnson uses the word *relationship* as a noun, she writes it as two words—*relation Ship*. She writes it as one word—*relationShip*—when using it as a verb, an adjective, or an adverb. *Ship* 1.

42. Johnson, *Ship* 3.

43. Johnson, *Ship* 177.

44. Johnson, *Ship* 214.

45. Johnson, *Ship* 176-77.

46. Johnson, *Ship* 223.

47. Johnson, *Ship* 225-26.

48. Johnson, *Ship* 67.

49. Sonia Johnson, letter to Karen A. Foss, 13 Jan. 1997.

50. Johnson, *Ship* 121.

51. Sonia Johnson and Jade DeForest, *Out of This World: A Fictionalized True-Life Adventure* (Estancia, NM: Wildfire, 1993) 354.

52. Johnson, *Wildfire* 148.

53. Johnson, *Going* 241.

54. Johnson, *Going* 256-57.

55. Johnson, *Going* 266.

56. Johnson, *Wildfire* 178.

57. Johnson, *Going* 265-66.

58. Johnson, *Wildfire* 102.

59. Johnson, *Wildfire* 85.

60. Johnson, *Wildfire* 86.

61. Johnson, *Wildfire* 85.

62. Johnson, *Ship* 83.

63. Johnson, *Going* 256.

64. Johnson, *Housewife* 94.

65. Johnson, *Wildfire* 87.

66. Johnson, *Going* 92.

67. Johnson, *Wildfire* 122-23.

68. Johnson and DeForest 10.

69. Johnson, *Going* 339.

70. Johnson, *Going* 339.

71. Johnson, *Going* 299.

72. Johnson, *Going* 330.

73. Johnson, *Wildfire* 38.

74. Johnson, *Wildfire* 38-39.

75. Johnson, *Wildfire* 37.

76. Johnson, *Wildfire* 196.

77. Johnson, *Wildfire* 196.

78. Johnson, *Wildfire* 197.

79. Johnson, *Wildfire* 39.

80. Johnson, *Wildfire* 179.

81. Sonia Johnson, *Living the Dream,* lecture, U of Alaska, Anchorage, Mar. 1990, video (Albuquerque, NM: Wildfire, 1990).

82. Johnson, *Wildfire* 95-96.

83. Johnson, *Wildfire* 100.

84. Johnson, *Going* 306.

85. Johnson, *Ship* 162.

86. Johnson and DeForest 239.

87. Johnson and DeForest 337.

88. Johnson and DeForest 337.

89. Johnson, *Going* 157.

90. Johnson, *Going* 164.

91. Johnson, *Wildfire* 39.

92. Johnson, *Wildfire* 222.

93. Johnson, *Wildfire* 112.

94. Johnson, *Wildfire* 112-13.

95. Johnson, *Wildfire* 112.

96. Johnson, *Ship* 175.

97. Johnson, *Ship* 250.

98. Johnson, *Ship* 250.

99. Johnson, *Ship* 125.

100. Johnson, *Ship* 242-44.

101. Johnson, *Ship* 245.

102. Johnson, *Ship* 248-49.

103. Johnson, *Ship* 250-51.

104. Johnson, *Going* 5.

105. Johnson, *Housewife* 111-12.
106. Johnson and DeForest 346-47.
107. Johnson, *Going* 237.
108. Johnson, *Going* 237.
109. Johnson, *Going* 111.
110. Johnson, *Housewife* 162.
111. Johnson, *Housewife* 382.
112. Johnson, *Housewife* 94.
113. Johnson, *Housewife* 95.
114. Johnson, *Going* 69.
115. Johnson, *Going* 188.
116. Johnson, *Housewife* 395.
117. Johnson, *Going* 120-21.
118. Johnson, *Housewife* 152.
119. Johnson, *Ship* 51-52.
120. Johnson, *Ship* 162.
121. Johnson, *Ship* 50.
122. Johnson and DeForest 131-32.
123. Johnson and DeForest 132.
124. Johnson and DeForest 299-300.
125. Johnson, *Ship* 163.
126. Johnson, *Ship* 157.
127. Johnson and DeForest 165.
128. Johnson and DeForest 167-68.
129. Johnson and DeForest 176.
130. Johnson and DeForest 176.
131. Johnson and DeForest 177.
132. Johnson, *Ship* 224.
133. Johnson, *Wildfire* 80.
134. Johnson, *Going* 26-27.
135. Johnson, *Wildfire* 16-17.
136. Johnson, *Wildfire* 17.
137. Johnson, *Going* 334.
138. Johnson, *Wildfire* 251.
139. Johnson, *Wildfire* 41.
140. Johnson, *Ship* 210.
141. Johnson, *Wildfire* 45.
142. Johnson, *Wildfire* 43.
143. Johnson, *Ship* 21.
144. Johnson, *Ship* 21.
145. Johnson, *Wildfire* 47.
146. Johnson, *Wildfire* 46-47.

147. Johnson, *Ship* 163.
148. Johnson, *Ship* 190.
149. Johnson, *Wildfire* 223.
150. Johnson, *Wildfire* 223.
151. Johnson, *Wildfire* 233.
152. Johnson, *Wildfire* 237.
153. Johnson, *Wildfire* 236.
154. Johnson, *Wildfire* 240.
155. Johnson, *Wildfire* 241.
156. Johnson, *Wildfire* 240-41.
157. Johnson and DeForest 64.
158. Johnson and DeForest 83.
159. Johnson and DeForest 62.
160. Johnson and DeForest 354.
161. Johnson, *Going* 19.
162. Johnson, *Housewife* 406.
163. Johnson, *Going* 348.
164. Johnson, *Wildfire* 272.
165. Johnson, *Housewife* 156.
166. Johnson, *Housewife* 158, 200.
167. Johnson, *Going* 8.
168. Johnson, *Going* 48.
169. Johnson, *Going* 48.
170. Johnson, *Going* 344-45.
171. Johnson, *Going* 347.
172. Johnson, *Wildfire* 107.
173. Johnson, *Wildfire* 109.
174. Johnson, *Going* 343.
175. Johnson, *Wildfire* 45.
176. Johnson, *Wildfire* 55.

Index

university system and, 32
See also Rhetorical studies
Communication theory/research, 33, 56-58
Communication, educational, 32, 42-43
Communicators. *See* Rhetoricians
Community outreach, 91-92
Condit, Celeste, 20, 28
Conference on Gender and Communication, 25
Confession, 86-87
Connectedness/estrangement, 48-49, 167,
    168-169
Conversational control in mainstream, 44-45
Creativity/mystery, 178-180
Critical consciousness, 83-84, 92-93
Cultural criticism, 89-91
Cultural intersection, 106-108

Daly, Mary, 129-130
    duality in society, 134-138
    education of, 130-132
    feminism, radical, 138-139
    feminist philosophy, elemental, 134
    literary output, 132-134
    professional obstacles, 132-134
    rhetorical theory, transformation of,
        154-156
    rhetoricians, foreground/background,
        139-141
Death culture, 198-201, 207-209, 210-213, 220
DeFrancisco, Victoria, 19
Dervin, Brenda, 26
Dialogue, 87-88
Diversity, 27-29
Dominant thought system, 235-236
Domination, culture of, 76-78, 92-93,
    134-136, 166-167, 233-235
Dow, Bonnie J., 21, 22, 28
Downey, Sharon D., 28-29
Duality, societal, 134-138

Ecofeminism, 170-171
Edson, Belle A., 30
Educational communication, 32, 42-43
Enactment, 85-86, 94
Enfoldment, 274-276
    assumptions of, 278-280
    communicative activities of, 280-285

persuasion as violence, 276-278, 289
Equal Rights Amendment (ERA), 18, 294-297
Estrangement, 167
Ethos, 122-123, 323-324
Exigence, 123, 154-155, 322

Feminism, 1-5, 52-53, 78-81, 104, 111-112
Feminist perspectives, 14-15
    acceptance of, 22
    acrostic vision, 169-170
    collectivism, 164, 170, 271-272
    communication discipline and, 22-23
    discourse, style of, 21-22
    diversity in, 27-29
    dominant thought system and, 235-236
    ecofeminism, 170-171
    inception, radical, 15-16
    linguistic practice and, 56-61
    mestiza consciousness, 109-111, 116-117,
        118
    minority women in, 27-28, 104, 236-237
    Native Americans and, 204-207
    radical, 138-139
    rhetoricians, women as, 17, 18-20
    social movements, 18
    See also Patriarchy
Feminist philosophy, elemental, 134
Feminist scholarship:
    arenas of exchange, 24-26
    diverse agendas, 28-29
    feminist reconstruction position, 28-29
    reconceptualization in, 29-32
    standpoint theory, 27-28
    theoretical frameworks, 26-27
Filmmaking, 230-233, 241-244, 245, 246-247
Foreground, 134-136
    rhetorical options, 142-147
    rhetoricians in, 139-140
Foss, Karen A., 19-20, 22, 24, 28, 31, 32
Foss, Sonja K., 18, 19-20, 22, 28, 30-31, 32
Friedan, Betty, 80
Fuller, Margaret, 18

Gay men. *See* Lesbians and gays
Gearhart, Sally Miller, 16, 257-258, 261
    academic life of, 258, 259
    Christianity and, 258

About the Authors

Sonja K. Foss, Karen A. Foss, and **Cindy L. Griffin** share research and teaching interests in contemporary rhetorical theory and criticism; feminist perspectives on communication; the incorporation of marginalized voices into rhetorical theory and practice; and issues of voice, identity, and power. They have authored numerous articles and book chapters on these topics; their coauthored article "Transforming Rhetoric through Feminist Reconstruction" (*Women's Studies in Communication,* 1997) summarizes their perspective on the intersection of rhetorical theory and feminism.

Sonja K. Foss is professor and chair of the Department of Communication at the University of Colorado at Denver. She received her Ph.D. in communication studies from Northwestern University and has taught at Virginia Tech, Norfolk State University, the University of Denver, the University of Oregon, St. Louis University, and Ohio State University. She is the author or coauthor of *Contemporary Perspectives on Rhetoric, Rhetorical Criticism, Women Speak,* and *Inviting Transformation.*

Karen A. Foss is professor and chair of the Communication and Journalism Department at the University of New Mexico in Albuquerque. She received her Ph.D. in speech and dramatic art from the University of Iowa and has taught at Humboldt State University and the University of Massachusetts at Amherst. She has served as director of women's studies at both Humboldt State University and the University of New Mexico. She is coauthor of *Contemporary Perspectives on Rhetoric, Women Speak,* and *Inviting Transformation.*

Cindy L. Griffin is associate professor in the Department of Speech Communication at Colorado State University in Fort Collins. She received her Ph.D. in speech communication from Indiana University and has taught at Northern Kentucky University. She has served as president of the Organization for Research on Women and Communication of the Western States Communication Association and received the Karl Wallace Award for public address scholarship from the National Communication Association.